The Emergence of Southern Multinationals

The Emergence of Southern Multinationals

Their Impact on Europe

Edited by

Louis Brennan
Associate Professor and Research Associate,
Institute for International Integration Studies, Trinity College, Dublin

palgrave
macmillan

First published 2011 by
PALGRAVE MACMILLAN

Palgrave Macmillan in the UK is an imprint of Macmillan Publishers Limited, registered in England, company number 785998, of Houndmills, Basingstoke, Hampshire RG21 6XS.

Palgrave Macmillan in the US is a division of St Martin's Press LLC, 175 Fifth Avenue, New York, NY 10010.

Palgrave Macmillan is the global academic imprint of the above companies and has companies and representatives throughout the world.

Palgrave® and Macmillan® are registered trademarks in the United States, the United Kingdom, Europe and other countries.

ISBN 978–0–230–23557–1 hardback

This book is printed on paper suitable for recycling and made from fully managed and sustained forest sources. Logging, pulping and manufacturing processes are expected to conform to the environmental regulations of the country of origin.

A catalogue record for this book is available from the British Library.

A catalog record for this book is available from the Library of Congress.

10 9 8 7 6 5 4 3 2 1
20 19 18 17 16 15 14 13 12 11

Printed and bound in Great Britain by
CPI Antony Rowe, Chippenham and Eastbourne

Contents

List of Tables

List of Figures

Preface

The emergence of Southern Multinationals (i.e. multinationals from the non-Triad economies) has garnered increasing attention in recent years. The nature of the response to this phenomenon has varied greatly. More enthusiastic responses foresee these firms as having the potential to transform the global economy in the coming decades. Some other responses are full of foreboding as these companies expand their activities and increasingly into the developed world. The number of emerging market companies in the Financial Times Global 500 increased from 68 in early 2007 to 119 in early 2010. In 2009, the takeovers by emerging market companies of developed world groups exceeded takeovers in the opposite direction for the first time, with the former exceeding the latter by some US$ 30 billion (*Financial Times*, 11 May 2010). As iconic companies in Europe are acquired by Southern Multinationals, there is heightened anxiety in relation to the motivations of the acquirers, with fears being expressed that such acquisitions are simply a precursor to a 'lift and shift' of some or all of the acquired companies' assets and technologies to the acquiring companies home country.

This volume seeks to offer some insights around the emergence of Southern Multinationals, and uniquely explores the impact of this growing phenomenon on the host region of Europe. Contributions are offered from both home and host region/country perspectives and from different disciplinary perspectives by distinguished experts in the topic. As such this volume advances the state of knowledge around this increasingly significant phenomenon in the global economy and provides some early considerations around its impact on Europe.

This volume had its genesis in an exploratory workshop on the topic of Southern Multinationals and their impact on Europe that I convened in October 2008. I acknowledge the support of the European Science Foundation in funding this workshop.

My sincere thanks are due to all the authors for their contributions to this volume. I also wish to thank most sincerely Palgrave Macmillan and in particular Paul Milner and Virginia Thorp from Palgrave Macmillan without whose support (and indeed pressure!) this volume would never have materialized.

Louis Brennan
June 2010

Notes on Contributors

Caner Bakir (PhD Monash University) is an Assistant Professor of International Political Economy in the Department of International Relations at Koc University, Istanbul, Turkey. His areas of research include institutional change, governance, globalization and public policy. His work has been published in *Governance* and *Public Administration* and many other academic journals. His new book *Globalization, Governance and Public Policy: Banking in Australia* is forthcoming from Palgrave Macmillan. He received the 2010 Encouragement Award given by the Scientific and Technological Research Council of Turkey (TUBITAK).

Filip de Beule is Assistant Professor of International Business at the Lessius University College, Antwerp, Belgium. He holds a BA and MA in Economics (UFSIA), and an MBA from the University of Antwerp Management School (UAMS). He got his PhD from the University of Antwerp on 'Belgian subsidiary management in the People's Republic of China: Strategic evolution, host country impact and policy'. Dr. de Beule has lectured as Visiting Professor at the University of Antwerp and the Catholic University of Leuven, where he also teaches courses on the economics and economic development of China. Dr. de Beule is a board member of the European International Business Academy, where he serves as national representative for Belgium. He is an affiliate researcher at the LICOS Centre for Institutions and Economic Performance at the Catholic University of Leuven, where he focuses his research on multinational companies and emerging economies.

Louis Brennan is a Fellow of Trinity College Dublin where he is an Associate Professor in the School of Business and a Research Associate in the Institute for International Integration Studies. He is the proposer and Chair of COST ACTION IS0905 on the Emergence of Southern Multinationals and their impact on Europe which currently consists of researchers from some twenty countries. Louis has lived and worked in several countries in Asia and Europe and in the US. His research interests are in global and operations strategy, global supply chain management and technology management.

Peter J. Buckley is Professor of International Business and Director of the Centre for International Business, University of Leeds. He was President of the Academy of International Business 2002–4. He is currently Chair of the European International Business Academy. He holds a Changjiang Scholarship at the University of International Business and Economics, Beijing.

Daniël Van Den Bulcke is Emeritus Professor at the University of Antwerp and former President of the Institute of Development Policy and Mananagement (IOB) at this university. He is Academic Director of the EuroChina Centre of the Antwerp Management School. He obtained his MA from the University of Toronto, Canada, and his Ph.D. from Ghent University, Belgium. He is a fellow of the Academy of International Business (AIB) and the European International Business Academy (EIBA). He also was Vice-President of AIB and Chairman of EIBA. Dr. Van Den Bulcke has published extensively on foreign direct investment issues and the activities of multinational enterprises in Western Europe and China. He has carried out research projects for several international organizations such as ILO, World Bank, UNCTC, OECD and EU. He received the Friendship Prize from the Chinese government for his contributions to the Chinese economy where he has been teaching since the beginning of the 1990s. He has been a visiting professor in a large number of universities in Belgium and The Netherlands and also in Asia. He still teaches at the Institute of European Studies in Macau. His most recent book is a co-edited volume (with A. Verbeke and W. Yuan) published by Edward Elgar, Cheltenham, UK, in 2009: *Handbook on Small Nations in the Global Economy. The Contribution of Multinational Enterprises to National Economic Success.*

Judith Clifton is Senior Lecturer at the Department of Economics, University of Cantabria. She previously lectured at Leeds, Oxford and Oviedo universities, and has been Visiting Research Fellow at the European University Institute in Florence, Consejo Superior de Investigaciones Científicas in Madrid, and Colegio de México in Mexico City, among others. Judith received her DPhil in the Political Economy of Latin America from the University of Oxford in 1997. Her research interests include economic and public policy, the public sector and public services. Judith has recently published in a number of leading specialist journals including *Revista de Economía Mundial, Journal of European Public Policy, Annals of Cooperative and Public Economics* and *Política y Gobierno* and has published books with Palgrave Macmillan and Kluwer Academic. She has also worked as a consultant for the 'World Investment Report', published by the United Nations annually.

Adam Cross is a Senior Lecturer in International Business at Leeds University Business School. Currently Adam's research interests concentrate mainly on cross-border licensing; the management of intellectual property as a business asset; outward foreign direct investment from emerging markets and foreign market entry analysis, with China as a major country focus for much of it. Adam teaches international business and intellectual capital management on a number of undergraduate and MBA programmes, both in the UK and overseas.

Erzsébet Czakó is Associate Professor at the Corvinus University of Budapest, Hungary, where she has been working since her graduation in 1986 where she obtained her Ph.D. in Business and Management. As visiting scholar she spent several semesters in US and European business schools. She teaches Business Economics, Strategic Management and International Business. Her fields of interest are contents of and approaches to competitiveness researches and programmes, competitiveness of various industries and enterprises and theories in international business. Professor Czakó is general secretary of the Competitiveness Research Center, which coordinates competitiveness surveys in Hungary since 1995. She has over 100 publications, among them eight books, including one on the competitiveness of the Hungarian economy in English.

Carl F. Fey is a Professor of International Business at the Center for Strategic and International Management and the China Economic Research Center at Stockholm School of Economics and Stockholm School of Economics Russia. For the past 12 years he has been helping Stockholm School of Economics to develop a branch campus for executive development work in St. Petersburg, Russia. Dr. Fey's research focuses primarily on how cultural and institutional differences effect what management practices work best in Russia and China (for example, strategic human resource management, organizational culture, cross-border merger and acquisition integration, knowledge transfer, firm internationalization and leadership). Dr. Fey is also a sought-after executive educator and consultant and has published over 40 articles in leading journals.

Don Fleet is a senior research associate at the Centre for International Manufacturing, Institute for Manufacturing, University of Cambridge. His primary interests are in international manufacturing networks, network design, mergers and acquisitions and the application of research frameworks in industry.

Afonso Fleury is Professor in the area of Work, Technology and Organisation at the University of Sao Paulo and (former) head of the Production Engineering Department. He was a research fellow at Institute of Development Studies (UK), Tokyo Institute of Technology, École Nationale des Ponts et Chaussées (France), Institute for Manufacturing, Cambridge University (UK), and prepared research projects for ILO, UNU, IDRC, UNDP, IDE, ECLAC as well as Brazilian institutions, covering different industries such as aeronautics, automobile, capital goods, computing and information, machine-tools, shoes, software, telecommunications and textile/apparel. He is currently researching about the internationalization of firms from Brazil as well as other emerging countries. He has published several books and articles on work organization, technology management, industrial policy and international business. He is associate editor of the *Journal of Manufacturing Technology Management* and of *Operations Management Research* and acts as Vice-President Americas for Production and Operations Management Society (POMS).

Maria Tereza Leme Fleury teaches in the area of Human Resources Management. She is the Dean of the School of Business Administration of Fundacao Getulio Vargas in Sao Paulo and former Dean of the School of Economics, Business Administration and Accountancy of the University of Sao Paulo. She was Visiting Professor at ESSEC (France) and at the Institute for Manufacturing, University of Cambridge, as well as Research Fellow at the Institute of Development Studies (UK) and Institute for Developing Economies (Tokyo). She has published several books and papers on strategy and competence management, internationalization of emerging countries possessive firms, human resources management, management of organizational culture and labour relations. She is a board member of the Business Association for Latin America Studies, of the Scientific Committee of Euromed Marseille, France, as well as the editorial boards of *The International Journal of Human Resources Management* and other Latin American journals.

Daniel Díaz-Fuentes is Professor of Economics at the University of Cantabria. He has also lectured at the universities of Oxford (1993–5), Carlos III (1990–3), Alcalá de Henares (1989–90) and Buenos Aires (1986–8). He was also Visiting Fellow at the European University Institute (2006) and the universities of Manchester-UMIST (1999), LSE (1996), Oxford, (1993–5) and Michigan (1992). Daniel received his PhD in Economics from the University of Alcalá-Madrid. His research interests include international economic policies (fiscal policy, public service privatization and regulation and Foreign Direct Investment) particularly in Europe and Latin America. He has published widely in a range of specialist academic journals, such as *Journal of European Public Policy, Public Management Review, International Review of Applied Economics* and *Revista de Economía Mundial*, as well as with several prestigious publishing houses such as Palgrave Macmillan, Kluwer Academic, Ashgate and Harvard Univeristy Press. He has served as consultant for the United Nations, the European Commission and CEEP (European Centre for Public Enterprises).

Axèle Giroud is Senior Lecturer in International Business at Manchester Business School. She is currently European Vice President of the Euro-Asia Management Studies Association, and is on the editorial board of several international business journals. She specializes in Asia, Asian and emerging multinational firms, inter-firm relations and linkages, knowledge transfer and FDI spillovers. She has published numerous articles, book chapters and two books: *Transnationals, Technology and Economic Development* (Edward Elgar, 2003) and *Multinationals and Asia: Organizational and Institutional Relationships* (Routledge, 2005).

Jörn-Carsten Gottwald joined University College Cork (UCC) in October 2006. He is a lecturer with the UCC School of Asian Studies / Irish Institute of

Chinese Studies. Jörn received his MA from LMU Munich in Chinese Studies, Political Science and Economics and holds a PhD (Dr. rer.pol.) in Political Science from FU Berlin. He was Assistant Professor at the University of Trier where he finished a post-PhD project on the politics of financial services regulation in Europe. Having worked in various projects of Sino-German technical and economic co-operation and being a regular visitor to China, his research interests are the political and economic developments in East Asia, particularly in China, and issues in financial market regulation in Asia and Europe.

Stephanie Graser has been working since May 2008 as an external doctoral candidate with Prof. Meckl (Chair of International Management at University of Bayreuth, Germany) on emerging market multinationals. She graduated (Diplom-Kauffrau) from the Leipzig Graduate School of Management in Leipzig, Germany, in 2001. She has work experience in consulting (permanent position in in-house consulting at BHW Holding AG, Hameln, Germany, and internship at The Boston Consulting Group GmbH, Munich, Germany) as well as in investment banking (internship at Goldman, Sachs & Co. oHG, Frankfurt am Main, Germany).

Michael W. Hansen is Associate Professor at the Center for Business and Development Studies, Copenhagen Business School. His main research interest is MNC strategy in emerging markets, in particular India, where he has worked with both the development implications of inward investment as well as outward investment strategies of Indian firms.

Françoise Hay is an Economist Researcher (PhD), associated with the Centre de Recherche en Economie et en Management of the CNRS (Scientific Research National Centre) at the University of Rennes 1. In recent years, she has carried out several studies on the Chinese economy and on FDI into and from China and India. She has (with her colleagues Christian Milelli and Yunnan Shi) performed some research studies for the French Ministry of Economy and Finance on the investments of Chinese and Indian firms in Europe (attractiveness of the European countries, European strategies and specificities of these investors, impacts).

Andreja Jaklič is Associate Professor and Researcher at the Center of International Relations at the Faculty of Social Sciences, University of Ljubljana where her teaching and research focus on internationalization, foreign direct investment, multinational enterprises and their effects on growth, productivity and innovation. She has been involved in several international research projects, consulting with international organizations such as UNCTAD and the OECD, as well as with national governmental agencies and business. Her publications include *Enhanced Transition through Outward Internationalization: Outward FDI by Slovenian Firms* (Ashgate Publishing, 2003), co-authored with Marjan Svetličič; several chapters in volumes published by Routledge, Edward Elgar, Palgrave Macmillan and Ashgate, among others; and articles in *Transnational Corporations, The Services Industries Journal, Eastern European Economics, Economics and Business Review, Journal for East Management Studies* and others.

Alexander Mansilya-Kruz has been consulting with major companies and doing research at the Moscow School of Management SKOLKOVO since 2007. His main area of expertise is foreign direct investment and the international expansion of multinationals from emerging markets. He graduated with honours from Moscow State University in 2003, after completing a yearly exchange programme at the Institute for Political Studies in Strasbourg. In 2004–6 he worked for the leading Russian business weekly *Expert,* covering various topics of economic policy and local development, and focusing in particular on telecommunications and transportation. In 2007, he obtained a full-time MBA from HEC Paris.

Reinhard Meckl studied economics at the University of Regensburg. His PhD thesis addressed cross-border cooperation among European companies. He joined Siemens AG Munich, Central Department for Strategic Planning and focused on the development of internationalization strategies for business units of Siemens AG and managed Mergers & Acquisitions projects for the company. His habilitation dealt with concepts for controlling foreign subsidiaries. In 2000 he became full Professor for International Management at Friedrich Schiller University in Jena. In 2004 he changed to a chair with the same denomination at the University of Bayreuth. Since 2007 he has been director of the Bavarian-Chinese Centre for Advanced Studies. In 2008 he was awarded a guest professorship at the Beijing Institute of Technology. His main research topics are mergers & acquisitions, knowledge management in international corporations and internationalization of renewable energies companies.

Christian Milelli is Research Fellow at the Centre National de la Recherche Scientifique, EconomiX, Université de Paris-Ouest Nanterre La Défense (France). He has a general interest in multinational companies. Over the last years, his research has focused on emerging multinational companies from China and India particularly across Europe. His work uses field research and comparative analysis.

Hafiz R. Mirza is chief, Investment Issues Section of the Investment Trends and Issues Branch within the Division on Investment and Enterprise at UNCTAD. In his role at UNCTAD, as well as working on the *World Investment Report,* Professor Mirza is responsible for research programmes related to TNCs, FDI and Development in the Division on Investment and Enterprise. He is deputy editor of *Transnational Corporations,* which is published by UNCTAD, and retains close research collaboration with his colleagues at Bradford University School of Management, as well as the wider research community. He is also responsible for the UNCTAD Symposium/Network on International Investment *for* Development, which aims to increase collaborative research and other activities between UNCTAD, academia and other researchers. Some recent research he has been directly involved with include regionalization; FDI and poverty alleviation (which focused on the impact of FDI in the electrical, electronic and garment industries in ASEAN); developing country TNCs; the impact of the internationalization of infrastructure industries on developing countries; TNCs and agricultural production in the South; and international investment in a low-carbon economy.

Germano Glufke Reis is a lecturer at the Sao Paulo Business School, Fundação Getulio Vargas, engaged in a doctoral programme at the School of Economics, Business and Accounting of the University of Sao Paulo. He holds a Master's in Business Administration from Fundação Getulio Vargas and a BA in Psychology from the University of Brasilia. He has professional experience as a consultant, working for multinationals and Brazilian firms (including state-owned and Brazilian multinationals). His research interests include global mindset and internationalization of emerging country firms.

Ruth Rios-Morales is Deputy Director of Research at Les Roches-Gruyére, University of Applied Sciences in Switzerland. Ruth is also Country Director for Switzerland of the EuroMed Research Business Institute (EMRBI). Ruth holds a BSc in Economics, MSc in International Economics and a PhD in Politics of International Business from the University of Ulster, UK. Before joining Les Roches-Gruyére, Ruth taught international business at the School of Business Studies, Trinity College Dublin. Ruth has also taught international business and finance in Universidad de Zaragoza, Spain. She has conducted advanced research in international business and finance, and her research has been acknowledged by the United Nation Conference for Trade and Development and the World Bank. Ruth contributed to *Oxford Analytica* and to the State Failure Task Force of NATO. Ruth is also member of the advisory committee of the Institute of International Trade of Ireland.

Andreas Nölke is Professor of International Political Economy at Goethe University Frankfurt. He has also taught at the Universities of Constance, Leipzig, Utrecht and Amsterdam; he was a visiting fellow to the Max Planck Institute for the Study of Societies (Cologne); and served as a consultant for the German Agency for Technical Cooperation (GTZ), the European Commission and the World Bank. Nölke also is an Associate of the Amsterdam Research Centre for International Political Economy (ARCIPE). His publications have appeared in journals such as the *Review of International Political Economy*, *World Politics* and the *Journal of Common Market Studies*.

Henrik Schaumburg-Müller is Professor in Business and Development Studies and Director of the Centre for Business and Development Studies at the Copenhagen Business School. He is working on strategies of developing country firms, their positions and upgrading in global value chains and their linkages to transnational corporations and has recently worked extensively with internationalization strategies of firms from Vietnam and Africa.

Jagjit Singh Srai is Head of the Centre for International Manufacturing, Institute for Manufacturing, University of Cambridge. His primary research interests are in international supply network design and operation, industry dynamics, value chain analysis and the industrial exploitation of emerging research models.

Marjan Svetličič is Professor at the Faculty of Social Sciences, University of Ljubljana (was also its Dean), Head of the Centre of International Relations and Ambassador of Science of the Republic of Slovenia, Fellow of the European Academy of International Business (EIBA). He also teaches at the Universities of Trento, Sarajevo, Skopje and Rijeka. He is vice chair of COST project The Emergence of Southern Multinationals, a member of FP7 Advisory Group for International Scientific Cooperation and a member of many editorial boards of scientific journals and a consultant to international organizations. He was president and vice president of the EIBA, a member of the Steering Committee of the Standing Group of the European Consortium for Political Research (ECPR). He has authored more than 300 articles and books.

Heather Taylor is a research associate specializing in International Political Economy at Goethe University Frankfurt. She has also worked at the Friedrich Ebert Foundation in Germany and at the Sardar Patel Institute for Economic and Social Research in Ahmedabad, India. Most recently, she was awarded a grant for a three-month research stay at Trinity College under the supervision of Louis Brennan. Her research is primarily focused on the impacts OFDI on industrial relations and national institutional comparative advantages. Her publications include several book chapters and journal articles on these issues.

Jens Erik Torp is a Senior Consultant at the Centre for Business and Development Studies at the Copenhagen Business School. He has previously worked with private sector development related issues both as a researcher and as a consultant and is currently conducting research on inward investment from developing countries in Scandinavia.

Kee Hwee Wee is Senior Economic Affairs Officer in the Investment Trends and Issues Branch of the Division on Investment and Enterprise at UNCTAD. Dr. Wee is a member of the World Investment Report team at the United Nations Conference on Trade and Development (UNCTAD) in Geneva. He joined UNCTAD in 2002 and prior to that he was Assistant

Director at the ASEAN Secretariat in Jakarta, responsible for matters on regional investment cooperation. He initiated, managed and published a number of key reports, articles and other publications on investment issues at the ASEAN Secretariat.

Changqi Wu is Associate Dean and the Head and Professor of Department of Strategic Management, Guanghua School of Management, Peking University. Professor Wu received his BA in Economics from Shandong University in China and earned his MBA with distinction and his Doctorate in Applied Economic Sciences from the Catholic University of Leuven in Belgium. He specializes in industrial economics, management strategy and international business. He has published two scholarly books and his research appears in leading international journals in the fields of economics and management, including *Rand Journal of Economics, International Journal of Industrial Organization* and *Journal of World Business*. Professor Wu has been a member of the editorial board of the *European Management Review* and *Journal of World Business*. He is a member of the research committee of the International Management division of the Academy of Management and the Chairman of the China Chapter of the Academy of International Business. Professor Wu has been invited to deliver executive seminars to major corporations and government agencies around the world. He sits on the boards of a number of listed companies.

Hinrich Voss (PhD, Leeds) is a Roberts Academic Research Fellow at the Centre for International Business University of Leeds (CIBUL) UK. He is currently conducting research on the internationalization and the international competitiveness of mainland Chinese companies. This research strand incorporates the influence of China's institutions on the international investment behaviour of Chinese firms. His other major research focus is on how international business strategies of multinational enterprises (MNEs) are affected by climate change policies and the institutional objectives to move towards 'Future Energies'. Hinrich is chairman of the advisory board of the NetImpact Chapter at Leeds University Business School.

H. Emre Yildiz is a PhD student at the Stockholm School of Economics, and a member of the Center for Strategic and International Management. His current research focuses on the management of sociocultural integration in cross-border mergers and acquisitions. He completed his Master's in International Business at the Norwegian School of Economics and Business administration and a Master's in Business Administration at Bogazici University in Turkey. He is a native of Turkey and has been living in Stockholm since 2007.

Haiyan Zhang is Associate Professor at Antwerp Management School and programme director of its Euro-China Centre. He holds an MA and a PhD in Public Administration and Management from the University of Antwerp.

Dr. Zhang's research interests include international business activities of Chinese companies and Chinese-owned overseas enterprises, foreign direct investment and management issues of international joint ventures in transition economies, industrial agglomeration in China, etc. He has published in journals and contributed to more than ten books on foreign direct investment in China and the internationalization of Chinese multinational enterprises. He is co-author of *European Direct Investment in China*, published by Routledge in 2002. He has consulted for several trade associations, government institutions and multinational companies on various topics, such as US direct investment in Belgium, strategic management of bilateral cooperation with Chinese local authorities, mergers and acquisitions in China, etc.

Part I
Introduction

1
Introducing Southern Multinationals and their Impact on Europe

Louis Brennan

This chapter serves to describe the content of this edited volume on the emergence of Southern Multinationals and their impact on Europe. The volume is divided into seven parts, including this introductory section and a concluding section. The five intervening parts contain contributions that address the following aspects:

- Quantification of the emergence of Southern Multinationals
- Southern Multinationals from a home country perspective
- Southern Multinationals from a host country/region perspective
- Innovative perspectives on Southern Multinationals and
- Implications for Theory and Theory Development.

Part Two on the quantification of Southern Multinationals consists of two contributions that appear as Chapters 2 and 3.

In Chapter 2, on the rise of transnational corporations (TNCs) from the South, Hafiz Mirza et al. present the trends, growth and characteristics of foreign direct investment (FDI) from developing countries. They consider the core concepts and issues related to the emergence of Southern Multinationals. They highlight that since these companies have recently embarked on their internationalization paths, their motivations, strategies and characteristics are yet to be clearly identified. They note, however, that these emerging TNCs have implications in terms of the competitive landscapes in both developed and developing host economies. Since traditionally FDI by developing country TNCs tended to be directed to neighbouring and developing economies, they focus their analysis on South–South aspects of such FDI. However, many of the issues and questions that they raise are also pertinent to the consideration of South–North FDI.

Peter Buckley, Adam Cross, and Hinrich Voss assemble the extant data in relation to foreign investment into Europe from the South in Chapter 3 'Data Constraints in the Analysis of Southern Multinationals: Evidence from the EU'. While highlighting that the analysis of the impact of Southern

Multinational Enterprises (MNEs) on Europe is severely constrained by the lack of available data, they do, however, offer some significant results in relation to the phenomenon. These include the significant and growing nature of such investment and that its impact is likely to differ from that of the 'typical' Northern MNE.

Part Three addresses Southern Multinationals and Europe from a home country perspective. The five chapters in this part include contributions from Brazil, China, Hungary, Russia and Slovenia.

Chapter 4 addresses the role of Europe in the internationalization strategies of the Multilatinas. Afonso Fleury, Maria Tereza Leme Fleury and Germano Glufke Reis utilize a framework based on the degree of cultural and development distance to elaborate on the choice of foreign region chosen by those Multilatinas included in the rankings of Fortune, Forbes, WIR and BCG. Of this set of 33 large Multilatinas, roughly 21 per cent had made their first investments in the European region, though these were overwhelmingly in Latin-Europe as opposed to Anglo-Saxon Europe. For those choosing the European region for their second or third international investment, their investments were more evenly balanced between Latin and Anglo-Saxon Europe. The authors argue that the relatively small presence of Multilatinas in Europe, particularly in the Anglo-Saxon region, can be attributed to cultural and institutional factors, while the lack of certain management competences, such as cross-cultural competences, also plays a role. They point to the need for further research to understand the impact of such factors on the strategies of Multilatinas in Europe.

Changqi Wu analyses the internationalization of China's enterprises and its implications for Europe in Chapter 5. In examining the motives for Chinese enterprises going global, he offers some insights into why China's enterprises have thus far limited their direct investment in the developed world as is evident from the roughly 2 per cent share of China's overall outward investment accounted for by Europe. Two case studies of China's enterprises' investments in Europe serve to illustrate the contrasting fortunes of China enterprises' direct investment into Europe. He concludes by arguing that European sophisticated technology-owning and innovative small firms, particularly in manufacturing sectors, remain attractive to Chinese companies that want to move up the technical ladder and to expand globally. This is consistent with the view that China's enterprises' direct investment into Europe is motivated by technology-seeking and concentrated in those sectors where the appropriated technologies are useful to China's next stage of domestic economic development.

In Chapter 6, Erzsébet Czakó characterizes the pattern of inward and emerging outward FDI (OFDI) in Hungary. She demonstrates that Hungary has an edge in both inward and outward investment in the region encompassing itself and Bulgaria, the Czech Republic, Poland and Romania. While typically some 80 per cent of inward investment originates from Europe, some investment has started to originate from Asia and Latin America. Similarly Europe accounts for the overwhelming bulk of OFDI by Hungary's companies, with the dominant destinations being other EU countries. The services sector predominates as the source of Hungary's OFDI, with financial enterprises being the largest contributor from the services sector. Outward investors are represented in three groups: MNE subsidiaries, large Hungarian enterprises and medium and small-size enterprises. She concludes that outward FDI may be attributed to the most experienced and largest enterprises while market- and strategic asset-seeking may be the dominant incentive for foreign market entry for such enterprises.

Chapter 7 by Alexander Mansilya-Kruz considers the westwards expansion of Russian multinationals. He describes the recent trends in outward investment in a sample of Russia's largest multinationals ranked by assets. For these top Russian MNEs, Europe is by far the most important investment destination. He describes and analyses such investment in Europe according to their motivation. Downstream integration is the motive for the strategic expansion into Europe of Russian commodity producers. While vertical integration is also a defining characteristic of the strategies in the metal mining sector, the companies focused not just on complementing their Russian upstream assets with downstream facilities in target markets, but bought up a wide range of mines and smelters throughout Europe in what was justified as scale-seeking expansion. The strategy that was pursued by companies mostly active in manufacturing industries was a strategic asset-seeking strategy, which he describes as product-line import. This consists of purchasing a relatively smaller, but technically modern manufacturer in a developed country and localizing the production of its main line of machines in Russia. The purpose, on the one hand, is to bridge quickly the technological gap between Russian manufacturers and their Western competitors, and, on the other, to benefit from lower costs and dynamic demand in Russia.

Andreja Jaklič and Svetličič Marjan consider the case of Southern Multinationals from Slovenia in Chapter 8. They argue that while FDI and internationalization theories traditionally emphasized firm-level determinants as the main drivers of the creation of MNEs, determinants outside the enterprise have become increasingly important. The authors report that the 'Top 25 Slovene MNEs' have 286 foreign affiliates across 53 countries, that is, 11 affiliates, and a presence in nine countries, on average, with more than 80 per cent of their foreign affiliates located in Europe. Eight of the 'Top 25 Slovene MNEs' are based exclusively in Europe. The authors conclude that in terms of development, smallness can be only outweighed by internationalization, and that in the light of the current global changes this is not only relevant for Slovenia, but also for Europe in general.

Part Four addresses Southern Multinationals and Europe from a host country/region perspective. The five chapters in this part include two contributions that address Chinese and Indian firms in Europe generally and also the case of Denmark for these two sets of firms. China's OFDI is also considered for the case of Belgium in a further chapter in this part, while the case of strategic industries in Europe and the European perspective on Sovereign Wealth Funds are considered in the final two chapters of this part.

In Chapter 9, Françoise Hay and Christian Milelli consider the presence of China's and India's firms in Europe from the perspectives of both theory and empirical evidence. Drawing on a proprietary database and face-to-face interviews, the authors examine the advantages of such firms, their motives and strategies. They consider that the main strategy followed by Chinese and Indian companies is based on the exploitation of distinctive assets, which combine firm-specific with home country advantages. However, while the asset exploitation strategy is still prominent for these companies in Europe, the authors conclude that the asset-augmenting strategy is emerging, and in many cases it goes hand in hand with the previous strategy. When companies embark on such a strategy they target a wide range of created assets: technology, brands, distribution network, R&D facilities or managerial capabilities. In considering the impact of such investments on European economies they discriminate between the complementary and competitive impacts on FDI from other sources, bilateral trade, employment and qualification and on competition in product and service markets.

In Chapter 10, Jens Erik Torp, Michael W. Hansen, and Henrik Schaumburg-Müller assess Chinese and Indian multinationals in Denmark with a view to establishing whether there is anything special about them in the context of the ongoing debate related to international business theory and MNEs emanating from the emerging economies. They assess the entry strategies of such firms in terns of their strategic intent, entry mode and organization to ascertain the extent to which they conform to the conventional international business perspective or the latecomer perspective. They include five case studies in their analysis. They find evidence of both Asian investments in Denmark conforming to latecomer and conventional types of investments, with investors being mainly asset seekers or market seekers. The authors note that Danish government actions have been crucial to securing the present wave of Asian investments. They particularly point to the promotion of clusters in this respect, and suggest that a possible policy implication could be that cluster development should focus not on general cluster development, but on building optimal conditions for the location of specific high value-added functions within these clusters.

Filip De Beule, Daniel Van Den Bulcke, and Haiyan Zhang consider in Chapter 11 the characteristics and policy issues relating to Chinese OFDI in Europe and specifically the case of Belgium. They offer an in-depth characterization of Chinese OFDI over time. They consider Chinese OFDI in Europe in terms of destination countries and of invested sectors, while acknowledging that such investment has up to the present been limited. The prospects for future Chinese investment in Europe are considered by the authors, and the history of Chinese investment in Belgium and the location factors affecting such investment based on earlier surveys and interviews by two of the authors are presented. The authors highlight some negative factors affecting Belgium's capacity to attract Chinese investment, including administrative burdens and shortcomings in promotional and marketing efforts, particularly its websites that promote inward investment. They identify some policy recommendations and offer some suggestions for European host countries around the promotion of inward investment from China.

Judith Clifton and Daniel Díaz-Fuentes consider the notion of IFDI into the EU from the non-triad economies as a potential threat to 'strategic industries', Chapter 12 on the the EU, Southern Multinationals and the question of the 'strategic industries' first considers the changing EU FDI regime for the energy and telecommunications sectors in an international context. The authors note that although marginal in terms of volume, IFDI from emerging markets into these two sectors has grown rapidly in recent years, with the BRIC (Brazil, Russia, India and China) economies accounting for the larger part of these flows. While they note that a considerable number of the attempts by multinationals from emerging markets to enter the European energy and telecommunications infrastructure have failed, so have many multinationals based within the EU failed in their efforts to enter these sectors in other member countries. Though the EU continues to enjoy one of the most liberal FDI regimes in the world, some countries such as France, Germany and Hungary have introduced additional screening and restrictions on IFDI on the grounds of security or 'strategic' industries. The authors find that it is difficult to conclude whether the EU is becoming increasingly more protectionist in the light of the emerging Southern Multinationals or whether its increased protectionism is more generally motivated.

Chapter 13 by Ruth Rios-Morales and Louis Brennan focuses on the emergence of sovereign wealth funds (SWFs) and the European perspective. The chapter considers the emergence of SWFs as global financial players and the response to these new important players, including the framework of generally accepted principles and practices that was established in 2008 as the Santiago Principles by the International Working Group established by the International Monetary Fund (IMF). The European response to these new players is addressed by the authors, particularly those of France and Germany, and also that of the European Commission, which has been active in supporting the principles and practices of the Santiago Principles. The authors conclude that the emergence of SWFs marks a significant change in the global economy, involving a shift in dominance away from the developed world to the emerging and developing countries and the financing of the private sector via public capital.

Part Five consists of two chapters that offer innovative perspectives on Southern Multinationals. The first chapter in this part considers emerging country multinationals from a value chain perspective while the second chapter considers the emergence of China's financial sector from the perspective of cadre-capitalism.

In Chapter 14, J. S. Srai and D. E. Fleet explore the configuration of emerging country multinationals using a value chain perspective. They suggest that the use of the value chain perspective can provide particular insights into different internationalization patterns of emerging multinationals that are not evident from the established FDI analytical approaches. A key goal of the study that they report was to understand whether Southern Multinationals have different investment patterns in developed and emerging economies and whether these investment patterns differ when compared with Western MNEs. Drawing on case studies representing around 100 individual international investments, the authors explore the investment behaviour across the manufacturing value chain for MNEs from both developed and emerging economies. The authors show how investment patterns differ between the two sets of MNES. Southern Multinationals' investments in emerging markets are largely supply-side resource- and demand-side market-seeking, and those in developed markets reflect objectives linked to network access (technology and markets) while traditional MNEs' international investments are driven by the need for *network efficiency* (particularly in the case of emerging markets) *and market access*-driven arrangements that integrate low-cost country (LCC) resources and emerging market potential.

In Chapter 15 on financial market reforms in China and the new role for the People's Republic of China in world markets, Jörn-Carsten Gottwald considers the progress of reform in the financial services sector in China and the overall approach adopted in relation to China's OFDI in this sector. The author suggests that the recent reforms and changes in China's financial sector highlight the continuing and deepening involvement of the party–state leadership in China's socialist market economy. While China's 'Go Global' policy, which the author addresses in this chapter, has been in place for almost a decade at the time of writing, only very recently has it been extended to include banks and investment companies. The steps China has taken, including the creation of nominally independent regulatory agencies, to make its financial sector globally competitive are described by the author. However he highlights that while the formal structure of financial services governance in the PRC leads to the state organs, crucial decisions concerning the scope, content, organization and staffing of the administration are decided by party organs, not by the state. The recent progress of the Big Four banks in China and that of the two direct government investments vehicles are described by the author, including their internationalization engagement.

Part Six considers the implications for theory and theory development. The first of four chapters in this part explores the issue as to whether the internationalization strategies of Southern Multinationals provide a strong case for theoretical extension. The second chapter applies the comparative capitalism framework to derive some hypotheses on home–host country interactions while the third chapter explores the impact of financial strategy on the internationalization of Southern Multinationals. The final chapter in this part links the comparative public policy and international business fields by modifying the state capacity framework and adapting it to the entry bargaining process.

Chapter 16 by H. Emre Yildiz and Carl F. Fey addresses whether the internationalization strategies of firms from emerging markets provide a strong case for theoretical extension. They consider whether or not an emerging multinational enterprise (EMNE) is a *sui generis* form of entity such that new theories and frameworks are needed to understand its international strategies and growth patterns. They contend that multiple factors, over and above institutional and economic development, need to be considered when trying to understand internationalization strategies of EMNEs. In particular, factors such as temporal shift and differences in scale rather than differences in home country environments may explain differences between EMNEs and MNEs in terms of their internationalization strategies. The authors argue that by comparing firms from different points in time and of different sizes, many recent studies on EMNEs' internationalization have not clearly shown whether the differences between MNEs from emerging economies and developed economies are really a result of country of origin difference or other factors. They advocate adopting multi-level research designs in future studies to single out the effects of difference factors on the international activities of EMNEs.

In Chapter 17, Andreas Nölke and Heather Taylor consider the case of Indian multinationals using the comparative capitalism perspective to study the implications for global and host country economic institutions. They apply the comparative capitalism framework to Indian MNCs, in order to first understand their domestic background and to identify the most important institutional factors that have contributed to the rise of Indian multinationals, and then to study their conflict potential in host economies and in global economic regulation. Given the early stage of studies on these issues, the authors focus on the identification of a specific agenda for further empirical research. They suggest that the most urgent case for empirical research is to be made for the issue of home–host country interactions. While the authors identify some specific issues of concern, they argue strongly for much more empirical research to be undertaken to confirm their initial findings.

Reinhard Meckl and Stephanie Graser in Chapter 18 consider the impact of financial strategy on the internationalization of EMNCs and whether this is a neglected factor in the study of the internationalization of EMNCs. They suggest that in the wake of the global financial crisis the role that financial strategies play in the internationalization of EMNCs has become a key question. They describe the motivation for a research agenda that seeks to empirically study the question of what role financial strategy plays in the internationalization of EMNCs. Their literature review points to the paucity of coverage around this topic. The few studies cited by the authors offer contrasting conclusions as to the relationship between financial strategy and internationalization, thus affirming in their view the need for research in this area.

Caner Bakir contribute to the literature on the entry bargaining process by considering in Chapter 19 the case of a Southern Multinational and an emerging European (transition) state. He argues that previous studies on entry bargaining have several major weaknesses, and so he seeks to provide a more complete account of how entry bargaining is a multi-actored and multi-level governance process, and why some interactions between the key actors generate an investment agreement, while others do not. He links the comparative public policy and International Business (IB) fields by modifying the state capacity framework and adapting it to entry bargaining. He suggests that an investment agreement is more likely to be the outcome of the entry bargaining process when state capacity exists, and that his work adds to the knowledge of the entry bargaining process from an interdisciplinary perspective. His results indicate that entry bargaining is a governance process where state-led steering is of utmost importance for its conclusion with an investment agreement. The chapter offers some important insights for both governments and Southern Multinationals.

The final chapter in the Conclusion section summarizes the main insights across the different contributions on the emergence of Southern Multinationals and their impact on Europe.

Part II

Quantifying the Emergence of Southern Multinationals

2
The Rise of TNCs from the South

Hafiz Mirza, Axèle Giroud, and Kee Hwee Wee

Transnational corporations (TNCs) from developing and transition economies ('Emerging TNCs') are rapidly strengthening their business links worldwide and contributing to the evolving global economic landscape. The core concepts and issues related to their emergence will be covered in this chapter. First, a large share of foreign direct investment (FDI) by developing country TNCs is directed to neighbouring and developing economies. Second, these companies have recently embarked on their internationalization paths, and the motivations, strategies, and characteristics are yet to be clearly identified. In particular, emerging TNCs have implications in terms of the competitive landscapes in developed and developing host economies. In the context of other developing host economies, some questions arise as to whether such competition will be beneficial. Third, in a regional context, as much FDI from Emerging TNCs is directed towards nearby countries, both national and regional institutional frameworks must be analysed to understand whether these TNCs' internationalization should be encouraged, how regional economies benefit, and the extent to which regional policies can be designed to support such regional cross-investments in view of enhancing the mutual beneficial impact on countries' development.

2.1 Trends, growth and characteristics of FDI from developing countries

2.1.1 Key trends and growth of FDI from developing countries

Developed economies are the leading sources of FDI, with outflows at US$ 820.7 billion in 2009, ahead of developing countries with outward foreign direct investment (OFDI) of US$ 229.2 billion (see Table 2.1) and transition and CIS economies with outflows of US$ 51.2 billion. The trends show that developing and transition countries have increased their share in the world's outward FDI from just 8.0 per cent in 1990, to 16.4 per cent in 2007, and further to 25.4 per cent in 2009. However, this last share will likely fall back a little in the next few years as global FDI bounces back after the financial and

Table 2.1 FDI outflows, by region and selected countries, 1986–2009 (billions of US$)

Region/Economy	Annual average			Outflows				
	1986–90	1991–5	1996–2000	2005	2006	2007	2008	2009
Developed economies	168.3	222.1	692.2	751.6	1,158.1	1,923.9	1,571.9	820.7
Europe	97.3	127.0	502.2	692.6	797.6	1367.6	992.1	439.6
European Union	90.5	116.7	470.0	612.9	694.9	1287.3	915.8	388.5
United States	27.4	63.6	132.6	15.4	224.2	393.5	330.5	248.1
Japan	33.4	20.7	25.6	45.8	50.3	73.5	128.0	74.7
Developing economies	11.1	35.7	78.4	127.1	228.7	292.1	296.3	229.2
Africa	.5	1.8	2.2	2.2	7.0	10.6	9.9	5.0
North Africa	.1	.0	.3	0.4	0.1	5.5	8.8	2.6
Other Africa	.4	1.8	1.9	1.9	6.8	5.1	1.2	2.3
West Africa	.3	.5	.5	0.5	0.3	0.9	1.5	0.5
Central Africa	–	–	–	0.1	0.1	0.1	0.2	0.1
East Africa	–	–	–	0.1	0.0	0.1	0.1	0.1
Southern Africa	.1	1.3	1.4	1.2	6.3	4.0	–0.6	1.6
Latin America and the Caribbean	1.5	5.8	23.9	33.9	67.7	56.0	82.0	47.4
South and Central America	1.2	3.2	8.9	19.6	43.6	23.2	37.3	13.9
South America	.6	2.6	6.9	11.8	35.5	12.1	34.1	3.8
Central America	.5	.6	2.0	7.7	8.2	11.2	3.2	10.1
Caribbean	.4	2.6	15.0	14.4	24.1	32.7	44.7	33.5
Asia and Oceania	9.0	28.1	52.3	91.0	154.0	225.5	204.3	176.8
Asia	9.0	28.1	52.3	90.9	154.0	225.5	204.2	176.7
West Asia	.8	–.2	1.3	19.4	28.0	47.3	38.0	23.3
South, East and South-East Asia	8.2	28.3	51.0	71.5	125.9	178.2	166.3	153.4

East Asia	7.2	22.2	40.8	49.8	82.3	110.3	131.9	116.8
South Asia	–	–	.3	3.5	14.8	17.7	19.0	15.3
South-East Asia	1.0	6.1	9.9	18.1	28.8	50.2	15.4	21.3
Oceania	–	–	–	0.1	0.0	0.0	0.1	0.1
South-East Europe and the CIS	–	.9	2.3	14.3	23.8	51.5	60.6	51.2
Southeast Europe	–	–	.1	0.3	0.4	1.4	1.9	1.4
CIS	–	.9	2.2	14.0	23.4	50.1	58.7	49.7
World	179.4	258.6	772.9	893.1	1410.6	2267.5	1928.8	1101.0
Memorandum: percentage share in world FDI flows								
Developed economies	93.8	85.9	89.6	84.2	82.1	84.8	81.5	74.5
Developing economies	6.2	13.8	10.1	14.2	16.2	12.9	15.4	20.8
South-East Europe and the CIS	*0*	*0.3*	*0.3*	*1.6*	*1.7*	*2.3*	*3.1*	*4.6*

Source: UNCTAD, FDI/TNC database.

economic crisis of recent years (the 2009 level of global OFDI was a half of the figure in 2007 (Table 2.1), with the lion-share of the fall among developed countries). Although a large share of OFDI from developing and transition economies originates from a small number of source economies, companies from more and more countries see the need to explore investment opportunities abroad to defend or build a competitive position. The value of the stock of FDI from developing and transition economies was estimated at US$ 2.97 trillion in 2009, or 15.7 per cent of the world total (see Table 2.2).

As recently as 1990, only six developing and transition economies recorded outward FDI stocks of more than US$ 5 billion. By 2007, that threshold had been exceeded by 27 developing and transition economies; ten of these had outward stocks exceeding US$ 50 billion. It is notable, first, that the number of large outward investor countries in the developing and transition economies has increased, and, second, that outward investments from *tax havens* such as the British Virgin Islands or Cayman Islands have also risen. Tax havens will not be investigated in depth in this chapter, owing to the specific nature of the business transactions. Instead, we will focus the successful development of key TNCs in other economies.

The top five home economies accounted for 68 per cent of the stock of FDI from developing and transition economies, and the top 20 for over 90 per cent (see Table 2.2). In 2007, the largest outward FDI stocks among developing and transition economies were found in Hong Kong (China), the Russian Federation, Taiwan Province of China, the British Virgin Islands, Singapore, and Brazil. Some variations by region can be identified.

2.1.2 OFDI by region

Asia and Oceania is the largest source region of OFDI among developing countries. The region's outward FDI stock was estimated at US$ 1.95. trillion in 2009 (see Table 2.3). *South, East and Southeast Asia* had the largest share of this, with stocks of US$ 1.79 trillion. This represents around 60 per cent of OFDI flows per cent and stocks from developing countries (see Tables 2.1, 2.2). East and Southeast Asia have seen their flows and stocks increase sharply over the past two decades. In 2007, OFDI stocks were of US$ 1,348 billion for East Asia and US$ 242 billion for Southeast Asia. By comparison, such stocks were of US$ 49 billion for East Asia and US$ 9 billion for Southeast Asia in 1990. Asian corporations engage in substantial intraregional investment, promoting the South–South (as well as both intraregional and interregional investment) trend.

This is likely to continue and intensify as a result of a strong performance by Asian firms, their commitment to further internationalization, and mergers and acquisitions (M&As) deals likely to take place. In terms of stocks, Hong Kong (China) is the largest source of OFDI from the region, followed by Singapore, Taiwan, China, the Republic of Korea, and Malaysia (Table 2.3). The picture varies if we consider OFDI flows. Hong Kong dominated in 2007,

Table 2.2 FDI outward stocks, by region and selected countries per cent

Region/Economy	Billions of US$					Percentage share to the global stock				
	1990	2000	2007	2008	2009	1990	2000	2007	2008	2009
Developing economies, the SEE & CIS	145.2	884.0	2,807.5	2,620.9	2,971.3	7.0	11.1	14.5	16.2	15.7
Developing economies	145.2	862.6	2,420.3	2,393.3	2,691.5	7.0	10.8	12.5	14.8	14.2
Africa	19.8	44.1	88.8	84.5	102.2	1.0	0.6	0.5	0.5	0.5
North Africa	1.8	3.3	9.2	17.7	20.3	0.09	0.04	0.05	0.11	0.11
Other Africa	18.0	40.9	79.6	66.8	81.9	0.9	0.5	0.4	0.4	0.4
West Africa	1.8	6.6	9.4	10.9	11.4	0.09	0.08	0.05	0.07	0.06
Central Africa	.4	.6	.8	.9	.9	0.02	0.01	0.00	0.01	0.00
East Africa	.2	.4	.7	.7	.8	0.01	0.00	0.00	0.00	0.00
Southern Africa	15.7	33.2	68.8	54.3	68.7	0.8	0.4	0.4	0.3	0.4
South Africa	15.0	32.3	65.9	49.8	64.3	0.7	0.4	0.3	0.3	0.3
Latin America and the Caribbean	57.6	204.4	511.4	589.3	643.3	2.8	2.6	2.6	3.6	3.4
South and Central America	56.0	115.1	295.2	328.5	349.0	2.7	1.4	1.5	2.0	1.8
South America	49.3	96.0	224.3	254.3	264.9	2.4	1.2	1.2	1.6	1.4
Caribbean	1.6	89.3	216.2	260.8	294.3	0.1	1.1	1.1	1.6	1.6
British Virgin Islands	.9	67.1	159.1	198.4	224.9	0.0	0.8	0.8	1.2	1.2
Brazil	41.0	51.9	136.1	162.2	157.7	2.0	0.7	0.7	1.0	0.8
Central America	6.7	19.1	70.9	74.2	84.1	0.3	0.2	0.4	0.5	0.4
Cayman Islands	.6	20.8	54.9	59.5	66.3	0.0	0.3	0.3	0.4	0.3
Mexico	2.7	8.3	44.7	45.9	53.5	0.1	0.1	0.2	0.3	0.3
Chile	.2	11.2	31.7	31.8	41.2	0.0	0.1	0.2	0.2	0.2
Argentina	6.1	21.1	27.5	28.7	29.4	0.3	0.3	0.1	0.2	0.2
Panama	3.9	10.5	24.8	26.8	29.2	0.2	0.1	0.1	0.2	0.2
Venezuela	1.2	7.7	14.9	15.8	17.7	0.1	0.1	0.1	0.1	0.1
Colombia	.4	3.0	10.9	13.2	16.2	0.0	0.0	0.1	0.1	0.1

(continued)

Table 2.2 Continued

	Billions of US$					Percentage share to the global stock				
Region/Economy	1990	2000	2007	2008	2009	1990	2000	2007	2008	2009
Asia and Oceania	67.7	614.1	1,820.1	1,719.5	1,946.0	3.2	7.7	9.4	10.6	10.3
Asia	67.4	613.5	1,819.3	1,718.6	1,945.2	3.2	7.7	9.4	10.6	10.2
West Asia	8.5	16.4	116.6	146.3	159.2	0.4	0.2	0.6	0.9	0.8
Turkey	1.2	3.7	12.1	13.7	14.8	0.1	0.0	0.1	0.1	0.1
United Arab Emirates	.0	1.9	35.0	50.8	53.5	0.0	0.0	0.2	0.3	0.3
South, East and South-East Asia	58.9	597.1	1,702.7	1,572.3	1,785.9	2.8	7.5	8.8	9.7	9.4
East Asia	49.0	509.6	1,341.3	1,184.1	1,361.5	2.3	6.4	6.9	7.3	7.2
China	4.5	27.8	95.8	147.9	229.6	0.2	0.3	0.5	0.9	1.2
Hong Kong, China	11.9	388.4	1,011.2	762.0	834.1	0.6	4.9	5.2	4.7	4.4
Korea, Republic of	2.3	26.8	74.8	97.9	115.6	0.1	0.3	0.4	0.6	0.6
Taiwan Province of China	30.4	66.7	158.4	175.1	181.0	1.5	0.8	0.8	1.1	1.0
South Asia	.4	2.9	47.2	67.1	82.0	0.0	0.0	0.2	0.4	0.4
India	.1	1.7	44.1	62.5	77.2	0.0	0.0	0.2	0.4	0.4
South-East Asia	9.5	84.5	314.3	321.2	342.4	0.5	1.1	1.6	2.0	1.8
Malaysia	.8	15.9	58.2	67.6	75.6	0.0	0.2	0.3	0.4	0.4
Singapore	7.8	56.8	218.2	207.1	213.1	0.4	0.7	1.1	1.3	1.1
Oceania	.3	.6	.8	.8	.9	0.01	0.01	0.00	0.01	0.00
South-East Europe and the CIS	.0	21.3	387.1	227.7	279.8	0.0	0.3	2.0	1.4	1.5
Southeast Europe	.0	.8	3.9	9.3	10.4	0.0	0.0	0.0	0.1	0.1
CIS	.0	20.5	383.3	218.4	269.4	0.0	0.3	2.0	1.3	1.4
Russian Federation	.0	20.1	370.2	202.8	248.9	0.0	0.3	1.9	1.3	1.3
World	2,086.8	7,967.5	19,314.0	16,206.8	18,982.1	100.00	100.00	100.00	100.00	100.00

Source: UNCTAD, FDI/TNC database.

with outflows of US$ 53 billion, followed by China, Republic of Korea, India, Singapore, Taiwan Province of China, and Malaysia. A large share of Hong Kong's outward investment is located in offshore financial centres, while 'round-tripping' is also common. Chinese TNCs are consolidating their position as investors in other developing African and Latin American countries. South, East, and Southeast Asia account for per cent about a half of all cross-border M&A purchases made by developing countries' TNCs.

West Asia OFDI has increased continuously over the last few years to reach OFDI stocks of US$ 159 billion in 2009 (Table 2.3). Key investors from the region include the United Arab Emirates, Saudi Arabia, Kuwait, Turkey, and Qatar. The Gulf Cooperation Council (GCC) countries represented over 90 per cent of regional outflows. TNCs from the region have invested in greenfield projects in other developing economies (predominantly South, East, and Southeast Asian countries such as China, India, and Malaysia). Intraregional FDI and investment to nearby Africa is also increasing. M&As are the dominant mode of investment (US$ 43 billion of the US$ 44 billion outflows in 2007). Large stocks of foreign assets were facilitated by substantial

Table 2.3 South, East and South-East Asia: FDI outward stocks from top 10 investors, in millions of US$

Economy/ Region	1990	1995	2005	2006	2007	2008	2009
Hong Kong, China	11,920	78,833	471,320	677,153	1,011,215	762,038	834,089
Singapore	7,808	35,050	121,392	160,668	218,201	207,130	213,110
Taiwan Province of China	30,356	42,612	106,511	126,963	158,361	175,140	181,008
China	4,455	17,768	57,206	73,330	95,799	147,949	229,600
Korea, Republic of	2,301	10,231	38,680	49,190	74,780	97,910	115,620
Malaysia	753	5,123	21,919	36,127	58,233	67,580	75,618
United Arab Emirates	14	710	9,542	20,433	35,001	50,801	53,524
Indonesia	86	5,896	13,932	16,658	21,333	27,233	30,183
India	124	495	9,741	27,036	44,080	62,451	77,207
Saudi Arabia	2,124	2,567	14,210	19,608	32,338	33,788	40,314
Kuwait	3,662	2,804	5,893	10,845	14,622	16,144	16,014
Turkey	1,150	1,418	8,302	8,892	12,146	13,745	14,790
Asia	67,395	210,074	901,558	1,254,706	1,819,310	1,718,628	1,945,163
East Asia	49,032	149,444	674,203	927,701	1,341,262	1,184,052	1,361,528
South-East Asia	9,471	50,127	165,271	222,942	314,272	321,207	342,367
West Asia	8,469	9,677	50,424	74,543	116,609	146,282	159,226
South Asia	422	826	11,660	29,520	47,167	67,087	82,042

Source: UNCTAD, FDI/TNC database.

revenues from oil exports in the early 2000s. Sovereign wealth funds (SWFs) are also important, many of them being Islamic private equity firms and other asset management companies from the Gulf Cooperation Council (GCC) countries. These funds have been investing in China and India, in some cases toward initial public offerings (IPOs) or real estate. SWFs invest in diverse industries, ranking from banking, telecoms, real estate, and manufacturing. For banking, North African countries (such as Egypt, Tunisia, and Morocco) have attracted investors from GCC countries.

Latin America and the Caribbean is the second largest investing region in the developing world. However, it saw its OFDI decrease to US$ 47 billion in 2009per cent because of the world financial and economic crisis. Outward FDI stocks reached US$ 643.3 billion the same year (Table 2.4). The leading investor countries in the region are Brazil, Mexico, Chile, Argentina, Panama, and Venezuela. Compared with the size of their economies, the level of outward FDI from Latin American economies remains low, but with prospects for increase given current investments plans by its TNCs.

Africa had the smallest stock of outward FDI in 2009, with a total of US$ 102.2 billion (Table 2.2). The key investing countries in the region are South Africa, Nigeria, Liberia, Morocco, and Egypt (see Table 2.5). South African TNCs are particularly active, acquiring stakes in major projects within the

Table 2.4 Latin America: FDI outward stocks from top 10-Investors (in millions of US$)

Economy	1990	1995	2005	2006	2007	2008	2009
British Virgin Islands	875	12,474	118,754	134,172	159,122	198,360	224,895
Brazil	41,044	44,474	79,259	113,925	136,103	162,218	157,667
Cayman Islands	648	1,384	39,125	47,335	54,908	59,516	66,313
Mexico	2,672	4,181	29,641	36,447	44,703	45,860	53,458
Chile	154	2,774	21,359	26,025	31,688	31,763	41,203
Argentina	6,057	10,696	23,340	25,897	27,544	28,749	29,428
Panama	3,876	5,484	19,839	22,048	24,751	26,846	29,182
Venezuela, Bolivarian Republic of	1,221	3,427	9,429	13,196	14,920	15,834	17,670
Colombia	402	1,027	8,915	10,013	10,926	13,180	16,204
Trinidad and Tobago	21	21	1,049	1,419	1,419	2,119	2,121
Peru	122	567	1,047	1,476	2,284	1,694	1,880
Jamaica	42	308	49	96	69	36	128
Latin America and the Caribbean	57,643	87,892	353,758	434,340	511,401	589,322	643,281
Caribbean	1,630	14,623	159,473	183,607	216,212	260,806	294,288
South America	49,344	63,432	143,927	191,214	224,314	254,275	264,888
Central America	6,668	9,837	50,357	59,518	70,875	74,240	84,104

Source: UNCTAD, FDI/TNC database.

Table 2.5 Africa: FDI outward stocks from top 10-Investors (in millions of US$)

Economy	1990	1995	2005	2006	2007	2008	2009
South Africa	15,004	23,288	37,706	50,826	65,878	49,788	64,309
Libyan Arab Jamahiriya	1,321	976	1,536	1,002	4,935	10,823	11,988
Nigeria	1,207	2,931	4,841	4,857	5,325	6,297	6,438
Liberia	453	1,370	2,929	3,237	3,599	3,981	4,345
Egypt	163	350	967	1,116	1,781	3,701	4,272
Angola	1	0	273	467	1,127	3,502	3,509
Morocco	155	269	666	1,054	1,337	1,699	2,169
Algeria	183	183	687	721	1,017	1,335	1,644
Botswana	447	650	796	758	1,323	545	400
Gabon	167	249	234	340	399	495	582
Africa	19,826	31,501	52,367	66,217	88,809	84,467	102,165
Southern Africa	15,653	24,220	39,136	52,458	68,836	54,336	68,714
North Africa	1,836	1,808	3,908	3,981	9,187	17,712	20,305
West Africa	1,799	4,561	8,158	8,476	9,365	10,871	11,385
Central Africa	372	590	606	711	768	866	944
East Africa	165	322	559	590	653	682	817

Source: UNCTAD, FDI/TNC database.

region and outside (essentially in banking, information and communications technology, infrastructure development, and natural resource industries).

Southeast Europe and the CIS increased their stock of outward investment substantially in the early 2000s to reach US$ 279 billion in 2009, representing, around 10 per cent of total stocks from the developing economies, SEE, and CIS. The Russian Federation is the main investor (Table 2.2), followed by Kazakhstan. Russian companies are consolidating their position regionally, as well as in developed and other developing countries. In Africa, they target raw material supplies and strategic commodities.

2.1.3 OFDI by sector

Table 2.6 shows that major TNCs have emerged in primary, secondary, and tertiary sectors. In the *tertiary sector*, firms from emerging markets invest primarily in finance and business activities (Brazil, China, Hong Kong, Singapore), in electricity, gas, and water (Turkey, Chile, Croatia), in transport, storage, and communication (Singapore, Croatia, Morocco), and in wholesale and retail trade (China, Hong Kong, Thailand). In the *secondary sector*, firms invest predominantly in chemical and chemical products (Thailand, Croatia), electrical and electronic equipment (Thailand, Singapore), food, beverages, and tobacco (Thailand, Turkey) and in textiles, clothing, and leather (Turkey). In the *primary sector*, firms have invested primarily in mining and quarrying (Chile, Morocco, Thailand).

Table 2.6 OFDI stock of selected emerging countries by sector, 2006 (percentage of total)

Investor country	Sector of activity	% of Total	Main sub-sectors concerned (in order of importance)
Brazil	Primary	2.10	
	Secondary	2.76	
	Tertiary	80.73	Finance and business activities
Chile	Primary	46.82	Mining and quarrying
	Secondary	11.23	
	Tertiary	41.95	Electricity, gas, and water, finance
China	Primary	20.65	Mining and quarrying
	Secondary	8.31	
	Tertiary	71.04	Business activities, wholesale and retail trade, finance
Hong Kong	Primary	...	
	Secondary	3.09	
	Tertiary	94.40	Business activities, wholesale and retail trade, finance
Croatia	Primary	9.11	
	Secondary	39.10	Chemical products and chemicals
	Tertiary	46.18	Electricity, gas, and water, transport, storage, communication
Morocco	Primary	5.85	Mining and quarrying
	Secondary	14.60	
	Tertiary	78.44	Transport, storage, communication, finance, business activities
Singapore	Primary	...	
	Secondary	22.67	
	Tertiary	75.57	Finance, transport, storage, communication, business activities
Thailand	Primary	2.71	Mining and quarrying
	Secondary	55.12	Food, beverages, and tobacco, electrical and electronic equipment, chemicals and chemical products
	Tertiary	36.89	Finance, wholesale and retail trade
Turkey	Primary	0.32	
	Secondary	19.01	Textiles, clothing and leather, coke, petroleum products and nuclear fuel, food, beverages, and tobacco
	Tertiary	79.19	Electricity, gas, and water; finance

Source: Calculated from figures available from the IT/FDI Database. Data extracted in November 2008.

Note: Figures may not add up to 100 per cent as some of the OFDI remains unspecified. Business activities can be in real estate, computer and related activities, R&D or other.

Overall, key players have emerged in the primary sector (oil, gas, and mining) and resource-based manufacturing (metals, steel, and petroleum refining), but the bulk of FDI from developing and transition economies has been directed at the tertiary sector, notably business activities and finance.

2.2 Characteristics of TNCs from developing countries

2.2.1 Large TNCs from developing countries

A large number of TNCs from the developing world have established themselves as key global competitors, and are now listed among the largest TNCs in the world. An analysis of the largest TNCs from the emerging world shows that their importance has increased in global rankings, their countries of origin are in line with overall flows and stocks, and they have different features when compared with developed countries' large TNCs (notably they are more diversified, their international activities are less important but increasing rapidly, and they have fewer overseas affiliates).

By 2006, Hutchinson Whampoa (Hong Kong, China), Petronas (Malaysia, Samsung Electronics (Republic of Korea), Cemex (Mexico), Hyundai Motor (Republic of Korea), and Singtel (Singapore) were among the top 100 non-financial TNCs. As a group, foreign assets by the 100 largest TNCs from developing economies were US$ 570 billion in that year. However, these foreign assets are unevenly distributed, with the 10 largest TNCs controlling over half of them.

There have been few changes in the origin composition of the top TNCs over the past decade. Of the top 100, three-quarters of TNCs are from South, East and Southeast Asia, most of the rest equally from Latin America and Africa, with 3–4 from West Asia (namely from Turkey and Kuwait). By origin the top TNCs, in order of importance, are Hong Kong, Taiwan Province of China, Singapore, South Africa, China, Mexico, and Malaysia.

The top TNCs from developing countries differentiate themselves from the general top 100 TNC list in two key areas. First, large TNCs from the South operate in a broader range of industries than the top developed countries' TNCs. Firms in the electrical/electronic and computer industries dominate the top 20, followed by the telecoms, petroleum, and food and beverages industries.

Second, their foreign operations have less importance in the overall level of operations, but are increasing at a much faster rate. Table 2.7 compares the world's largest 100 TNCs with the largest 100 TNCs from developing countries. The first group's share of foreign assets in total assets reached 56 per cent in 2006, the share of foreign sales 58 per cent, and that of employment 56 per cent. This meant that the share of foreign assets for TNCs from developing economies was 34 per cent, that of foreign sales 46 per cent, and foreign employment 41 per cent. However, in value terms foreign assets of developing countries' largest TNCs had increased by 21.3 per cent (compared to a 10.8 per cent increase for world's largest group), foreign

Table 2.7 Snapshot of the world's 100 largest TNCs and 100 largest TNCs from developing economies

Variable	World's largest 100 TNCs					Largest 100 TNCs from developing countries		
	2006	2007	2006–7 % change	2008	2007–8 % change	2006	2007	% change
Assets ($ billion)								
Foreign	5,245	6,116	16.6	6,094	−0.4	571	767	34.3
Total	9,239	10,702	15.8	10,687	−0.1	1694	2186	29.0
Foreign as % of total	*57*	*57*	*0.4*[a]	*57*	*−0.1*[a]	*34*	*35*	*1.4*[a]
Sales ($ billion)								
Foreign	4,078	4,936	21.0	5,208	5.5	605	737	21.8
Total	7,088	8,076	13.9	8,518	5.5	1304	1617	24.0
Foreign as % of total	*58*	*61*	*3.6*[a]	*61*	*0.0*[a]	*46*	*46*	*−0.8*[a]
Employment (thousands)								
Foreign	8,582	8,440	−1.7	8,896	5.4	2151	2638	22.6
Total	15,388	14,870	−3.4	15,302	2.9	5246	6082	15.9
Foreign as % of total	*56*	*57*	*0.8*[a]	*58*	*1.4*[a]	*41*	*43*	*2.4*[a]

Source: UNCTAD / Erasmus University database.

sales increased by 26.9 per cent (compared to 9.0 per cent), and foreign employment by 12.0 per cent (compared to 6.9 per cent).

Finally, developing countries' TNCs also differentiate themselves in having fewer foreign affiliates (nine on average). This pattern varies by company and by region (TNCs from East Asia are the most transnational, as shown in Table 2.8). Company exceptions in terms of geographical diversification include Cemex, Samsung Electronics Co., Flextronics International, LG Corporation, Singtel, Acer, and Neptune Orient Lines, all of which have operations in over 20 countries.

2.2.2 Key features of emerging TNCs

Despite the rising number of large TNCs from the developing and transition economies, most TNCs from developing countries are relatively small firms with a limited geographical reach. Additionally, a feature distinguishing the largest TNCs globally from those based in developing countries is the role of state ownership (such as CITIC Group, Petronas, Singtel). Many of the 100 largest developing-economy TNCs are state-owned, and they are particularly common in the primary sector.

Luo and Tung (2007: 483) subdivide developing countries' TNCs into four sub-categories, namely the world-stage aspirant, the niche entrepreneur, the transnational agent, and the commissioned specialist. These four categories are differentiated on their international diversification and whether or not

Table 2.8 Transnationality of the largest TNCs from developing economies, by region, 2007

Top 100 TNCs from developing economies	**Average TNI[a]**	
Region	**TNI**	**Number of TNCs**
Africa[a] (South Africa)	47.6	9
South-East Asia	49.9	19
South Asia	47.4	2
East Asia	59.2	57
West Asia	56.1	4
Latin America and the Caribbean	40.9	9
Total	**54.4**	**100**

Source: UNCTAD / Erasmus University database.
a: TNI is calculated as the average of the following three ratios: foreign assets to total assets foreign sales to total sales and foreign employment to total employment.

they are state-owned firms. World-stage aspirant and transnational agent have a broad international diversification, while niche entrepreneur and commissioned specialist have a narrow international diversification. Firms in the transnational agent and commissioned specialist categories are state-owned.

The *niche entrepreneurs* include companies such as ZTE (China), Patni Computer Systems Ltd (India), Kamaz (Russia), Mabe (Mexico) or Arcelik (Turkey). These firms typically do not benefit from government funding or possess a rich industrial experience, but focus on a narrow line of products and markets.

The *world-stage aspirants* include companies such as Lukoil (Russia), Haier (China), the Tata Group (India), Embraer (Brazil), Cemex (Mexico), Charoen Pokphand (Thailand), and Nando (South Africa). These firms are key global competitors with a cost advantage related to mass-manufactured and technologically mature products.

The *transnational agents* include International Trust & Investment Corp. (CITIC, China), Ocean Shipping Co. (COSCO, China), Gasprom and UES (Russia), Petrobras and Companhia Vale Do Rio Doce (Brazil), Hindustan Petroleum Co. Ltd and Oil & Natural Gas Corp. (HPCL and ONGC, India), and Pemex and Bancomext (Mexico). Governments are the major shareholders of these companies, and for this reason, although they seek international opportunities their internationalization plans also focus on supporting economic development at home.

The *commissioned specialists* include Minmetals and Sinopec (China), Rosneft and Alrosa (Russia), Bharat Heavy Electrical Ltd and National Thermal Power (India), Electrobras and Banco do Brasil (Brazil), Petronas (Malaysia), and Anglogold Limited (South Africa). These firms have a focused line of business, and as they are state-owned, pursue state-related mandates (Luo and Tung, 2007: 484).

2.3 Determinants and motivations of FDI from developing countries

2.3.1 Key types of TNC activity

There are four principal types of TNC activity, namely natural resource-seeking, market-seeking, efficiency-seeking, and strategic asset (capability)-seeking. Depending on the region and the investment some types of activity will dominate. For instance, in the case of TNCs entering Latin America, Casanova (2004) found that the three main objectives were efficiency-seeking, growth-seeking, and resource-seeking. In particular, it was noted that having a common history or language and physical proximity played a role in explaining relative success of TNCs in this part of the world. For SMEs from developing countries, motivation for internationalization lay predominantly in access to strategic assets, technology, skills, natural resources, markets, and improving efficiency (UNCTAD, 2006).

TNCs' activities abroad may be *aggressive* (that is, seeking to take a proactive action to advance strategic objectives) or *defensive* (that is, reacting to actions taken by competitors, foreign governments or others). Undoubtedly the reasons behind overseas expansion change over time and according to circumstances, and for a particular TNC, all four types of activity may be operationalized to varying intensities and geographical coverage. A good understanding of FDI determinants helps in grasping the complexity of FDI strategies and why and how TNCs wish to operate abroad (Meyer, 2004).

With more complex international strategies adopted by TNCs nowadays, the links and integration between headquarters and foreign affiliates are often important in determining the scope and potential of foreign activities. Firms exploit countries' comparative advantages, but also wish to be located in countries where they can combine their own mobile (firm-specific) assets efficiently with the locational factors. Thus, the type of value-added activity conducted by TNCs in a foreign location matters (WIR, 1998; Dicken, 2007; Dunning and Lundan, 2008).

2.3.2 Historical view on TNCs from the South

In the case of developing countries' TNCs, the literature identifies two waves of OFDI, the first being emerging TNCs that started to invest abroad in the 1960s and 1970s. At that time, the key drivers were mainly efficiency- and market-seeking, and the investment was primarily directed towards other developing countries (mostly neighbouring economies). The second wave of investment was initiated in the 1980s, and is ongoing. FDI is more strategic asset-seeking and driven by a combination of pull and push factors. As in developed countries' TNCs, emerging TNCs have become more strategic, and engage more in M&As. The direction of their FDI is more diversified, with substantial investment in developed countries, predominantly to gain access to key resources.

A Deloitte (2008) survey of Russian TNCs indicated that traditional motives such as secure sustainable sales markets, to gain access to scarce resources and advanced technologies dominate. Push factors rank low compared to the pull factors of host economies. Home country push factors included the insufficient quality of Russian materials or disadvantageous delivery terms, and absence of needed technologies and skills. Thus, political risks in the home Russian economy did not appear as a significant factor explaining Russian firm's internationalization. This contrasts to the situation experienced in the 1990s, when Russian companies did invest abroad to escape from political and economic risks at home. This turnaround exemplifies the changes that occur for TNCs depending on the level of economic development or openness of their home economy.

OFDI also depends on the region of origin. While Asian firms started their internationalization in the 1960s and 1970s, those from Eastern Europe only engaged in international business in the 1990s. In a study of both Hungarian and Estonian firms, Andreff (2003) thus finds that TNCs from transition economies share a number of common features with emerging TNCs in their first stage of development in the late 1970s.

2.3.3 Drivers and motives for TNCs from the South

The role of TNCs from the South in international markets has increased (Mirza, 2000; Sauvant, 2005; Khanna and Palepu, 2006; UNCTAD, 2006; Luo and Tung, 2007; UNCTAD, 2007). A number of studies have investigated the specific nature of drivers and motives of TNCs from the South. These studies find some clear similarities between the rationale for internationalization when compared to developed countries TNCs (Aykut and Ratha, 2003; Beausang, 2003), yet it is undeniable that differences occur, particularly when TNCs from the South invest in developed countries, where they face challenges of being late movers (Bartlett and Ghoshal, 2000).

The case of Russian TNCs highlight that home country consideration is important when analysing motivations of emerging TNCs. For instance, TNCs investing abroad because of limited home markets tend to invest in neighbouring countries through familiarity, or in other developing countries that have similar consumption patterns or institutions. Thus *market access* is a key motive for South–South investment (see Table 2.9). Market-seeking FDI is not solely related to a small home market, and can be attributed to aggressive plans by firms to increase market share in large and growing developing markets. Many Asian firms such as Samsung and Hyundai (Korea), TSMC (Taiwan) or Venture (Singapore) have invested abroad predominantly to gain access to foreign markets often because of a limited market at home.

Table 2.9 South–South FDI drivers and motives

S–S FDI drivers	Rationales	Industrial characteristics	Corporate examples
Lower factor costs	• Access to lower labour and other production costs • Access to natural and other resources	• Labour-Intensive manufacturing, e.g. clothing, toys, and electronics. • Extraction industries, e.g. oil and gas, minerals, and agriculture.	• Giordano (Hong Kong), Hon Hai Precision, Compal and Quanta (Taiwan), and WBL (Singapore) • Minmetal, CNOOC and Boasteel (China); ONGC (India); Petronas (Malaysia), PTT-EP (Thailand); RusAl and Norilsk Nickel (Russia)
Market access	• Small or saturated home markets • Follow-the-customer in global production networks • New growth via internationalization	• Manufacturing of finished and intermediate goods • Services, e.g. retail, telcoms, hotel, and property development	• Samsung and Hyundai (Korea), TSMC (Taiwan), Venture (Singapore) • CLP, Cheung Kong, Hutchison Whampoa (Hong Kong), YTL (Malaysia), SingTel and Capital and (Singapore)
Geographical proximity	• Familiarity and experience • Difficulty in penetrating into matured and industrialized economies	• Most manufacturing industries • Service industries, particularly consumer-oriented	• Hong Kong and Taiwanese TNCs in Greater China • Malaysian and Singaporean TNCs in Southeast Asia
Organizational change and entrepreneurship	• Succession in family business • Family networks spanning several DTEs	• More relevant to service industries, e.g. hotel and property development	• Hong Leong group of companies in Malaysia and Singapore • Sino Land (Hong Kong) and Far East Organization (Singapore) • Li Ka-shing (Hong Kong) and Richard Li's PCRD (Singapore)
Economic diplomacy	• National development assistance and regional solidarity • Political legitimacy	• More relevant to infrastructural projects and resource extraction industries	• China's OFDI in Africa • Taiwan's OFDI in Southeast Asia • Singapore's OFDI in China

For many investors, *geographical proximity* explains the ease of OFDI. For instance, Hong Kong and Taiwanese TNCs invest substantially in Greater China, and firms from ASEAN invest in neighbouring countries. Geographic proximity investment occurs because TNCs have a certain level of familiarity and understanding of markets that are close geographically. These are often also considered to be *psychically* close (although not always). In the case of ASEAN, proximity FDI is also encouraged and facilitated by favourable regional policies that make it easy for firms (from outside or within the region) to invest regionally.

When costs considerations are paramount, FDI seeks out developing countries that offer cheaper labour costs, TNCs invest to access *lower factor costs*. Cost-related FDI are commonly found in labour-intensive manufacturing (such as clothing, toys, and electronics) and extraction industries. One must further note that home country considerations can be related to external pressures, such as the presence of foreign competitors in the home market. Pressures of competition prompt various strategic options, including cost-cutting (leading to investment in the South) or an upgrading of capabilities (which could result in the acquisition of created assets in developed countries).

Emerging TNCs increasingly engage in FDI related to *organizational change and entrepreneurship*. This type of investment relates to key competitive advantages of emerging TNCs, such as family businesses and long-established relational networks. This is commonly found in service industries, and particularly for Asian firms with complex networks of relationships across the regions based on overseas Chinese businesses. The ethnic Chinese networks plays a role in international trade and FDI, especially in differentiated goods, and explains many cases of investment by Asian TNCs across Asia. As a result, it is estimated that over two-thirds of China's inward FDI come from developing Asia (Gao, 2005). Illustrations include the Hong Leong group (Malaysia/Singapore), Far East Organization and Richard Li's PCRD (Singapore), and Sino Land and Li Ka-Shing (Hong Kong).

Finally, when considering overseas FDI, the key role of liberalization of developing countries' policies toward inward FDI as well as the relaxation of home policies toward outward FDI has also played a significant role (the Government of China is promoting outward FDI by providing loans on preferential terms, tax rebates, and investment insurance). Such FDI is related to *economic diplomacy*. Home country government can also be directly involved in internationalization of firms, notably through SOEs, or in other cases the privatization of existing SOEs, giving rise to new private firms with internationalization potential. Such features are common in the South.

The factors driving outward FDI have been in place in some developing countries for some time. Perhaps the most significant driver for the recent surge in OFDI in the early 2000s from the South lies in the growing wealth in some emerging economies that has increased the supply of capital (Aykut and Ratha, 2004).

2.4 Home country policy and institutional development

TNCs from Asia differentiate themselves with their investment strategies and industrial coverage, but also because of the influence and encouragement of their home country governments and economic development (UNCTAD, 2008: 49). For instance, firms from China and India have incentives to venture abroad, while firms from Malaysia, Singapore, and the Republic of Korea have limited home markets. In this section, we focus on four key ways through which the home country policy and institutional development influences OFDI from emerging TNCs, namely liberalization efforts, government bodies and policies, cross-border initiatives, and governments' direct involvement in business.

2.4.1 Liberalization efforts

The first impact that governments in developing economies have had is related to the liberalization of markets. Liberalization programs have changed the competitive landscapes of national firms. In some cases, liberalization programs implemented were linked to efforts conducted by the WTO, the IMF, and the World Bank (some selected Latin American and African economies); in other cases, liberalization occurred in line with the economic development objectives of the home economy (as with many Asian economies) or as part of the transition to market economies (for China, Vietnam, the SEE, and CIS).

Many developing economies have implemented policies that have increased competition in the domestic marketplace, encouraged local firms to internationalize, and allowed foreign TNCs to enter the domestic market. Such changes have been particular salient in Eastern and Central Europe during the 1990s (Kalotay, 2003). In the case of Eastern European transition economies, it is less the process of transition *per se* than the resulting efforts by companies to integrate the global system, namely to gain market shares overseas and exploit firm-specific advantages that explain internationalization (Jaklič and Svetličič, 2001). Institutional changes varied from full privatization of SOEs as in the case of Eastern Europe to partial-privatization experienced in China (often through the mode of equity joint ventures). In other developing economies such as India, Brazil, and Mexico, support came through liberalization programs aimed at opening up markets and deregulating key sectors.

In a study of eight Turkish TNCs (including KOC Holding, Sabanci Holding, Haznedar Refrakter, Borova Ener Holding, Oynurden Kimya Emsas, and Aksan Kalip), Erdilek (2008: 746) finds that liberalization of the home regulatory environment ranked as a powerful driver to overseas investment. This can be explained by the liberalization of the foreign exchange regime, of foreign exchange controls, by the liberalization of the Turkish foreign trade regime, which allowed greater competition from imports.

2.4.2 Government bodies and policies

In addition to liberalization programs and improvements in the regulatory frameworks, developing countries have facilitated OFDI through a series of policies and supportive measures. First, government policies aimed at the competitive development of local firms indirectly support the development of competitive advantages by home TNCs. Second, policies targeting OFDI further support internationalization. For instance, China, India, the Republic of Korea, Thailand, and Vietnam have adopted outward FDI policies and regulations (UNCTAD, 2007). In general, fiscal and other incentives are frequently used to stimulate OFDI, as in the case of loans on preferential terms, tax rebates, and investment insurance provided by the Chinese government.

In some cases, regulations target specific host markets, as in the case of Chinese investment in Africa. To facilitate Chinese firms' investment in Africa, the Chinese government provides loan finance through the Export-Import Bank of China and has established the China–Africa Development Fund to support African countries' investments in agriculture, manufacturing, energy, transportation, telecommunications, urban infrastructure, and resource exploration (WIR08: 53). In other cases, regulations target specific sectors of activity. Vietnam recently ratified a new decree governing regulations and procedures on outward FDI in oil and gas. Governments can also influence investment by engaging in discussion with each other. In the case of Russian TNCs, they often try to secure government assistance abroad, especially in the production and processing of energy and mineral resources. These sectors are usually protected in host economies that consider them as strategic sectors. The Russian government would engage in preliminary discussion with foreign governments in view of protecting the investment interests of its firms abroad (Deloitte, 2008: 37).

Another area through which government policies have been influential is that of FDI in infrastructure. Many current leading TNCs in this industry are SOEs, having been created through government support in line with the economic development objectives of the country. Such firms can be found in Singapore (such as PSA) and Malaysia (MTD capital, Senai Airport Terminal Services) (UNCTAD, 2006).

2.4.3 Cross-border initiatives

Cross-border initiatives and participation in the global institutional framework contributes to the support provided by home government on their TNCs. First, by joining the World Trade Organization, countries engage in a series of further liberalization and harmonization programs that benefit local TNCs. This has been particularly important in the case of China and Vietnam. Secondly, governments engage in bilateral agreements, for trade and investment, which contribute to the ease of firms engaging in economic activities with partner countries. Governments are particularly proactive in terms of protection of their TNCs' foreign assets. In the South–South investment context, numerous new agreements are being signed, for instance, China's investment guarantee agreement was signed with the Republic of Korea. Also, the Mainland and Hong Kong Closer Economic Partnership Arrangement was implemented in 2008 and has opened 11 sectors to investors from Hong Kong in China. In other cases, double taxation agreements were signed between Singapore and China, the Republic of Korea, and Saudi Arabia.

Finally, governments facilitate OFDI within their regional contexts. The effect of such cross-border policy agreements is felt by investors from outside the region, or in some cases solely by investors from within the region. As an example, ASEAN has been in bilateral trade and investment agreements negotiations with the EU since 2007. ASEAN is also negotiating the deepening of an investment agreement among member countries, which would facilitate intraregional FDI, as well as negotiating agreements (such as the agreement for trade in services with the Republic of Korea signed in 2007) that promote South–South investments.

2.4.4 Governments' direct involvement in business

The recent surge in South FDI is also related to the significance of state-owned enterprises; in particular, strategies by SOE TNCs can be linked to the economic development objectives of the home government, to targeted firms' development programs or to sovereign wealth funds. Asia has a large number of SWFs, whose success is linked to rising foreign exchange reserves and government policies. Examples include Temasek (the company has large investments abroad, and controls numerous other international firms such as Singapore Telecommunications, PSA International, and SembCorp Industries); Khazanah Malaysia (linked to UEM, Telekom Malaysia International, Opus Group Berhad, and Bumiputra Commerce Bank), or China Investment Corporation. Local governments have also influenced overseas FDI by historical ties and development of local firms. These are not solely SOEs, but also include the Korean *chaebols*, which have received significant government support in the past and have become major international investors.

2.4.5 Institutional voids in emerging countries and OFDI

Another explanation is related to a set of business groups in emerging economies which have primarily arisen to fill institutional voids (Aulakh and Kotabe, 2008: 212), given that the value created by business groups varies depending on the type of resources and capabilities they are able to acquire. This is important in explaining why micro-institutions might develop, such as the Turkish *families*, Latin American and Spanish *grupos* or Indian business *groups*.

In this section, we focus on government policy and institutional development issues that have facilitated OFDI from the South. In the next section, we will address specific policies implemented in selected emerging countries to support TNCs in their internationalization strategies.

2.5 Modes of entry

There are many forms of operations that can be utilized by TNCs in foreign markets, ranging from arm's-length market transactions (that is, exports) to fully integrated vertical hierarchies (that is, FDI). Available data on cross-border M&As and greenfield investment expansion projects outside the developed world confirm the growing significance of TNCs from developing and transition economies. Joint ventures and acquisitions are perhaps the most common organizational modes for South–South FDI. These joint ventures may take the form of equity investment or non-equity cooperative agreements (for example, joint production arrangements). Acquisitions are also preferred by large emerging TNC conglomerates to control their foreign subsidiaries. Other cooperative strategies in internationalization, such as informal networks and strategic alliances, are also frequently adopted.

2.5.1 Greenfield investments

Emerging TNCs' share of all recorded greenfield (including expansion) projects exceeded 1 per cent in 2009. As a destination, developing countries account for around a half of total greenfield FDI projects (see Table 2.10). The largest number of greenfield projects originate and occur within Asian developing countries, with particularly high numbers found in China and India.

2.5.2 M&As

Emerging TNCs are also key players in terms of M&As. Between 1987 and 2005, emerging TNCs' share of global cross-border M&As rose from 4 per cent to 13 per cent in value terms, and from 5 per cent to 17 per cent in terms of the number of deals concluded. In 2007, the largest South–South M&A deal was the acquisition of National Mobile Telecommunications Co. KSC (Wataniya) of Kuwait by the Qatar firm Qatar Telecom QSC for US$ 3.8 billion (WIR08). Other large South–South M&A involved private equity firms and hedge funds, such as a Korean investor group investing US$ 1.5 billion in the Taiwanese China Network Systems Co. Ltd, the UAE Abraaj Capital Ltd investing in the Egyptian Fertilizers Co. SAE for US$ 1.4 billion, Global A&T Electronics Ltd investing from the Cayman Islands in the Singaporean United Test & Assembly Centre Ltd for US$ 1.17 billion, or the Brazilian GP Investimentos investing in the Argentinean Pride International Inc. for US$ 1.0 billion (UNCTAD cross-border M&A database).

SWFs have been key players in cross-border South–South M&As. The largest deal took place in 2005 with the International Petroleum Investment Co.

Table 2.10 Number of Greenfield FDI Projects, by Investor/Destination Region

	Source		Destination	
	2008	2009	2008	2009
World	16,147	13,727	16,147	13,727
Developed countries	13,219	11,250	7,386	6,249
Developing economies	2,629	2,235	7,595	6,646
Africa	197	171	840	689
South Africa	65	49	116	108
Latin America and the Caribbean	214	226	1,140	1,214
South and Central America	235	271	1,512	1,640
Brazil	101	63	250	271
Mexico	25	35	346	317
Caribbean	14	14	68	55
Asia	2,215	1,835	5,603	4,734
West Asia	580	433	1,093	1,004
Saudi Arabia	56	32	106	141
United Arab Emirates	267	230	486	394
South, East and South-East Asia	1,635	1,402	4,510	3,730
China	256	303	1,515	1,143
Hong Kong, China	170	133	216	253
India	359	260	965	742
Korea, Republic of	252	215	86	96
Malaysia	134	112	212	158
Singapore	175	117	295	309
Taiwan Province of China	156	131	87	87
Thailand	47	51	330	273
Viet Nam	36	24	348	255
Oceania	3	3	12	9
South-East Europe and the CIS	299	242	1,166	832
South-East Europe	31	21	231	131
Croatia	16	8	40	28
Serbia and Montenegro	15	9	128	58
CIS	268	221	935	701
Russian Federation	194	150	574	399
Ukraine	28	27	125	92

Source: UNCTAD, based on information from the OCO monitor website (www.ocomonitor.com).

(IPIC) from the UAE acquiring the Taiwanese firm Kuokwang Petrochemical Co. Ltd for US$ 2.3 billion. The largest South–South M&A deal conducted by SWFs in 2007 was that of the Dubai Financial LLC acquiring the Oman Bank Muscat Al Ahli Al Omani for US$ 621 million.

While large FDI deals take place at both intraregional and interregional levels, the bulk of South–South FDI is intraregional in nature. Cross-border M&As data corroborate this (see Figure 2.1). Intraregional FDI are large in South, East, and Southeast Asia, Latin America, and the Caribbean. At the

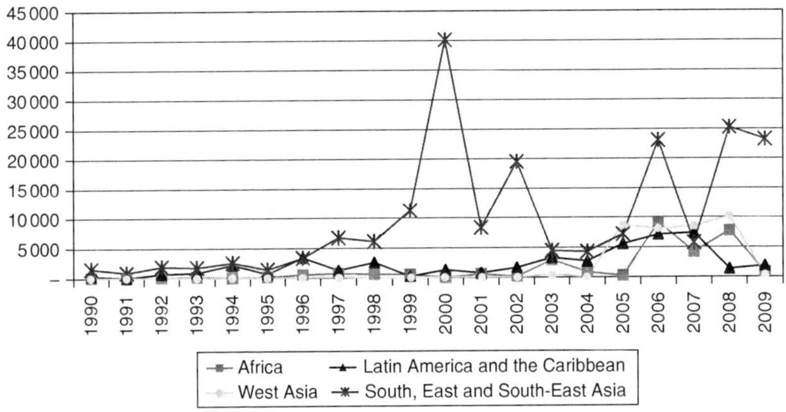

Figure 2.1 South–South cross-border M&As, by intraregional deals, 1990–2009 (millions of dollars)

interregional level, as far as data on cross-border M&As suggest, FDI from South, East, and Southeast Asia to Africa, from South, East, and Southeast Asia to Latin America and the Caribbean, and from Latin America and the Caribbean South, East, and Southeast Asia have increased over the past few years. Table 2.11 shows the geographical orientation of M&As by selected investing countries during the period 1990–2010. South-South acquisitions dominate, with a strong preference for particular regions by TNCs from some countries (e.g. Kuwait and the UAE). TNCs from other countries, however, are more wide-ranging in their acquisitions (e.g. Korea and Malaysia).

2.5.3 Factors explaining modes of entry

There are numerous factors that explain the choice of entry mode in South–South FDI. First, the home and host institutional contexts influence entry mode, as firms may face positive or negative discrimination and regulatory constraints. When TNCs are unfamiliar with the foreign market in which they invest, they often favour the acquisition mode, as a means to reduce unfamiliarity with the host market (for instance, Singapore's Keppel Corp. acquiring shipyards in Brazil). Acquisitions facilitate risk minimization, experience-building, and in turn will enhance the ability of emerging TNCs to further invest in the developing host.

A key feature of South–South FDI is that emerging TNCs can build firm-specific advantages through acquired knowledge on conducting business in unstable developing environments. TNCs also benefit from favored networks that facilitate their success in acquiring firms in other developing countries, or they might use acquisition to quickly gain economies of scale in the targeted host.

Table 2.11 Geographic M&A Orientation of Investors from Selected Asian Developing Countries, 1990–2010 (Number of Acquisitions)

Country	World	Developing countries	Africa	Main target countries in Africa
Kuwait	95	78	15	Egypt, Tunisia, Algeria, Morocco, Sudan, Mauritania, South Africa, Nigeria
Saudi Arabia	119	51	13	Egypt, Morocco, Algeria, Sudan, Nigeria, Botswana, ,
Turkey	84	7	2	Tunisia
UAE	276	124	21	Egypt, Morocco, Sudan, South Africa, Algeria, Libyan Arab Jamahiriya, Tunisia, Guinea, United Republic of Tanzania, Zambia
Indonesia	78	38	6	Mauritius, Tunisia
Korea	336	123	11	South Africa, Morocco, Sudan, Egypt, Congo, United Republic of Tanzania
Malaysia	1,138	865	36	South Africa, Egypt, Mauritius, Sudan, Ghana, Seychelles, Libyan Arab Jamahiriya, Guinea, Cameroon, Kenya, Madagascar, Uganda, Malawi, Mozambique
Singapore	1 530	978	12	South Africa, Mauritius, Nigeria, Cameroon
Thailand	116	69	2	Zimbabwe, Namibia, Mauritius
Taiwan	252	91	1	South Africa

Source: UNCTAD cross-border M&A database.

2.6 Some future research issues

The analysis of emerging TNCs has illustrated the increasing spread of foreign investment activities among companies of varying size, ownership or industrial origin. Outward FDI from emerging economies remains concentrated with a small number of key players, in terms of country of origin, and even in terms of number of TNCs from these countries (as demonstrated by the high concentration of OFDI among a small number of key TNCs in the case of the Russian Federation). However, the number of home developing economies has diversified over the past two decades, and there are increasing numbers of globally competitive TNCs from the emerging world. This confirms the new phase of emerging TNCs' integration into the global economy and the expected continuous growth of their position. Keeping this in mind, we would like to suggest a series of future research issues to be addressed to further understand emerging TNCs as well as the role and context of South–South FDI. Given the scale of South–South investment, and its growth prospect, further support ought to be provided by home and host governments alike, and in line with current regional integration trends, the role of regional groupings will also increase in the future. The role of international institutions and that of UNCTAD specifically, will also be addressed.

2.6.1 FDI and TNCs from developing countries

For policymakers in host governments, or for international organizations, the rise of FDI from developing countries has implications in terms of policy development. What are the implications of emerging competition between established (mostly developed country) and emerging (mostly developing and transition economy) TNCs for, among others, host countries and the international institutional framework? Will this competition be beneficial overall (for example, because of the wider diversity of assets that TNCs bring to developing host countries, for example, in setting up infrastructure) or problematic (for example, because intense competition might cause companies to pay less regard to corporate responsibility, for example, as is sometimes argued in extractive industries)? How can policies at the national and international level maximize benefits and simultaneously reduce costs?

2.6.2 South–South FDI

2.6.2.1 Nature of South–South FDI

Emerging TNCs tend to invest in neighbouring developing countries, in markets that are geographically, economically, and often culturally and linguistically close. This creates growth opportunities for developing host economies, particularly those for which South–South FDI is the major source of FDI. Host countries with the highest share of South–South FDI—as a proportion of total inward FDI—include Bangladesh, Ethiopia, Kyrgyzstan, Thailand, and the United Republic of Tanzania. Many of these are LDCs and, indeed, the evidence shows that South–South FDI is particularly significant for the poorest developing countries. Some important research questions arise from these patterns. What are the particular characteristics of Southern TNCs (for example, appropriate technology, a familiarity with institutions) that might be tapped to support the development policies of LDCs? When developed countries TNCs hesitate to invest in LDCs perceived as highly risky, can South–South FDI become a viable alternative source of investment?

2.6.2.2 *Understanding emerging TNCs in the South*

At the level of the firm, future research will need to identify whether or not emerging TNCs are indeed more familiar with and better placed to understand developing hosts and their business environment. Are they more able to manage risks in these environments, and do they benefit from enhanced competitive advantages compared to their developed country counterparts? Do they maximize their advantage in terms of technological and resources in other developing economies?

2.6.2.3 *Understanding the impact of South–South FDI*

Despite the increasing role of South–South FDI, there is still little evidence in terms of its long-term trend and impact on developing recipient. Further research in this area is needed to address a series of questions regarding the nature of the investments undertaken, the key strategies adopted in South–South FDI, the potential impact on developing hosts, and in return the impact on home developing economies. The type and level of impact from emerging TNCs in developing countries is yet to be fully understood, as existing studies are inconclusive (partly because of a lack of consistent and comparable country-level data). Are emerging TNCs beneficial to developing countries in terms of impact, and knowledge and technology transfer? With slowing market growth in the developed countries, many TNCs are now turning to developing countries as their main growth markets. They may, in turn, increase the competitive pressure for both emerging TNCs and for local firms in host developing environments. What will be the impact for the potential growth of local competitors in LDCs? Is South–South FDI beneficial for the home countries, and if so to what extent, and what areas ought to be targeted?

2.6.2.4 *Support by home governments*

Given the diversity of comparative advantages, political systems and levels of economic development (with related competitive environment and existing capabilities at firms and individual levels) and geographical features (in terms of climate or proximity to other markets), we acknowledge that there is no one-size-fits all policy that can be recommended to deal with outward FDI. Until now, little support has been provided to outward FDI from developing countries. This is, in part, related to other urgent developmental goals being pursued, yet when local TNCs are developed, they learn from their internationalization process, and can in return bring substantial resources back to their home country. This can further support economic development goals of home governments. Should home governments facilitate internationalization of their firms? If so, what can home governments do to facilitate this process? How can home developing countries integrate TNCs into their overall development strategies? and how can they best promote outward FDI? To what extent should FDI promotion target South–South FDI?

These questions relate to understanding resources and strategic assets that outward FDI can bring, and absorptive capabilities at home; they also relate to commitment in home markets to create dynamic business environment that can further support TNCs and local firms' capabilities. Thus, home governments must decide how OFDI promotion can be integrated into local competitive policies. How can UNCTAD provide support in this effort?

2.6.2.5 Support by host governments

Host governments in developing countries also need to consider the role of and benefits from emerging TNCs in their country. A key question is what developing host countries can do to leverage fully the expansion of FDI from the South. In terms of enhancing the positive impact of such FDI, they need to consider the full range of policies that can influence the behaviour of foreign affiliates, and their interaction with the local business environment. This requires taking into account the specific characteristics of different industries and activities in designing a strategy to attract desired kinds of FDI. In addition, it is important to promote the amount and quality of linkages between foreign affiliates and domestic firms. Host-country governments can use various measures to encourage linkages between domestic suppliers and foreign affiliates and strengthen the likelihood of spillovers in the areas of information, technology, and training. In terms of addressing potential concerns and negative effects associated with inward FDI, there is no principal difference between the policies to apply in the case of FDI from developed countries and in the case of FDI from developing and transition economies.

2.6.2.6 Key features for South–South investment promotion

South–South investment cooperation has increased, namely through international investment agreements. The increase of FDI from emerging TNCs is likely to generate growing demand from their business community for greater protection of their overseas investments. As a consequence, in addition to using international investment agreements as a means to promote inward FDI, some developing-country governments will increasingly consider using international investment agreements to protect and facilitate outward investments. This may influence the content of future treaties and result in an additional challenge for those developing country governments to balance their need for regulatory flexibility with the interests of their own TNCs investing abroad.

Beyond bilateral efforts, WIR 06 suggested the creation of a network of EXIM banks and development finance institutions. Such initiatives will take time, but would have long-term beneficial impact on the propensity, coordination and impact of South–South investment. Policy makers therefore need to investigate avenues for future collaboration.

2.7 South–South FDI in the regional context

Most FDI by developing country TNCs is in other countries in neighbouring countries. Given this, in addition to creating bigger markets, can regional policies be designed to support such regional cross-investments in order to facilitate the mutual development of countries? In particular, how can neighbouring countries use their regional division of labour to best effect, for example, in regional integrated production systems? Some regional groupings have been more proactive and successful in encouraging intraregional FDI, as in the case of ASEAN. How can other regional groupings learn from the intraregional trade and investment liberalization efforts conducted in successful regions and replicate these in their own region? Is intraregional investment more beneficial than interregional investment? Is intraregional investment a more reliable source of investment for LDCs and in the long term? Finally, can South–South FDI be facilitated on an interregional level, through negotiations taking place between regional groupings from the South as opposed to individual governments? At firm level, future research will also lead to better modelization of FDI flows at the aggregate level and at industry or firm levels, such models would support a better understanding of how regional integration impacts upon South–South FDI flows.

References

Andreff, W. (2003), 'The Newly Emerging TNCs from Economies in Transition: A Comparison with Third World Outward FDI', *Transnational Corporations*, 12 (2), 73–118.

Aulakh, P. S. and Kotabe, M. (2008), 'Institutional Changes and Organizational Transformation in Developing Economies', *Journal of International Management*, 14, 209–16.

Aykut, D. and Ratha, D. (2003), 'South–South FDI Flows: How Big are They?' *Transnational Corporations*, 13 (1), 149–76.

Bartlett, C. and Ghoshal, S. (2000), 'Going Global: Lessons from Late Movers', *Harvard Business Review*, 78, 132–42.

Beausang, F. (2003), *Third World Multinationals: Engine of Competitiveness or New Form of Dependency?* Basingstoke: Palgrave Macmillan.

Casanova, L. (2004), 'East Asian, European, and North American Multinational Firm Strategies in Latin America', *Business and Politics*, 6 (1), Article 6.

Deloitte (2008), *Russian Multinationals: New Plays in the Global Economy*. Moscow.

Dent, C. M. (2008), *East Asian Regionalism*. London: Routledge.

Dicken, P. (2007), *Global Shift: Reshaping the Global Economic Map in the 21st Century*, 5th edn. London/Thousand Oaks, CA/New Delhi: Sage Publications.

Erdilek, A. (2008), 'Internationalization of Turkish MNEs', *Journal of Management Development*, 27 (7), 744–60.

Gao, T. (2005), 'Foreign Direct Investment from Developing Asia: Some Distinctive Features', *Economics Letters*, 86 (1), 29–35.

Heinrich, A. (2004), 'EU Enlargement and the Challenges for the Internationalization of Companies from Central and Eastern Europe: Insiders and Outsiders in the Energy Sector', paper presented at the Elites and EU Enlargement Second International Conference, University of Bremen, May 1, mimeo.

Jaklič, A. and Svetličič, M. (2001), 'Does Transition Matter? FDI from the Czech Republic, Hungary and Slovenia', *Transnational Corporations*, 10 (2), 67–105.

Kalotay, K. (2003), 'Outward FDI from Central and Eastern European Europe', *Economics of Planning*, 37 (2), 141–72.

Khanna, T. and Palepu, K. G. (2006), 'Emerging Giants: Building World-Class Companies in Emerging Markets', *Harvard Business Review*, 84 (10), 60–9.

Luo, Y. and Tung, R. L. (2007), 'International Expansion of Emerging Market Enterprises: A Springboard Perspective', *Journal of International Business Studies*, 38 (4), 481–98.

Meyer, K. E. (2004), 'Perspectives on Multinational Enterprises in Emerging Economies', *Journal of International Business Studies*, 35 (4), 259–77.

Mirza, H. (2000), 'The Globalization of Business and East Asian Developing-Country Multinationals', in N. Hood and S. Young (eds), *The Globalization of Multinational Enterprise Activity and Economic Development*. Basingstoke: Macmillan Press Ltd.

Sauvant, K. P. (2005), 'New Sources of FDI: The BRICs. Outward FDI from Brazil, Russia, India and China', *The Journal of World Investment & Trade*, 6, 640–709.

UNCTAD (2006), *World Investment Chapter 2006: FDI from Developing and Transition Economies: Implications for Development*. New York/Geneva: United Nations.

UNCTAD (2007), *Global Players from Emerging Markets: Strengthening Enterprise Competitiveness through Outward Investment*. New York/Geneva: United Nations.

UNCTAD (2008), *World Investment Chapter 2008: Transnational Corporations and the Infrastructure Challenge*. New York/Geneva: United Nations.

Wong, J. and Chan, S. (2003), 'China's Outward Foreign Direct Investment: Expanding Worldwide', *China: An International Journal*, 1 (2), 273–301.

3

Data Constraints in the Analysis of Southern Multinationals: Evidence from the EU

Peter J. Buckley, Adam R. Cross, and Hinrich Voss

3.1 Introduction

The impact of Southern Multinational Enterprises (MNEs) on Europe is of pressing interest in the wake of the rapid internationalization of multinationals from the BRIC(S) countries (Brazil, Russia, India, China and South Africa) and other countries of the 'South'. It is of compelling interest to know the impact that Southern MNEs have on Europe and to examine if (and how) this impact differs from traditional inward investors such as the USA and Japan. However, this chapter shows that such efforts are severely constrained by the lack of reliable and consistent data. The chapter assembles the extant data and suggests that significant outcomes of inward foreign direct investment from the South are already occurring.

3.2 Paper tigers and shadow dragons (Empirical challenges)

Empirical research on the impact of Southern MNEs on Europe is constrained by the investment volume and availability of data. Here we discuss and interpret the available data and point out some empirical challenges.

Investment volume: The stock of FDI into the European Union by firms located in Southern countries has doubled over the period 2004 to 2008 but remains small overall. By the end of 2008, the stock of inward FDI by Southern countries accounted for about 3 per cent of all inward FDI to the EU-27, which is dwarfed by investments from North America, let alone intra-EU-27 FDI (see Table 3.1). This stock is heavily concentrated in a small set of countries of which the ten largest investor countries are Singapore, Brazil, Russia, Hong Kong, China (excluding Hong Kong), Mexico, South Korea, India, South Africa, and Turkey.[1] Although the investment volume is small, the presence of the BRIC(S) countries within the top ten Southern investors reaffirms the current focus on the growing economic strength of these countries and their outward investment behaviour (cf. UNCTAD, 2006). Indeed, all five countries have significantly increased their investments into Europe

Table 3.1 Inward FDI stock to the EU-27 (EUR mn and percentage of total)

	2004	2005	2006	2007	2008
All countries of the world	**4,810,733**	**5,653,692**	**6,508,521**	**7,441,574**	**7,514,753**
Summation check (%)	0.938	0.939	0.938	0.939	0.937
1 Africa	**0.17%**	**0.15%**	**0.11%**	**0.13%**	**0.21%**
1a Northern Africa	0.02%	0.02%	0.02%	0.02%	0.06%
1b Central and Southern Africa	0.14%	0.12%	0.09%	0.11%	0.15%
2 America	**17.69%**	**17.23%**	**16.31%**	**16.16%**	**16.17%**
2a North America	17.31%	16.82%	15.85%	15.42%	15.32%
2b Central America	0.17%	0.16%	0.15%	0.14%	0.15%
2c South America	0.20%	0.25%	0.31%	0.59%	0.69%
3 Asia	**2.60%**	**2.43%**	**2.45%**	**2.71%**	**2.88%**
3a Southern Asia	0.01%	0.04%	0.04%	0.06%	0.09%
3b Eastern and Southeastern Asia (excl. JP)	0.85%	0.95%	0.86%	0.98%	1.26%
3c Japan	1.70%	1.38%	1.50%	1.62%	1.46%
3d Near and Middle East	0.04%	0.04%	0.04%	0.04%	0.00%
4 Europe	**72.73%**	**73.71%**	**74.59%**	**74.52%**	**74.10%**
4a EU-27	67.24%	68.20%	69.10%	68.95%	68.55%
4b other Europe (incl. Israel)	5.49%	5.48%	5.48%	5.56%	5.55%
4c Transition economies (excl. CIS)	0.01%	0.04%	0.02%	0.01%	0.01%
4d Commonwealth of Independent States	0.18%	0.35%	0.31%	0.41%	0.46%
5 Oceania	**0.58%**	**0.42%**	**0.32%**	**0.35%**	**0.32%**
5a Australia	0.57%	0.40%	0.29%	0.33%	0.30%
Southern MNE home economies (1, 2b,c, 3a, b, d, & 4c, d)	**1.62%**	**1.98%**	**1.84%**	**2.36%**	**2.87%**

Source: Eurostat (2010).

since 2004. Investments from Brazil, China, and India increased tenfold during the period in question. The FDI stock from Brazil in Europe is now equivalent to the combined stock of Greece, Hungary, and Portugal in the rest of Europe. Chinese FDI stock is equivalent to that of Malta in the rest of Europe and India's FDI stock in Europe is as large as that of Polish FDI to the rest of Europe. Prima facie, the impact of Southern MNEs from these countries could be compared to similar intra-European investments.

The data and the prominence of certain countries highlights a problem intrinsic to the analysis of FDI data, namely the ownership of the investing company (Stephan and Pfaffmann, 2001). Singapore is a well-established Asian hub for regional headquarters (Yeung, Poon and Perry, 2001; Li, Yu and Seetoo, 2010), Mexico has attracted significant investments from firms who want to take advantage of its lower production cost and NAFTA membership (for example, Jordaan, 2008), and Turkey has attracted significant investments from firms who want to take advantage of its lower production cost and proximity to the European Union (Özdemir and Darby, 2009). Aggregated FDI statistics on outward investments from these countries cannot identify the ultimate investor. It is therefore possible that the available data show investments from Western MNEs through Southern countries as well as investments from genuine Southern firms. Inferring impacts of Southern MNEs on Europe from such secondary FDI statistics is therefore problematic.

Investment distribution: The limited data we have on the distribution of Southern FDI within the European Union indicate an interesting investment motivation pattern, which calls for further in-depth, firm-level analyses. Historically, investments by American and Japanese firms have been concentrated in the earliest members of the European Union (EU-15) as access and political and economic links between these countries already existed. Following our discussion on the theoretical challenges on Southern FDI to Europe and its potential impact, we establish here that firms from Southern countries predominantly invest in the EU-15 countries as well (see Table 3.2). For the years 2004–07 the share of EU-15 countries in investments to the EU-27 was well over 95 per cent of total investments from most Southern countries. Indeed, Russian firms, which had a considerable investment volume in Central and Eastern Europe up until 2004, today are concentrating their investments in Western European countries. The new accession countries from Central and Eastern Europe received a negligible share of investment with the exception of that from South Korea and Turkey. South Korean firms have relocated their business operations from Western European countries to Central and Eastern Europe or established new operations there. Firms from Turkey use their proximity to Southeast Europe (Romania in particular) to get a foothold in the European Common Market. In these two cases, it seems likely that firms intend to benefit from lower production costs than available elsewhere in the EU. Firms from the BRIC(S) that invest in the advanced European economies are not likely to invest for productive purposes but to support trade activities, establish 'listening posts', and seek to benefit from easier access to external capital (Buckley et al., 2007, 2008). The impact of Southern investments will therefore differ significantly by MNE home country as well as, distribution indicates, by host economy.

Foreign affiliates: The volume and distribution of Southern investments in the EU is further illustrated by available European disaggregated statistics.

Table 3.2 Share of total FDI stock to the EU-27 invested in the EU-15

	2004	2005	2006	2007	2008
Brazil	100.09%	100.01%	91.92%	96.05%	100.21%
China	92.64%	85.88%	94.99%	92.85%	30.83%
HK	99.43%	99.22%	98.74%	98.49%	98.31%
India	97.43%	99.20%	98.25%	96.03%	96.69%
Russia	66.68%	69.10%	79.82%	80.99%	86.42%
South Africa	99.86%	97.18%	99.74%	95.69%	99.97%
Egypt	89.90%	92.36%	91.50%	91.96%	98.45%
Korea	82.00%	78.58%	70.22%	67.40%	58.81%
Mexico	99.94%	99.99%	100.01%	101.00%	101.57%
Malaysia	94.43%	94.60%	96.84%	97.81%	96.03%
Nigeria	100.00%	99.96%	100.00%	99.97%	99.98%
Singapore	99.18%	99.57%	99.23%	99.50%	99.45%
Turkey	78.02%	87.88%	80.95%	74.35%	75.50%
Japan	97.92%	97.21%	97.21%	97.13%	96.95%
USA	98.55%	98.57%	98.20%	98.18%	98.51%

Note: These are the top 12 Southern investors and Japan and the USA.
Source: Eurostat (2010).

We use the European Foreign Affiliates Statistics (FATS). These data have been collected and reported by member countries on a voluntary basis since 1996 and are not available for Austria, Bulgaria, Germany, Finland, and the Netherlands. According to FATS, all reported Southern affiliates of the top 12 investor countries sum to 1,952 affiliates, which is slightly higher than the number for Japanese firms and considerably smaller than for the American investments. The largest number of Southern affiliates in Europe in 2006 is controlled by Russian firms with 433 affiliates, followed by Turkey with 302 affiliates, and mainland China with 222 affiliates (see Table 3.3). The other BRIC(S) countries have 64 (Brazil), 207 (India), and 149 (South Africa) affiliates in Europe, respectively.

The distribution of the foreign affiliates mirrors the earlier observation on aggregated FDI statistics. Russian firms have strongest presence in the former Comecon countries – Czech Republic, Hungary, Latvia, and Lithuania (87 per cent of total affiliates). Similarly, 68 per cent of Turkish affiliates are located in Romania, and South Korea has a strong presence in Central and Eastern Europe. While geographical proximity seems to be an important factor for Turkish firms, cultural and linguistic proximity appears to play a critical role for Brazilian, Indian, and South African firms. More than 60 per cent of Brazilian affiliates are located in Portugal, which formerly colonized Brazil, while 55 per cent of Indian and 48 per cent of South African affiliates are located in the UK. The UK is also attractive to Chinese, Korean, Malaysian, and Singaporean investors.

Table 3.3 Number of enterprises in industry and services in reporting EU-27 countries in 2006

	Brazil	China (incl. HK)	HK	India	Russia	South Africa	Egypt	Korea	Mexico	Malaysia	Nigeria	S'pore	Turkey	Japan	USA
Bulgaria	:	:	:	:	:	:	:	:	:	:	:	:	:	:	:
Czech Rep.	7	9	9	32	121	9	5	27	7	4	2	12	61	131	985
Denmark	0	:	10	9	:	2	0	0	1	3	0	8	:	31	378
Germany	:	:	:	:	:	:	:	:	:	:	:	:	:	:	:
Estonia	0	0	2	0	14	0	0	0	0	0	0	1	0	3	43
Spain	0	:	:	:	:	6	0	4	6	11	0	:	:	160	:
France	6	61	:	20	7	4	:	16	37	5	:	26	13	437	4,061
Italy	:	:	:	:	:	:	:	:	:	:	:	:	:	:	:
Cyprus	:	:	:	:	21	:	:	:	:	:	:	:	:	:	12
Latvia	:	:	3	1	129	:	:	1	1	1	:	3	6	1	348
Lithuania	1	25	2	2	86	0	0	2	0	0	0	1	8	8	136
Hungary	3	54	7	3	28	7	:	18	4	9	0	11	8	82	367
Netherlands	:	:	:	:	:	:	:	:	:	:	:	:	:	:	:
Austria	:	:	:	:	:	:	:	:	:	:	:	:	:	:	:
Portugal	39	1	7	2	2	7	1	3	1	0	0	3	1	31	291
Romania	0	31	1	2	5	0	2	5	0	0	0	0	204	14	172
Slovenia	:	:	:	:	:	:	:	:	:	:	:	:	:	:	:
Slovakia	:	:	:	:	10	0	0	:	:	:	0	3	:	17	109
Finland	:	:	:	:	:	:	:	:	:	:	:	:	:	:	:
Sweden	:	16	:	21	:	42	:	:	:	:	:	13	:	115	1,186
UK	8	25	116	113	10	72	5	36	3	40	:	78	8	750	4,611
Total	**64**	**222**	**157**	**207**	**433**	**149**	**13**	**112**	**60**	**73**	**2**	**158**	**302**	**1,780**	**12,700**

Notes: HK = Hong Kong (Special Administration Region of China); = not available; data for financial intermediation and public administration are not available. These are the top 12 Southern investors and Japan and the USA. HK is included to illustrate the data problem in the Eurostat database, and 2006 represents the latest available dataset.
Source: Eurostat (2010).

The impact of these affiliates is measurable through the available data on turnover per enterprise and turnover per person employed (see Tables 3.4 and 3.5). Firms from Russia, Malaysia, and Turkey report on average the lowest turnover per company and per person employed. In contrast, Mexican and mainland Chinese investors record turnover per enterprise of a value which is similar to that reported for American affiliates. The turnover per person employed of mainland Chinese firms even exceeds that of Japanese and American firms. It should be pointed out that the average figures hide stark inter-country differences. Indian companies in Sweden have significantly higher turnovers than in the UK, as do Mexican firms in Spain in comparison to their counterparts in France. These differences between countries and similarities with developed countries firms require in-depth, firm-level attention. They have the potential to reveal insights on the competitiveness of Southern MNEs and, by extension, on their impact on Europe.

The caveat for both data categories is the lack of data across the top 12 investor nations and for the USA and Japan. FATS data on the operations of foreign affiliates is sparse and often only recorded and published for two or three countries. This affects the usability of the data.

Case of Chinese firms: Data on mainland Chinese firms is more readily available in the FATS database than for other Southern MNEs. This allows us to compare the development of Chinese and American affiliates over a period of four years from 2003 to 2006 (see Table 3.6). Chinese affiliates in Europe numbered, as mentioned earlier, 222 by the end of 2006, which is an increase of 91 over the year 2003. The number of American affiliates increased in the same time frame by 2,441 to12,700 (despite non-reporting by Bulgaria, Finland, Italy, the Netherlands, and Spain for 2006). The larger presence of American firms, and hence their likely impact on the European economy, is most visible when numbers of persons employed are compared (see Tables 3.7 and 3.8). Chinese affiliates employed 824 persons in 2003, which increased to 2,800 by 2006 while American affiliates employed 943,273 and 2,112,347 persons, respectively (again, Bulgaria, Finland, Italy, the Netherlands and Spain do not report data for 2006). In terms of direct and indirect labour effects, the Chinese investments are likely to have a limited impact on Europe. It is noteworthy here that the numbers of persons employed is increasing rapidly for Chinese firms and the relative gap to American affiliates has shrunk.

Data availability: Using data published by Eurostat has the advantage that the methods of data collection and interpretation are homogenized across the European Union member countries. Nevertheless, data on Southern FDI into the EU is scarce and not consistent on a disaggregated level.

A good example for data inconsistency is the case of mainland Chinese investments. Eurostat reports 25 Chinese (inclusive of Hong Kong) affiliates in the UK and, at the same time, 116 Hong Kong affiliates in England. The disconnect between Chinese (inclusive Hong Kong) and Hong Kong data

Table 3.4 Turnover per enterprise in industry and services in reporting EU-27 countries in 2006

	Brazil	China (incl. HK)	HK	India	Russia	South Africa	Egypt	Korea	Mexico	Malaysia	Nigeria	S'pore	Turkey	Japan	USA
Bulgaria	:	:	:	:	:	:	:	:	:	:	:	:	:	:	:
Czech Rep.	:	:	:	:	:	:	:	:	:	:	:	:	:	:	:
Denmark	:	:	129,535	39,611	:	:	:	:	:	:	:	:	:	228,980	25,7579
Germany	:	:	:	:	:	:	:	:	:	:	:	:	:	:	:
Estonia	:	:	:	:	:	:	:	:	:	:	:	:	:	:	:
Spain	:	:	:	:	:	136,509	:	240,043	178,003	1,460	:	:	:	87,059	:
France	19,969	44,234	:	48,570	23,789	7,412	:	170,885	27,043	17,003	:	19,463	20,542	83,653	45,526
Italy	:	:	:	:	:	:	:	:	:	:	:	:	:	:	:
Cyprus	:	:	:	:	207	:	:	:	:	:	:	:	:	:	16,769
Latvia	:	:	:	:	5,363	:	:	:	:	:	:	:	:	:	1,982
Lithuania	:	:	:	:	50,177	:	:	:	:	:	:	:	1,107	70,399	18,396
Hungary	:	:	:	:	:	:	:	:	:	:	:	:	:	:	:
Netherlands	:	:	:	:	:	:	:	:	:	:	:	:	:	:	:
Austria	:	:	:	:	:	:	:	:	:	:	:	:	:	:	:
Portugal	:	:	:	:	:	:	:	:	:	:	:	:	:	:	:
Romania	:	:	:	:	:	:	:	:	:	:	:	:	:	:	:
Slovenia	:	:	:	:	:	:	:	:	:	:	:	:	:	:	:
Slovakia	:	:	:	:	:	:	:	:	:	:	:	:	:	:	:
Finland	:	:	:	:	:	:	:	:	:	:	:	:	:	:	:
Sweden	:	26,142	:	101,626	:	89,495	:	:	:	:	:	21,4469	:	280,655	340,640
UK	:	204,480	17,221	10,727	:	30,597	:	95,164	:	11,988	:	16,332	:	78,210	56,915
Average	**19,969**	**91,618**	**73,378**	**50,133**	**19,884**	**66,003**	**:**	**16,8697**	**102,523**	**10,151**	**:**	**83,422**	**10,825**	**138,159**	**105,401**

Notes: HK = Hong Kong (Special Administration Region of China); = not available; data for financial intermediation and public administration are not available.
These are the top 12 Southern investors and Japan and the USA.
Source: Eurostat (2010).

Table 3.5 Turnover per person employed in industry and services in reporting EU-27 countries in 2006

	Brazil	**China (incl. HK)**	**HK**	**India**	**Russia**	**South Africa**	**Egypt**	**Korea**	**Mexico**	**Malaysia**	**Nigeria**	**S'pore**	**Turkey**	**Japan**	**USA**
Bulgaria	:	:	:	:	:	:	:	:	:	:	:	:	:	:	:
Czech Rep.	:	:	:	:	:	:	:	:	:	:	:	:	:	:	:
Denmark	:	:	2,654	2,228	:	:	:	:	:	:	:	:	:	2,376	2,539
Germany	:	:	:	:	:	:	:	:	:	:	:	:	:	:	:
Estonia	:	:	:	:	:	:	:	:	:	:	:	:	:	:	:
Spain	:	:	:	:	:	332	:	1,437	431	328	:	:	:	602	:
France	:	:	:	:	:	:	:	:	:	:	:	:	:	:	:
Italy	:	:	:	:	:	:	:	:	:	:	:	:	:	:	:
Cyprus	:	:	:	:	42	:	:	:	:	:	:	:	:	:	312
Latvia	:	:	:	:	243	:	:	:	:	:	:	:	:	:	84
Lithuania	:	:	:	:	850	:	:	:	:	:	:	:	138	258	364
Hungary	:	:	:	:	:	:	:	:	:	:	:	:	:	:	:
Netherlands	:	:	:	:	:	:	:	:	:	:	:	:	:	:	:
Austria	:	:	:	:	:	:	:	:	:	:	:	:	:	:	:
Portugal	:	:	:	:	:	:	:	:	:	:	:	:	:	:	:
Romania	:	:	:	:	:	:	:	:	:	:	:	:	:	:	:
Slovenia	:	:	:	:	:	:	:	:	:	:	:	:	:	:	:
Slovakia	:	:	:	:	:	:	:	:	:	:	:	:	:	:	:
Finland	:	:	:	:	:	:	:	:	:	:	:	:	:	:	:
Sweden	:	1,367	:	1,695	:	4,813	:	:	:	:	:	499	:	4,323	3,134
UK	:	7,334	89	139	:	176	:	1,798	:	78	:	143	:	572	247
average	**:**	**4,351**	**1,3712**	**1,354**	**378**	**1,774**	**:**	**1,618**	**431**	**203**	**:**	**321**	**138**	**1,626**	**1,113**

Notes: HK = Hong Kong (Special Administration Region of China); = not available; data for financial intermediation and public administration are not available.
These are the top 12 Southern investors and Japan and the USA.
Source: Eurostat (2010).

Table 3.6 Number of Chinese and American affiliates in the EU-27

	USA				China				
	2003	2004	2005	2006		2003	2004	2005	2006
Austria	195	:	:	:	Austria	:	:	:	:
Bulgaria	234	278	277	:	Bulgaria	59	41	20	:
Cyprus	:	8	9	12	Cyprus	:	:	:	:
Czech Republic	530	763	874	985	Czech Republic	0	11	9	9
Denmark	:	:	:	379	Denmark	:	:	:	:
Estonia	42	46	41	43	Estonia	1	0	0	0
Finland	321	321	334	:	Finland	:	:	:	:
France	3,145	3,556	3,558	4,061	France	24	38	61	61
Germany	:	:	:	:	Germany	:	:	:	:
Hungary	208	249	244	367	Hungary	:	:	:	54
Italy	2,271	2,317	2,508	:	Italy	0	0	2	:
Latvia	391	407	327	348	Latvia	1	2	1	:
Lithuania	135	129	146	136	Lithuania	17	24	28	25
Netherlands	840	927	1,357	:	Netherlands	0	0	7	:
Portugal	164	133	239	291	Portugal	0	0	1	1
Romania	89	141	144	172	Romania	:	18	17	31
Slovakia	37	113	116	109	Slovakia	:	:	:	:
Slovenia	36	55	:	:	Slovenia	14	17	:	:
Spain	508	487	679	:	Spain	:	:	:	:
Sweden	1,113	1,129	1,184	1,186	Sweden	15	16	15	16
UK	:	:	:	4,611	UK	:	:	:	25
Total	**10,259**	**11,059**	**12,037**	**12,700**	**total**	**131**	**167**	**161**	**222**

Note: Data cover all industry and services (excluding financial intermediation and public administration).
Source: Eurostat (2010).

Table 3.7 Number of persons employed in Chinese and American affiliates in the EU-27

	USA				China				
	2003	2004	2005	2006		2003	2004	2005	2006
Bulgaria	17,385	19,096	18,051	:	Bulgaria	411	252	165	:
Czech Republic	72,055	87,596	85,398	98,326	Czech Republic	0	:	:	:
Denmark	:	:	:	38,964	Denmark	:	:	:	:
Germany	:	:	:	427,483	Germany	:	:	:	:
Estonia	4,318	5,857	5,837	5,664	Estonia	:	0	0	0
Spain	146,999	147,783	125,699	169,462	Spain	:	:	:	:
France	:	:	:	:	France	:	:	:	:
Italy	270,551	269,507	290,425	:	Italy	0	0	:	:
Cyprus	:	421	516	646	Cyprus	:	:	:	:
Latvia	9,592	10,645	8,476	8,264	Latvia	3	12	2	:
Lithuania	6,750	6,617	6,545	6,871	Lithuania	135	178	245	:
Hungary	63,184	71,426	68,206	72,131	Hungary	:	:	:	393
Netherlands	119,681	132,264	129,265	:	Netherlands	0	0	:	:
Austria	24,820	:	:	:	Austria	:	:	:	:
Portugal	39,452	22,855	25,163	24,121	Portugal	0	0	:	:
Romania	22,106	25,668	32,957	32,475	Romania	:	1,217	999	1,404
Slovenia	910	4,063	:	:	Slovenia	48	61	:	:
Slovakia	11,614	36,715	38,174	37,957	Slovakia	:	:	:	:
Finland	18,986	21,408	23,341	:	Finland	:	:	16	:
Sweden	114,870	119,611	120,966	128,919	Sweden	227	:	:	306
UK	:	:	:	1,061,064	UK	:	:	:	697
Total	**943,273**	**981,532**	**979,019**	**2,112,347**	**Total**	**824**	**1,720**	**1,427**	**2,800**

Note: Data cover all industry and services (excluding financial intermediation and public administration).
Source: Eurostat (2010).

Table 3.8 Number of persons employed per enterprise in Chinese and American affiliates in the EU-27

	USA					China			
	2003	2004	2005	2006		2003	2004	2005	2006
Bulgaria	:	69	:	:	Bulgaria	:	6	:	:
Czech Republic	:	115	:	:	Czech Republic	:	:	:	:
Denmark	:	:	:	102.8	Denmark	:	:	:	:
Germany	:	:	:	:	Germany	:	:	:	:
Estonia	:	127	:	:	Estonia	:	:	:	:
Spain	:	:	:	:	Spain	:	:	:	:
France	:	:	:	:	France	:	:	:	:
Italy	119.1	116.3	:	:	Italy	:	:	:	:
Cyprus	:	:	:	54	Cyprus	:	:	:	:
Latvia	:	26	:	24	Latvia	:	6	:	:
Lithuania	:	51	:	51	Lithuania	:	7	:	:
Hungary	:	287	:	:	Hungary	:	:	:	:
Netherlands	:	:	:	:	Netherlands	:	:	:	:
Austria	:	:	:	:	Austria	:	:	:	:
Portugal	:	171.8	:	:	Portugal	:	:	:	:
Romania	:	182	229	:	Romania	:	68	59	:
Slovenia	25	74	:	:	Slovenia	3	4	:	:
Slovakia	:	325	:	:	Slovakia	:	:	:	:
Finland	:	:	:	:	Finland	:	:	:	:
Sweden	103.2	105.9	102.2	108.7	Sweden	15.1	:	:	19.1
United Kingdom	:	:	:	230.1	United Kingdom	:	:	:	27.9
Average	**82.4**	**137.5**	**165.6**	**95.1**	**Average**	**9.1**	**18.2**	**59.0**	**23.5**

Note: Data cover all industry and services (excluding financial intermediation and public administration).
Source: Eurostat (2010).

also appears for a number of other host economies and other variables. The origin for this disconnect is unclear. A further disconnect exists between the European data and data reported by the British UK Trade & Investment (UKTI). According to Burghart and Rossi (2009), UKTI reported that, by 2006/7, 52 Chinese firms had invested in the UK while the Ernst & Young European Investment Monitor reports 101 investments. While the former is of somewhat similar magnitude, the latter figure is significantly higher. Comparing these data with cross-border merger and acquisition data uncovers further discrepancies between official datasets (Schüler and Schüler-Zhou, 2009). Similar discrepancies can be expected for other European countries as well.

Data availability decreases when operations related data is requested. Data on number of affiliates is generally available for the USA and China (USA: 63 out of 84 potential data fields; China: 43 out of 84) but falls for turnover per person employed (USA: 25 out of 84; China: 8 out of 84) and labour productivity (USA: 25 out of 84; China: 11 out of 84), for example, and seems incorrect in the case of Romania, which reports huge figures (see Tables 3.9 and 3.10). Data availability problems are not constrained to FATS but also prevail at the most aggregated level. We mentioned earlier that inward FDI stocks are reported for only 23 Southern countries in 2006. There are huge data gaps observable. For investments from Central America a stock of EUR 342bn is reported. The breakdown by countries shows, however, stock data for Mexico of EUR 12bn. Smaller but still significant gaps also exist for data from Africa (–EUR 9bn) and Asia (–EUR 49bn). Data covering the European Union, North America, and Oceania, that is, 'Northern MNEs', is consistent with the breakdown by country.

3.3 Conclusion

There is understandable frustration among researchers that the analysis of the impact of Southern MNEs on Europe is severely constrained by the lack of available data. However we are able to show several tentative results, which are of great interest:

1. Investment in Europe by Southern MNEs is significant and rapidly increasing.
2. It is a geographically uneven spread across Europe.
3. There are regularities in the patterns of inward investment by Southern MNEs by nationality of ownership and by location within Europe.

This chapter has suggested that the impact of Southern MNEs is likely to differ from that of the 'typical' Northern MNE. For the moment, Southern FDI in Europe is small and therefore its impact will be well below that of traditional investors in Europe, such as the USA. The employment effect

Table 3.9 Turnover per person employed in Chinese and American affiliates in the EU-27

	USA					China			
	2003	2004	2005	2006		2003	2004	2005	2006
Bulgaria	:	106.81	:	:	Bulgaria	:	:	:	:
Czech Republic	:	4,223.58	:	:	Czech Republic	:	:	:	:
Denmark	:	:	:	2,499.3	Denmark	:	:	:	:
Germany	:	:	:	417.8	Germany	:	:	:	:
Estonia	:	791.39	:	:	Estonia	:	:	:	:
Spain	:	:	:	:	Spain	:	:	:	:
France	:	:	:	:	France	:	:	:	:
Italy	313.5	321.8	:	:	Italy	:	:	:	:
Cyprus	:	:	:	311.49	Cyprus	:	:	:	:
Latvia	:	54.34	:	83.45	Latvia	:	:	:	:
Lithuania	:	392.53	:	364.12	Lithuania	:	82.10	:	:
Hungary	:	48,336.68	:	:	Hungary	:	:	:	:
Netherlands	:	:	:	:	Netherlands	:	:	:	:
Austria	:	:	:	:	Austria	:	:	:	:
Portugal	:	226.6	:	:	Portugal	:	:	:	:
Romania	:	2,092,953.09	196.68	:	Romania	:	1,827,288.41	159.58	:
Slovenia	67,171.26	43,743.63	:	:	Slovenia	6,889.00	9,744.25	:	:
Slovakia	:	4,504.00	:	:	Slovakia	:	:	:	:
Finland	:	:	:	:	Finland	:	:	:	:
Sweden	2,935.3	2,876.5	3,041.2	3,133.7	Sweden	4,306.8	:	:	1,366.9
UK	:	:	:	247.3	UK	:	:	:	7,334.3
Average	**23,473.35**	**183,210.91**	**1,618.94**	**1,008.17**	**Average**	**5,597.90**	**612,371.59**	**159.58**	**4,350.60**

Note: Data cover all industry and services (excluding financial intermediation and public administration).
Source: Eurostat (2010).

Table 3.10 Simple wage-adjusted labour productivity in Chinese and American affiliates in the EU-27 (gross value added by personnel costs) (per cent)

	USA				**China**				
	2003	**2004**	**2005**	**2006**		**2003**	**2004**	**2005**	**2006**
Bulgaria	:	273.08	:	:	Bulgaria	:	110.50	:	:
Czech Republic	:	226.09	:	:	Czech Republic	:	136.83	:	:
Denmark	:	:	:	197.3	Denmark	:	:	:	:
Germany	:	:	:	155.1	Germany	:	:	:	:
Estonia	:	165.94	:	:	Estonia	:	:	:	:
Spain	:	:	:	164.8	Spain	:	:	:	:
France	:	:	:	134.4	France	:	:	:	109.2
Italy	149.6	144.5	:	:	Italy	:	:	:	:
Cyprus	:	:	:	177.77	Cyprus	:	:	:	:
Latvia	:	276.60	:	253.33	Latvia	:	:	:	:
Lithuania	:	219.77	:	203.87	Lithuania	:	157.72	:	:
Hungary	:	259.60	:	:	Hungary	:	:	:	:
Netherlands	:	:	:	:	Netherlands	:	:	:	:
Austria	:	:	:	:	Austria	:	:	:	:
Portugal	:	170.5	:	:	Portugal	:	:	:	:
Romania	:	198.84	218.09	:	Romania	:	241.93	293.15	:
Slovenia	:	211.20	:	:	Slovenia	280.91	131.63	:	:
Slovakia	:	268.34	:	:	Slovakia	:	:	:	:
Finland	:	:	:	:	Finland	:	:	:	:
Sweden	139.4	133.4	140.7	139.4	Sweden	110.7	:	:	105.6
UK	:	:	:	190.1	UK	:	:	:	367.1
Average	**144.50**	**212.32**	**179.40**	**179.56**	**Average**	**195.81**	**155.72**	**293.15**	**193.97**

Note: Data cover all industry and services (excluding financial intermediation and public administration).
Source: Eurostat (2010).

is currently small and is also likely to be different in type from that of Northern MNEs, and this seems to be reflected in productivity differences (lower for Southern MNEs a).

The above represents a huge, unfulfilled research agenda. The implications of this potential agenda are immense both for Europe and for the internationalization of the South.

Note

1. Eurostat (2010), DS-070774-EU direct investment positions, breakdown by country and economic activity.

References

Buckley, P. J., Cross, A. R., Tan, H., Liu, X. and Voss, H. (2008), 'Historic and Emergent Trends in Chinese Outward Direct Investment', *Management International Review*, 48, 715–48.

Buckley, P. J., Clegg, L. J., Cross, A. R., Liu, X., Voss, H. and Zheng, P. (2007), 'The Determinants of Chinese Outward Foreign Direct Investment', *Journal of International Business Studies*, 38, 499–518.

Burghart, N. and Rossi, V. (2009), *China's Overseas Direct Investment in the UK*, Chatham House, Programme Paper IE PP, 2009/06.

Eurostat, European Union Direct Investments Statistics and Statistics on Foreign Control of Enterprises (2010), at ec.europa.eu/eurostat.

Jordaan, J. A. (2008), 'State Characteristics and the Locational Choice of Foreign Direct Investment: Evidence from Regional FDI in Mexico 1989–2006', *Growth and Change*, 39, 389–413.

Li, G. H., Yu, C. M. and Seetoo, D. H. (2010), 'Toward a Theory of Regional Organization', *Management International Review*, 50, 5–33.

Özdemir, D. and Darby, J. (2009), 'One Less Barrier to Foreign Direct Investment in Turkey?' *European Urban and Regional Studies*, 16, 87–99.

Schüler, M. and Schüler-Zhou, Y. (2009), 'The Internationalization of Chinese Companies: What Do Official Statistics Tell Us about Chinese Outward Foreign Direct Investment?' *Chinese Management Studies*, 1, 25–42.

Stephan, M. and Pfaffmann, E. (2001), 'Detecting the Pitfalls of Data on Foreign Direct Investment: Scope and Limits of FDI Data', *Management International Review*, 41, 189–218.

UNCTAD (2006), *World Investment Report 2006*. New York/Geneva: United Nations.

Yeung, H. W. C., Poon, J. and Perry, M. (2001), 'Towards a Regional Strategy: The Role of Regional Headquarters of Foreign Firms in Singapore', *Urban Studies*, 38, 157–83.

Part III
Southern Multinationals from a Home Country Perspective

4

Europe in the Internationalization Strategies of the Multilatinas

Afonso Fleury, Maria Tereza Leme Fleury, and Germano Glufke Reis

4.1 Introduction

The increasing presence of firms from emerging countries, especially from the BRIC group (Brazil, Russia, India, and China), in the world scenario, is a remarkable characteristic of the 'third wave' of internationalization. The two first ones were generated by the expansion of North American and European firms (in the 1950s and 1960s) and by Japanese firms (in the 1980s). Currently, the so-called emerging country multinationals are taking a stand in the global economy (Goldstein, 2007; Sauvant, Mendoza, and Irmak, 2008; Ramamurti and Singh, 2009).

The fast development of these countries caught policy makers, managers, and researchers, among others, by surprise. Firms that were considered to be lagging way behind, acting in less developed contexts, have started to challenge global leaders. This phenomenon has generated new questions: Would emerging country multinationals have distinct characteristics compared to classical multinationals? Which factors justify their competitiveness in the global markets? What would be the impacts on developed countries? These questions generated new approaches that sought to capture the common characteristics of the new multinationals (Mathews, 2006; Cuervo-Cazurra, 2008; Guillen and Garcia-Canal, 2009). This chapter seeks to answer the third question raised: 'What would be the impacts on developed countries?', regarding the Multilatinas, with a focus on the European case.

The studies on Multilatinas reveal two distinct trends. The first highlights the relative bashfulness of their internationalization processes, and, from comparative analyses of what occurred in developed countries some time ago and what occurs today in Asian countries, it questions whether Latin American firms and countries would fulfil the basic requisites to become truly international. Such is the case of the books *Can Latin American Firms Compete?* and *Can Latin America Compete?*, by Grosse and Mesquita (2007) and Haar and Price (2008), respectively.

The second approach focuses on the Multilatinas and, acknowledging their specificities, seeks to understand their trajectories and the factors that justify the internationalization process (Cuervo-Cazurra, 2010: 14). Within this context, the studies developed by Cuervo-Cazurra (2008) and Santiso (2008) are noteworthy. This is the path pursued in what follows.

For us, a particularly important study is that in which Cuervo-Cazurra (2008) examines the choice of country for the Multilatinas' first entries. The author selected 20 Multilatinas and justified their foreign entry choices using two dimensions: cultural distance and development distance or proximity. His work contributes in clarifying the firms' internationalization strategies: he identified four different trends, to be considered later. The fact that the author restricted himself only to the first entries of these firms, however, does not allow observation of how these strategies developed.

Aiming to advance with the argument, we focused on the movement of Multilatinas towards Europe, and subsequent decisions in terms of international expansion. Besides the cultural links between Latin America and the European countries, Europe is responsible for the largest share of Latin American FDI, according to official sources. So, we proceeded by: (a) increasing the number of Latin American firms under study (from 20 to 33); (b) examining the trajectories of these firms after the first move – that is, if the Multilatinas that started their internationalization going to Europe have strengthened their presence in the region, or if their strategic priorities have changed; also, if the firms that expanded initially to bordering countries have subsequently ventured to more distant locations, such as the European continent.

We begin the chapter with a discussion on what Latin America is, in order to characterize the Multilatinas. Seeking to establish the foundations for the competitiveness of these firms, we examine how local contexts have influenced the firms in general, and, particularly, those that have internationalized. Then, based on the study of Cuervo-Cazurra (2008), we analyse the favoured options of the Multilatinas, in terms of their entry and expansion abroad. From a comparison of the trajectories adopted by these firms, we seek to identify the role Europe performs. This allows raising a number of hypotheses that are discussed in the sections that follow. We then conclude with an overview of our course of action and suggestions for future research.

4.2 What is Latin America? Diversity germinated from common roots

Europe encompasses a diversity of national cultures; there is no singular European country, but cultural clusters: Anglo-Saxon, Latin, and East European (Ashkanasy, Trevor-Roberts, and Earnshaw, 2002; Bakacsi et al., 2002; Jesuino, 2002; Szabo et al., 2002; Muzychenco, 2008). The root of the Latin American culture is Iberian, but, unlike in Europe, the possibilities of integration are smaller.

The integration difficulties start from geographical barriers. In the southernmost point of Latin America lies Patagonia, at 53 degrees south latitude, and at the extreme north is Tijuana, in Mexico, neighbouring San Diego, at 32 degrees north latitude. The distance between these two points is 10,600 kilometres, approximately the same distance between Lisbon, Portugal and Tokyo, Japan.

The topography is rich and diverse with the Andes range, the Amazon, and Central America itself as geographical accidents that hamper mobility and transportation. Central America and the Caribbean are constituted by 20 countries and 16 territories, the largest of them being Nicaragua, equivalent in size to Greece.

Despite the religious and linguistic roots (Catholicism/Latin) that contribute to delineating the concept of Latin America, there are nuances that differentiate cultural contexts within the region, which reflect in its local corporations.

A classic study by Hofstede (1980) identified more cultural similarity of countries like Argentina and Brazil with Latin European countries surveyed (which include Belgium, France, Italy, and Spain) than with the Latin American countries (which include Chile, Colombia, Mexico, Peru, and Venezuela), disclosing specific cultural clusters. Ronen and Shenkar (1985), based on the assessment of eight empirical studies, situated Brazil in an independent cultural cluster, alongside countries like Japan, India, and Israel, countries which, given their diverse specificities, were not included within the other groups encountered. In this analysis, the Latin American cluster is composed of Argentina, Chile, Colombia, Mexico, Peru, and Venezuela. These groupings can be associated to three interconnected dimensions: language, religion, and geographical region; they are also related to technological development, as it influences managers' attitudes.

4.3 Economic development in Latin American countries

From the standpoint of macroeconomic development, the histories of Latin American countries have many points in common. The first is the predominance of agro-exporting economies, thanks to these countries' soil and climate, hence the development of the production of meat (in Argentina and Brazil), wine (in Chile and Argentina), coffee (in Colombia, Costa Rica, and Brazil), as well as minerals (copper in Chile and Bolivia; iron and ore in Brazil), among others.

At the beginning of the twentieth century, Argentina and Uruguay were the countries with the most dynamic economies. Uruguay was considered 'the southern Switzerland' and Argentina was the first to take steps towards the industrialization process. Argentinean firms, such as Bunge y Born and Siam di Tella, are considered the first South American multinationals. Bunge y Born played an important role in Brazilian industrialization, starting back in the nineteenth century.

In the most advanced Latin American countries, industrialization policies to substitute imports were implemented in the 1930s and 1940s, state-owned enterprises were created in the 1940s and 1950s in strategic industries, and subsidiaries of multinational enterprises were attracted to speed up the industrialization process in the 1960s and 1970s.

Brazil and Argentina, particularly the first, given the size of its domestic market, have always been more attractive to the MNEs. Argentina has a significantly smaller domestic market (about 25 per cent of the Brazilian market), but, for a long time, it had a comparative advantage over Brazil for its higher educational and cultural level. Thus, for most of the twentieth century, these two countries were chosen to host subsidiaries of large multinationals. The competition with the subsidiaries in local markets and the spillovers generated by the subsidiaries were important factors for the development of internationally competitive local firms.

The industrialization model for substitution of imports began to collapse in the 1970s and 1980s, leading to the region suffering successive economic crises. The upturn followed the IMF guidelines, since the countries were extremely indebted. However, the reduction of tariffs and opening of the domestic market advocated by the Washington Consensus had different repercussions among the various Latin American countries (Cuervo-Cazurra, 2008). Besides trade opening, privatization policies played a decisive role. Mexico, Brazil, and Chile were more successful than Argentina.

Though having many points in common in their economic history, the current political and economic options are very distinct. In the economic context, Mexico and the Central American countries and the Caribbean are encompassed within the sphere of influence exerted by the United States and Canada, articulated through NAFTA – North America Free Trade Agreement – and CAFTA – Central America Free Trade Agreement. The countries in northern South America, those that face the Pacific Ocean, have established commercial relations through the Andean Pact and also have bilateral agreements with Asian countries, especially Korea and China. The southern countries of South America, including Brazil, instituted Mercosur. The project of establishing the FTAA – Free Trade Agreement of Americas – failed, and, today, the European Community strives to close trade agreements with Mercosur countries, seeking to counterbalance the North American influence. Authors like Mortimore (1993) and Jank (2005) used the metaphor of the *flying geese and sitting ducks* to compare the behaviours of Latin American country heads of state to those of the Asians: conversely, to their Asian counterparts, Latin Americans are amicable, meet very frequently, but seldom come to any practical agreement.

Therefore, the Latin American countries are distinctively positioned in the world economic order. Chile is considered the most developed, according to economic–social indicators, but its presence in international markets occurs essentially through exports of primary products or primarily processed goods. Brazil, Mexico, and Argentina are considered the most dynamic, from the economic point of view, although their development indicators are lower than Chile's.

In summary, economic and industrial development had very different outcomes in each Latin American country owing to the different factor endowments, distinct political and economic contexts, and different national cultures. These resulted in differentiated management in each country and each region. Consequently, Latin American countries present dissimilar histories of the internationalization phenomenon.

4.4 The Latin American multinationals

When we compare Latin American firms to the well-known global players, we find that their positions are relatively modest, as Table 4.1 shows. There are only 11 Multilatinas among the Fortune 500 (including three Brazilian banks), 26 among the world's 2,000 largest firms according to Forbes, eight in the World Investment Report list of the 50 largest MNEs from emerging countries (financial enterprises excluded) and 24 in the '100 Global Challengers' list of the Boston Consulting Group. Fortune ranking considers sales income and profits, while Forbes assesses a composite of sales, profits, assets, and market value. WIR Report examines foreign assets and the levels of internationalization (Transnationality Index, TNI), while the 2009 BCG list is based on a broad set of qualitative and quantitative factors. Table 4.1 lists the 33 firms that are present in these rankings.

Thus, 2.5 per cent of the firms listed by Fortune and Forbes are from Latin America. By comparison, South Korea makes up 2.5 per cent of the total, while Australia accounts for 2 per cent of the total.

In Table 4.1, two-thirds of multinationals originated in Brazil and 27.2 per cent in Mexico. Chile and Argentina account for 3 per cent each. This proportion is in accordance with that identified by Boston Consulting Group regarding the 100 Global Challengers: Brazil has 14 firms, Mexico 6, and Argentina 1. It also agrees with the ranking provided by *América Economia* (see Table 4.2), which shows the share of countries in relation to the 500 Largest Latin American Firms. Brazil, Mexico, Chile, and Argentina head the ranking and have been expanding their share in the last few years.

The reasons for these differences involve aspects such as size of the countries and of their domestic markets, industrialization policies, and the national cultures.

4.5 How competitive are the Multilatinas?

The competitiveness of the Multilatinas is a divisive issue. For Grosse (2007), Latin firms are not very competitive, both in the domestic and in the international market: they are regarded as clones of the North American multinationals, though smaller, less efficient, and less competitive; besides,

Table 4.1 The Multilatinas

Firms	Industry	Fortune 500 2009/2008	Forbes 2000 (2008/2007)	WIR 2008		BCG 2009	Home country
				Foreign assets	TNI		
Petrobras	Petroleum	34/63	29/88	12	94	X	Brazil
Bradesco	Banking	148/204	85/208	–	–	–	Brazil
CVRD (Vale)	Mining & Quarrying	205/235	76/361	11	73	X	Brazil
Itaúsa – Investimentos	Banking	149/273	175/477	–	–	–	Brazil
Banco do Brasil	Banking	174/282	132/256	-	–	–	Brazil
América Móvil	Telecomm.	273/283	453	14	54	X	Mexico
Cemex	Cement	421/389	249/361	4	21	X	Mexico
Carso Global Telecom	Telecomm.	464	346/1171	–	–	–	Mexico
Gerdau	Metals	400	766/1496	39	47	X	Brazil
Falabella	Retailing	–	1238/1777	–	–	X	Chile
Femsa	Food & Beverages	–	582/809	47	84	X	Mexico
Braskem	Chemicals	–	1091/1170	–	–	X	Brazil
Embraer	Aerospace & Defence	–	1345/1467	–	–	X	Brazil
Grupo Bimbo	Food & Beverages	–	1312/1881	91	76	X	Mexico
Grupo Alfa	Conglomerates	–	1255/989	–	–	X	Mexico
CSN	Metals	–	809/1049	–	–	–	Brazil
Unibanco	Banking	–	233	–	–	–	Brazil

Grupo Elektra	Services		1278	–	–	–	Mexico
Sadia	Food	–	1733	–	–	X	Brazil
Votorantim Group	Diversified	–	1487	–	–	X	Brazil
WEG	Electric Engines	–	1824	–	–	X	Brazil
Aracruz Celulose	Pulp and Paper	–	1519	–	–	–	Brazil
Suzano	Pulp and Paper		1971	–	–	–	Brazil
Usiminas	Steel		736	–	–	–	Brazil
Gruma	Food and Beverages	–	–	81	38	X	Mexico
Coteminas	Textiles	–	–	–	–	X	Brazil
JBS-Friboi	Food	–	–	–	–	X	Brazil
Marcopolo	Vehicles and Parts	–	–	–	–	X	Brazil
Natura	Cosmetics	–	–	–	–	X	Brazil
Perdigão	Food	–	–	–	–	X	Brazil
Camargo Corrêa SA	Diversified	–	–	–	–	X	Brazil
Techint	Metals	–		–	–	X	Argentina
Grupo Modelo	Diversified	–	–	–	–	X	Mexico

Sources: Forbes (2008), Fortune (2009), Boston Consulting Group (2009), UNCTAD (2008).

Table 4.2 500 largest Latin American companies by country of origin

Rank 2007	Country	Number of firms						Share % 2007
		2002	2003	2004	2005	2006	2007	
1	Brazil	137	195	203	204	207	211	42.2
2	Mexico	241	170	154	138	111	134	33
3	Chile	45	48	48	54	63	55	8.1
4	Argentina	24	25	32	36	41	36	5.5
5	Colombia	25	18	28	30	35	31	3
6	Peru	7	8	11	12	18	15	1.5
7	Venezuela	10	9	11	11	12	7	5.6
8	Costa Rica	3	5	6	4	3	3	0.3
9	Ecuador	2	3	2	5	3	3	0.5
–	Guatemala	–	1	2	1	2	–	–
10	Panama	1	2	1	2	2	2	0.1
11	Uruguay	3	2	1	2	2	2	0.1
12	El Salvador	1	2	1	1	1	1	0.1
	Total	500	500	500	500	500	500	100

Source: *America Economia* (2008).

they lack competence in the technological and innovation fields. Another controversial assessment was made by Feldmann (2009). After categorizing 24 Multilatinas according to the technological intensity levels defined by OCDE (high, medium, and low technological intensity), he concludes that only Embraer can be considered as of high technology; he classifies four firms as of medium technological intensity and the great majority, that is, 19 organizations (80 per cent) are in sectors of low technological intensity.

From another standpoint, authors who apply the UNCTAD's Transnationality Index defend the idea that CEMEX is the only Latin American firm that can be considered as 'legitimate' multinational.

Notwithstanding, the Multilatinas are effectively competing internationally. How can this be explained?

It is well established that for firms to be successful in the global arena there must be a complex interaction of a set of factors: those present within the firms themselves (their competences, resources, and management style) and in the institutional environment (sociopolitical infrastructure, culture, and factors endowment).

If we consider the country-specific factors, Brazil, Chile, Mexico, and Argentina have presented quite distinct sets of country advantages and disadvantages. Natural resources represent a common advantage, but it is necessary to highlight that there is a significant percentage of Multilatinas that are not involved in industries based on natural resources.

Considering disadvantages, then, the political and institutional turbulence is a common factor, with less relevance to Chile. Conversely, Chile is the country that presents the smallest useful surface as well as a smaller market. Thus, there are distinct sets of country-specific factors playing a relevant role in Multilatinas' internationalization processes. This means that each country has developed a specific dynamic interplay between CSAs and FSAs to sustain the internationalization of their firms.

Yet, it is important to observe that the Multilatinas are more intensely present in Latin America itself (Tavares, 2007). Various factors have contributed to this situation. First, various leading firms are state-owned, exploring natural resources. Since the continent is rich, their internationalization is justified as resource-seeking strategies in the neighbouring countries, as happened to Petrobras in the 1970s.

Second, cultural differences seem to be another element that is worth considering in understanding the timidity of Latin firms in adventuring beyond frontiers. The prevalence of a *parochial mindset* regarding the global environment (Gupta and Govindarajan, 2002) is an indicator. This characteristic reflects an experience in which an emphasis on the domestic market and local environment prevailed, hindering the comprehension and interpretation of cultural differences and characteristics of other regions and, also, the access to relevant international networks (Johanson and Vahlne, 2009).

Despite those trends, Multilatinas have developed differentiated competences and managerial styles that supported new business models that were successful in the international markets. In synergy with the development of competences for efficient performance in highly complex environments, the Multilatinas developed internationally distinctive models in production and operations (for example, Bimbo, Arcor, Ambev, Companhia Nacional de Chocolates, Gerdau, Cemex), competence in product development (for example, Natura, Embraer), competence in marketing (for example, Ambev, Bimbo, Spoleto), technological competence (for example, Gruma, Petrobras), competence in retailing (for example, Ripley, Falabela), competence in managing mergers and acquisitions (for example, Bimbo, JBS-Friboi) and, overall, competence in performing in highly complex environments.

The multinationals that ventured beyond the limits of Latin America were those that were confident in their organizational competences and management styles as compatible with the demands and opportunities of global economy. Moreover, the entry of these firms in more culturally distant countries involved the development of new capabilities required in forming alliances, partnerships and acquisitions, in the development of global products or products in certain specialist niches. This is the case of firms in the food sector, such as Gruma, which has focused on the market for Mexican food in Asia, and in the cement industry, where Cemex became the third largest in the world (Lucea and Lessard, 2010).

4.6 The Multilatinas in Europe

The Multilatinas that have invested in Europe constitute a small group. Figure 4.1 shows examples of countries in which they operate and Table 4.3 presents four selected cases, illustrating why and how these Multilatinas entered in Europe. The table also shows key competences that companies already had, before internationalization, and competences developed throughout their expansion abroad.

Although the European countries in which they are located varies widely, their countries of origin are not so diverse. Indeed, most of them are from Argentina, Brazil, and Mexico. Brazil, in its turn, has a more significant presence than the other two countries, considering the number of Brazilian firms established in Europe.

Some Multilatinas operate in many countries and sub-regions, as is the case of Cemex (with the largest investment), Techint, Ambev, and Weg, among others.

The investment pattern, on the other hand, involves setting up offices, distribution centres, joint ventures, and the acquisition of plants. In fact, the emphasis on alliances and acquisitions as an entry mode (instead of greenfield subsidiaries) has been appointed as a common pattern among emerging country organizations (Guillen and Garcia-Canal, 2009). What the chart does not show, however, are the cases of Latin firms that left

Host countries	Brazil	Mexico	Argentina
Western Europe			
Portugal	Petrobras (JV), CSN (P), Weg (P), Marcopolo (P), Embraer (JV)		
Spain	Gerdau (P), Weg (O)	Cemex (P), Gruma (P)	Arcor (O)
France	CVRD (O)	Cemex (P),	
Germany	CVRD (O), Votorantim (O), Sabó (P), Weg (O), Inbev (JV), Romi (O),	Cemex (P),	
Netherlands	Weg (O), Inbev (JV), Perdigão (P)	Gruma (O)	
UK	Petrobras (O), CVRD (O), Votorantim (O), Sabó (O), Weg (O), Inbev (JV)	Cemex (P), Gruma (P)	Techint (O)
Norway	CVRD (O)	Cemex (O),	
Switzerland	CVRD (O), Votorantim (O),	Cemex (O),	
Italy	Sabó (O), Embraco (P), Romi (P)	Gruma (O)	Techint (P)
Austria	Sabó (P)	Cemex (P),	
Poland		Cemex (P),	Techint (P)
Ireland		Cemex (P),	
Belgium	Votorantim (O), Inbev (P)		
Finland		Cemex (O)	
Sweden	Weg (O)		
Southeast Europe and CIS			
Croatia		Cemex (P),	
Romania			Techint (P)
Hungary	Sabó (P)		

Key: O = offices; P = plant (acquisitions); JV = joint ventures; DC = distribution centres.

Figure 4.1 Multilatinas operating in Europe (examples)

Table 4.3 Examples of Multilatinas operating in Europe (selected cases)

Case	Country of entry in Europe	Objectives in Europe	Pre-existing competences	Competences acquired in international operations
GRUMA (Mex)	UK (offices 1997/98); tortillas' first plant, 2000).	Market-seeking, efficiency-seeking (optimization of cornmeal processing plants)	Process engineering technologies (cornmeal) Vertical integration and distribution	Absorption of technologies from acquired companies Development of products (flat breads)
CEMEX (Mex)	Spain (acquisition of two companies 1992)	Market-seeking, efficiency-seeking, financial resources-seeking	Information systems to support operational excellence Efficient logistics in complex environments Efficiency in M&A	Absorption of technologies from acquired companies Operating according to new technical standards
WEG (Bra)	Portugal	Market-seeking, efficiency-seeking, strategic asset-seeking	Business model Management model Technology (electric motors)	Brand management Costumer relationships management Moving up the value chain (as a solutions provider)
Techint (Arg)	Italy	Market-seeking, efficiency-seeking	Operational excellence	Supplier chain management Costumer relationship management

European countries, in recent years, as for example, Odebrecht in Germany, Marcopolo in Portugal, Embraco in Italy, and Sadia in Russia; furthermore, Marcopolo recently opted for postponing investments in Russia.

4.7 Multilatinas' first entry: The choice of country

Cuervo-Cazurra (2008) assessed the cultural distance or proximity between country of origin of multinationals and host country of the first value-added activity, as a way to measure psychic distance. This variable has been commonly used in other studies, starting with the analysis of the influence of culture on entry modes by Kogut and Singh (1988). In the same manner as these authors, Cuervo-Cazurra applied a composite index, based on the four indicators of work-related values developed by Hofstede (1980) – power distance, individualism, uncertainty avoidance, and masculinity. He also analysed the development distance or proximity between country of origin and host country of the first value-added activity; for such, he made use of the human development index developed by the United Nations, which considers three dimensions: education, health, and income (United Nations, 2009).

Considering cultural distance and development distance, Cuervo-Cazurra (2008) identified two dominant patterns or strategies for the first international entry mode and two secondary ones. The patterns that arose were:

(a) Firms that internationalized to countries that are proximate in both culture and development. These firms often sell products dependent upon government relationships and institutional/developmental conditions. In this case, the strategic focus is on countries in Latin America itself.
(b) Firms that started their internationalization in countries that are distant in both culture and development. These firms often sell products that are culturally bound but that need larger market opportunities. It involves destinations like Canada, the United States, and Anglo-Saxon European countries.

The secondary patterns, so called because of the limited number of firms using them, are:

(c) firms that invested in countries that are proximate in culture but distant in development. These firms sell products that are neither bound by development nor culture, or firms that are in search of assets and capabilities to complement their resource pools. It involves countries like Belgium, France, Italy, and Portugal (Latin Europe).
(d) firms that started their internationalization in countries that are distant in culture or proximate in development. These firms sell products adapted to the needs of consumers in developing countries but they are not culturally bound to these countries. It involves a strategic focus on African and Asian countries.

Our perspective is that other insights may be reached if Multilatinas developments are observed not only at the time of first value-added activity abroad, but also at subsequent stages. Although this is less studied in the literature, it casts light on the expansion of Multilatinas and contribute to the comprehension of their entry and expansion patterns.

4.8 Research design

Based on former studies on dimensions related to national culture (Hofstede, 1980; Ronen and Shenkar (1985); Kogut and Singh, 1988; Cuervo-Cazurra, 2008), and on levels of human development – very high, high, medium, and low human development (United Nations, 2009) – we adopted the general definitions indicated in Figure 4.2.

The firms selected for this analysis are those that are included in the rankings of *Fortune*, *Forbes*, WIR, and BCG. This compounds a set of 33 large Multilatinas, already shown in Table 4.1. Despite their relevance, these firms have received little attention in the international business literature (Cuervo-Cazurra, 2008), if compared to Asian or Eastern Europe firms.

As in the case of Cuervo-Cazurra (2008), this study used publicly available data – such as firm's websites, company documents, and information available in a broad range of press media – for examining the trajectories of these firms after their first move.

4.9 The trajectories of the Multilatinas

Table 4.4 presents the distribution of the 33 main multinationals in Latin America in the first three markets/regions in which they made investments. In the table, it is interesting to observe that 70 per cent of the firms assessed invested in a second region and only 42.4 per cent invested in a third. In the first entry, it was noted a preference of the Multilatinas for other Latin

Region	Cultural distance/development distance
Latin America	Lower/lower
North America	Higher/higher
South (Africa, Asia)	Higher/lower
Latin Europe	Lower/higher
Anglo-Saxon Europe	Higher/higher

Note: Only the home economies of firms mentioned in any of the four rankings analysed are considered for Argentina, Brazil, Chile, and Mexico.

Figure 4.2 Criteria for identifying choice of foreign region of operation

Table 4.4 Multilatinas: Sequence of entries in distinct global regions

Region	First entry	Second entry	Third entry
Latin America	17 (51.5%)	6 (26.0%)	2 (14.2%)
North America	9 (27.2%)	7 (30.4%)	1 (7.1%)
South (Africa, Asia)	0	2 (8.6%)	7 (50.0%)
Latin Europe	6 (18.1%)	3 (13.0%)	2 (14.2%)
Anglo-Saxon Europe	1 (3.0)	5 (21.7%)	2 (14.2%)
Total	33 (100%)	23 (100%)	14 (100%)

American countries (51 per cent of the firms). In fact, a significant number, nine firms (27.2 per cent), have not even carried out a second entry in another market, preferring to concentrate their strategic efforts in their own region: this is the case of firms such as Bradesco, Banco do Brasil, Braskem, Elektra, Falabella, Femsa, Gerdau, Unibanco, and Usiminas. The petrochemical firm, Braskem, for instance, has exported products to manufacturing industries worldwide; its core investments are, however, in proximate countries, such as Venezuela, in the search for resources and efficiency. In this case, the firms privileged regions with cultural differences and low development level, compared to their home countries.

In this first movement it is observed that, from those that entered Europe, the majority opted for Latin Europe (18.1 per cent), instead of Anglo-Saxon Europe (3 per cent). In this case, although the development level is distinct, there is greater cultural similarity, as in the example of Natura, a Brazilian cosmetics industry that operates under a network marketing model. It installed a store in France, clearly intending to learn how to approach the European market. Embraer, Modelo, and Marcopolo are other examples.

In terms of the first entry, some firms chose North America, notably Mexican industries, such as Bimbo and Alfa. The geographical proximity and the presence of a Hispanic consumer market in the United States (particularly for the food sector in which Bimbo and Alfa operate), are drivers for that movement. However, it is also the case of Brazilian firms searching for assets, resources, and markets, such as Votorantim, CSN, and CVRD (Vale). As a first choice, Anglo-Saxon Europe, Asia and Africa are the least preferred options.

Analysis of the second entry, however, reveals a different trend: Multilatinas started to direct their strategies toward the two European regions more frequently. Actually, one out of three Multilatinas chose Europe as the second platform for their internationalization process. It is the case, for example, of Perdigão and Techint. Conversely, Sadia moved to Asia and the construction firm Camargo Correa initiated activities in Africa.

As for the third entry, the focus moved to the South: among the 14 firms that proceeded into newer markets, most investments were concentrated in Asia, as in the case of Weg, Embraer, and CVRD (Vale). The motivations regarding this preference seem to involve mainly the search for markets, strategic assets, and resources. The European continent seems to be less attractive as a third platform for the Multilatinas that are already operating in two other continents.

4.10 The entry and expansion strategies of the Multilatinas

Assessment of the three entries of the Multilatinas in the Fortune, Forbes, WIR, and BCG rankings allows some insights to complement the observations of Cuervo-Cazurra (2008) in regard to their internationalization strategies.

The first entry movement suggests a cautious attitude of the firms that prioritize Latin America in their strategic choices, an environment in which similarities prevail. There are firms that opted for North America, most of them from Mexico (in this case, the geographical proximity and expressive Hispanic market in the USA play a relevant role). In terms of Europe, the focus, in this first move, is on countries with a lower cultural distance, specifically the countries of the Latin European cluster.

Yet, in the subsequent movements, an interesting effect is observed: the emergence of *multiple strategies* and *trajectories* from the second or third entry. While in the first movements the destination choice in which there were marked similarities seems to be more relevant (as in the case of the choice for Latin America and Latin Europe), in the subsequent expansions the movements seem to become rather erratic, spreading throughout the globe, as if reducing the significance of distances and differences (cultural and development level) on strategy choices.

In fact, our understanding is that this effect is related to a learning process, associated with entering into new networks, to acquiring new capabilities and to acknowledging previously unnoticed global opportunities, shifting the emphasis from avoidance of uncertainties to exploitation of global strategies. In this learning process, Latin firms have developed what Knight and Kim (2009) have denominated 'international business competence', which includes international orientation, international marketing skills, international innovativeness, and international market orientation. Additionally, they have developed international networking competences, that is, the firm-specific ability to handle, use, and exploit inter-organizational relationships (Ritter and Gemunden, 2003), as well as inter-cultural competences.

Furthermore, based on the literature (Dunning, 2000; Gereffi, Humphrey and Sturgeon, 2005; Fleury and Fleury, 2009), we observe that some drivers are especially important to understand the Multilatinas movements, and they can exert a combined influence on them (more than one driver simultaneously). They can be the *push* type, which attracts FDI, or a *pull*-type effect, compelling the organizations to internationalization ECLAC (2005).

One of these drivers refers to insertion into global production networks, following the sources of supply. In these cases, the Multilatinas follow the

Key drivers	Firms (selected examples)
Global production network (supply follower)	Automotive: Sabo (Brazil), Nemak (Mexico) Electric suppliers: Embraco and Weg (Brazil)
Resource-seeking	CVRD (Vale) (Brazil)
Market-seeking	Cement: Cemex (Mexico) Steel: Gerdau (Brazil), Techint (Argentina) Food: Bimbo and Gruma (Mexico), Ambev (Brazil) Textile: Santista/Tavex (Brazil) Machinery: Romi (Brazil) Engineering: Odebrecht (Brazil)
Asset-seeking	Marcopolo (Brazil)
Operational support	Embraer (Brazil)

Figure 4.3 Key drivers for the internationalization of Multilatinas to Europe

movements of their main clients and deploy capabilities and advantages that are progressively accumulated and developed in this relationship. There is also the search for resources (mainly raw materials), capital markets, and strategic assets. On the other hand, there is the search for new markets, owing to market opportunities/imperfections, competitiveness in the domestic market, and as a means of forging ahead of the competition in entering foreign markets. Finally, there is a driver related to operational support development. Figure 4.3 illustrates examples of Multilatinas' international trajectories relating to these different drivers.

4.11 Final remarks

The internationalization of Latin firms is still in its early ages; it is observed that these firms delayed their internationalization, which mostly occurred some decades after their foundation. There was a small movement in the 1980s, but the process really intensified at the end of the 1990s, and later, as events modified the context of their operations. As evidenced by the Multilatinas presented here, they internationalized autonomously, following their own decisions and strategies; there was no cooperation either among industrial firms or between them and financial institutions (as is the case of Spain), and there was no support from governments (as is the case of China). On the other hand, privatized firms outstood among them.

The arrival of Multilatinas in Europe has been timid, particularly in Anglo-Saxon regions. There are cultural and institutional factors that explain this. It is likely that the institutional complexity of Europe and the reliance on social and environmental rules and norms to defend the region against foreign competitors (Messner, 2004), as well as peculiarities of the consumer market and difficulties of accessing distribution channels, have also been inhibiting factors. The lack of certain management competences, such as cross-cultural competences (Johnson, Lenartowicz, and Apud, 2006) also plays a role. Understanding the significance of these factors on the strategies of Multilatinas in Europe is an area for future research.

It is unlikely that this timid presence of Multilatinas in Europe will be changed within the next few years. First, because the European reactions to the financial crisis are still difficult to predict, decreasing its attractiveness to foreign investment. Second, because Multilatinas, despite their exceptional capability to adapt, particularly in adverse situations and times of crises, as well as the disposition to quickly invest in new opportunities still have some homework to do, on various fronts, especially those referring to the need of developing technological and innovative capabilities with a higher level of sophistication.

However, it is quite possible that the demonstration effect and the maturing process of Latin firms, only recently present in the global arena, might stimulate increasing entries of new players from the same region.

References

America Economia (2008), '*As maiores empresas da América Latina*', 361, 21, *Julho*, 106–78.

Ashkanasy, N., Trevor-Roberts, E., and Earnshaw, L. (2002), 'The Anglo Cluster: Legacy of the British Empire', *Journal of World Business*, 37 (1), 28–39.

Bakacsi, G., Sándor, T., András, K., and Viktor, I. (2002), 'Eastern European Cluster: Tradition and Transition', *Journal of World Business*, 37 (1), 69–80.

Boston Consulting Group (2009), 'The New Global Challengers', *BCG Report*, January 2009, 38.

Cuervo-Cazurra, A. (2008), 'The Multinationalization of Developing Country MNEs: The Case of Multilatinas', *Journal of International Management*, 14, 138–54.

Cuervo-Cazurra, A. (2010), 'Multilatinas', *Universia Business Review*, 25, 1st Quarter, 14–33.

Dunning, J. H. (2000), 'The Eclectic Paradigm as an Envelope for Economic and Business Theories of MNE Activity', *International Business Review*, 9 (2), 163–90.

ECLAC (Economic Commission for Latin America and the Caribbean) (2005), *Foreign Investment in Latin America and the Caribbean 2005*. Santiago, Chile: United Nations.

Feldmann, P. (2009), '*O atraso tecnológico da América Latina como decorrência de aspectos geográficos e de fatores microeconômicos interligados*', *Economia e Sociedade*, 18 (1), 119–39.

Fleury, A. C. and Fleury, M. T. L (2009), 'The Brazilian Multinationals: Surfing the Waves of Internationalization', in R. Ramamurti and J. Singh (eds), *Emerging Multinationals from Emerging Countries*. Cambridge, UK: Cambridge University Press.

Forbes (2008), The Global 2000, available at: http://www.forbes.com/lists/2008/18/biz_2000global08_The-Global-2000_Rank.html [accessed 5 June 2009].

Fortune (2009), Global 500, available at: http://money.cnn.com/magazines/fortune/global500/2009/full_list [accessed 5 June 2009].

Gereffi, G., Humphrey, J., and Sturgeon, T. (2005), 'The Governance of Global Value Chains', *Review of International Political Economy*, 12 (1), 78–104.
Goldstein, A. (2007), *Multinational Firms from Emerging Economies*. New York: Palgrave Macmillan.
Grosse, R. (2007), 'Introduction: Can Latin American Firms Compete?' in R. Grosse and L. Mesquita (eds), *Can Latin American Firms Compete?* New York: Oxford University Press, 1–25.
Grosse, R. and Mesquita, L. (eds) (2007), *Can Latin American Firms Compete?* New York: Oxford University Press.
Guillen, M. and Garcia-Canal, E. (2009), 'The American Model of the Multinational Firm and the "New" Multinationals from Emerging Economies', *The Academy of Management Perspectives*, 23 (2), 23–35.
Gupta, A. K. and Govindarajan, V. (2002), 'Cultivating a Global Mindset', *The Academy of Management Executive*, 16 (1), 116–26.
Haar, J. and Price, J. (eds) (2008), *Can Latin America Compete? Confronting the Challenges of Globalization*. New York: Palgrave Macmillan.
Hofstede, G. (1980), *Culture's Consequences: International Differences in Work-Related Values*. Beverly Hills, CA: Sage.
Jank, M. (2005), 'Of Flying Geese and Sitting Ducks: Brazil Stares, East Asia Takes Off…' Yaleglobal Online, available at: http://yaleglobal.yale.edu/content/flying-geese-and-sitting-ducks-brazil-stares-east-asia-takes-off%E2%80%A6 [accessed 6 August 2009].
Jesuino, J. (2002), 'Latin Europe Cluster: from South to North', *Journal of World Business*, 37 (1), 81–9.
Johanson, J. and Vahlne, J. (2009), 'The Uppsala Internationalization Process Model Revisited: From Liability of Foreignness to Liability of Outsidership', *Journal of International Business Studies*, 40 (9), 1411–31.
Johnson, J., Lenartowicz, T., and Apud, S. (2006), 'Cross-Cultural Competence in International Business: Toward a Definition and a Model', *Journal of International Business Studies*, 37, 525–43.
Knight, G. and Kim, D. (2009), 'International Business Competence and the Contemporary Firm', *Journal of International Business Studies*, 40 (2), 255–73.
Kogut, B. and Singh, H. (1988), 'The Effect of National Culture on the Choice of Entry Mode', *Journal of International Business Studies*, 19, 411–32.
Lucea, R. and Lessard, D. (2010), 'Como mantienen su ventaja competitiva las multinacionales de economias emergentes?' El caso de CEMEX. *Universia Business Review*, 25, 1st quarter, 76–97.
Mathews, J. (2006), 'Dragon Multinationals: New Players in 21st-Century Globalization', *Asia-Pacific Journal of Management*, 23, 5–27.
Messner, D. (2004), 'Regions in the "World Economic Triangle"', in H. Schmitz (ed.), *Local Enterprises in the Global Economy: Issues of Governance and Upgrading*. Cheltenham, UK: Edward Elgar.
Mortimore, M. (1993), 'Flying Geese or Sitting Ducks? Transnationals and Industry in Developing Countries', *CEPAL Review*, 51, 15–34.
Muzychenco, O. (2008), 'Cross-Cultural Entrepreneurial Competence in Identifying International Business Opportunities', *European Management Journal*, 26 (6), 366–77.
Ramamurti, R. and Singh, J. (eds) (2009), *Emerging Multinationals from Emerging Countries*. Cambridge: Cambridge University Press.
Ritter, T. and Gemunden, H. (2003), 'Inter-Organizational Relationships and Networks', *Journal of Business Research*, 56 (9), 691–7.
Ronen, S. and Shenkar, O. (1985), 'Clustering Countries on Attitudinal Dimensions: A Review and Synthesis', *Academy of Management Review*, 10, 435–54.

Santiso, J. (2008), 'The Emergence of Latin Multinationals', *OECD Development Centre*, available at: http: www.oecd.org/dataoecd/4/40/40512615.pdf [accessed 20 October 2009].

Sauvant, K., Mendoza, K., and Irmak, I. (2008), *The Rise of Transnational Corporations from Emerging Markets: Threat or Opportunity?* Northampton, MA: Edward Elgar Publishing.

Szabo, E., Brodbeck, F., Hartog, D., Reber, G., Weibler, J., and Wunderer, R. (2002), 'The Germanic Europe Cluster: Where Employees Have a Voice', *Journal of World Business*, 37 (1), 55–68.

Tavares, M. (2007), 'Outward FDI and the Competitiveness of Latin American Firms', in R. Grosse and L. Mesquita (eds), *Can Latin American Firms Compete?* New York: Oxford University Press, 45–65.

UNCTAD (United Nations Conference on Trade and Development) (2008), *World Investment Report 2008*. New York: United Nations.

United Nations (2009), *Human Development Report*. New York: United Nations.

5

Internationalization of China's Enterprises and Its Implications for Europe

Changqi Wu

5.1 Introduction

The forces of globalization in the last three decades have greatly reshaped the landscape of the world economy. In that process, an increasing number of firms from emerging markets have undergone fundamental transformation and experienced a rapid growth. Some of them have started looking for investment opportunities across the national borders. Many of these kinds of investments go to countries with institutional environments that are similar to their home base, but a few also invest in developed economies. This South–North type of foreign direct investment is a new phenomenon that has caught the attentions of business scholars as well as policy makers. Although the stories of Southern Multinationals' expansion have been widely reported as the headlines in business news in recent times, systematic studies on this important phenomenon are scarce. Therefore it is worthwhile examining this new kind of multinational enterprise in order to gain a better understanding of its distinctive characteristics (UNCTAD, 2006).

When the global economy faced unprecedented challenges from 2008 onwards, the pace of overseas expansion of the Southern multinational quickened. That quickening has added to the urgency for the academic community to understand outward foreign direct investment from emerging economies and to assess its implications for the world economy in general and for Europe in particular.

Among the emerging market multinationals, enterprises from China stand out. It is not only because China, in comparison to other transition economies, has been the first to start its market-based transformation and therefore has richer experiences, it is also because China is a country that has integrated most closely into the world economy by measures such as international trade and openness to inward foreign direct investment. The lessons learnt from Chinese multinationals can help us to have a better understanding of the new multinationals from the South.

A number of questions naturally arise: What are the extents and patterns of China's outward direct investment in the last decade? Where do these investments go? What are the motives for Chinese enterprises going abroad? What is the impact of such outward investment on Europe?

In the next section, we take a historical perspective to review the evolution of outward foreign direct investment from China. Then, we will combine theoretical arguments and statistical facts to explain the motives for Chinese enterprises going global. A number of case studies are presented and discussed before concluding remarks are offered.

5.2 Evolution of internationalization of Chinese enterprises

To understand the background behind the surge in outwards direct investment from China, we can view retrospectively what has happened in the last three decades in China. As we know, starting from 1979, China has experienced one of the most profound economic reforms in its history. The central planning system was replaced by market mechanism, and the self-isolated China integrated itself rapidly with the rest of the world through trade and investment.

The reform and open-door policies also swept the Chinese industrial sector. At firm level, enterprises in China experienced fundamental reform. In that process, many state-owned enterprises were privatized while the largest ones were restructured and incorporated. More non-state firms were established. By the end of the twentieth century, China had almost completed the restructuring of its corporate sector. The numerous reform measures have changed the incentive structure within economic organization and led to much improved efficiency. The competitive pressure demands continuous improvement of the productivity of domestic firms.

Moreover, the open-door policy implemented at the beginning of China's economic reform unleashed the forces of globalization. Active measures were introduced to attract foreign direct investment. Multinational enterprises, which entered China initially through joint ventures, eventually developed their operations in the form of wholly owned subsidiaries. China's low labour costs combined with foreign capital, plus global best practices, made China the powerhouse for the export of manufactured goods. China's exports increased rapidly in both relative terms and its absolute value. The export to GDP ratio of China reached as high as 40 per cent in some years. China had become the workshop of the world. The export competitiveness of China strengthened after it joined the World Trade Organization in 2001 and integrated fully into the world economy.

In that process, Chinese enterprises were exposed to the forces of globalization. Most importantly, the foreign-invested enterprises brought the technologies and management skills willingly or unwillingly towards Chinese companies and improved the technical and competitive capabilities of Chinese enterprises.

Although China as a whole has exported manufactured goods for years, more than half of China's exports are so-called process trade. In other words, a large amount of intermediate products and raw materials are imported and processed in China, then exported to the rest of the world. The portion of the value-added created and retained in China is relatively small. When globalization and subsequently division of labour deepened, Chinese firms imported more raw materials and other inputs to meet the needs of expanding manufacturing sectors. To secure the supply of those production inputs, some Chinese companies considered expanding to upstream and/or downstream economic activities to become more vertically integrated.

Therefore, privatization, globalization, and the need for vertical integration lay the foundation for the more advantaged stage of internationalization of Chinese firms: outward foreign direct investment.

Although the term *'internationalization'* carries a broader set of meanings than foreign direct investment, in this particular context, we refer to it as the outward foreign direct investment made by Chinese indigenous enterprises. Lenovo's acquisition of IBM's PC business in 2004, Shanghai Automotive Industrial Corporation (SAIC)'s acquisition of Rover in 2005 and Geele's acquisition of Volvo of Sweden in 2010 are examples of such activities.

The public policy response of the Chinese government towards the changing global environment is to encourage those indigenous companies that are ready to carry out outward FDI. Hence in March 2001 the so-called Going Global policy was formally launched. Chinese Premier Wen Jiabao, in his government report to the annual general assembly of the People's Congress of China, announced that the Chinese government would encourage China's enterprises going global, that is, to invest abroad and to expand their overseas business.

This was a watershed in China's open-door policy, although it has taken time for the Chinese government to work out detailed policy measures. China has benefited enormously from globalization in its reform process via international trade and foreign direct investment in the first twenty years of economic reform. Then it was the time for Chinese firms going out to look for opportunities and resources.

Figure 5.1 shows the trends of outward foreign direct investment in the period 1990–2009. As the figure shows, China's outward FDI remained subdued in the period of 1990–2000 and accelerated afterwards. Following the introduction of the new policy to encourage Chinese firms going global, an increasing number of Chinese enterprises started exploring the investment opportunities in overseas markets. The average annual growth rate of China's outward FDI in a ten-year period from 2000 to 2009 was 45.8 per cent.

As outward FDI increased over time, its regional distribution also changed. Figure 5.2 illustrates China's outward FDI across regions in the period of 2006–8. The flows of outward FDI show a strong contrast between developed and developing economies as the destination of investment.

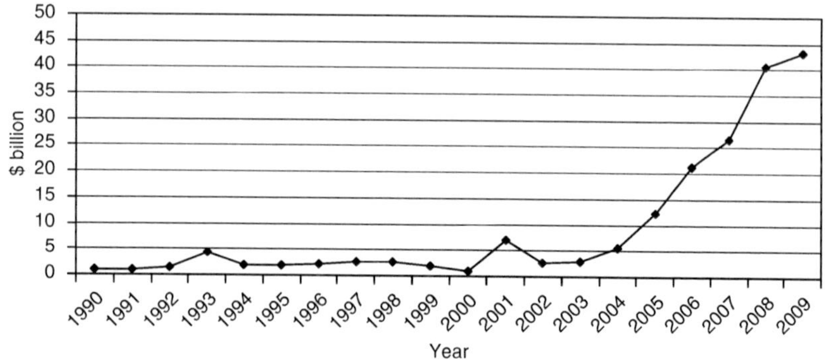

Figure 5.1 China's outward foreign direct investment
Source: The Statiscal Yearbook on China's/Outward Foreign Direct Investment.

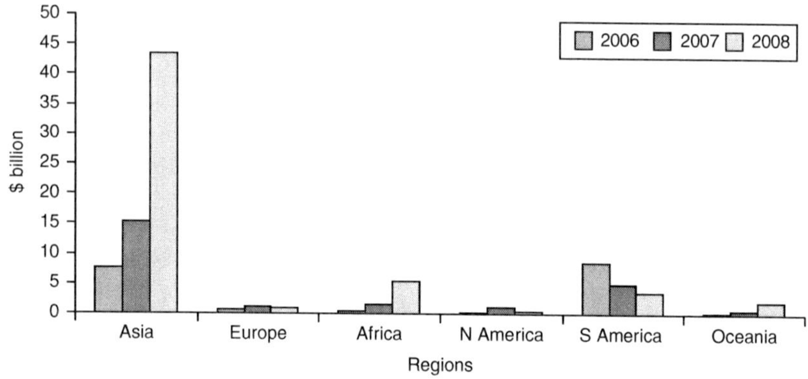

Figure 5.2 China's outward foreign direct investment across region
Source: The Statistical Yearbook on China's Outward Foreign Direct Investment.

Chinese outward FDI concentrates in Asia, particularly in China's Special Administrative Region of Hong Kong. South America and Africa also attract a noticeable amount of FDI from China. But it seems that Chinese multinational enterprises keep themselves away from developed economies such as Europe and North America. Over the years, China's direct investment in Europe was in the range of 2 per cent of total outward investment of China, almost negligible even without adjusting for the size of the European economy.

These figures help us to answer the questions regarding the motives of Chinese enterprises going global.

5.3 Motives for Chinese enterprises going global

Following Dunning (Dunning and Lundan, 2008), international business scholars often consider multinational enterprises' motives of investing abroad as resources-seeking, efficiency-seeking, assets-seeking, and market-seeking. Chinese multinationals as a whole share many of the aspects of multinational enterprises in general, but also have their own characteristics.

First of all, to understand the outward FDI from China, we have to understand the composition of Chinese enterprises. Different from other developed economies, Chinese firms can be roughly grouped into three categories: state-owned enterprises, private enterprise, and foreign invested enterprises. Because of the different nature of ownership, resources, objectives, and incentive structure, their motives for overseas expansion are also different. Child and Rodrigues (2005) call for theoretical extension to explain emerging Chinese multinationals. Some theories have been proposed in the existing literature, such as in Buckley et al. (2007), Morck et al. (2008), and Guillen and Garcia-Canal (2009). Moreover, the spring-board perspective (Luo and Tung, 2007) argues that overseas expansion is for indigenous companies jumping over the technical and market barriers, while the domestic restraint hypothesis proposes that private domestic firms expand overseas to escape from institutionalized discrimination (Witt and Lewin, 2007). These theories are useful for us to understand the phenomenon of emerging multinational enterprises from China. However, there are still some more special reasons, as we will discuss below.

5.3.1 Institutional void

Similar to other emerging economies, protection of private property rights and contract enforcement are far from sufficient in China. Because of the weak market institutions, enterprises in mainland China, particularly non-state-owned firms, have a strong incentive to relocate their assets to places with better protection of the property rights. Hong Kong, for instance, is one such location. Hong Kong moreover can provide those mainland-based companies more than better protection of property rights; it has a higher standard of contract enforcement than in the mainland of China. For a mainland China-based company, investing in Hong Kong and other Asian economies can fill the so-called institutional void. Special institutional environments explain the peculiar situation of the lion's share of outward FDI in Asia.

5.3.2 Transaction costs

A close look at the outward FDI data reveals that the destination that has attracted China's largest outward investment is Hong Kong, a special administrative region of China where the common law system inherited from British rule before 1997 is well established. The high proportion of direct investment in Hong Kong is consistent with the hypothesis of the institutional void. Moreover, proximity in location, culture, and institutions makes Asian economies in general an ideal choice in the internationalization process of Chinese firms. But property rights and the institutional void argument alone cannot explain why Hong Kong is the primary destination for outward FDI. The conditions for that to happen must include the difficulty or high costs of using other locations or means to seek better protection of property rights such as by listing these companies in Hong Kong as *red chip* companies, those listed companies with roots from the mainland of China, but registered in tax havens such as British Virgin Islands. When the Chinese government did not officially adopt the going global policy and put a lot of restrictions on outward FDI, some companies or individuals also used the methods of round-tripping, that is, to move money out of the country and bring it back as investment to the mainland of China as foreign invested enterprises so as to take advantage of preferred tax and other policies in place in order to attract inward FDI. These foreign invested enterprises typically receive better protection of property rights.

Moreover, although Europe can offer similar or better protection for property rights from the institutional theoretical perspective, the cost of long-distance travel and different languages and culture put Europe at disadvantage as the destination for Chinese companies to invest directly to seek institutional protection. Therefore, the institutional void theory provides an explanation why some companies in emerging market have incentives to invest money outside their home country, but it cannot explain satisfactorily why the outflow of capital must take the form of direct investment and where that investment goes.

5.3.3 Learning

In addition to the institution theoretical perspective, such a skewed allocation of outward FDI from China can be explained in the perspective of internationalization as a process framework. Many Chinese enterprises do not have the experience to manage their international operations when cultural distance and institutional distance are far from their home constituency. When those firm-based capabilities of international management improve, it is likely that they will venture to places far from their home countries.

The third theoretical perspective that is relevant to understand possible China's outward direct investment in Europe is the theory of the firm perspective. Following rapid economic growth, China's market became one of the major emerging markets in the world. Moreover, it also developed into the workshop of the world, which supplies manufactured goods to other parts of the world. China became a manufacturing centre partly because of its ample supply of cheap labour. In the early stages, multinational enterprises from developed economies invested directly in China by combining advanced technology as intangible assets and the abundant and inexpensive labour to make products to serve the world market. Complementarity of two sets of skills or capabilities leads to efficiency gains. In the early stage of China's development, multinational enterprises from developed economies had the upper hand in deciding whether the invested companies in China could succeed. As the Chinese economy continues to grow, so does the productivity of the local firms. These companies attempt to leapfrog on the technological front.

5.3.4 Local market knowledge advantages

The sophistication of the local markets also demands a good understanding of the local market conditions. The local companies may acquire companies located in developed economies in order to get access to the advanced technology and continuous creation of new products. Although the combination of manufacturing capability and advanced technology continue to produce benefits to the society, the real issue here is who should run those combined operations. In the past, multinational firms ran the operations in China because of superiority of technology and/or brand name. When China's markets become more mature and sophisticated, locally based companies may have an upper hand, partly because of their knowledge about the local markets. It is particularly the case when the companies in the developed countries that own the technology are relatively small in their operations and therefore lack the resources to explore China's market alone. Under this particular circumstance, Chinese companies will have an incentive to acquire those companies based in Europe and other developed economies. The improvement of domestic firms' productivity and their gradual moving up the technical ladder make those companies better able to utilize the technology that they tend to acquire. It is one of the reasons for Chinese firms to take over existing firms in developed economies. In other words, Chinese companies leverage the large domestic market and use outward investment to gain access to advanced technology.

5.3.5 Vertical integration advantage

In the standard theory of multinational enterprises à la Williamson, transaction cost economics is used to explain the existence of multinational enterprises in the context of intangible assets and opportunistic behaviour. Because the transaction costs for intangible assets are prohibitively high, those assets can be used at different locations across national borders, with horizontal internalization within firms becoming a natural outcome. For the multinational enterprises from emerging markets, the incentive is not the same. The economics of vertical integration can serve as a means to reduce transaction costs. The internalization perspective must answer the question as to why market transactions along the supply chain are inferior in term of transactions. The underlining condition for market transactions is that resources and inputs are competitively supplied. If they are not, vertical integration and control become important.

Let's look at what has happened in the case of China. Over the years, China has become the workshop of the world, partly because of its abundant and cheap labour. Foreign direct investment led to the fairly rapid industrialization of China's economy. The issue is that China itself cannot provide the resources domestically to support its globally focused industrial growth. It must rely on external supply of energy, raw materials, and other inputs. If the upstream markets are competitively structured, market transactions would turn out to be an efficient solution; unfortunately, most of these industries are highly concentrated, and therefore are not competitive markets. It makes sense for Chinese firms to integrate vertically in order to break up the potential monopoly in upstream industries. That explains why many China firms invest aggressively in Africa to guarantee the access to those natural resources.

Many Chinese companies in their early stages are subjects for outsourcing activities from firms in the developed economies and perform certain kind of tasks along the value chain. When these firms develop, they may have desired to move either downstream or upstream to in-sourcing some activities. To do that, those firms typically will start setting up distribution and commercial operations in their major markets. That may be one of the reasons that the majority of overseas operations of private enterprises from China fall in that category.

5.3.6 Monopoly power over the local market

Multinational enterprises must own some capabilities that can used to overcome the difficulties in their operations in foreign markets. Compared to firms from developed countries, Chinese firms are more familiar and more capable in dealing with poor public governance in transitional economies, developing economies, and transition economies.

Hymer's theory of multinational enterprises argues that monopoly power resulting from technology provides the incentive for firms to explore new markets and therefore to extend their monopoly power to these markets. In the case of emerging markets, the incentive may just be the opposite. The domestic markets of these economies are not as transparent and as open as similar markets in the developed economies, so the domestic firms, though lacking the advantage of technology, have a better understanding of the local market. Therefore they may extend their reach to acquire those technologies by taking over those firms that are relatively small in size, but control the technology that the local firms need. The ability to operate in the local markets give the indigenous companies comparative advantage to utilize these technologies in those emerging markets. It will be very costly for the foreign firms to serve those markets because they lack the necessary resources to explore those frontier markets.

For the majority of Chinese firms, which do not possess monopoly power over technology, they do enjoy the knowledge advantages over the local market that gives them the incentive to integrate vertically in order to capture more value-added along the value-chain. For instance, there are 34 Chinese companies among the 500 largest companies listed in *Fortune* magazine in 2009. Although many of these firms are domestically focused and are largely local monopolies, some indeed invest actively outside China.

5.3.7 Global supply network

A trend that has emerged in recent years is that some multinational enterprises in global industries want to reduce their number of suppliers and select a few to become global suppliers for their components and services. A variation of this incentive is that, as global suppliers of multinational enterprises, some Chinese companies must follow their major clients and invest in other countries to serve their clients better. Wanxiang and BYD fall in this category by investing in the US and European markets in order to serve their clients.

5.3.8 Institutional similarity

In the conventional theory of multinational enterprises, firms from developed economies enjoy competitive advantage over the local firms in host countries. This is essentially true in case of China outward FDI. The difference is that the characteristics of competitive strength may be multidimensional. When going abroad, firms from China must look for places where they enjoy comparative advantage over their competitors from developed economics and turn these comparative advantages into competitive advantage in particular countries. That interpretation is consistent with the statistical observations. Chinese multinational enterprises perform relatively well in those countries that share similar institutional environments, while, in general, they perform relatively unsatisfactorily in developed countries. High costs and rigid labour market conditions discourage Chinese firms from operating in these markets. This is consistent with the observation that the total direct investment in Europe from China is very small.

If we focus on Europe only, we can see Chinese enterprises' direct investment in Europe is unevenly distributed. Russia is the largest recipient country in Europe while UK and Germany have also attracted significant direct investments from China. Other European countries have received a relatively small amount of direct investment from China (Figure 5.3).

Although the statistics are patchy, with these figures in mind, we have to find explanations that are consistent with what we have observed. Some of these theoretical explanations may not be consistent with the existing theory of multinational enterprises.

Despite the relatively small size of China's outward investment in Europe, there are a number of interesting cases that can throw light on the challenges and obstacles for Chinese enterprises investing in Europe.

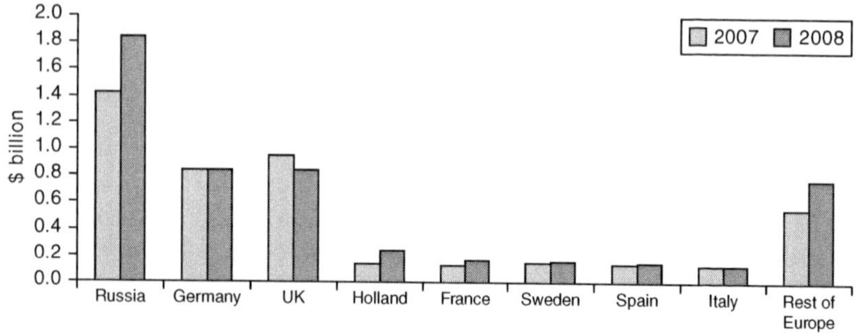

Figure 5.3 China's outward foreign direct investment in Europe
Source: The Statistical Yearbook on China's Outward Foreign Direct Investment.

5.4 Chinese multinational enterprises in Europe

Although the magnitude of China's direct investment is Europe is small, it has its particular features. Here we will discuss a few cases to highlight the characteristic of China's FDI in Europe. The cases are chosen partly because these cases are widely reported in the Chinese media and are considered as representative cases for Chinese companies to learn lessons from them. They include TCL's acquisitions in Germany and France, and Shenyang Machines Tools Company Limited's acquisition of Schiess, a German lathe machine manufacturing company. Through these cases, we can have a better understanding of China's investment in China.

5.4.1 TCL in Europe

TCL is one of the largest TV producers in China. In October 2002, it bought the then bankrupted operations of Schneider Electronics in Germany and absorbed its 120 employees. In November 2003, TCL bought the TV manufacturing operations of Thomson of France and formed a joint venture in which it held 70 per cent of the equity and became the largest producer of TV sets in the world at that time. TCL confronted major problems in both acquisitions, mainly because of its unfamiliarity with the operating environments, particularly in respect of labour relations. Moreover, the objectives of the overseas expansion were not clear. TCL did not have the capability to integrate both operations internationally. For instance, when the acquisition decision was made, there were not even sufficient interpreters who knew French. The senior management team did not have sufficient knowledge and experience of international operations when the decision was made, so TCL hastily organized training courses for the senior management team only after the acquisition decision. Moreover, rapid technical progress in television sets accelerated the obsolescence process of the acquired assets, which could only be used to produce bulky CRL television sets. So the acquisitions did not meet the strategic objectives of acquiring technology. Moreover, the corporate culture and management style of TCL, a private entrepreneur-controlled company based in Southern China, was not compatible with those acquired business units. All these factors combined to make TCL pay hefty tangible and intangible prices for both of these acquisitions.

The product life cycle theory of FDI predicts that when a product becomes mature and production processes become standard, there will be an efficiency gain by relocating the production to less developed economies so to reduce the production cost. China is in its mid-stage of the industrialization process, and it will receive some inward immigration of those industries. But this theory does not spell out how this process will be implemented. In the case of TCL, the company failed to notice the challenges of incompatible institutional arrangements and how to manage the transactions.

5.4.2 Shenyang Machine Tool Company Limited

A better-managed case is the acquisition of Schiess by Shenyang Machine Tool Company Limited (SMTCL). SMTCL is the largest machine tool manufacturing company in China. It produces over 10,000 units of machine tools annually, although the majority of these are small and medium-sized machine tools of low technical sophistication. Schiess is one of the oldest machine tool manufacturing companies, established in 1857 and located in Aschersleben, Magdeburg, Germany. Schiess enjoys a good reputation in machine tools industry and has its market niche. After several unsuccessful restructuring efforts, it declared bankruptcy in August 2004. SMTCL acquired Schiess's assets in November of the same year.

Because the product lines, R&D, product development, and manufacturing capability of both SMTCL and Schiess were so different before acquisition, they become very much complementary. Moreover, the merger fits perfectly the mould of the made-in-Germany and sold-in-China and made-in-China and sold-in-Europe concept, that is, German quality and industrial design plus China price. The technological intensity, cultural complexity, high barriers to international trade, and market penetration provide considerable potential benefits from this merger.

SMTCL-Schiess is one of a series of acquisitions made by Chinese companies in Europe, mainly in Germany. These purchases are usually small in scale and focus on particular technology where there is a huge market for sophisticated machine tools in China. The question is who should manage the combined company. It is obvious SMTCL can better manage the post-acquisition operation, because of the huge and growing China market. The intangible assets of Schiess are fully realized while SMTCL has acquired a piece of strategic assets for its future growth.

There are a quite a number of successful acquisition cases taking place in Europe. These include Zoomlion's acquisition of Compagnia Italiana Forme

Acciaio SPA (CIFA), a well-known concrete-mixing machine manufacturer based in Italy, and Blue Star Group's acquisition of Adisseo, a France-based bio-agricultural company. These mergers strengthen the competitiveness and technical competency of Chinese acquirers.

China's 'Going Global' strategy encourages Chinese firms' outward direct investment through merger and acquisitions, and in that process, a group of Chinese firms become world leaders in certain industries when they manage to transform China's comparative advantage into their competitive strengths. In recent years, a new generation of Chinese enterprises has emerged on the global stage. Companies, such as BYD, can take advantages of comparative advantage in China and develop into firm-specific capabilities. For instance, one of BYD's business lines is rechargeable batteries, of which it is the largest producer. After BYD became the global supplier for mobile phone handset manufacturing companies such as Nokia, it acquired a company in Hungary in order to serve its clients better.

5.5 Concluding remarks

Outward FDI from China is rising, but is insignificant in the world in general and in Europe in particular. Chinese firms have benefited from globalization and gained competitiveness in the process of the country's economic reform. Chinese companies in general may not have sufficient skills to manage cross-border operations, with a few exceptions. Most of China's companies are still at the phase of learning how to manage their rapidly expanding operations in an increasingly globalized world. Outward FDI to Europe is motivated by technology-seeking and is concentrated in those sectors where the appropriate technologies are useful to China's next stage of domestic economic development.

This situation makes the majority of outward FDI complementary in nature to the strengths of China's indigenous companies. As such it diverges from the theoretical model of horizontal investment proposed by Hymer and the OLI paradigm to explain the existence of multinational enterprises. It is important to notice that in the early stage of development many Chinese enterprises were in a narrow segment of the value-chain in order to specialize. For many Chinese companies, vertical direct investment can reduce transaction costs and expand value-adding activities. So some of these companies start investing abroad.

Through a number of closely observed cases, one can also note that sophisticated technology-owning and innovative small firms, particularly in manufacturing sectors, remain attractive to Chinese companies that want to move up the technical ladder, and to expand globally. They intend to leverage China's vast and expanding domestic market and manufacturing base. Europe can serve as an ideal innovation centre and location for marketing facilities. The constrained direct investment serves as a springboard to market Chinese products to the European market.

Chinese multinationals at this stage follow a very different model in comparison to those from industrialized economies. Even among Chinese companies, different ownership types and resource availability make them behave very differently. In any case, the rapid economic growth in the mainland of China remains the central theme of outward investment. The assets these companies acquire or the facilities that they build in other countries must be complementary to the economic activities that those firms engage in and must facilitate the next stage of economic growth in China.

Note

This research is partially funded by the National Science Foundation of China (70532005).

References

Buckley, P. J., Clegg, L. J., Cross, A. R., Liu, X., Voss, H., and Zheng, P. (2007), 'The Determinants of Chinese Outward Foreign Direct Investment', *Journal of International Business Studies*, 38(4), 499–518.

Child, J. and Rodrigues, S. (2005), 'The Internationalization of Chinese Firms: A Case for Theoretical Extension?' *Management and Organization Reviews*, 1 (3), 381–410.

Dunning, J. and Lundan, S. (2008), *Multinational Enterprises and the Global Economy*, 2nd edn. Cheltenham, UK: Edward Elgar.

Guillen, M. and Garcia-Canal E. (2009), 'The American Model of the Multinational Firm and the "New" Multinationals from Emerging Economies', *Academy of Management Perspectives*, 23, 23–35.

Luo, Y. and Tung, R. (2007), 'International Expansion of Emerging Market Enterprise: A Springboard Perspective', *Journal of International Business Studies*, 38 (4), 481–98.

Ministry of Commerce of China, *The Statistical Yearbooks on China's Outward Foreign Direct Investment*, various years.

Morck, R., Yeung, B., and Zhao, M. (2008), 'Perspectives on China's Outward Foreign Investment', *Journal of International Business Studies*, 39 (3), 337–50.

UNCTAD (2006), *World Investment Report 2006: FDI from Developing and Transition Economies*. Geneva: United Nations.

Witt, M. A. and Lewin, A. (2007), 'Outward Foreign Direct Investment as Escape Response to Home Country Institutional Constraints', *Journal of International Business Studies*, 38 (4), 579–94.

6
Characterizing the Patterns of Inward and Emerging Outward FDI in Hungary

Erzsébet Czakó

In terms of its size, Hungary has been a relatively open economy. This is indicated by high exports/GDP ratios that have prevailed since the 1970s. However, until the 1990s both inward and outward foreign direct investments (FDI) were negligible. The decade of the 1990s can be characterized by inward FDI, and in the 2000s fast-growing outward FDI can be observed. The impacts of inward FDI on Hungary and transition economies are widely discussed in both comparative economics and international business literature. Outward FDI has attracted lesser attention, especially in Central and Eastern Europe so far. The political and economic situation of some countries in the region has been changed by EU membership. This chapter provides an overview on the inward and outward FDI of selected Central and Eastern European countries and focuses on Hungary. In the 1990s Hungary was a success story in attracting FDI. The description of the source countries and recipient branches will show that the inward FDI is concentrated. Emerging Hungarian outward FDI put Hungary ahead in the region in the 2000s. However, the values are small and volatile. Time series data is used to depict these trends. Recipient countries and source branches will be analysed. The shaping patterns will be described and evaluated in the light of international business and Hungarian literature on MNEs.

6.1 Introduction

There has been an abundance of literature published on FDI in Central and Eastern Europe and in transition economies (Meyer, 2001a). The early works studied the phenomena of transition (Buckley and Ghaury, 1994) and the latter ones focused on FDI (Kalotay, 2001; Rojec, 2001; Uminski, 2001; Zemplinerová and Jaromlím, 2001; Demekas et al., 2007). A large part of the literature applies a comparative approach to transition economies (Bevan and Estrin, 2004). They cover Central and Eastern European countries and also countries from other part of the world. A smaller part of the literature focuses on the MNEs' activity (Meyer, 2001; Estrin et al., 2008). They either provide comparative analyses or validate the research paradigms. The third and recently evolving group of the literature examines issues relating to policy implications (Kalotay, 2000 and 2003; Szanyi, 2003; Svetličič and Sicherl, 2006). They indicate that there may be a shift from transition. There are several examples of both quantitative and qualitative methods-based papers. As statistics became reliable and time series became available econometric analyses have emerged (Holland et al., 2000; Demekas et al., 2007). A sensitive point relating to these papers is the difficulty of managing temporal business environment changes influencing variables.

The literature on Hungarian FDIs has been also proliferating since 1990. In the 1990s it focused on the relationships of inward FDI and privatization (Fahy et al., 1998; Antalóczy and Sass, 2001; Éltető, 2001; Szanyi 2001). Case research was also frequently employed (Woodside and Somogyi, 1995; Estrin, Hughes and Todd, 1997). The angle of FDI papers altered in the 2000s. Multinational enterprises (MNEs) came into focus and the approaches of papers resembled that of international business (Meyer, 2001b; Meyer and Estrin, 2001; Antalóczy and Éltető, 2002; Kalotay, 2003; Incze, 2005; Viszt and Vanicsek, 2005; Szanyi, 2006; Estrin et al., 2008, Sass et al., 2009). They provide insights from different angles and reveal mosaics on the whole picture. Even so, it was recognized that there are many more missing pieces on Hungarian FDI and MNEs. Analysis of FDI statistics may serve as a starting point to give an orientation on selecting topics, directions, and paradigms for further research. This chapter may be instructive for scholars in the field of similarly developed medium-sized and transition economies.

The FDI flows started from scratch in Central and Eastern European countries. As FDI statistics are available for more than a decade it is possible to reveal long-term trends and propose patterns. This chapter focuses on FDI statistics as a starting point. Data for comparison are taken from the UNCTAD (2008) database. For Hungarian FDIs the database of the Hungarian National Bank (2007) statistics was used. The time span of FDI stock analysis is 1995–2007. For interpretation purposes and arriving at conclusions the international business literature and studies of Hungarian scholars after 2001 will also be reviewed.

The chapter is organized into four sections. Section 6.2 provides an overview on the trends of inward and outward FDI in Hungary in comparison with the latest EU member countries in her region (Bulgaria, Czech Republic, Poland, and Romania. Slovenia is not included as it is the subject of a separate chapter.) Based on the statistics, Hungary has an edge in both inward and outward FDI in her region. Section 6.3 focuses on Hungary. Initially inward FDI will be analysed. The biggest and fastest-growing source countries and the recipient branches will be highlighted. The literature on international joint ventures and MNE subsidiaries will be reviewed here. Then the fairly new phenomenon for Hungary of outward FDI is analysed for the period 1998–2007. One conclusion is that both inward and outward

FDI are concentrated by both partner countries and branches. Section 6.4 is devoted to the findings on Hungarian MNEs, and the final section summarizes the conclusions. One methodological conclusion is that when available data are small and volatile in value it is worthwhile analysing time series to uncover patterns though the parsimonious presentation is hard. The findings may support concepts on internationalization and serve as the basis for exploring topics for further research.

6.2 A comparative view on FDI statistics

This section provides the main trends for inward and outward FDI for six selected countries. The Czech Republic, Hungary, Poland, and Slovakia accessed the European Union in 2004, and Bulgaria and Romania in 2007. The inward and outward FDI stocks are for 1995–2007. Data for the 1990s are widely used and ones for the 2000s are not. A premise here is that time series for more than a decade may depict trends and reveal patterns. The volumes in US$ at current prices are taken from UNCTAD (2008).

Figure 6.1 on inward FDI stocks show that there has been an exponential growth of inward FDI for the six selected countries since 1995. In 1995 the total inward FDI stocks was 21 billion, and it was 20 times bigger, 442 billion

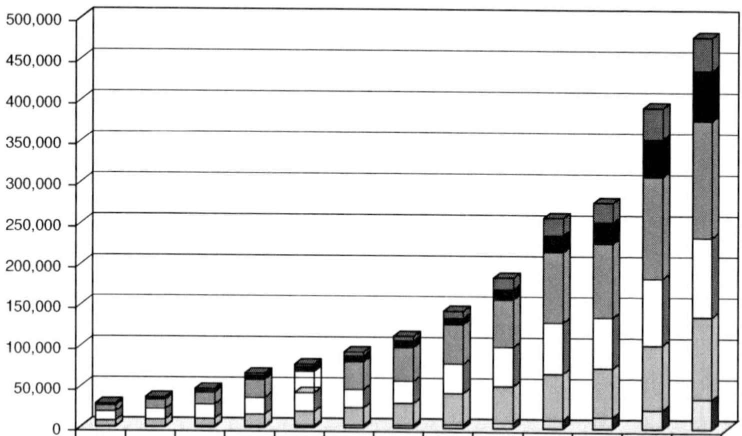

	1995	1996	1997	1998	1999	2000	2001	2002	2003	2004	2005	2006	2007
Slovakia	1,297	2,046	2,103	2,920	3,188	4,746	5,582	8,530	14,576	20,910	23,656	38,335	40,702
Romania	821	1,097	2,417	4,527	5,671	6,951	8,339	7,846	12,202	20,486	25,817	45,452	60,921
Poland	7,843	11,463	14,587	22,461	26,075	34,227	41,247	48,320	57,877	86,623	90,711	124,530	142,110
Hungary	11,304	13,282	17,968	20,733	23,260	22,870	27,407	36,224	48,340	62,585	61,970	81,586	97,397
Czech Republic	7,350	8,572	9,234	14,375	17,552	21,644	27,092	38,669	45,287	57,259	60,662	79,841	101,074
Bulgaria	445	554	1,059	1,597	2,184	2,704	2,945	4,074	6,371	10,108	13,851	22,867	36,508

Figure 6.1 Inward FDI stock in selected countries (US$ at current prices, million, 1995–2007)
Source: UNCTAD (2008).
Note: Data for 2007 are estimations.

in 2007. The largest inward FDI was received by Poland, Czech Republic, and Hungary in that order and they received 76 per cent of total stock. Data shows that Bulgaria, Romania, and Slovakia were late movers.

When inward FDI stock per capita is examined, as in Figure 6.2, two patterns are visible. The Czech Republic and Hungary reveal similar trends, and since 2002 Slovakia has been closing up on them. They have the highest stocks of 7,000–9,000 US$ per capita, and represented the fastest growth rate. Data indicate that Bulgaria, Poland, and Romania have a somewhat different pattern. Their growth trends started to accelerate in 2001 and their values are half those of the members of the previous group.

What do the data series in Figures 6.1 and 6.2 suggest? One of the widely shared propositions in the literature is that the divergences in launch, speed, and techniques of privatization explain the differences. This proposition was tested for Czech Republic, Hungary, and Poland for the 1990s. A newly emerging explanation is that EU membership has an impact on inward FDI. The depicted trends after 2001 support that proposition.

Outward FDI is a newly observed phenomenon in these countries. In the 1990s its volume in the six countries was negligible. In 1995 outward FDI was 1.5 billion for the six countries, and it has increased to 48 billion by 2007, representing a 31 times growth. The growth rate accelerated in the 2000s, as Figure 6.3 shows. Poland and Hungary are by far the largest source countries, accounting for 78 per cent of the value. The third largest source country is the Czech Republic, and the decreasing order of the remaining three is Slovakia, Romania, and Bulgaria. GDP per outward FDI per capita data is

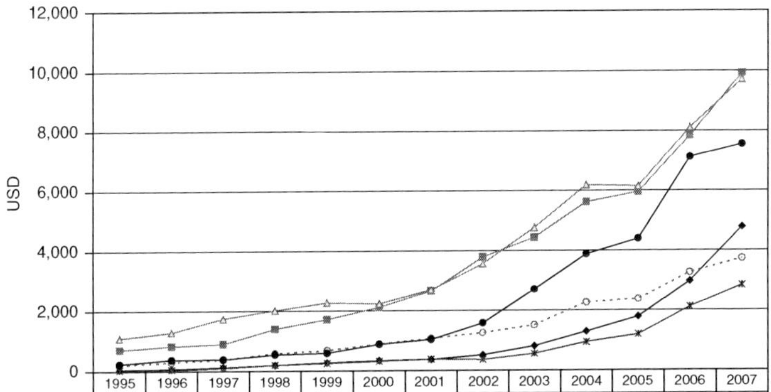

	1995	1996	1997	1998	1999	2000	2001	2002	2003	2004	2005	2006	2007
Bulgaria	53	67	129	196	271	338	371	516	812	1,297	1,788	2,973	4,779
Czech Republic	713	833	898	1,401	1,715	2,118	2,654	3,790	4,441	5,617	5,952	7,836	9,923
Hungary	1,094	1,288	1,746	2,019	2,271	2,239	2,690	3,564	4,768	6,188	6,144	8,111	9,711
Poland	203	297	378	583	678	891	1,075	1,260	1,511	2,265	2,375	3,265	3,732
Romania	36	49	108	203	255	314	378	358	559	943	1,194	2,111	2,842
Slovakia	242	381	391	542	592	881	1,036	1,583	2,706	3,882	4,391	7,115	7,551

Figure 6.2 Inward FDI stock per capita
Source: UNCTAD (2008).
Note: Data for 2007 are estimations.

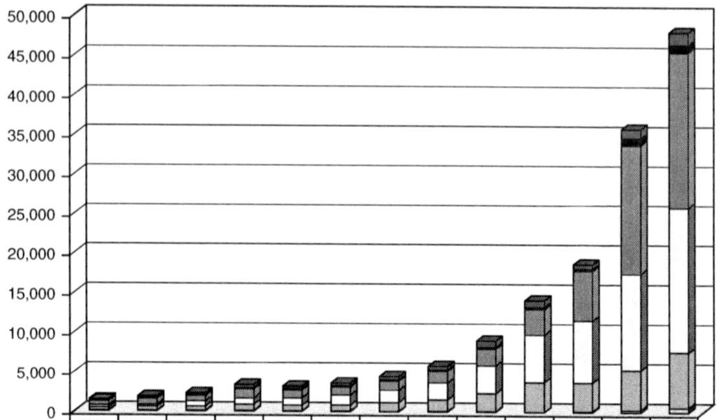

	1995	1996	1997	1998	1999	2000	2001	2002	2003	2004	2005	2006	2007
Slovakia	139	183	236	408	346	374	449	485	823	835	597	1,154	1,609
Romania	121	120	126	135	144	136	116	145	208	272	214	880	917
Poland	539	735	678	1,165	1,024	1,018	1,156	1,453	2,147	3,228	6,279	16,291	19,644
Hungary	278	265	647	784	924	1,280	1,556	2,166	3,509	6,018	7,836	12,177	18,282
Czech Republic	345	498	548	804	698	738	1,136	1,473	2,284	3,760	3,610	5,017	6,971
Bulgaria	105	76	74	75	69	67	34	40	52	0	123	228	599

Figure 6.3 Outward FDI stock (US$ at current prices, million)
Source: UNCTAD (2008).
Note: Data for 2007 are estimations.

below US$ 500 in these countries, for the Czech Republic and Poland it is between US$ 500 and US$ 1,000, while for Hungary it is above US$ 1,000.

The trends for outward FDI as percentage of GDP reveal a very similar pattern to that of outward FDI per capita. Figure 6.4 shows that outward FDI as percentage of GDP was below 2 per cent for each country until 1999. The year of 2000 seems to be a turning point. The close-moving trends of the countries diverged and faster growth rates are indicated. The value reached 13 per cent in Hungary in 2007. In Czech Republic and Poland it doubled and attained a level of around 4 per cent.

The statistical data series can signal stages of the development path for the analysed countries, as proposed by Dunning (1988). He set out the following five-stage development path for countries: (i) no FDIs, (ii) inward FDI, (iii) both inward and outward FDIs, (iv) net outward FDI, and finally (v) when FDI is based on not country- but firm-specific advantages. Statistical data indicated that in the 1990s the examined CEE countries were in stage (i) and the beginning of the 2000s saw their entry into stage (ii). Bourdier-Bensebba (2008) has conducted an empirical test on Dunning's development path model on 28 CEEC countries. Using 2004 FDI and GDP data, he found that net FDI and GDP per capita were correlated. He identified five groups, with Slovenia standing alone in the first, most developed group, Czech Republic and Hungary in the second, Poland and Slovakia in the third, and Bulgaria and Romania in the fourth group.

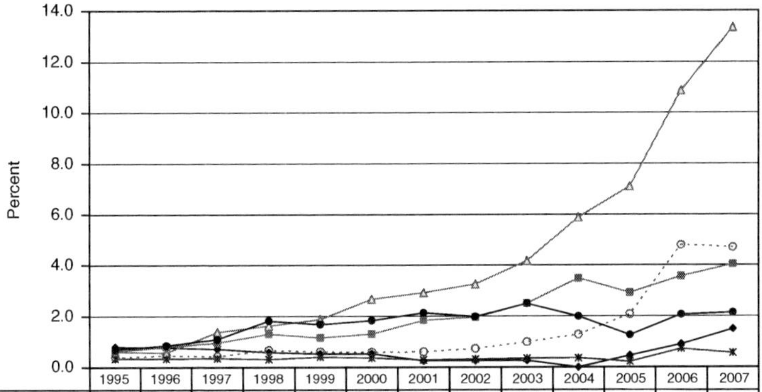

	1995	1996	1997	1998	1999	2000	2001	2002	2003	2004	2005	2006	2007
Bulgaria	0.8	0.8	0.7	0.6	0.5	0.5	0.2	0.3	0.3	0.0	0.5	0.9	1.5
Czech Republic	0.6	0.8	1.0	1.3	1.2	1.3	1.8	2.0	2.5	3.5	2.9	3.6	4.0
Hungary	0.8	0.6	1.4	1.6	1.9	2.7	2.9	3.2	4.2	5.9	7.1	10.9	13.3
Poland	0.4	0.5	0.4	0.7	0.6	0.6	0.6	0.7	1.0	1.3	2.1	4.8	4.7
Romania	0.3	0.3	0.4	0.3	0.4	0.4	0.3	0.3	0.4	0.4	0.2	0.7	0.6
Slovakia	0.7	0.9	1.1	1.8	1.7	1.8	2.1	2.0	2.5	2.0	1.3	2.1	2.1

Figure 6.4 Outward FDI as percentage of GDP
Source: UNCTAD (2008).
Note: Data for 2007 are estimations.

Cartensen and Toubal (2003) analysed six Central European (Czech Republic, Hungary, Poland, Slovakia, and Slovenia) and two Southern and Eastern European (Bulgaria and Romania) countries in the period 1993–9. They identified two sets of determinants for FDI. The traditional set included market size, trade costs, plant- and firm-specific costs, and relative factor endowments. The transitional set included share of private business, method of privatization, and risk associated with the recipient country. They found that 'both traditional variables suggested by theory and transition-specific variables have significant and plausible effect on FDI' (2003: 17). Based on their econometric analyses they suggest that the countries should be divided into two groups, first of five Central European countries, and second of two Southern and Eastern European (Bulgaria and Romania).

A similar approach was employed by Demaks et al. (2007) in their analysis of 16 countries for the period 1995–2003. Their sample included all of the countries studied by Caratensen and Toubal (2003), and their analysis added policy variables including trade barriers, labour cost, trade and foreign exchange liberalization, infrastructure reform, corporate tax burden, human capital, and corruption. They concluded, that 'these results suggest that when a host country first opens its door to foreign investors, geographical and cultural proximity, cheap labour, and satisfactory infrastructure are among the key determinant of FDI. As the country's income level increases, however, the importance of these factors declines and other factors come increasingly into play, such as the size of the domestic market and the business environment'. (2007: 378).

6.3 Inward and outward FDI in Hungary

To gain a greater insight on Hungarian FDI this section cites statistics gathered by the Hungarian National Bank (2007). The Hungarian National Bank (HNB) is responsible for compiling statistics on inward and outward FDI for the balance of payments. Their yearly upgraded database is based on OECD methodology. Time series are available on inward and outward FDI stocks in HUF and Euro for 1995–2007, and accessible via the HNB home page. The stock FDI data of HNB will be analysed by four selected years to reveal the trends. The time span of the analyses is 1998–2007. This period was selected since the literature does not cover it entirely. The selected years are 1998, 2001, 2004, and 2007, and the focus will be on partner countries and branches.

6.3.1 Inward FDI

There are 25,000 enterprises with more than 10 per cent foreign equity in Hungary, as reported by the Hungarian Statistical Office. Out of these, 1,800–2,000 enterprises are surveyed by the HNB. The owners' equity of selected enterprises is above 300 million HUF (1–1.2 million Euro). The equity data are based on the financial statements submitted to the Hungarian taxation authority. Antalóczy and Éltető (2002) made a calculation on enterprise data by checking the total inward FDI stock. Their inward FDI data were 2 billion Euro higher than that of HNB. In spite of that difference the time series data of HNB will be applied to reveal patterns. Their data series are consistent since 1995 and suitable for depicting the main trends.

Table 6.1 shows that between 1998 and 2007 there was a 3.9 times increase in inward FDI on current Euro prices, and the growth rate was lower in 2004–7 than it had been previously. These figures suggest that it is hard to measure and estimate the absorption capacity of FDI. Kalotay (2003) and Szanyi (2003) assumed that as inward FDI was attributed to privatization, growth was not sustainable. They also noted that there may be a new development path in Hungary. The source of the inward FDI is concentrated and the composition seems to be stabilized. Characterizing the figures on the inward FDI stock, 82 per cent is from countries of continental Europe, 8 per cent from the Americas and 2 per cent from Asia. The ratios of North and South America and that of Far East Asia have increased since 1998. This may signal the emergence of the Southern multinationals. The investments of international organizations was originally included with privatization, but this facet of investment has practically disappeared with only one privatization deal by HNB since 2000. It follows that inward FDI may be assigned to investment of multinational enterprises (MNEs).

In analysing the biggest source countries of inward FDI, countries with close to or above 1 billion Euro of investment were selected. Table 6.2 shows that altogether 15 countries belong to this group and they represent

Table 6.1 Inward FDI stock by source regions (million Euro and per cent)

Source	1998		2001		2004		2007	
	Mio €	%	Mio €	%	Mio €	%	Mio €	%
Europe	**12,494**	**81.6%**	**20,069**	**78.6%**	**33,805**	**83.6%**	**48,853**	**81.6%**
America	**1,187**	**7.8%**	**2,508**	**9.8%**	**2,094**	**5.2%**	**4,582**	**7.7%**
North America	1,133	7.4%	2,396	9.4%	1,925	4.8%	3,211	5.4%
Middle America	54	0.4%	111	0.4%	170	0.4%	570	1.0%
South America	0	0.0%	0	0.0%	0	0.0%	802	1.3%
Asia	**208**	**1.4%**	**622**	**2.4%**	**1,065**	**2.6%**	**1,439**	**2.4%**
Middle East	14	0.1%	4	0.0%	45	0.1%	63	0.1%
Far East	194	1.3%	618	2.4%	1,019	2.5%	1,375	2.3%
Africa	**0**	**0.0%**	**22**	**0.1%**	**12**	**0.0%**	**28**	**0.0%**
Australia	**–1**	**0.0%**	**–6**	**0.0%**	**3**	**0.0%**	**10**	**0.0%**
International organizations	**103**	**0.7%**	**53**	**0.2%**	**45**	**0.1%**	**7**	**0.0%**
Not known	**1,314**	**8.6%**	**2,275**	**8.9%**	**3,401**	**8.4%**	**4,936**	**8.2%**
Total	**15,306**	**100.0%**	**25,543**	**100.0%**	**40,426**	**100.0%**	**59,855**	**100.0%**

Source: Hungarian National Bank (2007).

Table 6.2 The biggest source countries of inward FDI

Source countries	Million, Euro			
	1998	2001	2004	2007
Europe	**12,493.6**	**20,068.9**	**33,805.2**	**48,853.2**
Austria	1,369.6	2,754.6	4,593.5	7,764.9
Belgium	259.5	564.3	826.8	1,461.4
Cyprus	84.4	182.6	221.9	1,424.9
United Kingdom	256.4	280.7	322.8	1,564.0
France	864.6	1,391.5	1,904.7	3,095.0
The Netherlands	2,182.8	3,827.6	7,174.1	8,516.1
Luxemburg	127.5	317.0	1,802.1	3,396.2
Germany	6,317.2	8,575.9	11,807.9	14,718.0
Norway	13.5	55.2	933.4	927.4
Italy	322.4	572.5	693.8	988.5
Spain	10.7	32.3	737.2	959.9
Switzerland	279.7	378.0	458.6	879.5
Subtotal, 12 European	*12,088.4*	*18,932.1*	*31,476.6*	*45,695.8*
Subtotal Europe	96.8%	94.3%	93.1%	93.5%
Americas	**1,187.1**	**2,507.6**	**2,094.5**	**4,582.5**
United States	1,050.3	2,273.2	1,805.0	2,950.3
Brazil	–	–	–	801.5
Asia	**207.9**	**622.0**	**1,064.7**	**1,438.6**
Japan	121.8	426.4	674.9	782.4
Subtotal, 15	*13,260.4*	*21,631.7*	*33,956.6*	*50,230.0*
Subtotal 15/Total	86.6%	84.7%	84.0%	83.9%
Total	**15,306.3**	**25,543.3**	**40,425.9**	**59,855.2**

Source: Hungarian National Bank (2007).

84 per cent of the total inward FDI stock. The majority of them, 12, are from continental Europe, two from the Americas, and one from Asia. Accession to the EU maintained the dominance of the European countries, and the growth in IFDI is attributed to EU members. The share of some of these countries such as Cyprus, United Kingdom, France, Luxemburg, and Spain increased substantially. It can be proposed the Hungarian EU membership resulted in closer ties with EU members via foreign investments. Brazil is among the newcomers. From a base of zero, its inward FDI was 800 million Euro in 2007.

Sectors with around or above 1 million Euro inward FDI stock in 2007 were selected for analysis. The selected sectors represent 65.5 per cent of the total inward FDI stock. The manufacturing sector accounted for 36 per cent and the services sector 55 per cent in 2007. Table 6.3 shows that the manufacturing sector has a lower share and growth rate than that of services. The coke and oil manufacturing sector shows the largest increase, with its value rising from zero to above 2 million Euro. The automotive and metallurgy manufacturing sectors are ranked next. Both the share and growth rate of

Table 6.3 The main recipient branches of inward FDI and their growth

Recipient branches	Million, Euro				Growth, 1998 = 1		
	1998	2001	2004	2007	2001	2004	2007
Manufacturing (F)	**5,732.8**	**11,587.8**	**17,861.8**	**21,514.3**	**2.0**	**3.1**	**3.8**
Coke and oil	1.9	201.9	586.8	2,145.9	109.0	316.7	1,158.2
Gum and plastic	218.4	462.1	646.2	895.5	2.1	3.0	4.1
Metallurgy	337.8	491.1	1,188.5	1,691.1	1.5	3.5	5.0
Automotive	849.3	2,833.1	4,387.4	6,468.1	3.3	5.2	7.6
Services (G-Q)	**7,438.8**	**11,493.2**	**19,684.0**	**33,164.9**	**1.5**	**2.6**	**4.5**
Trade (G)	1,357.8	2,649.2	4,066.9	8,773.0	2.0	3.0	6.5
Financial (J)	1,557.8	2,688.8	4,261.6	7,415.8	1.7	2.7	4.8
Out of: Monetary activity	*1,201.4*	*2,073.4*	*3,411.8*	*5,954.0*	*1.7*	*2.8*	*5.0*
Other financials	*71.2*	*120.9*	*105.4*	*330.4*	*1.7*	*1.5*	*4.6*
Insurance	*273.4*	*454.1*	*684.9*	*1,043.8*	*1.7*	*2.5*	*3.8*
Property and other business services (K)	887.5	2,672.2	6,797.8	11,847.1	3.0	7.7	13.3
Out of: Property	*407.6*	*1063.6*	*2,620.3*	*3,497.9*	*2.6*	*6.4*	*8.6*
IT services	*41.2*	*133.8*	*224.1*	*437.0*	*3.2*	*5.4*	*10.6*
Business services	*422.8*	*1420.5*	*3,835.9*	*7,716.6*	*3.4*	*9.1*	*18.3*
Out of: Equity management	*132.6*	*949.0*	*2,135.5*	*3,028.3*	*7.2*	*16.1*	*22.8*
Total	**15,306.3**	**25,543.3**	**40,425.9**	**59,855.2**	**1.7**	**2.6**	**3.9**

Source: Hungarian National Bank (2007).
Letters in parenthesis denote NACE classification.

services have accelerated since Hungary accessed EU membership. Property and other business service sectors led, representing 20 per cent of inward FDI stock, and they had the highest growth rate. Trade and financial services followed, with 14 and 12 per cent share respectively, and with above-average growth rates.

6.3.2 Outward FDI

The procedure for calculation of outward FDI differs from that of inward FDI. Until 2001 registration on inward FDI was compulsory and the register was modified by the data of commercial banks. Since 2001 registrations by commercial banks have served as a basis. All enterprises with above 10 million HUF (33,000–40,000 Euro) foreign investments are included in the database.

Outward FDI has been increasing since 2000, and was above 11 billion Euro in 2007. Its growth was greatest in 2005–7 when outward FDI stock almost doubled. Table 6.4 shows data for 2000–7 by recipient countries. The biggest 15 destinations are in continental Europe, representing 95 per cent in 2007. Slovakia is the largest recipient country, accounting for 25 per cent of total Hungarian outward FDI stock. The United Kingdom is the second and Croatia is the third largest, with over one billion Euro stock. Besides the UK there are three more developed European countries among the 15 (The Netherlands, Luxemburg, and Switzerland), and nine recipient countries are EU members. The data indicate a similar pattern to that of inward FDI stock. Since accession to the EU outward FDI stock increased faster than before and the dominant destinations are EU members. Non EU-member neighbouring or close countries like Croatia, Russia, Serbia, and Ukraine are also among the recipient countries.

Two tables are presented for examining outward FDI by sector. Table 6.5 gives an overview on the sectors with the biggest outward FDI stock for four selected years. Altogether five areas of activity represent 94 per cent of outward FDI. Of these, 83 per cent are from services (G, J, and K), with more than half of outward FDI stock in financial services.

As the values are small and volatile Table 6.6 provides data on the activities with the most stable outward FDI stock. All activities and sub-activities were selected where the values were over 100 million Euro. Mining and coke and oil manufacturing have a 30 per cent share. It can be proposed that the larger part of the outward FDI stock is attributed to MOL, the Hungarian oil company. The second biggest sub-branch is Business services, and third is Financial services. OTP, the largest Hungarian retail bank, may be responsible for the latter growth.

Outward FDI is an emerging phenomenon in Hungary. The year 2000 may be considered as a turning point. Since then outward FDI stock has exceeded one million Euro and growth has accelerated. The time series data suggest that the EU accession might have an impact on that. The data show

Table 6.4 Outward FDI by recipient countries (million euro, 2000–2007)

Recipient countries	**2000**	**2001**	**2002**	**2003**	**2004**	**2005**	**2006**	**2007**
Bulgaria	4.1	0.8	11.4	136.4	218.2	306.6	431.0	577.1
Cyprus	92.2	67.3	98.0	64.8	107.9	105.3	265.4	413.2
Czech Republic	71.9	98.2	96.3	81.3	86.7	96.3	139.7	121.5
United Kingdom	10.6	12.1	12.1	12.0	41.8	96.1	479.4	1,392.2
The Netherlands	424.5	384.6	374.1	341.8	362.4	1,116.1	1,060.3	561.1
Croatia	17.6	23.5	51.7	323.4	359.9	522.4	969.7	1,054.8
Poland	14.4	32.5	60.5	59.3	297.9	184.5	265.9	241.9
Luxemburg	1.5	44.9	46.6	46.2	47.7	23.9	54.5	246.8
Macedonia	–	319.9	281.2	255.6	355.4	397.5	404.6	475.1
Russia	6.7	12.7	12.4	11.6	19.5	16.6	139.6	160.9
Romania	65.7	95.4	151.6	165.9	202.5	312.9	429.5	519.6
Serbia and Montenegro	–	0.4	0.3	5.0	14.9	146.6	405.0	Na
Serbia	Na	Na	Na	Na	Na	Na	Na	432.5
Switzerland	4.6	5.9	3.2	3.2	2.9	2.2	509.9	482.0
Slovakia	115.7	182.1	262.5	558.2	1,643.6	2,076.0	2,536.9	2,795.5
Ukraine	16.2	23.4	19.0	19.9	21.2	28.3	213.0	305.5
BIG15 Total	*845.8*	*1,303.6*	*1,480.9*	*2,084.4*	*3,782.5*	*5,431.3*	*8,304.3*	*9,779.8*
European countries	**1,162.0**	**1,527.0**	**1,694.0**	**2,334.2**	**3,911.1**	**5,599.3**	**8,464.9**	**10,328.8**
BIG15/EU, %	72.8%	85.4%	87.4%	89.3%	96.7%	97.0%	98.1%	94.7%
Americas	**65.8**	**65.8**	**70.2**	**55.0**	**15.6**	**−3.0**	**145.3**	**166.3**
United States	64.0	62.8	67.0	53.8	14.4	−3.2	143.8	125.5
Asia	**3.4**	**3.2**	**17.5**	**9.4**	**9.0**	**643.5**	**393.8**	**512.9**
South Korea	–	–	14.6	5.8	6.3	37.2	378.4	496.0
Not known	**92.8**	**77.6**	**124.5**	**140.4**	**172.1**	**213.5**	**219.7**	**285.3**
Total	**1,326.4**	**1,675.4**	**1,908.1**	**2,541.0**	**4,107.8**	**6,453.2**	**9,223.8**	**11,293.3**

Source: Hungarian National Bank (2007).
Na denotes not appropriate; the countries were separated.
Serbia and Montenegro and Serbia are accounted as one country in the table.

Table 6.5 Biggest outward FDI stock by activity, 1998–2007

Activity	1998		2001		2004		2007	
	Mio €	%	Mio €	%	Mio €	%	Mio €	%
Mining (C)	8.1	1.4%	4.5	1.4%	25.1	0.3%	990.1	1.4%
Manufacturing (F)	50.4	8.7%	201.3	8.7%	2,192.4	12.4%	3,413.3	8.7%
Trade services (G)	99.5	17.2%	271.5	17.2%	476.4	16.8%	1,052.6	17.2%
Financial services (J)	307.0	53.1%	670.7	53.1%	1,087.8	41.4%	1,917.4	53.1%
Property and business services (K)	5.2	14.7%	394.0	14.7%	74.7	24.3%	3,192.2	14.7%
Subtotal	*550.2*	*94.5%*	*1,541.9*	*94.5%*	*3,856.4*	*92.0%*	*10,565.6*	*94.5%*
Property and household investment abroad	16.8	2.9%	74.5	2.9%	161.1	4.6%	285.3	2.9%
Not known	11.1	1.9%	3.1	1.9%	11.0	0.2%	6.3	1.9%
Total	**582.4**	100.0%	**1,675.4**	100.0%	**4,107.8**	100.0%	**11,293.3**	100.0%

Source: Hungarian National Bank (2007).
Letters in parenthesis denote NACE classification.

Table 6.6 Activities with stable FDI stock, 1998–2007

Branches	1998	1999	2000	2001	2002	2003	2004	2005	2006	2007
Mining (C)	**8.1**	**14.7**	**25.1**	**4.5**	**7.2**	**12.6**	**25.1**	**401.2**	**890.1**	**990.9**
Manufacturing (F)										
Oil and coke						473.6	1,818.9	1,924.6	2,350.0	2,500.7
Chemicals	3.0	3.7	32.7	48.0	101.8	102.8	125.6	150.9	249.9	249.4
Metallurgy		24.1	30.2	32.4	82.0	104.0	128.0	100.5	113.5	175.2
Electricity	1.0	7.3	2.3	– 1.0	8.4	10.5	35.6	90.6	56.8	340.5
Trade services (G)	**99.5**	**107.9**	**259.6**	**271.5**	**293.0**	**413.3**	**476.4**	**64.0**	**875.3**	**1,052.6**
Transportation, telecom (F)	**0.2**	**13.8**	**17.1**	**13.9**	**21.8**	**3.7**	**5.6**	**114.6**	**227.2**	**241.0**
Financial services (J)	**307.0**	**396.6**	**605.4**	**670.7**	**731.0**	**1,056.6**	**1,087.8**	**2,080.7**	**2,614.8**	**1,917.4**
Monetary	7.7	67.6	48.5	86.7	127.9	182.1	295.2	1,600.9	2,075.7	1,737.4
Property and business services (K)	**85.2**	**97.5**	**158.1**	**394.0**	**357.0**	**54.1**	**74.7**	**170.6**	**1,303.3**	**3,192.2**
Business services	80.5	82.7	118.7	373.0	319.1	29.6	47.9	138.7	1,222.9	3,131.2
Equity management	4.2	29.0	63.0	12.6	40.2	31.8	42.6	130.9	833.0	1,877.8
Subtotal	503.9	665.6	1,130.5	1,433.9	1,602.1	2,231.3	3,777.7	5,997.8	8,680.8	10,659.9
Subtotal/Total	86.5%	82.2%	85.2%	85.6%	84.0%	87.8%	92.0%	92.9%	94.1%	94.4%
Total	**582.4**	**810.1**	**1,326.4**	**1,675.4**	**1,908.1**	**2,541.0**	**4,107.8**	**6,453.2**	**9,223.8**	**11,293.3**

Source: Hungarian National Bank (2007).
Letters in parenthesis denote NACE classification.

a fast-growing and concentrated pattern by both recipient countries and activities. The regional distribution of the outward FDI reflects regionalization (Mirza, 1998; Rugman and Verbeke, 2004). What motivates Hungarian outward FDI? Three of the four FDI seeking patterns of Dunning (1998 and 1988) may be proposed. Resources-seeking may be signalled by mining (especially oil mining), market-seeking by oil manufacturing and financial services, and efficiency-seeking by business services activities. Both market- and efficiency-seeking patterns are widely shared and supported theory (Rojec, 2001; Bevan and Estrin, 2004). The resource-seeking pattern may be explained by country- and firm-specific factors.

Buckley and Casson (1976) proposed that internalization of market imperfection is one of the main attributes of MNEs. Since then a stream of theories on internalization has been developed in the international business literature. Buckley and Casson proposed four sets of factors the interplay of which induces internalization (1976: 44–5): (i) industry-specific, (ii) region-specific, (iii) nation-specific, and (iv) firm-specific factors. Nation (or country)- and firm-specific factors are widely researched. The depicted trends suggest topics for further research on region-specific and industry-specific factors.

6.4 What is known on Hungarian MNEs?

The phenomenon of multinational enterprises (MNE) came with transition into Hungary. The Transnationality index of Hungary is among the highest (UNCTAD, 2008). The index correlates with the size of the economy, and in the case of Hungary it can be attributed to selected privatization techniques. Sales of state-owned equity were favored with the expectation of importing financial, management, and technological assets (Mihály, 2001). Deals resulted in international joint ventures that were characterized as brownfield entry from the MNEs' side by Meyer and Estrin (2001). The privatization was completed by the late 1990s and Hungary became an EU member.

In Hungarian terminology 'multi' (short for multinational) refers to the subsidiaries of MNEs. These have been intensively researched especially in light of privatization and in comparison with non-foreign-owned enterprises. There is much evidence that their profitability and productivity is higher than that of enterprises with no foreign equity (Chikán and Czakó, 1998; Antalóczy and Sass, 2001; Éltető, 2001; Chikán et al., 2002; Chikán and Czakó, 2009). There has not been much research on the Hungarian-headquartered MNEs that have subsidiaries abroad. They have existed for less than a decade and their number may be small. The issue of which enterprises may or should be called Hungarian MNEs has been raised, reflecting recent trends among MNEs as revealed in the international business literature. Three big groups can be considered: (i) those that are registered in Hungary, (ii) those that have Hungarian majority ownership by equity, and (iii) those that are controlled by Hungary-based management. Mapping them statistically becomes more complicated as one proceeds from group (i) to group (iii). Some of the emerging MNEs, like MOL or OTP, are referred to as regional MNEs by denoting that they have subsidiaries in the neighboring countries. This section gives an overview on what has been published by Hungarian researchers on both MNE subsidiaries and the Hungarian MNEs in the 2000s.

Casson (1994) predicted that formal institutions (laws, authorities, and agencies) are the first and the easy step in transition. Evolution of entrepreneurship as the essence of market systems, however, takes much time. Czakó (1993) showed that practically all of the necessary market system-required laws and rules on enterprises were in force by the end of 1992. A group of papers based on consecutive competitiveness enterprise surveys in 1996, 1999, and 2004 fall into the category of Casson-defined entrepreneurship in medium and large-scale enterprises. Chikán and Czakó (1998) showed that enterprises worked under the market mechanism and transition was practically over for them. Their findings were based on a survey of 324 medium and large-scale enterprises representing 50 per cent of the Hungarian GDP in 1996. Their findings also indicated that the phenomena of globalization became the main challenge of the enterprises. The 1996 survey was repeated in 1999, and the comparison of the 1996 and 1999 surveys were published in Chikán et al. (2002). Two main conclusions are highlighted here. The first is that the advanced management techniques spread and were employed widely, and the second is that the most spectacular development was achieved in the field of information management. Foreign investment was not signalled until 2004.

Studies on outward FDI and MNEs rely on small samples. Probably the first study on outward FDI and Hungarian MNEs is by Antalóczy and Éltető (2002). Their study is based on a 2001 survey in Hungary. The project was supported by the EU-financed PHARE-ACE. Their sample included 22 enterprises. They found that market- and strategic assets-seeking was the most important motivator for foreign entry. The foreign subsidiaries contributed to their host country's market share and profitability increase. The 2004 competitiveness survey showed 31 enterprises with more than a 10 per cent equity stake in foreign enterprises, representing 10 per cent of the sample. Their composition was the following: 20 were large by size, 16 were privately owned and 10 MNE subsidiary, and 10 were in the chemical industry. Their host countries covered the largest destinations described in the outward FDI section of this chapter. Market- and strategic assets-seeking were their top priority in foreign market entry. Previous experiences and contacts in host countries, and export experiences were mentioned as among their firm-specific advantages. Their strategic attitudes were compared with the rest of the sample. They were significantly much more prepared for managing changes in their own industry and the broader environment, and they were capable of altering their own positions in their industry value network (Incze, 2005).

Viszt and Vanicsek (2005) studied outward FDI from 2004 data. Their findings underpin the concentration of outward FDI, with 80 per cent of outward FDI stock attributed to 15 enterprises. They identified three main groups of investors: MNE subsidiaries, large Hungarian enterprises (like MOL and OTP), and medium and small-size enterprises. These findings suggest that enterprises with international experiences and knowledge take the lead. Market- and strategic assets-seeking foreign entry seem to be dominant.

A range of studies may be interpreted in terms of the embeddedness of MNE subsidiaries (Forsgren et al., 2005). Demeter et al. (2006) analysed the supply chains of Audi (German) and Suzuki (Japanese) subsidiaries in the automotive industry in Hungary. They found that the two companies have different strategies that impact on the contacts and relationship with local suppliers. The market-seeking Suzuki relies more on local suppliers. Audi follows an efficient-seeking strategy that gives less room for local suppliers. Their results underpin the proposition by Dyker (2004),based on interviews with a dozen European large-scale Eastern European investors. Dyker found that enterprises follow their own strategies; they are active in-house, make efforts to support their own supply and infrastructure base, and enjoy high process productivity. The FDI-driven process of catch-up results in a dualistic development of Eastern European EU members that may lead to social tensions. There are substantial differences in the level of real wages and productivity among foreign and domestically owned enterprises. This phenomenon is recognized in Hungary, as well. Szanyi (2002) discusses the lessons of the Hungarian government-initiated supplier target programme announced in 1998. It was to support suppliers of domestically owned small and medium-sized enterprises to MNE subsidiaries. Szanyi's findings depict a learning process in government and missing capacities on the SME side. Sass et al. (2009) have studied cluster development. They propose that cluster development is in its early stages in Hungary, the first programme being announced by the Hungarian government in 2000. The clusters at their stage are not supported by MNE subsidiaries.

6.5 Conclusions

FDI statistics are proxies for revealing the internationalization process of MNEs in a country. Their parsimonious interpretation is challenging but they may serve as indicators for research topics. Time series data may explore turning points and uncover trends. As international FDI statistics are available they are good starting points for comparisons. This chapter took Hungary as a case study, and the indicated turning points and trends were explored in the context of the extant literature.

The inward and outward FDI of the latest Central and Eastern European EU members was discussed. The patterns of the FDI show a similarity. Hungary's pattern is closest to that of Czech Republic and Poland. Trends signal the year 2000 as a turning point. Outward FDI has been accelerating since then. The values are small and volatile, but outward FDI became a new phenomenon in the examined countries. These countries may enter into their second development phase when inward FDI is followed by outward FDI. The completion of privatization and transition at normative institutions, and EU accession might have contributed to that.

Hungary has been ahead in terms of both inward and outward FDI stock in her region. Its outward FDI was the biggest among neighboring new EU members at the beginning of the 2000s. Inward and outward FDI were analysed by countries and sectors. Hungarian FDI is concentrated both by countries and sectors. EU members have dominant shares in both cases. EU accession might have brought a new stage in inward FDI. Existing EU members dominated among the biggest source countries. There are signs that some of the new, Southern FDI source countries' shares are increasing. Neighboring non-EU member countries are the second largest group of recipient countries. The services sector is the biggest recipient and source in FDI. Firm-level research suggests that outward FDI is attributed to a couple of enterprises.

Buckley and Casson (1976: 109) argued that 'the main rationale for the MNE is the existence of widespread market imperfections which make the production and diffusion of knowledge and skills difficult to achieve except through internalization.' This theory has been widely shared and verified since then in the international business literature. Buckley and Casson also pointed that communication costs in an MNE internal market are much higher than in external markets. Some conclusions may be proposed in light of their perspective and by the depicted trends and the literature. The transition period resulted in formal market institutions known and expected by MNEs in Central and Eastern Europe. It may be suggested that the transition period and their being less developed EU members involved several markets with imperfections in the region. It may be proposed that the differences in the economic development of countries may support imperfections in several markets and their segments in comparison with more developed countries. The information and communication revolution at the end of the 1990s decreased communication costs and offered new and efficient techniques for knowledge development and dissemination within MNEs. As Castells (2000) has argued, information and communication technologies may preserve market imperfections among markets and countries. These developments *ceteris paribus* may anticipate further FDI development in the analysed countries.

The reviewed papers suggest that the decade of the 1990s was about learning management techniques. Outward FDI may be attributed to the most experienced and largest enterprises. Market- and strategic assets-seeking may be the dominant incentive for their foreign market entry. So far research evidence indicates the role of knowledge in internationalization. Studying knowledge development and dissemination within MNEs and their subsidiaries, MNE subsidiaries and their suppliers are feasible research topics.

Hungary may be regarded as an FDI-driven economy, as might be the case with small and medium-sized economies. Inward FDI absorptive capacity is hard to predict, but developed countries of the same size suggest room for more growth. The Buckley and Casson theory on the MNEs also supports that growth. Besides factor endowments created factors may have an influential impact. Research has indicated that foreign-owned enterprises have enjoyed better performance measures since 1990. This may result in social tensions and debates on the benefits and best features of MNEs. The economic role of MNE subsidiaries and the emerging outward FDI require an alteration in the research focus towards international business. International business is not without a tradition in Hungary. It is less cultivated than the MNEs' role in the Hungarian economy would anticipate. There is a tradition of transition economies in international business literature (Buckley and Ghauri, 1994; Meyer and Peng, 2005) that can be taken as an orientation. As presented in this chapter, international business theories may provide explorations and explanations for observed phenomena, and enhance their understanding. Recent changes in Hungarian inward and outward FDI suggest some topics. One of them is the embeddedness of MNE subsidiaries that have antecedents in the Hungarian literature.

Inward and outward FDI trends have policy implications. Kalotay (2003) proposes that a new stage is required in investment incentive policy. He analysed FDI world trends and positioned Hungary by UNCTAD data in the period 1990–2001. He noted that in phase 1 the investment incentive policies are about setting up institutions; in phase 2 investment promotion institutions have the preeminent role, and in phase 3 coordinated investment initiatives take the lead. Hungary was placed between phase 2 and phase 3.

References

Antalóczy, K. and Éltető, A. (2002), 'Internationalization of Hungarian Enterprises – Incentives, Impacts and Problems', *Közgazdasági Szemle*, 39/2, 158–72 (in Hungarian).

Antalóczy, K. and Sass, M. (2001), 'Greenfield Investments in Hungary: Are they Different from Privatization FDI?' *Transnational Corporations*, 10 (3), 39–59.

Bevan, A. A. and Estrin, S. (2004), 'The Determinants of Foreign Direct Investment into European Transition Economies', *Journal of Comparative Economics*, 32, 775–87.

Boudier-Bensebaa, F. (2008), 'FDI-assisted Development in the Light of the Investment Development Path Paradigm: Evidence from Central and Eastern European Countries', *Transnational Corporations*, 17 (1), 37–67.

Buckley, P. J. and Casson, M. (1976), *The Future of the Multinational Enterprise*. New York: Holmes & Meier Publishers.

Buckley, P. J. and Ghauri, P. N. (eds) (1994), *The Economics of Change in East and Central Europe: Its Impact on International Business*. London: Academic Press/Harcourt Brace Jovanovich.

Cartensen, K. and Toubal, F. (2003), 'Foreign Direct Investment in Central and Eastern European Countries: A Dynamic Panel Analysis', *Journal of Comparative Economics*, 32, 3–22.

Casson, M. (1994), 'Enterprise Culture and Institutional Change in Eastern Europe', in P. J. Buckley and P. N. Ghauri (eds), *The Economics of Change in East and Central Europe. Its Impact on International Business*. London: Academic Press/Harcourt Brace Jovanovich, 33–55.

Castells, M. (2000), *The Rise of the Network Society*, 2nd edn. Oxford: Blackwell Publishing.

Chikán, A. and Czakó, E. (1998), 'Competitiveness and Industry Restructuring: The Case of Hungary', in J.-P. Larçon (ed.), *Entrepreneurship and Economic Transition in Central Europe*, HEC School of Management, Boston, MA/Dordrecht/London/Paris: Kluwer Academic Publishers, 71–92.

Chikán, A. and Czakó, E. (eds) (2009), *In Global Competition: Competitiveness of the Hungarian Enterprises at the Turn of the New Millennium*. Budapest: Akadémiai Kiadó (in Hungarian).

Chikán, A., Czakó, E., and Zoltay-Paprika, Z. (eds) (2002), *National Competitiveness in Global Economy: The Case of Hungary*. Budapest: Akadémiai Kiadó.

Czakó, E. (1993), *Hungarian Experiences with the Market System: Privatization and Social Aspects*, The Leuven Institute for Central and East European Studies, Working Paper, KUL, Leuven, 1993.

Demekas, D. G., Horváth, B., Ribakova, E., and Wu, Y. (2007), 'Foreign Direct Investment in European Transitional Economies – The Role of Policies', *Journal of Comparative Economics*, 35, 369–86.

Demeter, K., Gelei, A., and Jenei, I. (2006), 'The Effect of Strategy on Supply Chain Configuration and Management Practices on the Basis of Two Supply Chains in the Hungarian Automotive Industry', *International Journal of Production Economics*, 104, 555–70.

Dunning, J. H. (1988), 'The Eclectic Paradigm of International Production: A Restatement and Some Possible Extension', *Journal of International Business Studies*, 19, 1–31.

Dunning, J. H. (1998), 'Location and the Multinational Enterprise: A Neglected Factor?' *Journal of International Business Studies*, 29, 45–66.

Dyker, D. A. (2004), 'Closing the Productivity Gap between Eastern and Western Europe: The Role of Foreign Direct Investment', *Science and Public Policy*, 31, 279–87.

Éltető, A. (2001), *The Competitiveness of Hungarian Companies*, HAS Institute for World Economics, Working Papers No. 118, Budapest, August.

Estrin, S., Hughes, K., and Todd, S. (1997), *Foreign Direct Investment in Central and Eastern Europe*. London: Cassell.

Estrin, S., Meyer, K. E., Wright, M., and Foliano, F. (2008), 'Export Propensity and Intensity of Subsidiaries in Emerging Economies', *International Business Review*, 17, 574–86.

Fahy, J., Shipley, D., Egan, C., and Neale, B. (1998), 'Motives and Experiences of International Joint Venture Partners in Hungary', *Journal of Business and Industrial Marketing*, 13 (2), 155–6.

Forsgren, M., Holm, U., and Johanson, J. (2005), *Managing the Embedded Multinational: A Business Network View*. Cheltenham, UK/Northampton, MA: Edward Elgar.

Holland, D., Sass, M., Benacek, V., and Gronicki, M. (2000), 'The Determinants and Impact of FDI in Central and Eastern Europe: A Comparison of Survey and Econometric Evidence', *Transnational Corporations*, 9 (3), 163–212.

Hungarian National Bank (2007), *FDI Statistics. Hungary, 1995–2005*. Budapest, April (in Hungarian), available at: http://www.mnb.hu. [accessed 10 March, 2009].

Incze, E. (2005), *International Expansion Strategies of Hungarian Enterprises*, CUB Competitiveness Research Center, Working Paper Series No. 18, November (in Hungarian).

Kalotay, K. (2000), 'Is the Sky the Limit? The Absorptive Capacity of Central Europe for FDI', *Transnational Corporations*, 9 (3), 137–62.

Kalotay, K. (2001), 'Privatization and Greenfield FDI in Central and Eastern Europe: Does the Mode of Entry Matter?' *Transnational Corporations*, 10 (3), vii–xii.

Kalotay, K. (2003), 'FDI – In Crisis?' *Közgazdasági Szemle*, 50 (1), 35–55 (in Hungarian).

Meyer, K. E. (2001a), 'International Business Research on Transition Economies', in A. M. Rugman and Th. L. Brewer (eds), *The Oxford Handbook of International Business*. New York: Oxford University Press, 716–59.

Meyer, K. E. (2001b), 'Institutions, Transaction Costs, and Entry Mode Choice in Eastern Europe', *Journal of International Business Studies*, 32, 357–67.

Meyer, K. E. and Estrin, S. (2001), 'Brownfield Entry in Emerging Markets', *Journal of International Business Studies*, 32, 575–84.

Meyer, K. E. and Peng, M. W. (2005), 'Probing Theoretically into Central and Eastern Europe: Transactions, Resources, and Institutions', *Journal of International Business*, 36, 600–21.

Mihályi, P. (2001), 'The Evolution of Hungary's Approach to FDI in Post-Communist Privatization', *Transnational Corporations*, 10 (3), 61–73.

Mirza, H. (ed.) (1998), *Global Competitive Strategies in the New World Economy*. Cheltenham, UK/Northampton, MA: Edward Elgar.

Rojec, M. (2001), 'The Restructuring of Firms in Foreign Privatization in Central and Eastern European Countries', *Transnational Corporations*, 10 (3), 1–24.

Rugman, A. R. and Verbeke, A. (2004), 'A Perspective on Regional and Global Strategies of Multinational Enterprises', *Journal of International Business Studies*, 35 (1), 3–18.

Sass, M., Szanyi, M., Csizmadia, P., Illésy, M., Iwasaki, I., and Makó, C. (2009), *Clusters and the Development of Supplier Networks for Transnational Companies*, Institute for World Economics, Hungarian Academy of Sciences, Working Paper No. 187, March.

Svetličič, M. and Sicherl, P. (2006), 'Slovenian Catching up with the Developed Countries: When and How?', *International Journal of Emerging Markets*, 1 (1), 48–63.

Szanyi, M. (2001), 'Privatization and Greenfield FDI in the Economic Restructuring of Hungary', *Transnational Corporations*, 10 (3), 25–37.

Szanyi, M. (2002), *Spillover Effects and Business Linkages of Foreign-Owned Firms in Hungary*, HAS Institute for World Economics, Working Papers No. 126, Budapest, May.

Szanyi, M. (2003), *An FDI-based Development Model for Hungary – New Challenge*, HAS Institute for World Economics, Working Papers No. 141, Budapest, February.

Szanyi, M. (2006), *Competitiveness and Industrial Renewal via Production Relocation by Global Multinational Networks: Post-1990s Development in Hungary's Electrical Industry*, HAS Institute for World Economics, Working Papers No. 166, Budapest, February.

Uminski, S. (2001), 'Foreign Capital in the Privatization Process of Poland', *Transnational Corporations*, 10 (3), 75–93.

UNCTAD (2003), *World Investment Directory, Volume VIII—Central and Eastern Europe, 2003*. New York/Geneva: United Nations.

UNCTAD (2008), *World Investment Report: Major FDI Indicators*, available at: http://stats.unctad.org/FDI [accessed May 2009].

Viszt, E. and Vanicsek, M. (2005), *Outward FDI in Hungary: Value, Trends, Experiences*. GKI Gazdaságkutató Rt, January (in Hungarian).

Woodside, A. G. and Somogyi, P. (1994), 'Creating International Joint Ventures: Strategic Insights from Case Research on a Successful Hungarian–Japanese Industrial Enterprise', in P. J. Buckley and P. N. Ghauri (eds), *The Economics of Change in East and Central Europe: Its Impact on International Business*. London: Academic Press/ Harcourt Brace Jovanovich, 185–202.

Zemplinerová, A. and Jaromlím, M. (2001), 'Modes of FDI Entry and Firm Performance: The Czech Case', *Transnational Corporations*, 10 (3), 95–111.

7

The Westwards Expansion of Russian Multinationals

Alexander Mansilya-Kruz

The expansion of multinationals from emerging markets in the 2000s has become a somewhat fashionable topic in the last few years. The appearance of Russian multinationals, in particular, has attracted a very intense interest not only from the business, policymaking, and academic communities, but also from the media and even the general public in many countries. At the same time, until very recently, quantitative data has been essentially limited to aggregate quarterly foreign direct investment (FDI) figures. Beyond that, even the basic breakdowns – such as by country or by industry – while available from the official statistics body Rosstat, are widely seen as reflecting off-shoring, 'tax optimization' and similar practices at least as much as actual FDI (Aris, 2006; Nessmann and Orlova, 2008). It is to partially fill this void that the Moscow School of Management, SKOLKOVO, in cooperation with the Vale Columbia Center for Sustainable International Investment, has started the research project that has provided the data for this chapter.

The primary method chosen was to observe the recent outward investment trend in a sample of Russia's largest multinationals ranked by foreign assets. It should be noted immediately that such sampling is far from neutral. It focuses on the leaders in terms of absolute amount invested, overlooking smaller companies. Moreover, using foreign assets as the main ranking variable gives advantage not only to large companies (not necessarily the most transnational ones), but also to capital-intensive and relatively concentrated industries.

In addition, owing to methodological constraints, the study was limited to the non-financial sector, excluding not only banks, but also private equity funds and similar diversified investment holdings. For this reason, major holdings such as Oleg Deripaska's Basel, Vladimir Evtushenkov's Sistema, Mikhail Fridman's Alfa, Vladimir Potanin's Interros, Mikhail Prokhorov's Onexim, Viktor Vekselberg's Renova and so on, are featured in the study through companies they own, rather than directly. Incidentally, these methodological limitations entail certain consequences on the analysis of strategic objectives, which will be discussed later.

To be considered, a company had to be based in Russia (that is, maintain headquarters there from which primary decisions are made) and own physical assets in at least one other country. A group of companies is considered as a single enterprise, except for the aforementioned diversified holdings. A company included in the ranking may be publicly, privately or government owned, which will not affect its position in the ranking. However, Russian firms fully controlled (over 50 per cent of voting shares, or the equivalent) by companies based outside Russia were not included.

The ranking of companies, and consequently the composition of the sample, were based on foreign assets as of end-2007. Since the vast majority of Russian companies use accounting procedures matching the financial year to the calendar year, evening out the timing of the data posed no challenge. Any amounts in roubles or euros were converted to US dollars using a single exchange rate. Information was collected on several key indicators for years 2004 through 2007.

For practical reasons of information availability, the sample was limited to 25 companies, with the cutoff point conveniently happening to be at $200 million in assets outside Russia. Table 7.1 displays companies ranked by this variable. For illustrative purposes, it also shows the place of each company in our previous ranking, based on data as of end-2006 and published in 2007.

7.1 Main findings

The study has shown that Russian multinationals have been growing very rapidly between 2004 and 2007: in three years, their aggregate foreign assets grew four times, to US$ 90bn; their foreign sales (including exports) increased 2.5 times, to nearly US$ 220bn; and foreign employment tripled to 140,000 people (see Appendix for details). The annual growth rates of the aggregated foreign assets have consistently exceeded 50 per cent.

In absolute dollar terms, a handful of companies account for most of the international direct investment from Russia. The three-firm concentration ratio for the foreign assets of the top 25 companies is at 57 per cent, and has been quite stable for the three years to 2007. Even in the top 25 group, designed to include only the largest investors, the bottom seven companies together only have one-tenth of Gazprom's foreign assets. The concentration is even more obvious when we take into account that some of the top 25 companies, like MTS and Sitronics or Rusal and GAZ, have the same controlling shareholders.

The aggregate Transnationality Index of the top 25 has risen from 28.5 to 35 per cent; this relatively slow growth rate reflects the fact that domestic operations have also grown rapidly. Historical Transnationality indices of the top 25 multinationals for 2004–7 are shown in Table 7.2.

The Transnationality Index is a composite ratio used by the United Nations Conference on Trade and Development (UNCTAD) to assess multinationals.

Table 7.1 SKOLKOVO ranking of Russian multinationals in terms of foreign assets, 2007 (millions of US$)

Rank	Prev. rank	Name	Foreign assets
1	1 →	Lukoil	20,805
2	2 →	Gazprom	17,236
3	6 ↑	Norilsk Nickel	12,843
4	11 ↑↑	Evraz	6,221
5	3 ↓	Severstal	5,130
6	5 ↓	Sovcomflot	4,874
7	4 ↓	Rusal	4,533
8	7 ↓	MTS	3,812
9	8 ↑	VimpelCom	3,572
10	14 ↑	Novolipetsk Steel	1,594
11	13 ↑	PriSCo	1,208
12	10 ↓	TNK-BP	1,150
13	12 ↓	FESCO	1,055
14	NEW	IMH/OAO Koks	978
15	17 ↑	Eurochem	901
16	15 ↓	InterRAO	799
17	16 ↓	TMK	606
18	NEW	Mirax	470
19	18 ↓	GAZ	384
20	21 ↑	ChTPZ	262
21	23 ↑	Acron	261
22	20 ↓	Alrosa	231
23	NEW	Sitronics	226
24	19 ↓	OMZ	207
25	NEW	Ritzio Entertainment	200
TOTAL			**89 558**

Source: SKOLKOVO ranking of Russian multinationals.

It is calculated by averaging the relative shares of foreign assets, foreign employees, and foreign sales as a percentage of their respective totals (UNCTAD, 1995: 24, 41; Ietto-Gillies, 1997). Evidently, the Transnationality Index shows a rather different picture compared to the ranking by foreign assets. For instance, Gazprom, a leader in the ranking (Table 7.1), only has about 23 per cent of its business abroad, as measured by the Index.

While the internationalization of management lags somewhat behind that of assets and sales, it also shows a clear, if uneven, trend. The SKOLKOVO survey and desk research found that the top 25 Russian multinationals have an average of 28 per cent foreigners on their boards of directors. Among executives (first level from the CEO), the share is only 10 per cent. One of the reasons is probably that keeping highly qualified foreign managers in Moscow on a permanent basis is a luxury: according to Mercer's 2008 Cost of Living survey, Moscow was the world's most

Table 7.2 Transnationality indices for the top 25 Russian multinationals

	Transnationality Index (%)			
Name	**2007**	**2006**	**2005**	**2004**
Lukoil	44	46	44	41
Gazprom	23	29	28	24
Norilsk Nickel	44	39	35	34
Evraz	34	23	18	15
Severstal	33	33	38	23
Sovcomflot	64	66	66	66
Rusal	39	38		34
MTS	27	23	22	18
VimpelCom	29	23	11	6
Novolipetsk Steel	26		21	22
PriSCo	60	60	57	58
TNK-BP	30	27	21	21
FESCO				
IMH/OAO Koks	36	17	15	5
Eurochem	39	34	35	26
InterRAO	66	68	72	81
TMK	16	17	16	9
Mirax				
GAZ	12	12	6	
ChTPZ	12	13	3	3
Acron	41	40	45	45
Alrosa	20	19	20	15
Sitronics	40	40	19	
OMZ	39	35	34	33
Ritzio Entertainment	34	26	18	20

Source: SKOLKOVO ranking of Russian multinationals.

expensive city for expatriates (Mercer, 2008). Another reason might be the trivial language barrier: at least nine out of the top 25 cite Russian as their only official language.

The financing of Russian multinationals is also quite internationalized. Out of the 25, 11 have their shares listed on stock exchanges outside the country; another six are only listed in Russia (see Table 7.3 for details). Loans from Western banks are common practice, although due to the credit crunch some of those are currently being refinanced by Russian government-controlled financial institutions.

It is noteworthy that nearly all of the companies on the list have only started investing abroad after 2000. This confirms the widely accepted notion that the international expansion of Russian companies is a relatively recent phenomenon. Figure 7.1, showing the yearly amounts of outward international investment over the last decade, makes the post-2002 boom quite evident. Figure 7.2 shows in more detail how it unfolded in 2004–7

Table 7.3 Supplementary information on the top 25 companies

Company name	HQ location	Industry	Main exchanges	Govt control**	Official language	Foreigners on board	Expats in top management
Lukoil	Moscow	oil/gas	RTS, MICEX, LSE	–	Russian	18%	0%
Gazprom	Moscow	oil/gas	RTS, MICEX, LSE	*50,002%*	Rus/Eng	9%	0%
Norilsk Nickel	Moscow	metals/mining	RTS, MICEX, LSE	–		33%	0%
Evraz	Moscow	metals/mining	LSE	–		40%	23%
Severstal	Cherepovets	metals/mining	RTS, MICEX, LSE	–	Rus/Eng	60%	20%
Sovcomflot	St Petersburg	transport	–	*100%*	Rus/Eng	9%	25%
Rusal	Moscow	metals/mining	–	–		50%	0%
MTS	Moscow	telecoms	NYSE, LSE, MICEX	–	Russian	33%	18%
VimpelCom*	Moscow	telecoms	NYSE, RTS	–	Russian	56%	25%
Novolipetsk Steel	Lipetsk	metals/mining	RTS, MICEX, LSE	–	Russian	33%	42%
PriSCo	Nahodka	transport	RTS, MICEX	–		0%	0%
TNK-BP*	Moscow	oil/gas	–	–	Rus/Eng	80%	50%
FESCO	Vladivostok	transport	RTS	–		22%	0%
IMH/OAO Koks	Moscow	metals/mining	RTS, MICEX	–		0%	0%
Eurochem	Moscow	agrichemicals	–	–		57%	0%
InterRAO	Moscow	electricity	RTS, MICEX	*58%*	Russian	0%	11%
TMK	Moscow	metals/mining	RTS, MICEX, LSE	–		30%	5%
Mirax	Moscow	development	–	–		0%	0%
GAZ	Moscow	automotive	RTS	–	Russian	33%	0%
ChTPZ	Chelyabinsk	metals/mining	–	–	Russian	n.a.	n.a.
Acron	Novgorod	agrichemicals	RTS, MICEX	–		0%	0%
Alrosa	Mirny	metals/mining	–	*47,63% fed. + 40% local*		0%	0%
Sitronics	Moscow	hi-tech	RTS, LSE	–	Russian	56%	20%
OMZ	Moscow	engineering	RTS, MICEX, LSE	–	Russian	11%	0%
Ritzio Entertainment	Moscow	entertainment	–	–	Rus/Eng	33%	0%

Source: SKOLKOVO ranking of Russian multinationals.
*TNK-BP is a joint venture between BP and a consortium of Russian investors. Telenor of Norway owns 33.6 per cent of VympelCom.
** A dash means the government does not have a significant stake in the company, to the best of our knowledge. It may, however, hold small minority stakes in many companies through state-owned financial institutions.

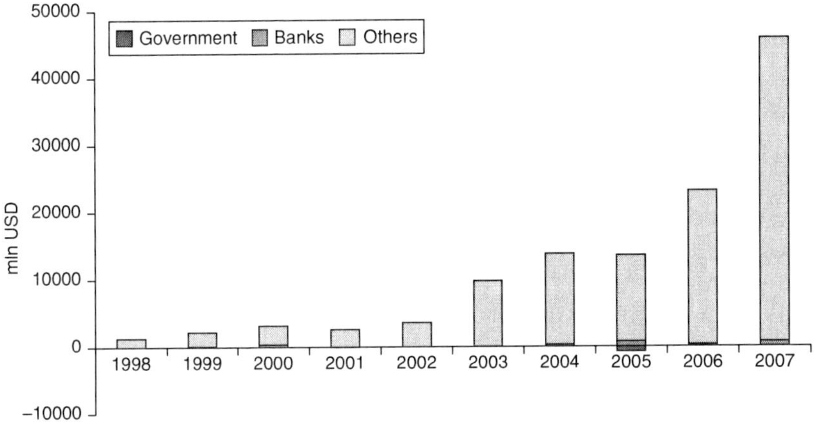

Figure 7.1 Direct investment from Russia by sector, 1998–2007, by year, according to Bank of Russia

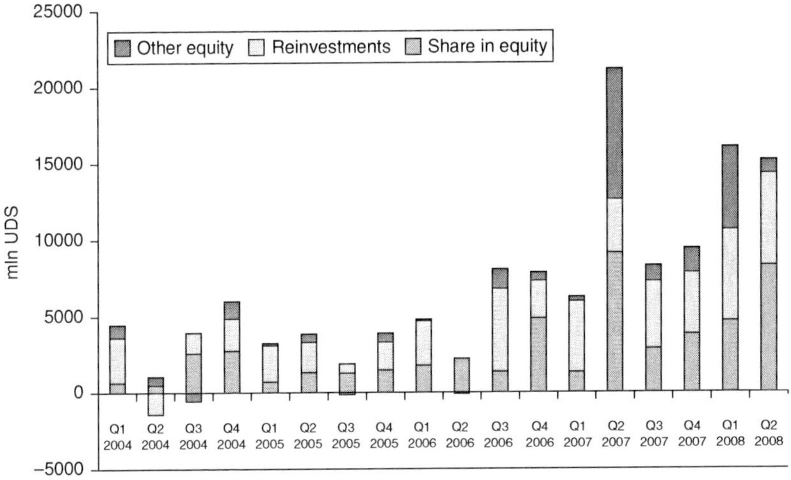

Figure 7.2 Direct investment from Russia by non-banking companies, 2004–1H2008, by quarter, according to Bank of Russia

(as covered by SKOLKOVO ranking data). Several factors have contributed to its surge, one of the most important one being clearly the increased operational cash flows arising from high commodity prices and rapid domestic economic growth.

Another positive factor has been the turnaround in public policy. The Russian government has begun to view outward investment more favourably since the early 2000s. The new federal law on currency exchange

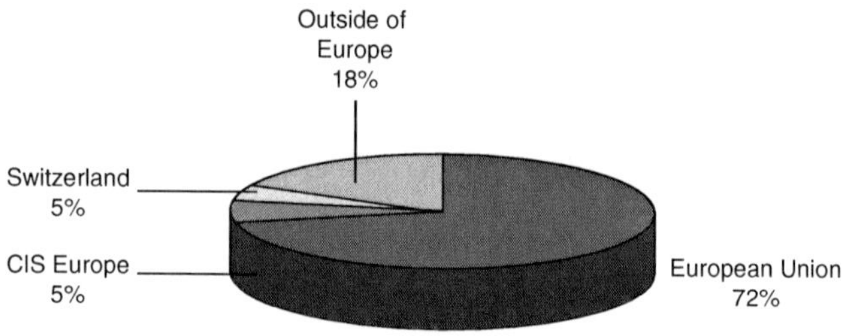

Figure 7.3 According to Rosstat, nearly 82 per cent of FDI from Russia in 2007 went to Europe

regulation, passed in 2003, has gradually lifted most formal restrictions on capital export. In contrast to a previously strong stand against 'the flight of capital', state leaders have come to show public support for companies investing abroad and, at one time, even considered establishing an agency to promote and support such projects.

It would be incorrect, however, to see this expansion as driven by the state. Most of the investment from Russia is being made by private companies: only four out of the top 25 companies are majority-owned by the state, and only one of them is wholly state-owned, as are, for example, many Chinese multinationals. These four state-controlled firms – the energy conglomerate Gazprom (#2), the shipping corporation Sovcomflot (#6), the power producer and trader InterRAO (#16), and the diamond mining company Alrosa (#22)—account for about 30 per cent of the aggregate foreign assets of the top 25.

Europe remains by far the most important investment destination for Russian business. European Union countries alone account for nearly half of the aggregate foreign assets of the top 25 multinationals; and non-member countries such as Belarus, Turkey, Ukraine, or even small Montenegro, are also significant investment targets. Official data from Rosstat show an even more tilted picture (see Figure 7.3), with as much as 82 per cent of all direct investment from Russia going to Europe.[1] The leading countries are Cyprus and the Netherlands, with the US only in third place. Europe's predominant role stems naturally from its geographic and economic proximity to Russia: over 65 per cent of Russian exports in 2007 went to Europe, according to Rosstat.

While Europe remains the destination of choice, the role of the more remote regions of the world, such as North America, Africa, and Australia, is definitely increasing (see Figure 7.4). This is mainly driven by the major Russian metals/mining groups, which invest in mines in resource-rich Southern countries and buy up smelters to penetrate the large North American market.[2]

Both SKOLKOVO data and official statistics show a decreasing share for the Commonwealth of Independent States (CIS) countries. The main reason for this tendency seems to be that the leading Russian multinationals, having

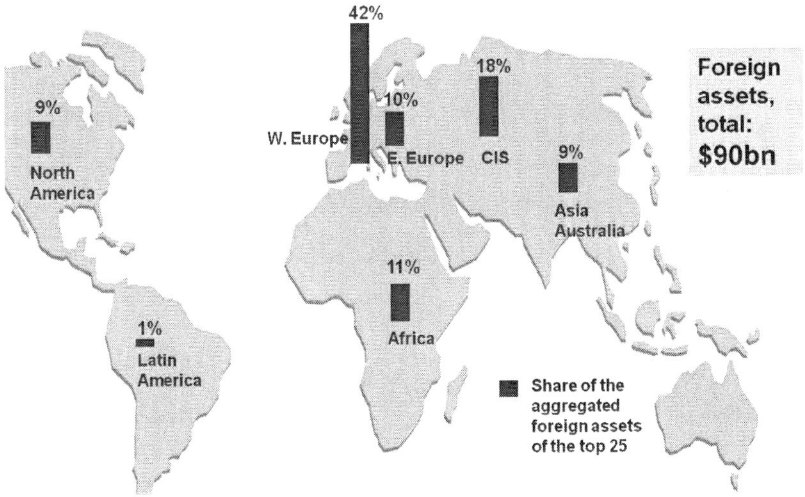

Figure 7.4 Geographic distribution of the foreign assets of the top 25 Russian multinationals, as of 2007
Source: SKOLKOVO. Data as of 2007.

acquired more experience in international business, are less compelled to limit their expansion to familiar, culturally close locations. However, smaller companies, especially in consumer industries such as retail or fast-moving consumer goods (FMCG), still focus on neighbouring countries; and the large fossil and mineral deposits of Central Asia continue to attract the attention of Russian oil and mining companies. One example is the recent contested acquisition of the controlling stake in KazakhGold by Polyus Gold for $187 million plus about 1 per cent of Polyus's shares. Most of Asia, on the other hand, is only now being discovered by Russian investors, with telecom operators beating the way to low-income consumer markets.

Official statistics also show a high degree of geographic concentration in outbound investment: the top 10 destinations accounted for 95 per cent of outward FDI in 2008. Predictably, the world's leading economies such as the United States feature on the list, as do immediate neighbours and trade partners. However, the prominent positions on those lists of countries such as the British Virgin Islands (identified by the UK National Audit Office as the 'world leader in provision of offshore companies' – see National Audit Office, 2007) underscore the limitations of official FDI statistics.

7.2 Downstream integration v. product-line import

FDI in general and Russian outward direct investment in particular include a wide variety of projects – not only in terms of scale, industry, and organizational and legal structure, but also in terms of strategic significance to the acquirer. In a very general sense, it is customary to distinguish market-seeking, resource-seeking, efficiency-seeking (including, in particular, scale-seeking), and strategic asset-seeking international investment (Dunning, 1993: 375). Of course, another powerful motive, not covered by this classification, is the geographic diversification of assets, which enables a group to gain some solidity against country-specific risks. Keeping in mind that our data does not include financial institutions or diversified private equity holdings, we are not going to examine this aspect of Russian outward FDI.

The aforementioned four types of strategic motives are closely linked to the geographic and industrial characteristics of the relevant markets. On a macro level, these motivations are influenced by country-specific comparative advantages and disadvantages of home and host markets. On a micro level, these same motivations are, to a large degree, derived from the profit drivers (to the extent that the management is aware of them) and therefore from the structure of a particular industry.

In the present chapter, we shall focus mostly on those motives and strategies that lead to significant investment in Europe. That is why we will not describe in any detail the market-seeking expansion into foreign consumer markets, typical of leading Russian companies in such industries as telecommunications, retail, food products, entertainment or media. This expansion is directed mostly to emerging markets, outside of the EU, because the business models these companies are trying to replicate abroad are expected to work best in an environment of dynamic consumer income growth.

For the same reason, we will only briefly mention resource-seeking, although it is one of the important motives of the international expansion of Russian companies. Very little of this investment takes place in the European Union, probably because the region has comparatively very few attractive deposits left.

The same commodity producers that engage in resource-seeking investment are also actively engaged in another type of strategic expansion, more relevant for Europe, which we call 'downstream integration'. It is characteristic of large Russian mining and energy corporations, both government-controlled and private. Companies such as Lukoil, Gazprom, InterRAO or Novolipetsk Steel have been using the competitive advantage of the country's natural resource endowments to build a strong presence on foreign markets. Throughout the 2000s, they have been buying and building refining, rolling, transportation, and distribution assets in their key destination markets. Combining market-seeking and strategic-asset seeking, this strategy enabled them to appropriate more value-adding activities and often to push up their market share.

The key role of this strategy in the international expansion of Russian business is illustrated by the fact that oil/gas and mining/metallurgy account for the greatest share of foreign assets of the top 25 multinationals: 44 per cent of the aggregate foreign assets belong to three oil and gas companies and

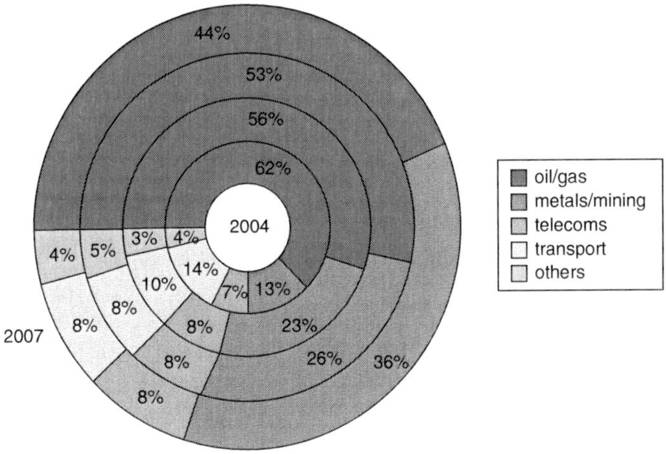

Figure 7.5 Foreign assets of the top 25 Russian multinationals by year industry, 2004–2007

36 per cent to nine metal and mining firms. The dominance of oil and gas conglomerates in the transnationalization process is clearly decreasing: in 2004, they accounted for as much as 63 per cent of aggregate foreign assets of the top 25 compared to 44 per cent in 2007 (see Figure 7.5).

The main reason why the share of the oil and gas groups in the growing foreign asset pool does not look as impressive as in 2004 is the astonishing pace of expansion of the metal/mining sector, namely such groups as Norilsk Nickel, Severstal or Rusal. Vertical integration is also a defining characteristic of their strategies. However, rather than just focusing on complementing their Russian upstream assets with downstream facilities in target markets, they have bought up a wide range of mines and smelters throughout the globe, including Europe. Within a few years, these groups broke into the peloton of the world's largest miners, thanks to a series of large acquisitions. While this trend has been part of a powerful global consolidation process, its motives and rationales are not clear-cut. Typically, the deals were justified as *scale-seeking expansion*. In principle, that may include economies in consolidated purchasing; more effective resource reallocation within the group in a volatile market; optimization of administrative costs; economies of scope derived from a fuller product range; consolidating sufficient cash flows to afford new large-scale investment projects; and, last but not least, access to cheaper capital. In practice, however, most of these benefits (possibly with the exception of lower financing costs) are hard to realize and not always sufficient to offset the cost of the deal. The contagious 'eat or be eaten' logic has probably been part of the motivations at work in this industry.

Those companies that have been engaging in such an aggressive scale-seeking expansion have apparently been the ones the most severely affected by the current downturn. Participating in the consolidation race, they and their shareholders had accumulated considerable debts, and the current financing, more expensive and less accessible, is putting them in a difficult situation. At the same time, a severe fall in metals prices has cut their operating cash flows dramatically. They are now forced to close down money-losing overseas operations, as in the case of Rusal or Norilsk Nickel, which has announced the discharge of about 1,500 employees from its foreign units. Capital expenditures are being 'reduced to critical committed amounts', according to a Norilsk Nickel presentation. Their shareholders have been trying to sell interests in some of the non-core businesses, both at home and abroad, to decrease overall consolidated leverage. For example, Oleg Deripaska's debt-ridden holding Basel has been forced to sell its stakes in Magna, the international automotive company, and in Holcim, the construction group. Currently, these companies rely on emergency loans from Russian state banks to keep afloat, large chunks of their shares are pledged, and the government has a significant say in the management. While they have so far resisted the threat of disintegration, and are still demonstrating global ambitions, they are unlikely to be able to finance any new expansion project in the near future.

The situation is somewhat different for those companies – like Lukoil, for instance – that had focused primarily on *downstream* integration. They are usually less indebted, and their moves into more value-added products (and services) may have made them somewhat less exposed to the volatility of commodity prices. In terms of capability to invest, they are therefore in a better position. By December 2008 Lukoil had closed a deal, financed by a consortium of international banks, to purchase Sicilian refinery assets for €1.3 billion; another refinery deal in the Netherlands, worth over US$ 700 million, was expected to close before the end of 2009. By 3 February 2009, Gazprom had completed a deal to purchase a controlling stake in Serbia's oil company NIS. State-controlled groups in the energy sector, such as Gazprom, Rosneft and InterRAO, are not only pushing on with previously planned international investments, but are also negotiating new projects in remote regions of Latin America, Africa, and Southeast Asia. The gas monopoly's revised budget for 2009 includes investments in Vietnam, India, and Turkmenistan.

A very different strategy was pursued by a range companies mostly active in manufacturing industries, such as GAZ Group (automotive), CTP, Rostselmash (both agricultural equipment), TransmashHolding (railway equipment) etc. This strategic asset-seeking strategy, which can be described as *product-line import,* consists of purchasing a relatively smaller, but technically modern manufacturer in a developed country and localizing the production of its main line of machines in Russia. The purpose is, on the one hand, to bridge quickly the technological gap between Russian manufacturers and their Western competitors, and, on the other, to benefit from lower costs and dynamic demand in Russia.

Typically, the plan is to start by importing products from the acquired plant into Russia to test demand and train potential clients, then to start production from imported parts (considerably reducing import taxation), and then finally localize most of the value chain as suppliers adapt. None of that means, of course, that the acquired company should necessarily discontinue production or sales in the existing markets; on the contrary, the new owners tend to do their best to keep and expand the existing operations, if at all possible. One example is GAZ, one of Russia's largest automotive groups, which in 2006 purchased LDV, a British minivan producer, with the intention to eventually start making a model based on LDV designs in Russia. While this particular strategy is most characteristic of engineering and vehicle production, it is also found in other industries where technology is both crucial and transferable. One example is Kalina, a Russian cosmetics company that acquired the German Dr. Scheller in 2005 and is now making and selling its products in Russia.

Unfortunately, product-line import projects initiated by Russian groups seem to have a rather low success rate, especially now that the downturn is affecting the plans. Several adverse factors are at work: decreased demand in both Western and CIS markets undercuts revenue of existing production facilities; dwindling investment programs threaten localization plans; and clients' preferences switch towards cheaper models rather than fancy advanced ones. As a result, many of the acquirers are getting rid of Western assets. For instance, Amtel, the tyre producer, has sold its Vredestein Banden plant in the Netherlands to the Indian company Apollo Tyres. The alternative to selling the Western plants is bankruptcy, which has recently happened to FTD Fahrzeugtechnik Dessau GmbH, previously owned by the Russian TransmashHolding. Similarly, LDV's assets have been sold to a Chinese company after a bankruptcy procedure. GAZ has announced that its next minivan model will be a 'more economical' one, and will not be based on the design by LDV. Another product-line import project by GAZ, centred on the Italian diesel maker VM Motori, has been cancelled even before the purchase went through. For troubled European manufacturers, a Russian investor is usually less of a chance for resurrection than both the locals and the newcomers would like to think.

It is much too early, however, to dismiss the idea of product-line import altogether. If they are to be successful in the marketplace, Russian manufacturers need to build up their product portfolios with more technologically advanced products, and they will continue to seek participation in the capital of European engineering companies in order to approach that goal. It remains to be seen whether a successful management model emerges for such projects.

Appendix: Top 25 Russian multinationals: Historical assets, employment, and sales, 2004–2007

Table A.1 Assets

	All asset figures are in millions of US$							
Name	Foreign assets 2007	F.A. 2006	F.A. 2005	F.A. 2004	*Total assets 2007*	*T.A. 2006*	*T.A. 2005*	*T.A. 2004*
Lukoil	20,805	18,921	14,361	10,579	59,632	48,237	40,345	29,761
Gazprom	17,236	10,572	5,445	2,951	276,485	204,228	166,888	115,524
Norilsk Nickel	12,843	3,855	1,600	1,413	35,696	16,279	14,730	13,632
Evraz	6,221	1,322	778	0	16,380	8,522	6,754	4,253
Severstal	5130	4538	4161	666	16717	14714	11812	6584
Sovcomflot	4,874	2,530	1,845	1,762	5,300	2,601	1,908	1,820
Rusal	4,533	4,138	1,453	743	15,631	14,100	7,261	6,544
MTS	3,812	2,316	2,015	994	10,967	8,574	7,546	5,581
VimpeCom	3,572	2,103	982	602	10,569	8,437	6,307	4,780
Novolipetsk Steel	1,594	n.a.	159	0	13,076	8,717	6,211	5,166
PriSCo	1,208	1,055	976	657	1,252	1,093	1,012	697
TNK-BP	1,150	1,212	904	438	29,128	23,600	21,624	18,244
FESCO	1,055	1,074	718	675	2,331	1,685	832	753
IMH/OAO Koks	978	7	0	0	2,901	1,391	638	449
Eurochem	901	456	407	0	2,646	1,850	1,547	1,507
InterRAO	799	670	281	261	1,188	983	681	351
TMK	606	490	392	0	4,676	3,548	2,453	2,494
Mirax	470	n.a.	n.a.	0	n.a.	n.a.	n.a.	n.a.
GAZ	384	366	0	–	2,969	2,162	1,807	–
ChTPZ	262	244	0	0	2,708	1,978	1,611	1,111
Acron	261	200	172	119	1,692	1,073	778	578
Alrosa	231	294	158	31	9,274	7,556	6,058	5,414
Sitronics	226	224	47	31	1,887	1,647	566	301
OMZ	207	356	318	347	398	913	832	901
Ritzio Entertainment	200	138	63	47	397	402	357	269

Table A.2 Employment

Name	All employment figures are in thousands							
	Foreign employment 2007	F.E. 2006	F.E. 2005	F.E. 2004	***Total employment 2007***	*T.E. 2006*	*T.E. 2005*	*T.E. 2004*
Lukoil	22	22	19	14	150	149	145	131
Gazprom	9	5	5	5	445	432	397	333
Norilsk Nickel	4	1.9	1.8	1.8	88	84	96	101
Evraz	13	4.4	1.7	0.0	127	110	110	107
Severstal	11	8	8	2	96	100	58	51
Sovcomflot	0.2	0.2	0.2	0.2	5.2	4	3	4
Rusal	15	11	8,5	5	100	100	n.a.	63
MTS	5.3	3.9	3.4	3.4	24.7	24.1	27.7	22.3
VimpelCom	8.6	7.6	1.4	0.4	23.2	21.3	13.3	10.9
Novolipetsk Steel	2.8	2.8	0.4	0	60	71	53	53
PriSCo	0	0	0	0	1	1	1	1
TNK-BP	5.5	5	1	1	63	65	91	96
FESCO	0.6	0.5	0.5	0.0	3.2	3.8	4.1	4
IMH/OAO Koks	3.4	0	0	0	23	20	14	13
Eurochem	1.0	1.2	1.2	1.0	24	26	30	31
InterRAO	14.0	16.0	16.7	4.3	16	16	17	4
TMK	3.1	2.8	0.1	0	48	49	50	50
Mirax	n.a.	n.a.	n.a.	n.a.	n.a.	n.a.	n.a.	n.a.
GAZ	0.9	0.9	0	–	115	110	99	–
ChTPZ	1.7	1.8	0	0	25	25	24	10
Acron	4	4	4	4	12	13	13	13
Alrosa	0	0	0	0	35	36	35	49
Sitronics	5.1	4.8	n.a.	n.a.	11	10	n.a.	n.a.
OMZ	1.9	2.0	1.9	2.0	11.4	17	18	22
Ritzio Entertainment	6.9	5.3	3.3	1.5	19	17	14	6

Table A.3 Sales

Name	All sales figures are in millions of US$							
	Foreign sales 2007	F.S. 2006	F.S. 2005	F.S. 2004	*Total sales 2007*	*T.S. 2006*	*T.S. 2005*	*T.S. 2004*
Lukoil	68,577	56,706	46,899	26,428	81,891	67,684	55,774	33,845
Gazprom	58,415	66,909	42,151	24,563	97,302	82,774	53,213	36,422
Norilsk Nickel	14,582	10,569	6,520	5,968	15,909	11,550	7,169	6,591
Evraz	6,856	4,075	2,603	2,645	12,808	8,292	6,508	5,933
Severstal	8,501	7,536	6,667	3,594	15,245	12,449	10,452	6,664
Sovcomflot	1,200	489	391	379	1,243	511	412	393
Rusal	10,500	9,572	5,520	4,412	14,300	12,900	6,650	5,436
MTS	2,071	1,717	1,322	859	8,252	6,384	5,011	3,887
VimpelCom	1,081	468	178	45	7,171	4,868	3,211	2,113
Novolipetsk Steel	4,816	3,572	2,606	2,911	7,719	6,045	4,375	4,460
PriSCo	137	150	130	120	164	177	175	150
TNK-BP	29,906	24,092	17,722	10,018	38,665	35,512	30,025	17,097
FESCO	n.a.	n.a.	n.a.	n.a.	872	577	541	450
IMH/OAO Koks	1,142	302	323	43	1,888	604	732	541
Eurochem	2,373	1,452	1,415	1,171	3,005	1,964	1,890	1,564
InterRAO	598	539	739	493	1,472	1,359	943	671
TMK	1,185	1,076	897	558	4,179	3,402	2,938	1,984
Mirax	55	n.a.	n.a.	n.a.	1,300	500	n.a.	n.a.
GAZ	1,353	885	683	–	6,224	4,512	3,592	–
ChTPZ	693	509	187	87	3,481	2,632	2,254	852
Acron	938	650	649	516	1,266	897	792	625
Alrosa	2,133	1,912	1,893	1,258	3,693	3,584	3,369	2,807
Sitronics	1,020	909	457	271	1,620	1,611	953	474
OMZ	419	356	314	271	863	667	602	524
Ritzio Entertainment	274	162	91	64	1,598	1,158	697	324

Notes

1. Turkey not included. Rosstat does not indicate any substantial investment from Russia to Norway, Iceland or the Balkan non-EU member countries in 2008.
2. See next section for discussion of this downstream strategy.

References

Aris, B. (2006), *A Row Over Russia's FDI Figures.* London: Business New Europe.

Dunning, J. H. (1993), *The Globalization of Business.* London: Routledge.

Ietto-Gillies, G. (1997), *What do Internationalization Indices Measure?* London: South Bank University CIBS.

Mercer (2008), *Cost of Living 2008.* New York: Mercer.

National Audit Office (2007), *Managing Risk in the Overseas Territories.* London: The Stationery office.

Nessmann, T. and Orlova, D. (2008), *Russia's Outward Investment.* Frankfurt am Main: Deutsche Bank Research.

UNCTAD (1995), *World Investment Report: Transnational Corporations and Competitiveness.* New York and Geneva: United Nations.

8
Multinationals from Slovenia – Nano Size, but Giga Important

Andreja Jaklič and Svetličič Marjan

8.1 Introduction

Creation of multinational enterprises (MNEs) seems an inevitable phenomenon of development, and their existence speeds up changes. Also emerging and many transition economies have increasingly invested abroad. New MNEs have emerged. Since communist and socialist regimes frequently hampered MNEs (interpreting the creation of domestic MNEs as an adverse export of capital needed at home and foreign MNEs as a synonym for the large exploiting enterprises from Western industrialized countries), many found the process of internationalization in these economies as surprisingly quick. Yet the case of Slovenia shows that escaping from the system may itself serve as a strong incentive for direct investment abroad (Svetličič, Rojec, and Lebar, 1994; Jaklič and Svetličič, 2003). Firm-level, bottom-up initiatives were taken after the change of the system, slowly accompanied by economic policy and also influenced by changes in the global environment. The speed of emergence in some economies has thus challenged traditional theories and patterns of internationalization as well as existing knowledge on changes and developments brought about by their existence (Dunning et al., 2008; Rugman, 2008).

While FDI and internationalization theories traditionally emphasized firm-level determinants as the main drivers of creation of MNEs, the determinants outside enterprise have become increasingly important with rapid globalization and development of information and communication technology (ICT). Not only the increasing opportunities in the international environment (L-advantages) but rapid changes and increasing competition in domestic business environment also act as a stimulus to outward internationalization. Enterprises from small countries, on the other hand, face additional incentives for outward internationalization from a small domestic market, as limited partners (buyers and suppliers) and scale economies demand their internationalization.

FDI trends were often found as unexpected, and even declinations from traditional investment development paths were identified, like the reverse development path in Slovenia. The firm-level determinants remain very important and still play a major role in international growth and survival of those MNEs in the longer run, yet other factors gained weight. Understanding the main factors important for the creation of MNEs, as well as the effects of outward internationalization through FDI, is important for business strategies and economic policy. This chapter reveals the experience of the emergence of MNEs in Slovenia. The next part presents trends of FDI and creation of MNEs since the transition period in the 1990s and introduces the top Slovenian MNEs. The third part describes changes and restructuring process driven by outward internationalization, the fourth discusses the reaction of the largest MNEs to the global economic crises and the fifth part presents our conclusions.

8.2 FDI trends and creation of MNEs

In 1991, when Slovenia became an independent country, FDI was insignificant. As in many past socialist countries the capital flow was restricted, though Slovenia was quite specifically compared to other transition economies (Svetličič and Jaklič, 2003: 34–46). The 'reverse investment development path', with outward foreign direct investment (OFDI) starting before inward FDI (IFDI) was system-specific (some forms of IFDI were only allowed in 1965) as were was direct investment abroad, that were 'system escape motivated' (Svetličič, Rojec, and Lebar, 1994). Those were, however, crucial for reorientation to Western markets, the accumulation of internationalization knowledge, and stimulation of transition. Many of the largest Slovene MNEs, as presented in the next part, originate from the socialist period.

8.2.1 FDI trends and structure

The loss of markets in former Yugoslavia put Slovenian enterprises, which traditionally sold there, into a very difficult position.[1] Limited resources together with the need for technological and organizational restructuring were poor companions for a rapid reorientation to more demanding markets that seemed the only way to survive. Export promotion and OFDI had proven as survival strategies and a means to return to former Yugoslav markets. Four stages of the internationalization process can be identified in the last two decades, predominantly characterized by institutional/legal and political developments, mostly privatization and accession to the EU:

1. Early transition stage (1990–3) – the first wave of internationalization – marked by a rapid increase of outward investment on one hand, and divestments and restructuring on the other.
2. Consolidation phase in the mid-1990s (1994–8) characterized by slow progress in outward investment activity, which was mostly carried out by

existing multinational companies, which consolidated and strengthened their foreign affiliates' network.
3. A new wave of internationalization (1999–2008) that speeded up the outward investments of existing multinationals and newcomers in terms of broadening and strengthening their foreign affiliate networks and rapid expansion into the former Yugoslav markets.
4. Consolidation, diversification, and internationalization hold-up stage (2009–).

The process has been predominantly bottom-up and external environment-driven, and policy measures were designed only after 1997 (see Jaklič and Svetličič, 2003: 45–63). Though Slovenia started to invest abroad earlier than other transition economies the net outward position (OFDI stock minus IFDI stock) remained negative (Figure 8.1). Yet the FDI outflows have exceeded the FDI inflows continuously since 2005 (Figure 8.2) until 2008 when the impact of the crises on OFDI seemed to be stronger than on the inflow of FDI.

Most of the investments were directed to the markets of former Yugoslavia. The major recipient countries are Serbia, Croatia, Bosnia and Herzegovina, Germany, and the Netherlands.[2] More than 70 per cent of OFDI stock in the studied period has been located in the countries of former Yugoslavia. These markets have also been normally the first entry markets. Increasing Slovenian FDI outflows were directed to some EU countries, Russia (which hosts 5 per cent of total outward stock), and in recent years also to China, yet the latter still host less than half of one per cent of total Slovenian stock. Industry structure has also remained quite stable since 1990s. In terms of volume the most important direct investors are from pharmaceutical and chemical industry, both wholesale and retail. The structure of OFDI is

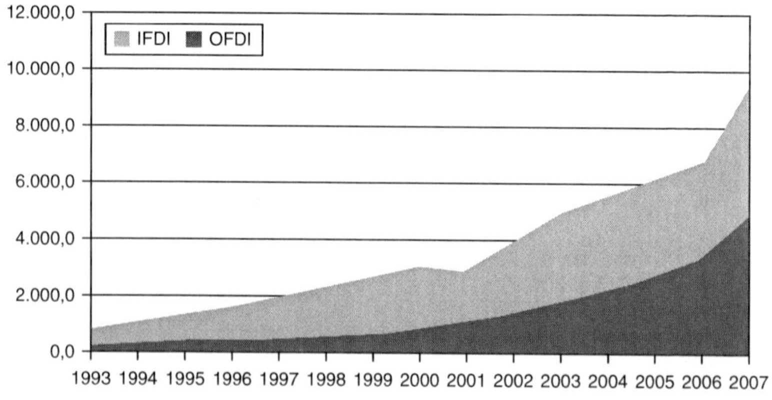

Figure 8.1 FDI stocks in Slovenia 1993–2007 (end-year stock in EUR million)

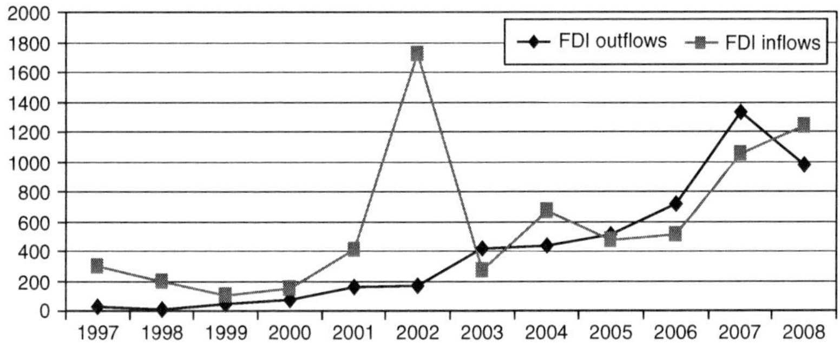

Figure 8.2 Slovenian FDI outflows and inflows, 1997–2006 (millions of EUR)
Source: Bank of Slovenia.

significantly determined by a handful of large investors. The fastest was growth by financial and other business services.

8.2.2 The top Slovene MNEs[3]

In spite of rapid expansion of OFDI, investors abroad represented a small share in the total corporate sector. Their share increased from 1.4 in 1993 to 2.4 per cent in 2007 (Bank of Slovenia, 2008). OFDI was not reserved only for large enterprises,[4] as SMEs have increasingly entered outward investment activity and show dynamic growth. SMEs represent three-quarters of the number of investors; however, the largest Slovenian MNEs remains the major creators of OFDI trends.[5]

The survey of the 'Top 25 Slovene MNEs' carried out in October 2007 covers only indigenous Slovene firms, ranked by the value of foreign assets abroad.[6] Even the largest Slovenian MNEs are not large when compared to MNEs in developed economies or other transition economies,[7] but they play a vital role in Slovenia's economy. The 'Top 25 Slovene MNEs' (Table 8.1) include old and young MNEs: seven MNEs have pre-transition experience in OFDI;[8] nine Slovene MNEs made their first investment abroad in the mid-1990s, and nine others established their first foreign affiliate after 1999 (although the firms were established in the pre-transition period).

Slovenia's 'Top 25 MNEs', valued by foreign assets, had almost US$4 billion[9] in assets abroad (Table 8.2), almost US$4 billion in foreign sales (including exports), and employed 23,616 people abroad. Their foreign assets and employment have each more than doubled since 2004, while foreign sales increased by 60 per cent. Foreign assets are concentrated in Europe. The top three MNEs account for more than half of the total assets of the 'Top 25', and the top five MNEs account for 68 per cent of the 'Top 25's' total foreign assets. As a rule, they are private firms (with the exception of one public company, accounting for only about 2 per cent of the aggregate foreign assets).

Table 8.1 CIR-CPII ranking of the 'Top 25 Slovene MNEs' in terms of foreign assets, 2006 (millions of US$)

Rank	Name	Industry	Foreign assets
1	Mercator	Retail trade	954
2	Gorenje	Electricity supply, manufacturing	668
3	Krka	Manufacturing	439
4	Droga Kolinska[a]	Manufacturing	352
5	Petrol	Oil supply	307
6	Merkur	Retail trade	203
7	Intereuropa	Transportation	127
8	Helios	Manufacturing	121
9	Iskra Avtoelektrika	Manufacturing	80
10	Elan	Manufacturing	75
11	Unior	Manufacturing	66
12	Lesnina	Retail trade	66
13	Kolektor Group	Manufacturing	59
14	Prevent	Manufacturing	50
15	Trimo	Manufacturing	46
16	Viator & Vektor	Transportation	40
17	HIT	Entertainment	37
18	JUB	Manufacturing	35
19	Hidria	Manufacturing	33
20	Perutnina Ptuj	Manufacturing	32
21	Kovintrade	Manufacturing	28
22	ERA	Retail trade	22
23	ETI Elektroelement	Manufacturing	21
24	Alpina	Manufacturing, retail trade	20
25	Kompas	Travel and related activities	20
Total			3,903

(a) Droga and 'Kolinska merged in 2004.
Source: CIR-CPII survey of Slovene multinationals.

Obviously, Slovene MNEs are much smaller than other international competitors (and could be called *nano* MNEs). Not one of the Slovene 'Top 25' makes it into the 'Top 50 MNEs from developing countries' (LDCs).[10] Yet, their expansion has been rapid. Between 2004 and 2006 their aggregate foreign assets doubled, their foreign sales grew by more than 50 per cent to US$7.3 billion (comprising more than half of the 'Top 25's' total sales), and foreign employment doubled to 23,616 people (Table 8.2). Foreign expansion is the engine of growth of the 'Top 25'. Their domestic sales dropped from 59 per cent to only 48 per cent of total sales, in 2006. For the top two manufacturing firms, foreign sales amounted to 86 per cent of their total sales, which demonstrates the extent to which trading companies, and manufacturers of white goods, are dependent on global markets.

A breakdown by industry[11] reveals the predominance of manufacturing among the top MNEs. This can be explained by the structure of the

Table 8.2 A snapshot of Slovenia's 25 largest MNEs, 2004–2006 (millions of US$ and no. of employees)

Variable	**2004**	**2005**	**2006**	**% change 2006/2005**
Assets				
Foreign	2,068	2,680	3,903	31
Total	9,061	9,407	11,777	12
Share of foreign in total (%)	23	28	33	16
Employment				
Foreign	11,699	18,972	23,616	24
Total	69,655	77,027	81,349	6
Share of foreign in total (%)	17	25	29	18
Sales (incl. exports)				
Foreign	4,730	5,093	7,256	28
Total	11,497	11,045	13,885	13
Share of foreign in total (%)	41	46	52	13

Source: CIR-CPII 2008 survey of Slovene multinationals.

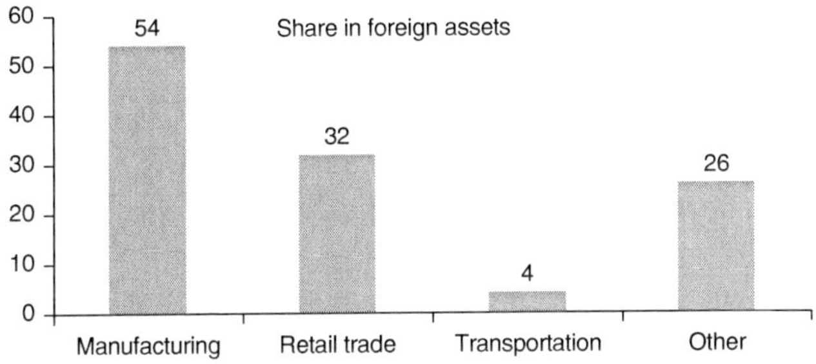

Figure 8.3 Breakdown of the 'Top 25 Slovene MNEs' foreign assets by industry, 2006 (percentage)
Source: CIR-CPII 2008 survey of Slovene multinationals.

economy, wherein traditional mature industries, with strong cost competition and accelerating globalization, dominate. Firms in these sectors have been under greater pressure to internationalize, in order to reduce costs. Less internationalized industries, on the other hand, faced slower restructuring. Manufacturing[12] is by far the most important industry in the 'Top 25 Slovene MNEs', with 16 of the 25 MNEs. It is followed by retail trade, with five MNEs. Other industries include transportation, electricity supply, oil supply, entertainment, travel, and related activities.

The 'Top 25 Slovene MNEs' have 286 foreign affiliates across 53 countries, that is, 11 affiliates and a presence in nine countries, on average (see Table 8A.1). The aggregate Transnationality Index[13] of the 'Top 25 Slovene MNEs' increased between 2004 and 2006, from 36 to 45 per cent, reflecting the rapid growth of international operations. These statistics show that Slovene MNEs do not lag far behind the largest firms in the world. They are more multinational than firms from other transition economies. The most internationalized Slovene company is Droga-Kolinska, a food manufacturer, with a Transnationality Index of 68 per cent. For a small country of two million people, foreign growth through FDI means survival, and is a vital engine of growth for Slovene firms.

Along with a small number of global players, such as Kolektor and Iskra-avtoelektrika, many companies from the 'Top 25 Slovene MNEs' are regional multinationals. Slovene MNEs are generally regional market-seekers, with trade and production affiliates, in the Western Balkan countries. For most of them it is the final strategy, for others a stepping stone to more global orientation. More than 80 per cent of their foreign affiliates are located in Europe. Eight of the 'Top 25 Slovene MNEs' are based exclusively in Europe, as revealed by the Regionality Index (see Table 8A.2), while five operate on at least four different continents, and ten of them are present on at least three continents. Recently, Slovene firms have shown a growing interest in Russia, China, and other, more distant, Asian locations.

In spite of high geographical spread the internationalization level of management is relatively low, and, with the exception of one MNE, all other CEOs are Slovene. Only eight out of the 'Top 25 Slovene MNEs', have more than 10 per cent of foreign senior management.[14] In 17 firms, senior management is entirely Slovenian. The 'Top 25 Slovene MNEs' all use Slovenian as their official language, although 15 MNEs also use foreign languages. Ten MNEs have Slovenian and English as official languages, two have three official languages (Slovenian, English, and German), and one has five official languages (Slovenian, English, German, Russian, and Croatian).

Low internationalization of management along with fully or majority-owned foreign affiliates, slow development of joint ventures and modest cooperation with foreign partners are frequently seen as their weaknesses and difficulties in their future development. Many Slovenian MNEs are too small, their managers too young and not mobile enough to grow global networks (Jaklič and Svetličič, 2008: 46–7). But in spite of numerous challenges that lie ahead for Slovenian and MNEs in their future growth (discussed below), the effects by existing investment activity are extremely important.

8.3 Changes driven by OFDI internationalization

Though their share in the total corporate sector is minor (2.4 per cent), Slovene MNEs are vital for the export-oriented Slovenian economy (exports exceed 70 per cent of GDP). Outward investors alone provide over 40 per cent of exports in the total Slovenian corporate sector and over 30 per cent employees of the total corporate sector (Jaklič, 2004). Several econometric studies show that outward investors are significantly more successful than the average Slovenian firm, exporting firm or comparable firms without investment abroad (Jaklič and Svetličič, 2003; Jaklič, 2004; Damijan et al., 2004; Burger, Jaklič and Rojec, 2006; Burger, 2009). Companies investing abroad are larger, more capital-intensive, have a better assets structure and are more export-oriented. Investing firms performed better than non-investing firms. The growth of investing companies was much faster than that of non-investing firms. Investing abroad considerably speeded up companies' restructuring, especially as regards value-added and export propensity (Jaklič and Svetličič, 2003: 100–4). The share of innovative firms among outward investors (42 per cent) is much higher than the share among exporters (35 per cent) or total corporate sector (21 per cent) (Jaklič, 2004).

Investing companies have generally experienced a positive net effect of OFDI, and their related success was mostly in line with expectations. Similarly, as econometric studies that emphasized export and productivity increases and surveys among investing firms (1999, 2001, 2004) revealed that trade and competitiveness effects were far more important than any other effects. Market-seeking investments resulted in increased market shares, growth of exports, and increased domestic production levels. Intra-firm trade grew, though the impact on imports was smaller (and heterogeneous) compared to export increases. Consequently, outward FDI enhanced efficiency and restructuring of investors, although these were not the initial motives. Investing companies introduced new products, product differentiation, and also increased the quality of products/services, since direct presence in a foreign market helped them respond to customers' needs more rapidly. By investing abroad, firms also achieved other positive asset-creation effects. They have improved their image and enhanced and broadened their marketing, management, and organizational skills. Studies on ICT use also demonstrated that more internationalized firms use ICT earlier and efficiently than non-internationalized firms (Stare et al., 2006). On the contrary, MNEs assessed technological expertise that was only modest on average, a finding also related to the fact that the majority of host countries are less developed than Slovenia. The employment effect was less important, with the majority of firms seeing no changes here as a result of OFDI. However, Slovene MNCs are significant employers in the domestic economy. International growth provides much better development opportunities than growth limited to the domestic setting only.

Firm-level effects of OFDI spill over to the whole domestic economy and influence the trade balance, the level and structure of industrial production, investment, and employment, with related development implications. OFDI was found to be a mode complementary to exports and had not crowded out domestic investment (Jaklič, 2004). Investing firms have the highest growth potential, while exposure to foreign competition forces them to pursue high-quality adaptations and innovations, which are also introduced into the home economy. As welfare depends much more on innovation and knowledge creation than the accumulation of physical capital, OFDI is also growth and development instrumental. Companies evaluated that OFDI improved the competitiveness and transformation of Slovenian economies and also stimulated EU integration. Investing firms speeded up the transition process and reduced the gap between transition and developed industrial countries. The restructuring and development benefits of OFDI can be seen more in the long term, and in the increasing number of investing firms. The effects on the home economy are stronger if investing firms develop more links with other firms and exploit scale and factor differences internationally.

The first study on international sourcing in Slovenia (Statistical Office of the Republic of Slovenia, 2009)[15] revealed relatively modest international fragmentation of production. Only 16 per cent of Slovenian enterprises source internationally, though growth from 2001–3 to 2004–6 had increased. International sourcing follows a sequential pattern, and increases with the level of internationalization. MNEs are the most involved in international sourcing. More than 36 per cent of the largest Slovenian MNEs source internationally. Activities are more frequently sourced within than outside the enterprise group (Figure 8A.1). Marketing, sales, distribution and logistics, and production were the most frequently sourcing activities (Table 8A.3).

In line with the geographical concentration of OFDI countries of former Yugoslavia (mostly Serbia and Croatia) are followed by new EU member states (Poland, Hungary, Romania) as the most important hosts for international sourcing, while selected developed countries (Austria, Ireland) and China are gaining importance. The main motivations for sourcing decisions were improved competitiveness, access to new markets, position on the market and reduction of costs, while the main barriers were overall concerns that the costs of the sourcing operation would exceed the expected benefits, the high risk of sourcing internationally, and a lack of management resources and know-how. Interestingly, the lack of knowledge, personnel, and difficulties with partner selection were especially emphasized by the largest MNEs, which may demonstrate that smaller companies are not yet in the stage to realize these gaps or are not yet aware of them. Differences in the assessment of the results of outsourcing activities by firms suggests the conclusion that Slovenian enterprises in general realized the positive impact of international sourcing, which contributed to their competitive advantage. Although negative experiences can be found in total sample, all the largest MNEs reported positive results in line with or even above expectations.

8.4 Slovene MNEs' response to the global economic crises

MNEs were among the first to face the global financial crisis, yet the consequences were not fatal for them. A survey on the global economic crisis among 'Top 25 Slovenian MNEs' (launched in June 2009 and supplemented by interviews[16]) revealed that the consequences of the crisis varies considerably among the top MNEs and the scale of effects had been less dramatic than daily media reports would suggest. Generally, lower sales were accompanied by cost-cutting, reduced investment and employment. Frequently the pool of unemployed people included those who might have been dismissed before the crisis but management had postponed dismissal decisions during more profitable times.

The most significant consequence of the crises for the largest MNEs has been a decease in sales (80 per cent of surveyed firms reported sales decreases, most frequently of between 20 and 49 per cent) and lower profits. Conversely, none of the surveyed MNEs experienced a decrease in market share, and none had lost suppliers or key personnel. Even laying off was not universal: 40 per cent reduced the number of employees below 20 per cent, or used the instrument of a shortened working week (partly subsidized by government), while the majority did not reduce the number of employees.

The initial reaction to the global crisis was cost-cutting and increasing sales activity. Long-term investment was postponed, and investment in R&D and marketing reduced. Sales promotion activities were focused on key customers, maintaining good relationships with leading business partners and rationalizing the product portfolio.

Rising uncertainty and scarcity of capital has proven less painful to more internationalized firms. One of the most efficient remedies was diversification of markets, since the crisis showed its teeth differently by markets and over time. Enterprises with more diversified sales could help themselves by managing the 'lags in the effects of the crisis'. Many Slovene MNEs' sales decreases in Europe lag behind sales decreases in the USA, while the responses in the Middle East, Russia, and other Asian markets were slower, less intensive, and showed large differences by industries.

Entry to new markets by variety of modes (keeping and/or increasing diversification of markets) has thus been selected as a response by all the top MNEs. None of the top MNEs has withdrawn from foreign markets, but on the contrary had increased international economic cooperation. Strategic alliances, international R&D cooperation, outsourcing, and captive offshoring have been identified as the most promising responses to the crisis and are expected to be more used in the future. As much as 40 per cent of surveyed enterprises planned to increase (or had recently invested) OFDI in new markets owing to the crisis.[17]

Entry to new and more distant markets is increasing not only among large but also among medium-sized and small direct investors. Expansion to BRICs is demonstrated also by the number of affiliations and representative offices[18] of firms established in the BRICs nations (Table 8A.4). The majority of them have been established only recently, particularly by the state-sponsored agency, JAPTI. Facilitating business cooperation and entry to more distant markets has been identified as a strategic need in Slovene national economic policy.

Recognizing that Slovenia has the lowest share of trade with China among all EU members, economic policy (particularly of the Chamber of Commerce) started to promote cooperation with BRICs in view of current tectonic changes in the world. Several activities have been undertaken, and most of the Slovene MNCs have participated. The climate of neglecting cooperation outside EU, which dominated the first years of transition – also as a reaction, perhaps, to too much political attention being given to cooperation with non-aligned and developing countries during the socialist period – has been changing into active promotion of strengthened economic ties with BRICS and other developing countries. Current economic crises will damage BRICs relatively less than industrial countries in general, which has been an additional incentive beside the fact that BRICS will grow much faster and be drivers of new demand in years to come, becoming the major source of additional demand.

8.5 Conclusion: MNEs face rising challenges

The creation of MNEs is certainly only the beginning of challenges that come along with international growth. They substantially facilitated the development of this new, small state, which faced the loss of almost half of its former market. Slovene MNEs, though still assuming a minor place in the Slovene economy, remain important employers, investors, and innovators. Owing to its small size and openness, it is expected that the Slovenian economy will be dominated by highly internationalized firms, both domestic and foreign-owned. If, it follows the pattern in more developed small countries, the ownership structure of the corporate sector in Slovenia in future may be composed of 40 per cent foreign-owned firms, possibly 40 per cent Slovene MNCs and the remaining 20 per cent local market-oriented firms. Local firms, operating mostly in the domestic market, will eventually be in the minority. Slovene MNEs, therefore, became an important development instrument, which was not the case some fifteen years earlier, when many attitudinal barriers restricted outward internationalization. Over time, even the most sceptical policy-makers and managers have realized that, in the era of globalization, outward internationalization has become a precondition for growth and enhanced competitiveness. Investing and exporting firms miss incentives, and systemic long-term support by economic policy, however, admit that several barriers are intra-firm.

Managing human resources is one of the most important challenges within existing MNEs and for creation of new MNEs. Several MNEs, even among the top MNEs, still lack systematic internal HRM and replace it by ad hoc activity. Lack of skilled and internationally mobile managers, which has proven to be the major barrier to internationalization, is a message for existing education and training programmes. These shortages highlight the need for holistic education that provides interdisciplinary knowledge of many areas of international business.

Opportunities for existing Slovenian MNEs also lie in improved corporate governance, international integration of activities, international sourcing, organization, and management. The largest publicly owned MNEs in particular face difficulties of higher international risk and the need for swift response and strategy adaptation. While the largest MNEs fear the possibilities of hostile takeovers or face inefficient governance, SMEs and niche players mostly lack financial and human resources, and a supportive business environment.

International mindset is strongly related to openness, and here Slovenia still has unexploited potential. Enhancing inward internationalization and improving the business environment (especially labour market rigidities, the tax regime, and administration procedures, traditionally criticized by foreign investors) would add to the desired openness. The present global economic crisis has, of course, influenced the outward internationalization strategies of firms, but has not halted their long-term orientation. The top MNEs are responding to this crisis with further outward internationalization, which should be an incentive also for policy-makers. In development, smallness can be only outweighed by internationalization. In current global changes this is not relevant only for Slovenia, but also for Europe in general.

Appendix

Table 8A.1 CIR-CPII ranking of the Top 25 Slovenian multinationals, key variables, 2006 (millions of US$ and no. of employees)

Ranking		Name	Industry	Assets		Sales		Employment		Trans-nationality Index	No. of foreign affiliates	No. of host countries
Foreign assets	Trans-nationality Index			Foreign	Total	Foreign	Total	Foreign	Total			
1	20	**Mercator**	Retail trade	954	2,456	585	2,725	5,892	19,539	30	5	5
2	6	**Gorenje**	Electricity supply, manufacturing	668	1,194	1,254	1,466	2,109	10,556	54	41	26
3	7	**Krka**	Manufacturing	439	1,160	759	881	2,113	5,759	54	14	12
4	2	**Droga Kolinska**	Manufacturing	352	577	315	446	2,605	3,577	68	11	6
5	24	**Petrol**	Oil supply	307	1,112	354	2,561	363	2,768	18	6	5
6	23	**Merkur**	Retail trade	203	1,153	464	1,318	661	4,075	23	8	7
7	13	**Intereuropa**	Transportation	127	383	194	290	1,018	2,310	48	12	10
8	3	**Helios**	Manufacturing	121	340	416	342	920	2,211	66	21	13
9	17	**Iskra Avtoelektrika**	Manufacturing	80	223	199	261	443	2,534	43	12	11
10	4	**Elan**	Manufacturing	75	161	145	162	337	1,267	54	7	6
11	19	**Unior**	Manufacturing	66	513	255	376	645	3,796	33	21	17
12	12	**Lesnina**	Retail trade	66	129	94	182	303	683	49	6	2
13	10	**Kolektor Group**	Manufacturing	59	235	302	327	1,110	2,879	52	10	9
14	11	**Prevent**	Manufacturing	50	285	468	435	1,143	3,817	52	5	5
15	5	**Trimo**	Manufacturing	46	162	231	222	278	979	54	12	12

16	15	**Viator & Vektor**	Transportation	40	289	322	315	549	2,554	46	11	9
17	25	**HIT**	Entertainment	37	400	25	300	236	2,548	9	3	3
18	1	**JUB**	Manufacturing	35	68	84	116	136	342	77	9	9
19	18	**Hidria**	Manufacturing	33	238	182	243	330	2,400	34	21	17
20	21	**Perutnina Ptuj**	Manufacturing	32	249	98	219	625	2,289	28	5	3
21	16	**Kovintrade**	Manufacturing	28	146	166	235	134	294	45	10	9
22	22	**ERA**	Retail trade	22	91	12	107	163	371	27	2	2
23	14	**ETI Elektro-element**	Manufacturing	21	83	84	94	431	1,745	47	10	10
24	8	**Alpina**	Manufacturing, retail trade	20	80	62	75	866	1,625	54	8	7
25	3	**Kompas**	Travel and related activities	20	51	152	216	206	431	52	16	16
TOTAL				3,903	11,777	7,256	13,885	23,616	81,349		286	53

Source: CIR-CPII survey of Slovenian multinationals.

Table 8A.2 The Top 25 Slovenian MNEs: Regionality Index,[a] 2006

Name	Europe	CIS	Middle East	Africa	North America	Latin America	Southeast Asia	Australia
Mercator	100	–	–	–	–	–	–	–
Gorenje	98	–	2	–	–	–	–	–
Krka	79	14	–	–	7	–	–	–
Droga Kolinska	100	9	–	–	–	–	–	–
Petrol	100	–	–	–	–	–	–	–
Merkur	100	–	–	–	–	–	–	–
Intereuropa	83	17	–	–	–	–	–	–
Helios	81	19	–	–	–	–	–	–
Iskra Avtoelektrika	42	17	8	–	8	8	17	–
Elan	71	–	–	–	14	–	14	–
Unior	71	–	–	–	5	–	19	5
Lesnina	100	–	–	–	–	–	–	–
Kolektor Group	50	–	–	–	20	10	20	–
Prevent	40	–	–	–	–	20	20	–
Trimo	75	25	–	20	–	–	–	–
Viator & Vektor	91	9	–	–	–	–	–	–
HIT	100	–	–	–	–	–	–	–
JUB	89	11	–	–	–	–	–	–
Hidria	67	5	–	–	5	14	10	–
Perutnina Ptuj	100	–	–	–	–	–	–	–
Kovintrade	100	–	–	–	–	–	–	–
ERA	100	–	–	–	–	–	–	–
ETI Elektroelement	80	–	–	–	–	–	20	–
Alpina	63	13	–	–	13	–	13	–
Kompas	88	6	–	–	6	–	–	–

[a] The Regionality Index is calculated by dividing the number of a firm's foreign affiliates in a particular region of the world by its total number of foreign affiliates and multiplying the result by 100.
Source: CIR-CPII survey of Slovenian multinationals.

Table 8A.3 International sourcing of Slovene enterprises by activity, in 2001–2003 and 2004–2006

	Top MNEs (N=25)		Total sample (N=827)	
	2001–2003	2004–2006	2001–2004	2004–2007
Production	25,9	40,7	3,6	8,3
Distribution and logistics	22,2	33,3	3,5	6,0
Marketing, sales, aftersales services	29,6	44,4	5,8	9,3
ICT services	7,4	14,8	1,5	3,9
Administrative services	7,4	18,5	2,2	3,9
Engineering	7,4	18,5	1,0	2,1
Research and development services	11,1	7,4	1,2	1,7

Source: Statistical Office of the Republic of Slovenia.

Table 8A.4 Slovene investment and representative offices in BRIC countries (value in millions of EUR)

	China	Russia	India	Brazil	Total
Affiliations (Number)	13 (7 SLO MNCs)	8 (5 Slo MNcs)	4 (2 SLO MNCs)	5 (4 SLO MNcs)	
Slovene OFDI stock 2007, mill. EUR	10.4	249	4.0	4.1	267.5 (5.5%)
Representative offices	11 (3 SLO MNCs)	80	5 (1 Slo MNCs)		
Representative offices of JAPTI (established)	Shanghai (2008)	Kazan (2008)	Mumbai (planned)	Sao Paulo (2008)	

Source: Bank of Slovenia, Direct investment 2007: 61, and Chamber of Commerce.

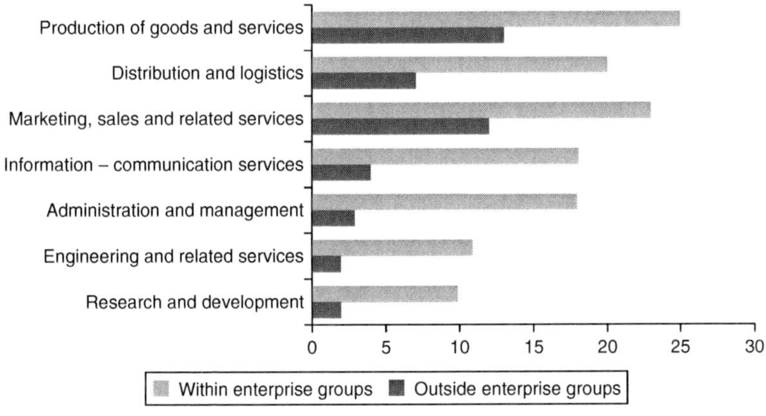

Figure 8A.1 International sourcing within and outside of enterprise groups (per cent), Slovenia, 2001–2009
Source: Statistical Office of the Republic of Slovenia.

Notes

1. Many of entrepreneurs and older managers have seen the situation in the early 1990s as more difficult than the current economic crisis. Sales were drastically cut, as the formerly 'domestic' Yugoslav market represents more than 50 per cent of total sales.
2. The Netherlands is a special case since it attracts mostly financial investment for tax minimization purposes and is not part of 'real' developmentally or structurally motivated internationalization.
3. See Jaklič and Svetličič (2008 and 2009) for more details.
4. Direct investors abroad with more than 500 employees represent about 25 per cent in terms of number of investors, but a majority in terms of value of capital invested.
5. The top Slovene MNEs are also among the most respected companies in Slovenia, according to *DELO*, a major newspaper in Slovenia. Six of the ten most respected firms also feature on the 'Top 25 Slovene MNEs'. The list of the 63 most successful firms in Slovenia, based on 18 indicators, also includes 14 of the 'Top 25 Slovene MNEs' (DELO, 26 November 2007: 23). The largest Slovene MNEs are also among the largest 101 Slovene companies. Of the largest ten, five are Top 25 MNEs (see Finance 2007, 28 May). Although large in Slovenia, these MNEs do not rank highly in the ranking of the most profitable companies. They account for second, fourth, sixth, fourteenth, seventeenth, and nineteenth place among the 20 most profitable firms in Slovenia (DELO, 21 May 2007: 31), and consequently, they also fail to rank highly in terms of value added per employee.

   There are several reasons for this. First, these MNEs are mainly older companies, and many operate in medium technology-intensive industries, where cost competitiveness is essential and profit rates are, by definition, lower. Second, strategically they are long-term, and not short-term, profit-maximization-oriented.
6. Even if foreign-owned MNEs that are located in Slovenia and invest abroad (indirect investors) were included, only a few would qualify. Slovene MNEs are, therefore, more home-grown than in other transition economies, where foreign-owned companies have played a greater role in outward investment. Only 11 per cent of companies investing abroad were foreign-owned (Jaklič and Svetličič, 2003: 59; 2009). The only substantial foreign-owned investor abroad would be Lek, a pharmaceutical company acquired by Novartis in November 2002. Even Lek developed its internationalization strategy as a Slovene firm and became an acquisition target for that reason. It was acquired already having 27 affiliates abroad. An opposite example is that of Kolektor, which started as a Slovene firm, later entered into a joint venture with a foreign partner, and in 2002 took over the foreign partner's share and bought its factory in Germany as well, and hence again became a Slovene firm and now an MNE (Jaklič and Svetličič, 2003: 251–62; Svetličič, 2008).
7. Slovenia was included in Emerging Markets Global Players project (EMGP). The foreign assets of the Top 25 are roughly 5 per cent of the Top 25 in Russia and the Top 20 in Brazil (the ranking lists for Brazilian and Russian MNEs were released in December 2007 – see www.cpii.columbia.edu).
8. Gorenje, for example, undertook OFDI in the 1960s; Krka established a pharmaceutical firm near Nairobi in the mid-1970s, and Elan has produced skis in Sweden since the 1970s.
9. The following EUR/USD exchange rates, based on XE.com Universal Currency Converter (http://www.xe.com/ucc/), were used throughout: 1.31954 (2006); 1.18395 (2005); 1.35338 (2004).

This includes food and beverages, chemical and pharmaceutical products, machinery and equipment, electrical equipment, and sports apparel.

10. See UNCTAD, *World Investment Report 2007* (Geneva: United Nations, 2007). Data for 2005 are the latest available at the time of writing.
11. MNCs in financial services were not included in this project. If included, Nova Ljubljanska Banka would be leading the list of Slovene MNCs in terms of volume of assets abroad.
12. This includes food and beverages, chemical and pharmaceutical products, machinery and equipment, electrical equipment, and sports apparel.
13. The Transnationality Index is a composite ratio calculated by averaging the relative shares of foreign assets, foreign employees, and foreign sales as a percentage of their respective totals. See UNCTAD, 2007.
14. In these eight MNEs the breakdown is as follows: 40 per cent or more of top management that is foreign: three MNEs; 30 per cent or more of top management that is foreign: two MNEs; 20 per cent or more of top management that is foreign: two MNEs; 10 per cent or more of top management that is foreign: one MNE.
15. The pilot survey on the reasons, extent, and consequences of international sourcing was conducted as a part of Eurostat surveys and is one of the first attempts to estimate the extent of international sourcing in the EU.
16. Eleven enterprises out of top 25 MNEs responded in detail, while some information on the rest was taken from public information.
17. Recent acquisition of ECS GmbH from Essen (Germany) by Kolektor (June 2009) has been realized as a joint venture with a Chinese partner. Recent investments by Trimo were oriented toward investment hubs important the for Middle East and Africa (Turkey and North Africa).
18. It is part of internationalization promotion strategy launched a few years ago by the government.

References

Bank of Slovenia (2008), *Direct Investment 2007*. Ljubljana: Bank of Slovenia.

Burger, A. (2009) 'Dynamic Effects of International Fragmentation of Production: Empirical Analysis of Slovenian Manufacturing Firms', doctoral dissertation, Ljubljana: Faculty of Economics.

Burger, A., Jaklič, A. and Rojec, M. (2006), *Dinamični učinki izhodne internacionalizacije* (Dynamic effects of outward internationalization). Ljubljana, Faculty of Social Sciences, mimeo.

Damijan, J.P., Polanec, S.& Prašnikar, J. (2004), Self Selection, export market heterogeneity and productivity improvements: Firm level evidence from Slovenia.LICOS Discussion Paper 14804, LICOS, K. U. Leuven.

Dunning, J. H, Kim, C. and Park, D. (2008), 'Old Wine in New Bottles: A Comparison of Emerging-market TNCs Today and Developing Country TNCs Thirty Years Ago', in K. Sauvant (ed.), *The Rise of Transnational Corporations from Emerging Markets: Threat or Opportunity?*. Cheltenham, UK: Edward Elgar, 158–82.

Jaklič, A., Svetličič, M. (2003) *Enhanced transition through outward internationalization: outward FDI by Slovenian firms* (Transition and development). Aldershot; Burlington (VT): Ashgate.

Jaklič, A. (2004), 'The Impact of Factor Endowments on the Creation of MNEs', doctoral dissertation, Ljubljana, Faculty of Economics.

Jaklič, A. and Svetličič, M. (2009), 'Unknown Multinationals: Top MNEs from Slovenia', in K. Sauvant (ed.), *Thinking Outward: Global Players from Emerging Markets*. Cheltenham, UK: Edward Elgar.

Jaklič, A. and Svetličič, M. (2008), 'Unknown Multinationals: The Case of Slovenia, V: Best Practices in Promoting Investment for Development', paper presented at OECD Investment Forum, available at: http://www.oecd.org/dataoecd/34/53/40408028.pdf.

Rugman, A. M. (2008), 'Do We Need a New Theory to Explain Emerging Market Multinationals?' in K. Sauvant (ed.), *The Rise of Transnational Corporations from Emerging Markets: Threat or Opportunity?*. Cheltenham, UK: Edward Elgar, 86–106.

Stare, M., Jaklič, A. and Kotnik, P. (2006), 'Exploiting ICT Potential in Service Firms in Transition Economies', *Service Industries Journal*, 26 (3), April, 287–302.

Statistical Office of the Republic of Slovenia (2009), *International Sourcing, Slovenia, 2001–2009*, January, available at: http://www.stat.si/eng/novica_prikazi.aspx?id=2125.

Svetličič, M. (2008), 'Reversed Internationalization Path: The Case of Slovenia', *AIB Insights*, 8 (1), 3–9.

Svetličič, M. and Jaklič, A. (2003), 'Outward FDI by Transition Economies: Basic Features, Trends and Development Implications', in M. Svetličič and M. Rojec (eds), *Facilitating Transition by Internationalisation*. Aldershot/Burlington, VT/Singapore/Sydney: Ashgate Publishing.

Svetličič, M., Rojec, M. and Lebar, S. (1994), 'Internationalisation Strategies of Slovenian Firms: The German Market Case', in K. Obloj (ed.), *High Speed Competition in a New Europe*, Proceedings of the 20th Conference of EIBA, Warsaw, December.

UNCTAD (2007), *World Investment Report 2007*. Geneva/New York: United Nations.

Part IV

Southern Multinationals from a Host Country/Region Perspective

9

Chinese and Indian Firms in Europe: Main Characteristics and Presumed Impacts

Françoise Hay and Christian Milelli

Introduction

Since the beginning of the millennium, companies from fast-growing emerging economies – that is, Brazil, China, India or Russia – have grown more confident on the global stage. By securing bold acquisitions and delivering the innovative products that strengthen their market positions, they have turned themselves into formidable competitors to the incumbent multinational companies. Moreover, as 'latecomers', they are fully cognizant of the changing world environment.

This chapter deals with investments by Chinese and Indian companies across Europe. It explains why those companies are now at the forefront of the 'new wave' of investments from emerging economies. Even though their involvement is still of modest magnitude[1] it is expanding rapidly. It then makes good economic sense to take into consideration the distinct advantages, motives and strategies as well as the potential impacts of Indian and Chinese companies on the European zone. To date, the European Union area is the world's largest FDI recipient, and it has established significant trade exchanges with both China and India. In addition, as firms from those two Asian countries developed in an unstable and changing economic environment they have become very flexible and resilient to shocks. Such features will possibly confer on them the competitive advantage required to manage through the worrisome global crisis that erupted in mid-September 2008.

9.1 The presence of Chinese and Indian companies in Europe: theory, empirical evidence and characteristics

9.1.1 The theoretical background

This section provides a brief overview of the theoretical foundations and their relevance to the internationalization of Chinese and Indian companies into mature markets – with Europe as a case study – and helps to better understand as well as characterize this twofold phenomenon.

Over the last decades, the theory has provided several approaches to interpret the internationalization of firms. 'Business international', which represents by far the more representative strand of the literature, is largely based on the so-called 'OLI' eclectic paradigm (Dunning, 1972, 1977). Accordingly, a firm has to meet three basic conditions before investing abroad: a specific Ownership advantage, a Location advantage when comparing its domestic market to that of the recipient country, and an Internalization advantage through transaction costs.

Notwithstanding some adaptation and extension, this approach is still valid to explain the rise of multinational firms from developing countries. More advances were made in 1998 when J. Dunning and R. Narula proposed the 'Investment Development Path' hypothesis that ascertains some causal link between outward FDI, inward FDI and the country's relative stage of development measured through GDP per capita. Of course, this supports outward FDI by Chinese and Indian firms, but only partially. It is also true that inward FDI has expanded in China and India in the last few years. Finally, GDP per capita is still low in both countries, and it can be argued that this is the very reason that prompted Chinese and Indian firms to seek new markets abroad.

Two other proposals, *inter alia*, are worth considering for our current purpose. First, the 'Developmental approach'[2] stresses the significance of experiential knowledge (Johanson and Vahlne, 1977; among others) and claims that learning about internationalization is a cumulative, path-dependent process in which each step abroad adds to the firm's knowledge. Hence, firms gradually have to overcome a 'psychic distance' covering a broad range of gaps, namely the geographical, cultural, linguistic, institutional or developmental aspects, between the home and the host country. Firms first invest in neighbouring or similar markets with low commitment before expanding to more remote places with larger engagement. Such an approach definitely tallies with the strategies of Hong Kong firms when they invest in Mainland China (extensive proximity), and, as far as cultural and ethnic links are concerned, it also true of both firms from Hong Kong and India when they invest in the United Kingdom. Yet, the 'Developmental approach' does not apply to firms from Mainland China insofar as in many instances they were 'born global': they made inroads into Europe, the United States, Latin America or Africa. So, it is no surprise that many of them often have a large cultural gap to fill before they can shore up their investments.

Second, the approach developed by S. Mathews (2006)[3] is also quite interesting for our case study. Widely acknowledged as the 'Linkage, Leverage, and Learning' framework, it accounts for the firms' accelerated internationalization that unrelenting globalization has caused in emerging countries. In such a pervasive context, the strategic goal of the 'latecomers' is to catch up with incumbent multinationals and move up to innovation as fast as possible. The underlying rationale is that a country or a firm arriving late on the industrial stage has the potential advantage to directly access advanced technologies and use them, sometimes faster and at a lower cost than the very firms that originally initiated the innovation. In some cases, the 'latecomer' can catch up with the lesser-advanced firms and switch from imitation to innovation. The critical dimension of such leverage is the development in the home country of the appropriate institutions that foster the catching-up process. Through 'Linkage', a 'latecomer' firm can tap into a larger pool of resources and thus absorb the technology and specific know-how. This ability to grasp more required resources from outside through relationships rather than from in-house mobilization is called 'Leverage'. By repeated sequences of 'Linkage' and 'Leverage', the firm can upgrade its capabilities – which is paramount to industrial 'Learning'.

9.1.2 Empirical evidence

First-hand evidence about the characteristics of Chinese and Indian affiliates in Europe – competitive advantages, motives and strategies – was drawn from a proprietary database. The dataset encompasses new investments (*Greenfield*, acquisitions or joint ventures) or further expansions; it includes more than 1,000 entities of significant importance controlled by Chinese and Indian companies.[4] The time period runs from early 1980 to 2007.[5] As a complement to the dataset, face-to-face interviews were conducted in some European countries during the second half of 2007.

9.1.3 The advantages at play

Overall, the advantages for firms when they invest or expand abroad can be firm-specific or stem from the home country environment. As far as Chinese and Indian investments are concerned, the path development followed by the home country and the derived industrial specificities are of utmost importance.

The main advantage for Chinese companies operating in Europe – and, to a lesser extent, for Indian companies too – lies in production process skills. This advantage does not stand alone as it is increasingly combined with the technological expertise and/or linkage with some of the specific activities that are expanding in the Asian companies' home markets.

Obviously, China and India are not trapped in low technological-intensive products or services. There is plenty of evidence that companies from both countries are rapidly climbing the technological ladder.[6] Thus, Chinese consumer electrical (Haier, Lenovo or BYD Co.[7]) and equipment telecommunication manufacturers (Huawei Technologies or ZTE) are already established in Europe. Similarly, Indian transport equipment manufacturers (Mahindra & Mahindra or Bharat Forge) have made sizeable investments. Last, Chinese and Indian companies can benefit from the particular activities that are expanding in their domestic markets. Chinese telecommunication equipment manufacturers are here a case in point since their growth was spurred by huge investments made at home in telecom infrastructure (mobile phone networks).

In addition to the advantages that are not ownership-specific, several Chinese and Indian companies also benefit from their proprietary assets. For the former it generally arises from the public nature of their status, while for the latter it is because they are family-controlled businesses.

Last, it can be noticed that international expansion is shaped by the strategic choices made by top management. As such, Chinese and Indian firms are very good at seizing opportunities and developing the 'dynamic capabilities' needed to integrate, build and reconfigure their internal and external skills so as to address a rapidly changing environment (Teece and Pisano, 1994).

9.1.4 The underlying motives

The Chinese and Indian firms entering Europe respond directly to the pressures felt both at home and in the host countries. An overcrowded and highly competitive market as well as strong government support are the main 'push' factors that drive these companies to increasingly operate abroad. At micro level, both countries' firms have capitalized on the competitive advantages prevailing at macro level.

In the case of China, companies benefit from an impressive array of government support measures (tax rebates, privilege loans, economic diplomacy...) and institutions (SASAC,[8] SAFE,[9] Chinese Academy of Science, and so on), not to mention the sovereign wealth funds that channel part of China's gargantuan forex reserves[10] into strategic investments. As for India, the National Association of Software and Service Company and the software technological parks created by the government played a key role in development of the IT sector.

Dunning (1993) provided a widely accepted typology including four types of motives for investing abroad, namely resource-seeking, market-seeking, efficiency-seeking or asset-seeking. Europe's developed countries, with their sophisticated economies, offer a more restrained set of worthwhile motives, and we intend to limit our analysis to the market-seeking and the created asset-seeking motives[11] because they largely predominate over the others, and also often simultaneously prevail.

9.1.4.1 Market-seeking motivations

Basically, most Chinese and Indian firms investing in Europe seek to improve their market access or to respond to market growth prospects. This is often manifest in the setting up of sales offices and distribution centres, regional headquarters or technical centres to back up their exports and get closer to European customers or even to circumvent antidumping measures (for television sets, for instance).

For the Chinese and Indian companies targeting the European area, market access is the primary motivation. For the Chinese, this includes product flexibility so that Chinese firms can meet the technical specifications or safety standards required and offer better after-sales services. They also serve as trade support thanks to their many sales units whose primary motivation is to facilitate and promote the influx of 'made in China' products into Europe.

Indian companies, particularly in such sectors as software and IT-enabled services and pharmaceuticals (generics) – which represent the lion's share of their sector distribution in Europe – are basically driven by market access. Indeed, they have to pursue (or get new) customers for niche markets and also provide their clients with technical support. Indian software companies have developed a specific 'business model' that combines local presence in overseas market – that is to say 90 per cent of their total annual revenues – with exports of software and related services from their home base.

Figures 9.1 and 9.2 illustrate the expansion of Chinese and Indian firms into Europe, taking 2002 as a yardstick.

Needless to say, the largest European countries mostly concerned are the United Kingdom, Germany, France and, to a lesser extent, Italy: together they have attracted about three-quarters of the total amount of Chinese and Indian investments since the 1990s. The relatively high level of investment in the Netherlands is a consequence of that country's sophisticated transport facilities (for example, Rotterdam Sea Port), its logistics system and a special VAT policy for distribution businesses.

9.1.4.2 Created asset-seeking motivations

These assets include management capabilities, technological know-how, marketing expertise and brand awareness. They rank second in the motivations of Chinese and Indian companies for coming to Europe, and they somewhat reflect those companies' ability to convert their competitive disadvantage (no brand, no fame, no efficient distribution networks or lack of organizational capabilities) into competitive advantages, and their wish to neutralize the incumbency advantages of the advanced multinationals (Filippov and Saebi, 2008).

Acquisitions are the main route to tap intangible assets, but organic expansion is also used to set up development centres and design institutes within/or close to technological clusters in recipient countries. Both modes of entry have their advantages and drawbacks. *Greenfield* investment and wholly owned subsidiaries allow for complete control on activities, but constitutes a slower route to be operational in a distant cognitive context or to product recognition by consumers. In contrast, acquisitions allow firms to rapidly tap specific assets, particularly intangible ones, but this also has its disadvantages as the foreign company has to run the acquired firm (liability, cultural gap). If some Chinese firms display a keen interest in setting up R&D activities in Europe, their subsidiaries are mostly 'observation outposts': basically, they bring back new sources of knowledge to the parent company.

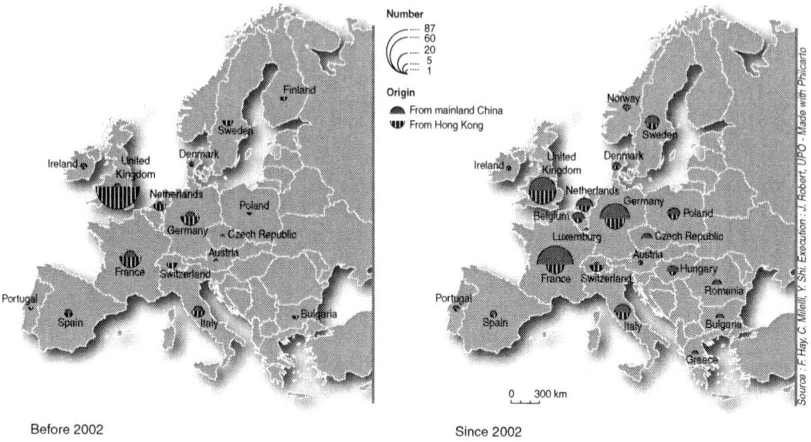

Figure 9.1 Chinese firms

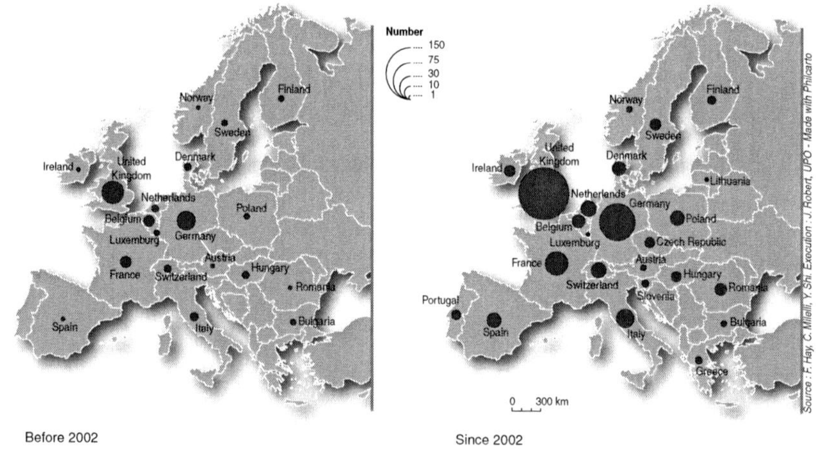

Figure 9.2 Indian firms

Indian firms also look for specific assets when they set up a company in Europe, but in the majority of cases this motivation is associated with market access motivations. For example, when Wipro Technologies made the decision to come to France, it chose scientific parks located in the southern (Biot) and western parts (Rennes) of the country, in order to get either the right connections and capture technological spillovers or to provide appropriate business services to large European companies.

9.1.5 The companies' strategies

The internationalization of firms usually follows the conventional pattern of setting up a new unit or of acquiring a domestic company. The available data on Chinese and Indian affiliates in Europe support this premise, with some nuances since Chinese companies have so far privileged *de novo* investments whereas Indian companies have relied more on acquisitions (Table 9.1). However, a convergence trend has emerged since 2007, with Chinese firms clinching to more acquisitions while their Indian counterparts engage in more *Greenfield* investments.

The main strategy followed by Chinese and Indian companies is based on the exploitation of distinctive assets, which combine firm-specific with home country advantages. It is well known that numerous Chinese companies have founded their competitive advantage on efficient production processes (Zeng and Williamson, 2007) whereas most Indian companies drew their strength from superior expertise in technology (IT and pharmaceuticals).

If the asset exploitation strategy is still prominent for both company types in Europe, the asset-augmenting strategy is emerging, and in many cases it goes hand in hand with the previous strategy. Indian companies somehow took the lead over Chinese companies but, over recent years, Chinese companies have also jumped on the bandwagon. When companies embark on such a strategy they target a wide range of created assets: technology, brands, distribution network, R&D facilities or managerial capabilities.

9.2 The impact of Chinese and Indian FDI on European economies

FDI in general affects host countries in a number of ways, through direct routes or indirect ones and through spillovers (UNCTAD, 2006). To begin with, the impact depends on the basic characteristics of Chinese and Indian investments, the institutional framework of each European recipient country – some differences undoubtedly still remain between close member countries within the EU area such as Germany and France – and the world economic environment.

Table 9.1 Form of entry into Europe for Chinese and Indian companies, 1965–2007 (percentage)

	Greenfield	Acquisition	Joint venture
China	61%	34%	5%
India	47%	51%	2%

Source: Authors' own calculations.

Indeed, Chinese and Indian FDI in Europe raises a basic question: can it really be compared to FDI of other origin, from the developed or Asian countries that had previously started venturing abroad?

Because of their huge, yet low-marketized domestic markets, and with their overseas drive occurring at a stage of lesser national development when compared with Western countries or Japan, China and India's FDI displays several characteristics that largely mirror these countries' own national path development.

Overall, the impact of FDI on recipient economies is not easy to gauge because direct and indirect effects often overlap, and consequences vary according to the period considered, the countries and the groups within each country: for instance, the interests of the producers are not the same as those of the consumers or of the workers. There is no way to specify a counterfactual and, as a result, to imagine what would happen if (a) foreign firm(s) had not invested in a particular country or region. Some new activities may well not have been created or would have disappeared, or domestic companies would have taken their place.

In order to clarify the issue and proceed, we adopted a qualitative approach derived from the framework by Kaplinsky and Messner (2008).[12] Interestingly, these authors have discriminated between the complementary impacts – generally viewed as positive or neutral – and the competitive impacts, as equivalent to damping effects.

We focus on some of the four economic aspects within the European economies that could be significantly impinged on by Chinese and Indian FDI: (1) FDI from other origin, (2) bilateral trade, (3) employment and qualifications, (4) and competition on product or service markets. The impacts on these four economic aspects are summarized in Tables 9.2 to 9.5 below.

9.2.1 The impact of Chinese and Indian investments on other FDI

Basically, FDI flows from China and India to Europe are to be viewed as a fresh source of investment, hence producing a complementary effect, but they can also compete with FDI from other countries, and therefore trigger a kind of crowding-out effect. For example, in low or mid-technological intensity sectors, Chinese or Indian companies on the eve of investing in Europe are in direct competition with companies from countries enjoying the same level of development, for example, Brazil or the Russian Federation.

Table 9.2 Impacts on other FDI

Impacts	On other FDI
Complementary	A fresh source of FDI for European economies
Competitive	Competition with FDI from other countries, particularly from developing countries

By way of illustration, India's Tata Steel was outbid by Brazil's Companhia Siderurgica Nacional when it made the decision to acquire the Anglo-Dutch steel producer Corus in 2006 and it had to pay a premium ($13 billion) to clinch the deal.

9.2.2 The impact on bilateral trade

International trade is the domain that would be most affected by FDI. Why? Two main reasons can be advanced.

In the first place, FDI is growingly intertwined with trade as a consequence of the fragmentation of manufacturing processes in several industries (Feenstra, 1998), and the development of transnational manufacturing networks (Gereffi, Humphrey and Sturgeon, 2005). In recent years, between one-third and one-half of overall worldwide trade in non-agricultural products has been internalized within multinational companies (Dunning, 2009).

In the second place, FDI could have detrimental side effects in the political arena. If India is not concerned because of its satisfactory trade balanced figure and low share of EU external merchandise trade (less than two per cent in 2007),[13] it is a different matter for China because of its gaping trade surplus and growing share of EU external merchandise trade.[14] Complementary effects result here from the numerous sales offices supporting the import of cheap consumer or intermediate goods from China.

This dynamic also unveiled a competitive dimension when, for example, Chinese companies on their way up the value ladder consequently displace European firms at the lower end in their effort to get direct contact with European consumers or venture into marketing activities. Esprit clothing or AS Watson (Hutchinson-Whampoa) perfumeries chains are recent examples. Indian software companies, particularly large ones (Tata Consultancy Services, Infosys or Wipro Technologies) have set up numerous offices and development centres across Europe and could therefore produce similar outcomes in the near future. Even Continental Europe and in particular France

Table 9.3 Impacts on bilateral trade

Impacts	On bilateral trade
Complementary	Cheap consumer goods and inputs (China) and services (India) Trade deficit decreases when production activities are created
Competitive	Chinese and Indian imports of goods or services potentially displace local producers, and increase the trade deficit particularly when sales subsidiaries are created Increasing influence of developing countries within multilateral organizations (WTO)

whose companies had resisted outsourcing IT services to Indian companies have changed their behaviour since 2007.

Furthermore, not only do Chinese exports increase the European bilateral trade deficit but they also contribute to strengthening the role of developing countries within multilateral organizations and, as a result, they alter the traditional geostrategic maps (Kaplinsky and Messner, 2008).

However, when Chinese firms create, acquire and maintain production activities in Europe the trade imbalance can be reduced (substitution effect): this is the case with the set-up of assembly lines for television sets in Europe.

9.2.3 The impact on employment and qualifications

It has to be said that employment (and unemployment) is a very sensitive issue in Europe. If Chinese and Indian affiliates generate extra jobs in some activities, they safeguard them in many cases too. Indeed, the entry into Europe and the development through fresh investments of Chinese telecom equipment manufacturers and maritime transport companies or of Indian software firms conspicuously contribute to the hiring of local employees. For example, Huawei Technologies has 2,000 employees in its European subsidiaries while COSCO has 800. They also create skilled jobs in R&D activities. As far as Chinese companies are concerned several examples can be advanced, such as ROSE (bio-industry) in Germany, Jac Anhui and Johnson Electric (automotive industry) in Italy, Huawei Technologies and ZTE (telecommunication equipment) in Sweden and France, or Hisense (television sets) in the Netherlands. Additionally, in Germany, many Chinese and Indian buyouts have allowed the sustaining or the survival of SMEs in the engineering and metal products sectors.

As expected, mergers and acquisitions affect the job toll with, in some cases, the relocation of manufacturing lines to the home country. That usually occurs with European production activities in low technological intensity sectors. As it is well acknowledged, Chinese firms produce at a lower cost on their home ground and reap benefits from the synergy between home assets and those of the acquired European firms (brand recognition or sales network). In some cases, the reverse prevails, with existing jobs being kept on or even extra jobs being created. The case of Nanjing Automobile, which first relocated its production of MG Rover cars to China before moving it back to the United Kingdom two years later, is worth mentioning, with the fame of the brand and the 'made in UK' label being of most importance for customers.

Similarly, some Indian investors also fare rather well in Europe. For example, the acquisition in 2005 of Imatra Kilsta,[15] a Swedish company, by Bharat Forge boosted the efficiency of the acquired European plants through process and management innovation, and expanded the parent company's market share.

Table 9.4 Impacts on employment and qualification

Impacts	**On employment and qualifications**
Complementary	Extra jobs created, existing jobs safeguarded Vacant niches occupied Some industries revived (Chinamex in the UK)
Competitive	Layoffs or displacement of employees resulting from plant closure or the relocation of manufacturing lines (Chinese companies mostly involved)

At times, Chinese firms maintain the acquired firm's European activity with the aim of duplicating it in China where the market is larger than in Europe and where it is critical to have a firm-specific advantage over domestic competitors. The case of China National BlueStar, through its French acquisitions, is a clear-cut illustration of this strategy. The investment made in Sweden by the Chinese electric utility company State Grid in the bio-energy industry is yet another example.

Overall, the results are contingent upon the individual country or region, sector or period of time. For example, France and Germany did not exhibit similar effects when confronted with the arrival of Chinese companies: activities are more often maintained in Germany than they are in France because in the former, the machinery and equipment industries encompass more activities around a highly competitive core.

9.2.4 The impact on competition in product or service markets

European firms increasingly compete in their home markets with Chinese and Indian affiliates. On the plus side, increased innovation along with rationalization programmes and consolidation might boost across-the-board efficiency in European companies, while on the minus side, it can lead to the relocation of manufacturing lines to the home country and thus cause layoffs that could severely affect deprived areas.

By setting up wholly owned subsidiaries, Chinese and Indian firms closely interact with consumers. In sectors such as telecom equipment, as mentioned previously, they can displace incumbent companies through aggressive strategies based on discount prices or particularly short lead time. The case in point here is the arrival of companies such as Huawei Technologies and ZTE whose behaviour is particularly disruptive for large European companies (Ericsson, Alcatel-Lucent, British Telecom, France Telecom and so on).

Indeed, Chinese and Indian firms are awesome competitors for European firms because they have many distinct advantages, such as low production costs, large domestic markets and valuable support from their governments. As already mentioned, they can combine the advantages of their home base with new investments made overseas. The Indian software companies that

Table 9.5 Impacts on competition in product or service markets

Impacts	On competition in product or service markets
Complementary	European firms are encouraged to innovate through more efficient manufacturing processes and to deliver new products
Competitive	New competitors for European firms (own advantage: low production costs, local support and large home market) Capacity to optimize the technology and know-how acquired or absorbed from Western companies, and to duplicate it in a more efficient way

have developed an original 'business model' in the United States attempt to duplicate it across Europe. This is based on a mix of onshore and offshore activities. The former are usually conducted on customer sites with Indian expatriates on short contracts (six to 12 months, owing to visa limits), while the latter are pursued in India to benefit from competitive labour costs and the fiscal advantages available more especially in 'special economic zones'.

In the case of Chinese companies, Zeng and Williamson (2007) have pointed out a 'business model' combining low prices, mass consumption, reduced margins and innovation. In their view these firms are formidable challengers for Western multinationals because they target the market segments within which those companies are potentially more vulnerable ('loose bricks').

9.3 Conclusion

Chinese and Indian firms in Europe display distinct characteristics which are to a large extent related to the development path followed by their respective home country. Chinese and Indian investments have both complementary and competitive effects on European economies. To date, these have been not too ominous for European firms, although they are often underestimated as Chinese and Indian investors are discreet and sometimes operate from a third country. For example, the purchase in 2007 by Aluminium Corp. of China (Chinalco) of a stake in the Anglo-Australian mining group Rio Tinto for $14.3 billion was channelled through a Singapore-based joint venture.

For the future, it is not easy to forecast the whole effects of the current global crisis on the investments made by (and to come from) Chinese and Indian firms across Europe. On the one hand, they will become more conspicuous because of their focus on domestic markets and the effort to diversify operations, while the investments will not be limited by real financial restraints and still benefit from their governments' incentives to invest abroad. On the other hand, Chinese and Indian firms will presumably seek to acquire strategic created assets at discount prices in developed economies. This is a particularly acute perspective for Chinese firms given China's large foreign exchange reserves and appropriate financial vehicles – 'sovereign wealth funds', public banks and financial institutions, or large state-owned enterprises – which ought to help Chinese companies get through the current economic crisis.

Notes

Françoise Hay is Associate Research Fellow, Centre de Recherche en Economie et en Management, CNRS and University of Rennes 1, France. Contact author: hay35@aliceadsl.fr

Christian Milelli is Research Fellow, EconomiX, CNRS and University of Paris Ouest Nanterre La Défense, France. Contact author: christian.milelli@u-paris10.fr

The authors are indebted to the French Ministry of the Economy, which has supported previous field research on the same topic. F. Hay, C. Milelli and Y. Shi (2008), *Présence et stratégies des firmes chinoises et indiennes en Europe: une perspective dynamique et comparative*. Paris: Ministère de l'Economie, des Finances et de l'Emploi.

1. By the end of 2007, India, Mainland China and SAR Hong Kong respectively held 0.2 per cent, 0.6 per cent, and 6.5 per cent of FDI world stocks (UNCTAD, 2008).
2. Also known as the 'Uppsala model'.
3. His argument is based on the classic concept of 'latecomer development' (Gerschenkron, 1962).
4. The cut-off was drawn at ten employees, and only the most important sales subsidiaries were selected.
5. There is evidence of Indian companies with affiliates abroad in the early 1960s (Pradhan, 2007).
6. It is reported that between 2005 and 2006 the number of patent filings worldwide by applicants from China increased by 32.1 per cent (UN/World Intellectual Property Organization). http://www.wipo.int/pressroom/en/articles/2008/article_0042.html, accessed November 4th, 2010.
7. In 2008, it was the world's third largest portable rechargeable battery producer.
8. For State Owned Assets Supervision and Administration Commission.
9. For State Administration of Foreign Exchange.
10. At the end of 2008 they reached US$ 2,000 billion.
11. Some Chinese and Indian 'resources-seeking' motives are punctually met in Europe: for instance, when State Grid created a large complex of bio-energy (thermal power) in Sweden or when Chinalco took stakes in the Anglo-Australian group Rio Tinto, or India's ONGC in Imperial Energy (UK). Also, as far as the efficiency-seeking reasons are concerned, we could evoke some investment-building production facilities in Eastern Europe by Chinese firms (Li Fan, Athletic Group), but this remains marginal.
12. This scheme intends to capture the different interactions (and resulting impacts) between the Chinese and Indian 'drivers' and the global economy in general, and it lays a special stress on some African countries.
13. The outcome is similar for services.
14. This trade soared from 7.5 per cent in 2000 to 16.2 per cent in 2007 (Eurostat). http://epp.eurostat.ec.europa.eu, accessed November 4th, 2010.
15. With, respectively, two plants in Sweden and Scotland.

References

Dunning, J. H. (1972), *Multinational Enterprises and the Global Economy*. Wokingham, UK: Addison-Wesley.

Dunning, J. H. (1977), 'Trade, Location of Economic Activity and the MNE: A Search for an Eclectic Approach', in B. Ohlin, P. Hesselborn and M. Wijkman (eds), *The International Allocation of Economic Activity*. New York: Holmes & Meier.

Dunning, J. H. (2009), 'Location and the Multinational Enterprise: A Neglected Factor?' *Journal of International Business Studies*, 40 (1), 5–19.

Dunning, J. H. and Narula, R. (1998), 'The Investment Development Path Revisited: Some Emerging Issues', in J. H. Dunning and R. Narula (eds), *Foreign Direct Investment and Governments: Catalysts for Economic Restructuring*. London: Routledge.

Feenstra, R. (1998), 'Integration of Trade and Disintegration of Production in the Global Economy', *Journal of Economic Perspectives*, 12 (4), 31–50.

Filippov, S. and Saebi, T. (2008), *Europeanization Strategy of Chinese Companies: Its Perils and Promises*, UNU-MERIT Working Paper No. 55, Maastricht.

Gereffi, G., Humphrey, J. and Sturgeon, T. (2005), 'The Governance of Global Value Chains', *Review of International Political Economy*, 12 (1), 78–104.

Gerschenkron, A. (1962), *Economic Backwardness in Historical Perspective*. Cambridge, MA: Belknap Press.

Hay, F., Milelli, C. and Shi, Y. (2008), *Présence et stratégies des firmes chinoises et indiennes en Europe: une perspective dynamique et comparative*. Paris: Ministère de l'Economie, des Finances et de l'Emploi.

Johanson, J. and Vahlne, J.-E. (1977), 'The Internationalisation Process of the Firm: A Model of Knowledge Development and Increasing Market Commitment', *Journal of International Business Studies*, 8, 23–32.

Kaplinsky, R. and Messner, D. (2008), 'The Impacts of Asian Drivers on the Developing World', *World Development*, 36 (2), 197–209.

Mathews, S. A. (2006), 'Dragon Multinationals: New Players in 21st Century Globalization', *Asia Pacific Journal of Management*, 23, 93–113.

Pradhan, J. P. (2007), *Growth of Indian Multinationals in the World Economy*, ISID Working Paper No. 04, New Delhi.

Teece, D. and Pisano, G. (1994), 'The Dynamic Capabilities of Firms: An Introduction', *Industrial and Corporate Change*, 3, 537–56.

UNCTAD (2006), *World Investment Report 2006*. Geneva: United Nations.

UNCTAD (2008), *World Investment Report 20-089*. Geneva: United Nations.

Zeng, M. and Williamson, P. J. (2007), *Dragons at our Door: How Chinese Cost Innovation is Disrupting Global Competition*. Cambridge, MA: Harvard Business School Press.

10
Chinese and Indian Multinationals in Denmark: Is There Anything Special About Them?

Jens Erik Torp, Michael W. Hansen, and Henrik Schaumburg-Müller

10.1 Introduction

Foreign direct investment (FDI) stock from developing countries has surged in recent decades, with a six-fold increase in the period 1990–2000, and a threefold increase between 2001 and 2008 (UNCTAD, 2006, 2009). Developing country FDI flows have increased from a level around US$ 30 billion in 1990–5 (annual average) to a level around $90 billion in 2000–5; and as a share of global FDI, FDI from these countries has doubled since the 1990s so that they by 2009 account for more than 20 per cent of global FDI (UNCTAD, 2010). The developing country investors are not merely small firms: 99 of the Fortune 500 companies are by 2009 from developing countries. The surge in developing country FDI is mainly derived from investment from Asian developing countries; in the early stages, Hong Kong, Singapore, Taiwan, and South Korea were leading, but more recently, India and China have become the leading Asian outward investors. This chapter will focus on the rise of Chinese and Indian investments.

Chinese and Indian MNCs are latecomers in the sense that they are late arrivals to the international economy, not really embarking on large-scale FDI before the 2000s. But then we saw a quite dramatic surge in investment from these countries: Chinese investments have grown from $5.5 billion in 2004 to almost $25 billion in 2007 and an estimated $40 billion in 2008 (UNCTAD, 2009). In spite of financial crises, it seems that Chinese investments continue to climb (Pietrobelli et al., 2009). The Chinese investments are concentrated in natural resource extraction and in manufacturing activities such as textiles and electronics. Chinese companies like Haier, Lenovo, Nanjing, and Huawei Technologies Co. are becoming household names. Many of the Chinese outward foreign direct investment (OFDI) are state owned enterprises (SOEs) or heavily supported by the Chinese state, for example, through the China Investment Corporation (CIC). The development in FDI from India is even more dramatic: where global FDI stock grew moderately in the period 2000–7, developing country stock increased 2½ times faster and Indian stock

16 times faster (Singh and Jain, 2009), although it should be noted that the Indian investment started from a very low base. Newcomer Indian firms are moving into IT, pharmaceuticals and services in developed countries, and hitherto protected Indian conglomerates such as Tata, Birla, and Reliance are diversifying into the knowledge industry and/or acquiring 'crown jewels' of European and US manufacturing (Pradhan, 2007).

While Indian and Chinese firms are large investors in other developing countries, the lion's share of their FDI is placed in developed countries. We have thus seen very large acquisitions in Europe and the US by companies including Tata (Jaguar, Corus Steel, Tetley), Mittal (Arcelor), Lenovo (IBM Thinkpad), and Tengzhong (Hummer), but also greenfield investments have been common, for example, with renewables and IT. The Asian investments in developed countries are puzzling in several ways, seen from an international business (IB) perspective. What, for instance, explains that FDI from these countries within a very short time span has risen from virtually nothing to becoming a significant phenomenon in global FDI? And how do these firms overcome the liability not only of being foreign but of coming from a developing country? And what will be the implications for incumbent MNCs of the arrival of Asian MNCs? Are these MNCs the vanguard of a new breed of MNCs that base their expansion on hard-to-imitate advantages deriving from their developing country home context or are they fairly conventional firms, basing their expansion on traditional competitive advantage? In this chapter we will discuss these and other puzzles and questions posed by the arrival of Asian MNCs in Western countries.

Empirically, the analysis will focus on the entry strategies of Indian and Chinese MNCs in Denmark. Denmark, a small, open, and highly affluent Western European economy, has in recent years seen the arrival of Chinese and Indian investors. While still modest, numerous Indian and Chinese companies have, within a very short time span, established subsidiaries in Denmark. In the chapter we will analyse the entry strategies of these firms, focusing on three key aspects of their entry strategies, namely 'Investment Motive', 'Entry Mode', and 'Organizational Strategy'. The analysis is based on detailed case studies of Asian investments in Denmark conducted in the autumn of 2009 as well as on general FDI data obtained from various databases.[1] While there are studies of Asian investments in large European countries,[2] this study is, to the best of our knowledge, unique in the sense that it focuses on Asian FDI in a small European host country.

10.2 Theory on developing country MNCs

In recent years, a substantial literature has evolved focusing on the rise of MNCs from developing countries (see, for example, Hobday, 1995; Mathews, 2006; Ramamurti and Singh, 2008; Tolentino, 2008). This literature refers back to and extends an earlier literature on MNCs from developing countries—the so-called

Third World Multinational literature (Lall, 1983; Wells, 1983)—that emerged in the early 1980s to explain the then surge in FDI from developing countries. Also more conventional IB theories such as those of the Product Cycle (Vernon, 1966), the Uppsala model (Johanson and Vahlne, 1977) and the Investment Development Path (Dunning and Narula, 1996) have been invoked to explain the rise of developing country firms (Beausang, 2003). A heated debate has taken place in recent years in academic journals as to the importance and explanations of developing country MNCs (see, for example, Dunning et al., 2008; Mathews, 2006; Narula, 2006). In this regard, we can identify two generic perspectives on developing country multinational corporations (DCMNCs). One perspective is the conventional perspective. According to this perspective, DCMNCS are MNCs like any other MNCs, subject to the same dynamics and subject to the same explanations as Western MNCs. Contrast this perspective to what we will label 'the latecomer perspective'. According to this perspective, DCMNCs are a new breed of firms, adopting internationalization paths that defy conventional FDI theory.

10.2.1 The conventional perspective

From the conventional FDI perspective, FDI from developing countries is akin to any kind of FDI (Giddy and Young, 1982; Lecraw, 1993). MNEs internalize to exploit their firm-specific advantages in locations where factor cost and demand conditions make it profitable to do so. From a conventional FDI theory perspective, we would expect little FDI from developing countries as firms from such locations would lack the resources, experience, capital, and technology that normally explain why and how MNCs embark on FDI. If FDI would take place, it would mainly be directed towards other developing countries, partly to exploit advantages in business models and technologies adapted to developing country factor and consumer market conditions (Lall, 1983; Wells, 1983), and partly to maintain a cost advantage that is eroding in the home market due to economic growth and development (Dunning and Narula, 1996).

To the extent that DCMNCs invest in developed countries, it would be explained with generic types of advantage such as privileged access to capital or low cost bases. For instance, Rugman and Li (2007) make a distinction between 'firm-specific advantages' (FSAs) and 'country-specific advantages' (CSAs).[3] They argue that OFDI from developing countries is mainly based on CSAs such as natural resources, cheap capital, and low labour costs, whereas Western MNCs mainly base their FDI on FSAs such as propriety technology, strong organizational capabilities, or unique capabilities to manage complex network organizations across borders. Only rarely will DCMNCs possess genuine FSAs, and such cases will generally be treated as outliers. Moreover, as DCMNCs have not been able to develop the complex networked and functionally concentrated global organizations that characterize Western MNCs, these firms will have great problems integrating and benefitting from their acquisitions.

Another interpretation of DCMNCs is offered by the Investment Development Path (IDP) theory (Dunning, 1981; Dunning and Narula, 1996, 2004). This theory can be seen as an attempt to build a specific theory of the relationship between the development level of a given country and FDI. The idea is that FDI patterns interact with locational factors in a dynamic fashion. The model makes a distinction between five stages of economic development, going from least developed countries to advanced countries, which each will produce a particular inward and outward FDI pattern. In regard to DCMNCs, the theory predicts that only when developing countries have built a domestic industry with its own ownership-specific advantages, will we see FDI, mainly in other developing countries. When FDI takes place from developing countries to developed countries it will mainly be aimed at acquiring complementary technology and brands (Dunning and Narula, 1996).

The IDP's macro level sequential FDI perspective is mirrored at the micro (firm) level by the so-called Uppsala model. This model focused on the sociology of firm internationalization and argued that firms appear to be internationalizing in a staged manner, starting from a strong home market position, investing first in nearby countries, then moving into increasingly distant locations and committing growing resources as they gain more and more internationalization experience (Johanson and Vahlne, 1977). Originally developed on the basis of studies on Scandinavian firms, this line of thinking has recently been applied to developing country firm internationalization (see, for example, Kuada, 2004 or Beausang, 2003). Here the argument is that developing country firms would initially invest in nearby developing markets and only with a low commitment. Only gradually would these firms build the experience and resources needed to take on culturally and technologically 'distant' Western markets and when doing that, only in an incremental manner.

A final conventional view of DCMNCs is based in Vernon's (1966) classical product-cycle theory of FDI. According to this theory, developing countries will start becoming outward investors as technologies and production travel from advanced to increasingly less advanced countries through imitation and diffusion. From this perspective, we can expect DCMNC investments in developed countries to exploit an advantage obtained in technological sunset industries, where the West no longer has any interest or production. This could, for instance, be labour- or natural resource-intensive types of industries, roughly what Ramamurti (2009) calls 'mature mid technologies.'

10.2.2 The latecomer perspective

Spurred by the surge in FDI from developing countries in the 1990s and 2000s, and echoing Gerschenkron's (1962) notion of 'latecomer' advantage of 'backwardness', a literature has recently evolved, trying to explain why growing numbers of firms from developing countries are successful in competing with Western firms in their own markets, in spite of, or maybe because of their latecomer status. This literature argues that, in light of the rapidly growing presence of DCMNEs in global industries, we need to revisit and revise our theoretical tools and conceptions of FDI (Hobday, 1997; Ernst, 2000; Mathews, 2006; Li, 2007). Where previous theories of FDI focused on transaction costs and oligopolistic competition, the latecomer theories are rooted in resource- and knowledge-based theory (Barney, 1991; Grant, Almeida, and Song, 2000), network theory (Anderson et al., 1997), theories of learning (Kuada, 2004), and dynamic capabilities theory (Teece, 2000). Where conventional theories tend to view firm internationalization in isolation of the development level of the home country context, the latecomer literature explicitly relates to the influence of the home country context (Ramamurti, 2008). And where conventional theory would predict DCMNCs to internationalize in a staged and incremental manner, latecomer theory draws heavily on 'born global' theory and its notion of accelerated internationalization paths (Oviatt and McDougall, 1994.)

Four aspects of latecomer firms in particular are emphasized by this literature: (1) their ability to access complementary assets through internationalization; (2) their ability to undertake organizational and strategic innovation; (3) their ability to combine advanced technology with a low cost base; and (4) as a consequence of the above, their ability to embark on accelerated paths of internationalization that defy the gradualist patterns of earlier internationalization incidents. They possess a number of advantages emanating from their developing country context, including flexibility, low overheads, cost effectiveness, and network-based business models (Buckley, Wang, and Clegg, 2007). Several authors stress the advantages related to the low cost base, however not as a generic advantage (a CSA), but as a firm-specific advantage (FSA) that it is very difficult for Western MNCs to copy (Buckley, Wang, and Clegg, 2007; Ramamurti, 2008; Ramamurti and Singh, 2008). Latecomer firms are not constrained by Western management orthodoxies and are therefore positioned, much more effectively than incumbents, to take in new ideas and innovations. Just like their Japanese predecessors, which introduced JIT and flexible production two decades before, these firms bring in strategic and organizational innovations. Where they have gaps in their knowledge base, they are effective in closing these gaps, what Mathews (2006) calls 'linkage', 'leverage', and 'learning'. Thus, even if their initial capabilities may be weak, globalization offers ample opportunities to acquire complementary capabilities, for example, through acquisitions of Western firms (Buckley, 2009), through learning by linking up to foreign MNCs in global value chains (Gereffi et al., 2001; Buckley, 2009) or by acquiring assets in the market (Teece, 2000).

10.2.3 Analytical framework

In this chapter we will discuss whether the entry strategies of the Asian investors in Denmark are more in line with the latecomer or the

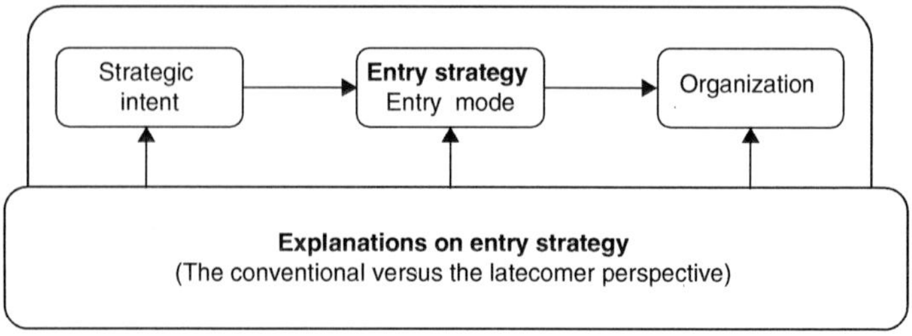

Figure 10.1 Entry strategy

conventional perspective. Entry strategy is about the strategic intent, mode, and organization of the entry into a foreign market (Meyer, 2002; Lasserre, 2007). Strategic intent or what is labelled 'investment motive' in the IB literature is typically of four types: resource-seeking, market-seeking, efficiency-seeking, or strategic asset-seeking. Entry mode can either concern ownership configuration of the investment (100 per cent ownership versus joint venture), or the way in which assets are deployed (greenfield or acquisition). The organization dimension concerns the way in which the investor organizes and integrates the investment in its global value chain and strategy (Figure 10.1).

10.3 The entry strategies of Chinese and Indian MNCs in Denmark

In the following, we will provide a profile of Indian and Chinese investments in Denmark and describe the entry strategies of Indian and Chinese MNCs in Denmark. This will be based on four sources of data: FDI flow and stock data from the Danish National Bank; lists of individual investments in Denmark from embassies; information from the Danish business press; and interviews with representatives of the more important Indian and Chinese investors in Denmark. The analysis encompasses the entire population of Indian and Chinese investments in Denmark. Five detailed case studies of some of the most proliferated and largest of those investments are provided.

10.3.1 Chinese and Indian FDI in Denmark

It is only from around the year 2000 that we can see an FDI inflow of some size from China and India to Denmark. Throughout that period the Chinese stock of FDI in Denmark has constantly been six to eight times higher than the stock of Indian FDI, as can be seen from Table 10.1.

It is clear that the stock of investments has grown since 2000 but for the investments from India the amounts are still very small. In particular

Table 10.1 Stock of foreign direct investment in Denmark (billion DKK)

	2000	2005	2006	2007	2008
Total Danish inward stock	359.0	580.0	630.0	688.0	693.0
Inward stock from China	0.1	1.5	2.3	2.5	3.0
Inward stock from India	0.0	0.2	0.3	0.3	0.3
Inward stock from India+China	0.1	1.7	2.6	2.8	3.3
India+China inward stock share of total Danish inward stock	*0.03%*	*0.29%*	*0.41%*	*0.41%*	*0.48%*

Source: Denmark National Bank statistics.

during the first half of the first decade of the 2000s we also see a fast relative increase in the share of investments coming from China and India compared to investments from the rest of the non-OECD countries. But the share in recent years has seemed to stagnate. Likewise, the share of India and China in the total FDI stock in Denmark has grown but the share remains very small (only 0.5 per cent) and again is growing only very slowly. The modest magnitude of Asian FDI in Denmark is confirmed by a recent survey of employment effect in Denmark (Danmarks Statistik, 2009). Overall, the employment share of investments from all BRIC countries compared to all foreign investments in Denmark is less than 1 percentage point; this is much lower than in Sweden and the Netherlands where the BRIC countries appear to be more active investors.

10.3.2 Chinese and Indian subsidiaries in Denmark

While the investment amounts have been quite different for FDIs from China and India, the number of firms in Denmark with Indian and Chinese ownership has been more similar, at around 17–18 for each country. This of course implies that average Chinese investments have been much higher than the average investment by Indian companies and also in terms of distribution on industries and investment motives there are important differences between the two portfolios.

The Chinese portfolio comprises by the end of 2009 of 18 companies broadly distributed within manufacturing (electronics, automotive and engineering), transport companies, IT software, trade and other services. (Table 10.2). The two subsidiaries from the electronics industry represent large global Chinese-owned companies: Lenovo, producing PCs and laptops based on IBM technology and owned by the Chinese Legend Holding Company, and Huawei Technologies, producing telecommunication equipment and software services. Both affiliates in Denmark are marketing and sales offices. The BYD Denmark affiliate in the automotive industry is also a sales subsidiary, established in Denmark to test the market for BYD's electric and hybrid electric auto models. This case is further

Table 10.2 Chinese firms in Denmark

Name of investor company	Name of company in Denmark	Sector	Business activity in Denmark
Air China	Air China	Airline industry	Sales office
Air China Cargo Co. Ltd	Air China Cargo Denmark	Logistics	Services
BYD	BYD Denmark ApS	Automotive industry	Sales office
Envision Energy	Envision Energy Denmark ApS	Renewable power industry	R&D
Huawei Technologies Co.	Huawei Technologies Denmark ApS	Telecom industry	Sales office
Lenovo	Lenovo Danmark ApS	IT hardware	Sales office
COSCO Group	Penta Shipping A/S	Shipping	Services
Zhejiang New Jialian Electronics Co.	NJL Acoustics ApS	Electronics	R&D
Dragon Power Co. Ltd	DP CleanTech Europe A/S	Bioenergy	Manufacturing and services
Bright Star Fireworks	Bright Star Fireworks Import A/S	Fireworks	Import
Shanghai ChemPartner Co. Ltd	ChemPartner Europe	Pharmaceutical and biotech	Contract research (European HQ)
China International Marine Containers Group Ltd (CIMC)	Holvrieka Danmark A/S	Manufacturing of stainless steel tanks/containers	Manufacturing and services
Guangdong Ming Yang Wind Power Industry Group Co. Ltd	Ming Yang Wind Power European R&D Centre ApS	N/A	N/A
China International Travel Service (CITS)	CITS Travel Denmark A/S	Tourism/travel	Sales & services
BMC SYS China	Dancom IT solutions ApS	IT software & solutions	Sales & services
Shanghai Worldbest Investment Development Group Co. Ltd.	Everbest ApS	Textiles	N/A
Brothers Pyrotechnics Inc.	LCH Fireworks A/S	Fireworks	Import
NCO China Consult	NCO China Consult ApS	Consulting	Sales & services

analysed below. The two engineering companies are Envision Energy in the wind-energy industry, and Zhejiang New Jialian in the acoustics component industry, which have recently established subsidiaries in Denmark, not for sales reasons, but to develop R&D units in Denmark. Envision is established in Silkeborg, a provincial town in the Danish windmill cluster close to the Danish leading global company, Vestas. Ming Yang Wind Power European R&D Centre, a private limited company (ApS), is also linked to R&D in the Danish windmill industry. The Zhejiang New Jialian affiliate is located in the Copenhagen region where the leading Danish hearing-aid companies are located. Both had considered locating in Germany, where they had major customers but chose Denmark to tap into the Danish R&D base. ChemPartner Europe is a newly established subsidiary locating its European office in Denmark to undertake contractual preclinical R&D. Finally, we have two transport firms located in Denmark. The Penta Shipping company is a joint venture in the shipping business, having its Scandinavian sales office in Denmark. This case is further detailed below. And the large Chinese airline company Air China has a sales office in Copenhagen. Both these transport investors have only needed limited financial investment for their establishments in Denmark, and their contribution to Chinese investment in Denmark is therefore very modest. Generally, investments in trade and services appear to be small, and in some cases it has not been possible to trace information on company activities.

The number of Indian establishments in Denmark was 17 by the end of 2009 (see Table 10.3). However, this number is fluctuating and it is hard at a given time to identify precisely how many operate and have invested in Denmark. Many Indian IT and pharmaceutical companies had concrete investment plans in the mid-2000s; before the financial crises, the Indian branch of the Danish investment promotion agency 'Invest in Denmark' expected 10 to 15 Indian high tech companies in telecommunication, energy, and biotechnology to arrive in Denmark. Twelve out of the 17 Indian companies are IT software companies. They have arrived as a result of the outsourcing and off shoring drive, where the main motive has been to capture clients. Seen from an Indian company perspective, the European market was interesting to balance dependency on the Asian and North American markets. To be convincing as suppliers, Indian software firms had to be close to the new clients either going into alliances with Danish providers or establishing their own offices in Denmark. A representative office also facilitated the tasks, where the Indian company brought their staff to work at the site of the clients in Denmark. The larger Indian IT companies like Tata Consultancy Services, Infosys, ITC Infotech, and Larsen & Toubro established themselves in this way. Satyam, which was smaller and came later than the other companies, went into an alliance with the Danish IT company KMD. It targeted smaller Danish clients, who could see an interest in outsourcing specific IT tasks, being too small to build up their own IT organization. Since

Table 10.3 Indian companies in Denmark

Name of investor company	Name of company in Denmark	Sector	Business activity in Denmark
Air-India	Air-India	Airline industry	Sales office
Four Soft	Four Soft Nordic A/S	Logistics software	Sales office
Infosys	Infosys Technologies Limited	Software services	Sales office
ITC Infotech India Limited	ITC Infotech Denmark	IT services & solutions	Sales & services
Larsen & Toubro Limited (L&T)	Larsen & Toubro Infotech Denmark	Software services	Sales office
Polaris Software Lab.	Polaris Software Lab. Ltd.	IT services & consulting	Regional manager
Reliance Industries Limited	Trevira Neckelmann A/S	Petrochemical products	Production subsidiary
Suzlon Energy	Suzlon Wind Energy A/S	Renewable Power industry	Regional HQ & R&D
Tata Group	Tata Consultancy Services Denmark Ltd.	IT services & consulting	Regional office
Cognizant Technologies	Cognizant Technologies	IT services & consulting	Sales office
Mahindra Tech	Mahindra Satyam	IT services & consulting	Sales office
Hikal Ltd	Hikal Marsing Pharma	Pharmaceutical	Marketing & distribution
Polaris Software Lab Ltd	Polaris Software	IT services & consulting	Sales & services
Infinite Computer Solutions	Infinite Computer Solutions	IT services & consulting	N/A
Tooltech Solutions	Tooltech Denmark	Engineering services	Manufacturing, sales & services
Wipro Technologies	Wipro Technologies	IT services & consulting	N/A
Lister Technologies	Lister Technologies	Software services	Sales & services

its entry, Satyam has been acquired by the Mahindra Group. Yet another entry model has been to acquire a Danish company which is what the Four Soft company did. This case is further studied below.

Indian biotech firms have also been interested in locating in Denmark, and in particular in the Oeresund medicon valley cluster. An example is the Indian firm Hikal, which has acquired a majority stake in the Danish pharmaceutical trading company Marsing, which essentially trades in active ingredients for the pharmaceutical industry. This allowed Hikal to find a European outlet for its generic drugs. In 2004 the up-start Indian biotechnology firm Avesthagen from Bangalore announced the opening of Avesta Nordic Research office in Copenhagen in a strategic joint venture with the Danish Centre for Clinical & Basic Research (CCBR). This also led to the establishment of a joint venture company in India together with the Danish Industrialization Fund for Developing Countries (IFU). The motive for Avesthagen was for its office in Copenhagen to attract Nordic partners to move outsourcing activities to its facilities in India. However, the office in Copenhagen and the joint venture in India with CCBR closed down in 2007.

Two Indian companies outside the software industry have been established in Denmark: Suzlon Energy in the wind energy industry and the large Indian conglomerate Reliance Industries Limited from Mumbai. Both companies had a strategy to use their establishment in Denmark to source knowledge, and the cases are elaborated below.

10.4 Case studies of Chinese and Indian investments in Denmark

In the following we will provide five detailed case studies of significant Indian and Chinese investments in Denmark. The case companies are Four Soft, an Indian IT company; Cosco, a Chinese shipping giant; Suzlon, an Indian wind turbine producer; BYD, a Chinese battery manufacturer; and Reliance, an Indian conglomerate that has invested in textile production. The case study firms have been selected because they represent a variety of different types of Asian MNCs both in terms of sector and strategic intent, and because they all represent significant and well-publicized investments.

10.4.1 Four Soft[4]

Based on a business platform to provide IT solutions for international transportation and logistics through the development of systems, services, and consultancies, a Danish company named Transaxiom Holding A/S was formed in 1992 with the Danish founder as sole owner. The company managed soon after its foundation to attract internationally well-known companies, such as DHL, TNT, Maersk Logistics, and Blue Water Shipping as clients. In order to enlarge its market further the company found it useful to complement its headquarters located in Denmark with a number of subsidiaries, notably in the US, Australia, and the UK.

Concomitantly with the formation of Transaxiom other newly established companies with a similar platform merged internationally. Hence in the year 2000, an Indian company named Four Soft Ltd was formed by an Indian businessman, who as a former senior employee of United Parcel Service America (UPS) had observed a need for mainframe Enterprise Resource Planning systems. Based on an equity capital equivalent to DKK 140 million, the founder provided DKK 40 million of the equity capital himself, while the remaining DKK 100 million was raised on the National Stock Exchange India and on the Bombay Stock Exchange. The increasing number of entrants to the business area of IT systems for international transportation and logistics during the 1990s led unavoidably to a process of mergers and acquisitions within the industry, and as part of this wider process Four Soft undertook an acquisition of Transaxiom Holding, in January 2007.

10.4.1.1 Strategic intent

During the first years of its existence, Four Soft based its growth strategy on acquisition of companies with technological know-how and a presence in geographical areas perceived to represent new business opportunities for Four Soft's products. Transaxiom became an important target for a Four Soft acquisition, since Transaxiom had developed one of the IT systems most widely used within the industry, had obtained a global market share of more than 50 per cent for some products, and possessed what Four Soft considered to be strategically important subsidiaries. For the Danish owner of Transaxiom the opportunity to sell his company to Four Soft in 2006 came at an opportune moment since it would permit the owner to cash in on his investment and put an end to continuous financial insecurity. In line with its growth strategy, in parallel with the acquisition of Transaxiom Four Soft also acquired some of Transaxiom's competitors in Holland and the UK, thereby providing Four Soft with a globally dominant position for some segments within the industry and a notable presence in others.

10.4.1.2 Entry mode and organization

The acquisition agreement stipulated that Four Soft became the owner of 95 per cent of the shares in Transaxiom Holding, while the former Danish owner became a minority shareholder and retained 5 per cent of the shares. Following the acquisition Transaxiom's name was changed to Four Soft Nordic, which continued as the owner of Transaxiom's subsidiaries in USA, and Australia respectively, which hence became Four Soft Group companies. Following the acquisition the former Danish owner became a member of Four Soft Nordic's Supervisory Board and maintained an important role in the day-to day management of Four Soft Nordic as Vice President. However, contrary to initial expectations that the acquisition would benefit from synergy between the

Indian HQ and the Danish subsidiary, serious difficulties in the day-to-day cooperation between these two parts of the Four Soft's organization soon emerged and prevented such synergies materializing. Apparently some of the contradictions were based on a mutual lack of understanding of the respective business cultures in the Indian HQ and in the Danish subsidiary.

Having implemented its initial growth strategy, Four Soft is at present in the process of adjusting its consolidation strategy with emphasis on technological development and market-seeking based on in-house know-how. As part of this new strategy and in order to make better use of the assets of Four Soft Nordic, the Danish subsidiary has begun to send groups of up to 15 engineers for longer stays at Four Soft HQ, in order to develop new products. The global R&D centre for Internet-based solutions will be consolidated in India, whereas the older mainframe technology will be based in Denmark. In a similar intention to capitalize on sales and marketing competencies in Denmark, the Four Soft HQ has begun sending some of its key commercial staff to stay at Four Soft Nordic's offices in Denmark for longer periods so that they can learn about Western sales and marketing practices. And in order to achieve Four Soft Group's ambitious goal of tripling its turnover in three years, the five most important group subsidiaries, which include Four Soft Nordic, have adopted a common strategy of undertaking acquisitions within their market segment and geographic area.

10.4.1.3 Status

From Four Soft's Annual Report for 2008–9, it appears that Europe is the major contributor to company revenues and profits, and Four Soft Nordic generated more than 50 per cent of the turnover. Four Soft Nordic itself generated yearly revenue of DKK 44.87 million, with a net profit of DKK 9.2 million, which is approximately 5 per cent above the results from its first year as a group company in 2007–8, and indications were that turnover in 2009–10 would lead to a further 20 per cent growth. Nearly three years after the acquisition, Four Soft Nordic has still been able to maintain most of Transaxiom's key costumers to the degree that some clients, including DHL, in some areas have all of their logistics and freight transport IT systems developed by Four Soft Nordic, while some other previously important clients, such as Maersk, have developed their own logistics division and hence have become less important customers.

10.4.2 Cosco and Penta Shipping[5]

Chinese shipping firms are among the world leaders. As the markets for Chinese manufacturing are in Europe, Chinese shipping firms also need to be present. The development of the Chinese shipping industry directly results from dedicated investment by Chinese authorities in the 1980s and 1990s to develop China's maritime sector (Hay, Milelli, and Shi, 2008). Among the largest Chinese shipping companies are the China Ocean

Shipping Company, Cosco. Cosco is a Chinese state-owned shipping company group, which in 2009 included more than 1,200 companies and 80,000 employees worldwide. In 2008, Cosco was listed at the Hong Kong Stock Exchange. In 1996, Cosco acquired a majority share in the Danish shipping company Penta Shipping.

10.4.2.1 Strategic intent

In order to undertake business activities within container shipping and related transport services and with a focus on business opportunities in China, a group of Danish partners founded the company Penta Shipping in September 1985. Soon after its establishment Penta Shipping opened a sales office in Beijing and entered into an agency agreement for Scandinavia with Cosco. In 1996, Penta Shipping became a joint venture company between Cosco Europe, a German subsidiary of Cosco's Container Lines Company and the Danish partners in Penta Shipping. For Cosco it was important to be present in Scandinavia either through an agent or a sales subsidiary, since Scandinavia represents an important and stable 'out of port' market for container shipping, which could provide Cosco with container cargo for its vessels in the ports of Hamburg and Rotterdam. Penta Shipping, on the other hand, needed a partner company that could provide financial muscle during downturns of markets and secure stability in its business activities.

10.4.2.2 Entry mode and organization

In the ensuing joint venture, Cosco holds 75 per cent of the JV company shares and the Danish partners 25 per cent. In general, Cosco prefers to enter into JV companies with its successful agents and not fully owned subsidiaries, since Cosco finds that the JV mode provides a better possibility for becoming acquainted with JV partner countries' business culture. When Cosco enters into a JV company such as Penta Shipping it also prefers that its JV partner's management maintains a commercial incentive to develop the business and not hold positions as company employees with a fixed salary. From a Danish JV partner perspective the JV has assured financial back-up during difficult market periods in 2002–3 and 2008–9, better job security for company employees, and an interested potential buyer of company shares held by Danish partners who might want to leave the company, as happened when a Danish partner left the company and an initial 50–50 per cent division of company shares was changed to the present 75–25 per cent.

Penta Shipping refers to the European HQ of Cosco Container Lines in Hamburg for day-to-day decisions, to Cosco Container Lines Company HQ in Shanghai for major decisions within the container shipping business area, and to Cosco Group HQ in Beijing for strategic decisions. However, there is widespread decentralization of decision-making to the Danish subsidiary. One of the main synergies from acquiring Penta Shipping has been that it could benefit from its competences concerning container management to development new business areas with project logistics for larger projects. Penta has two managing directors, one of them an experienced Chinese manager from Cosco China, who is responsible for relations with the Chinese parent company, and the other a Danish partner who is responsible for company relations in Denmark.

10.4.2.3 Status

Since its foundation, Penta Shipping has developed into a group company with approximately 50 employees and three offices in Denmark, Gothenburg (Sweden), and in Oslo (Norway). The volume of Penta Shipping's container shipping has increased from an annual 3,000–4,000 teus[6] before the formation of the JV to a present level of an annual 100,000 teus, which means that Penta Shipping now ranks among the four top container shipping companies in Scandinavia. A new promising business area of project logistics for larger projects has been taken up by Penta Shipping, while a previous business area of air freight was abandoned a few years after the formation of the JV.

10.4.3 Suzlon[7]

Based on a business platform to develop wind turbines, manufacture all key components, install, and undertake maintenance of windmills, an Indian wind power energy company named Suzlon Energy Ltd has become a major player within the global windmill industry. However, for a number of years up to 80 per cent of its revenues were derived from the Indian home market. The company therefore had an interest and a need to internationalize its activities in order to promote further growth. Since Suzlon India neither had experience nor in-house competence to undertake such an effort, it undertook a screening of suitable modes of creating a platform in Denmark, which has a reputation and strong position within the wind energy industry. Hence in August 2004, Suzlon India undertook a greenfield investment in Denmark in order to establish its international business headquarters, named Suzlon Energy A/S, with the mandate to develop and manage an expansion of Suzlon's activities outside India. Subsequently during the course of 2004 and 2005, Suzlon India undertook a further greenfield investment in Denmark in order to set up its European business headquarters, named Suzlon Wind Energy A/S, and located together with the international business HQ. By November 2005, Suzlon India's investments in the two new international business headquarters reached DKK 142,213,700, equivalent to US$ 24 million. Further, in 2009, Suzlon India undertook an additional investment project creating 30 jobs in a new R&D centre for new technologies, which is located at the vicinity of the two international business headquarters.

10.4.3.1 Strategic intent

The choice of Denmark as the hub for Suzlon's international expansion was based on several considerations: many years of experience with wind turbine technology on the manufacturing and supplier side; the extensive research carried out at Danish universities; and management competences within wind engineering, project execution, operations, financial engineering, service, and maintenance. Denmark has gained a leading position within the wind turbine industry, which Suzlon wished to tap into. Furthermore, Denmark allegedly has Europe's most flexible labour market, which allows companies to operate all 365 days of the year and to lay off redundant staff relatively easy. When the two major Danish wind power companies, Vestas and Micon, merged in 2004, and ran into problems as a consequence, Suzlon saw an opportunity to enter the Danish wind turbine cluster. Thus, several senior employees with long experience within the industry were inclined to leave the newly merged company and therefore responded positively when approached by Suzlon India with the suggestion that they form the core staff of a Suzlon subsidiary company in Denmark. Hence, based on a greenfield investment, Suzlon's international business HQ was formed and located in Denmark's second largest city, Aarhus. In accordance with its mandate, Suzlon Energy A/S established a number of sales business centres in USA, Australia, and China as greenfield investments. Likewise, Suzlon Wind Energy A/S opened a number of sales business centres in Europe with a total of 365 employees.

10.4.3.2 Entry mode and organization

Suzlon's investments in Denmark are all greenfield investments. Suzlon Energy A/S and Suzlon Wind Energy A/S have a high degree of autonomy within their mandate. There are normally four to five staff members from Suzlon India stationed at the Danish HQ in Aarhus in order to be acquainted with Western business methods and organization principles. Allegedly, this type of stay has proved to be useful in defusing emerging conflicts between Suzlon India and the two Danish business HQs. There is no Danish staff members stationed permanently in Suzlon India, but obviously shorter visits to India in order to discuss the company's business strategy do often occur. The Danish operations perform global and regional mandates for Suzlon in sales and marketing and R&D.

10.4.3.3 Status

The location of Suzlon's business HQ in Denmark has proven by and large to offer the anticipated advantages but has also encountered some unexpected difficulties. On the one hand, among the positive factors the proximity of Aarhus to the northern part of Europe has made it relatively easy to identify Northern European companies in which Suzlon could either be interested to enter into closer co-operation or target as objects for acquisition. It has also proven useful for Suzlon to initiate cooperation with two Danish technological universities in order for them to include in their curricula research and teaching regarding wind turbine technology, hence forming a new generation of engineers with acquired competence within the area. Another perceived advantage of a location in Denmark has also proven to be fulfilled by Suzlon's ability to outsource research on new technology to a number of Danish technological institutes and technical universities on a consultancy contract basis. Another advantage of the Danish location is related to the financial crises: the present economic crisis has led to a situation in which some clients have difficulties in honouring their contractual payments. In this regard the location in Denmark has given Suzlon access to the Danish export credit guarantee system, which guarantees payments to Suzlon in case clients do not undertake payments.

On the other hand, an unforeseen difficulty has been detected in an alleged tendency by some Danish authorities to discriminate against Suzlon as an international company and not a genuinely Danish-rooted company. An example given relates to the common interest of Suzlon and its major Danish competitor Vestas to test turbine technology for sea windmills along the coast of Denmark. Allegedly, Vestas received permission to undertake such tests in Danish waters, while Suzlon's request was declined and left the company with a need to undertake such tests in Spain, where its request for permission to undertake the tests was readily accepted.

10.4.4 BYD[8]

Founded in 1995, the Chinese company BYD (Build Your Dreams) became the world's second largest battery company in 2002, producing 65 per cent of the global rechargeable nickel-cadmium batteries and 30 per cent of the lithium-ion mobile phone batteries. After creating the affiliate BYD Auto in 2003, this Hong Kong Exchange-listed company started its production of conventional gasoline cars through the acquisition of a bankrupt state-owned automaker in China. Most of its cars appear initially to have been based on imitations of best-selling Japanese cars. However, in 2008 and one year ahead of Toyota and General Motors, BYD announced the commercialization of a mass-produced plug-in hybrid electric car known as F3DM that is not dependent on a commercial charging station. Soon after, in April 2009, the prototype of a pure electric car, the E6, was exhibited by BYD at the Shanghai International Auto Show with the intention of being introduced on the European market within two to three years. In Denmark BYD Denmark ApS was established as a sales office in 2005 through a DKK 125,000 greenfield investment of BYD Europe BV, the BYD European regional headquarters located in the Netherlands.

10.4.4.1 Strategic intent

BYD has chosen Denmark as a test-bed for its European market penetration of electric cars, on the basis of a perceived interest among the Danish people in green solutions. Furthermore, favourable tax policies towards green energy, including tax-exemption status on electric cars until at least

2012, and Denmark's lead position within the use of wind energy to generate electricity were decisive factors in BYD's decision to undertake a greenfield investment in a sales office. Further, BYD planned to enter the Danish market with electric or hybrid electric car models in relation with the UN Climate Change Conference COP15, held in December 2009 in Copenhagen. In Denmark the two investment promotion agencies (IPAs), 'Invest in Denmark' and 'Copenhagen Capacity' respectively, perceive the interest of BYD to invest in Denmark as a strategically important investment in order to advance the implementation of a Danish industrial policy to further industrial clusters in the area of renewable energy.

BYD and other producers of electrical car solutions, such as the Danish competitor Better Place, are involved in technical discussions and negotiations with Danish battery producers, Danish public authorities, and pertinent Danish industrial associations on how best to organize the introduction of electric cars into Denmark. Of particular interest is which methods to use in order to make it as easy as possible for the car user to recharge or change car batteries, either in special recharging stations or alternatively to exchange a fully discharged battery with another, which is already recharged. The Danish IPAs at the same time are undertaking a dialogue with the car companies in order to identify complementary needs within the sector, where it would be useful to attract further foreign direct investments. In this regard, it is of particular interest from a Danish industrial policy point of view that the world's largest battery producer, the Taiwanese company Amita, is actively pursuing the option to initiate production in Denmark of up to 40,000 batteries for electric cars annually. Thus, Amita will exploit Danish know-how within this area and Danish tax exemption until 2012 for electric cars. The high costs for transportation of batteries, which transported as ship cargo are considered to be 'explosive goods' with exorbitant freight rates counterbalance differences in wages between Denmark and Taiwan and hence makes a production of batteries in Denmark cost-effective.

10.4.4.2 Status

The technical discussions, *inter alia*, on how best to recharge batteries for electric cars within the Danish and broader European market appear at the time of writing to be inconclusive. Hence, it is not possible yet fully to assess the outcome of BYD's investment. However, BYD's interest in investing in Denmark has as a side effect stimulated producers of components for electric cars such as Taiwanese Amita to consider the option of undertaking their own investments in Denmark in relation to the introduction of electric cars

10.4.5 Reliance Industries Limited[9]

In 2004, Reliance Industries Limited, India's largest private sector enterprise, acquired from Deutsche Bank the large German Trevira Group based in

Germany. Earlier Trevira was owned by Hoechst Group. Trevira produces branded polyester fibre and yarn products, supplying among others the auto industry and has its own R&D facilities. The acquisition would lead to the creation of the world's largest polyester fibre and yarn producer. As an incidental outcome of the acquisition, Reliance also acquired the Danish company Treviara Neckelmann.

10.4.5.1 Strategic intent and organization

Trevira had different locations in Europe, including Treviara Neckelmann in Silkeborg, Denmark. The production at Treviara Neckelmann was at the same time knowledge- and labour-intensive. For Reliance, the plan was to tap into the knowledge- and R&D-intensive part of the group and reorganize it. For Trevira, the acquisition would potentially imply access to new markets and raw materials.

In 2007, production activities in Silkeborg were moved to the group's plant in Poland, leading to 300 jobs being lost. The reason cited by management was high production costs compared to low-cost locations and pressures from the group's main customers in the car industry. The R&D part was maintained as a Trevira Competence Center in Silkeborg, accounting for a mere 60–70 jobs by the middle of 2009; additional investments of DKK 50 million were made in developing this unit.

10.4.5.2 Status

In 2009, the financial crisis and in particular the downturn in the auto industry led to Reliance declaring the Trevira Group insolvent and to sell the group in a restructuring. In the restructuring, the plants in Germany and Poland have acquired new owners. Reliance also wants to sell the remaining R&D facility in Silkeborg. There may be an opportunity for a management buy-out for the plants in Belgium and Denmark, particularly if the links can be maintained to the earlier sister companies in the Trevira Group.

10.5 Analysis

In the following, we will try to extract some general patterns in regard to the entry strategies of Chinese and Indian MNCs in Denmark. We will first examine the profile and entry strategies of the Asian MNCs in Denmark, and then move on to discuss whether the investments appear to be more in line with conventional or latecomer theory.

10.5.1 The level of Chinese and Indian investments

The above description of Chinese and Indian FDI in Denmark suggested that FDI from these countries is relatively low; even relative to the size of the Danish economy, the investments are smaller than others we see in other OECD countries, and in spite of many companies expressing interest in investing in Denmark, the bottom line is that only just over 30 investments, many very small, have been realized. The low level of Asian investment could be related to the fact that small EU countries such as Denmark may have greater problems coming 'onto the radar screen' of Asian investors looking for investment opportunities in Europe than have countries with large home markets. Moreover, although Denmark has pursued an uncompromising policy of pegging the Kroner to the Euro, the fact that Denmark is not a member of the Euro may introduce a level of uncertainty, especially among investors with little or no previous experience from Europe. Finally, the low level of investment could be attributed to a bad match between China's and India's industrial strengths in large-scale production within manufacturing and services and Denmark's industrial strengths in niche and high-quality-oriented activities.

10.5.2 Investment motives

The investment motives of the Asian giants are exclusively related to market- and strategic asset-seeking, and there are no examples of resource- or efficiency-seeking investments.

10.5.3 Market seekers

It seems that there are two types of market seekers present in the sample. One is a traditional market seeker, who invests mainly to support trade; the other is a more strategic market seeker that uses the investment as a platform to develop a new European market. The Chinese investors in electronics, Lenovo and Huawei technologies, are examples of the former type, opening sales and service offices in Denmark to support exports. Another example is the Indian IT firms Infosys, ITC Infotech, Wipro, and Tata, which all try to support their export of IT services by creating sales and service offices close to their Danish and Scandinavian customers. Only by having close proximity to customers was it possible to effectively exploit the home country advantage in IT services employing highly qualified but comparatively lower-paid software engineers to undertake outsourcing tasks both in India and in Denmark for the Danish clients (Jensen, 2009). Since labour is mobile for undertaking the software outsourcing tasks, the IT software supplier firm needs to be present to organize the labour force transfer when the tasks are done inside the client's firm in Denmark.

Several of the market-seeking investors had ambitions beyond the relatively small Danish market. Thus, Asian investors appear to find Denmark a suitable gateway for expanding trade into the Northern European and Baltic markets. Cosco acquired Penta Shipping in order to use this acquisition as a hub for its Scandinavian activities. Four Soft wanted to use the Danish investment to strengthen its European platform in markets for IT for the shipping industry. And Suzlon not only aimed at creating a regional hub, but also to establish a global sales and marketing centre in Denmark.

10.5.4 Strategic asset-seeking

One of the most striking aspects of the Asian investments in Denmark is that many of them are strategic asset-seeking in one sense or another. Strategic asset-seeking investments are investments where the purpose of the investment is to build new advantages, rather than exploiting existing ownership-specific advantages. Apparently the Asian investors see opportunities of acquiring complementary assets in Denmark that can support them in their catch-up strategies and enhance their global and regional presence and capabilities. The strategic asset-seeking investments in Denmark were typically aimed at accessing high-end, high-value-added activities, upstream and downstream in the value chain. Whereas Asian strategic asset-seeking investments in other European countries have been aimed at acquiring well-known brands (for example, Tetleys or Jaguar), there are really no examples from Denmark of Asian acquisitions of brands, which is partly a reflection of the fact that Danish industry has its main strength in business-to-business markets, partly that most Danish brands are related to industries where only few Asian firms invest.

There are essentially two types of assets sought in Denmark, namely R&D capabilities, and sales and marketing capabilities. Examples of the former are Reliance expanding its R&D activities in Denmark (but outsourcing everything else), Suzlon investing in building a global R&D centre in Denmark, or BYD, which, through its Danish investment in development and testing of battery-driven cars, attempt to move from a low-cost imitator to a technological lead company in a niche sector within the automotive industry. Examples of the latter are that Suzlon head-hunted previous Vestas/NEG staff to build its global sales and marketing HQ in Denmark, or that Four Soft tapped into the Danish partner's strong sales and marketing capabilities in the European market, eventually making the Danish subsidiary a main revenue centre of the corporation. The value for the Asian firms of accessing such sales and marketing skills should not be underestimated; often a main barrier to expansion and upgrading of DCMNCs will be the huge market entry barriers in Western markets.

A final aspect of the strategic Asian investments is that several of them can be interpreted as examples of strategic positioning vis-à-vis global competitors. This is clearly the case with Suzlon, which through its massive investment in Denmark clearly sought to check its main competitors, Siemens and Vestas. In addition Four Soft's acquisition of Transaxiom and Cosco's acquisition of Penta Shipping can be seen as attempts to build and consolidate positions in oligopolistic industries.

The strategic asset-seeking investments are made in activities closely related to well-known Danish clusters such as Blue Denmark (shipping), renewable energy, and biotech (Table 10.4). Through their investments in Denmark, Indian Suzlon and Chinese Envision Energy not only obtained access to experienced sales, marketing, and R&D people, they also accessed

Table 10.4 Strategic intent

	Strategic intent	Entry mode	Organization and integration
Cosco	Market-seeking (access to the Scandinavian market) Strategic asset-seeking (part of Blue Denmark cluster)	Acquisition. Joint venture, 75% ownership. Former Danish owners partners	Widespread decentralization. Chinese MD jointly with Danish MD Denmark has special competencies in logistics that Cosco utilizes
Suzlon	Strategic asset-seeking into the Danish wind turbine cluster, both for sales and marketing experience and later for R&D capabilities	Greenfield (but acquisition of former employees of Vestas/NEG Micon)	Denmark global sales and marketing HQ Strong integration in Indian operation; Indian staff permanently stationed in Denmark
Four Soft	Market-seeking (access to Western European market); Danish subsidiary currently a cash cow for owner Strategic asset-seeking (part of Blue Denmark cluster. Establishment of dominant market position)	Acquisition. Joint venture (95% control). Former Danish owner partner	Attempts to integrate in Indian operation lead to initial cultural problems The Danish operation now specializes in sales and marketing. The Indian operation specializes in R&D
BYD	Strategic asset-seeking (tap into the Danish renewable energy cluster)	Greenfield	Sales office, referring to European HQ
Reliance	Strategic asset-seeking: maintain Denmark as R&D centre while outsourcing production	Indirect acquisition	Functional division of labour within Europe. Production moved to Eastern Europe, R&D maintained in Denmark

other advantages related to the Danish renewable energy cluster, Danish export subsidies, knowledge at Danish universities and a well-developed supply and service industry within wind turbines. Similarly, BYD had located its test facility in Denmark mainly on the basis of Danish subsidies for electrical cars, favourable tax policies, and an excellent infrastructure in the Danish renewable energy cluster. Many, especially Indian, pharmaceutical companies have in various ways contemplated investing in the Danish biotech cluster, and one company, Hikal, eventually bought a majority share in the Danish pharmaceutical trading company, Marsing. Cosco and Four Soft, through their acquisitions in Denmark, have been able to tap into the excellent physical, commercial, regulatory, and human infrastructure supporting the Blue Denmark cluster.

While there are several examples of strategic asset-seeking investments in Denmark, there are also numerous examples of such investments that never materialized. For instance, during the boom in the Indian investments to Denmark in 2004/5, several strategic asset-seeking investors in the biotech industry appeared to be about to invest, but the investments were never realized, with one or two exceptions.

10.5.5 Entry modes

Most of the investments were acquisitions, either partial or full acquisition. Many acquisitions maintain Danish ownership after the acquisition and thus became joint ventures, although in all cases, the Asians have majority ownership. The reason why the Asian investors maintain Danish ownership could be that they have few experiences with operating and integrating a European activity and therefore want to maintain a committed local management. It could also be in order to ensure a smooth transition to foreign ownership. Thus, it appears that downstream-oriented investments maintain Danish ownership, which could be in order to align the incentive structure of the previous owner with the interest of the new owner. Those investments that were R&D-oriented, for example, Reliance, Suzlon, and Zhejiang New Jialian, were always fully controlled by the Asian promoter, most likely on IPR concerns. Apart from Reliance, the R&D oriented investments were greenfield.

Several unconventional entry modes were detected, for instance, that the Danish acquisitions in some cases were incidental consequences of acquisitions in other countries (Reliance) or that the investments essentially were representative offices to support strategic alliances in the home country (Indian IT).

10.5.6 Organization and integration

Strategic asset-seeking investments need to be integrated in the global organization of the investing firm, as the whole purpose is to learn and upgrade based on the investment. So in particular the R&D-oriented subsidiaries were strongly integrated in the Asian owners' global strategies, partly through full ownership control, and partly through direct management oversight by the Asian owners. The need for integration of the market-seeking investments appeared to be less pertinent. Thus, initially market-seeking acquisitions such as Four Soft and Penta Shipping were running rather independently. The need for internal strategic and organizational alignment was modest as long as the subsidiaries generated revenues. However, as the acquisition matured, it appears that the Asian owners attempted to integrate the acquisitions and obtain synergies with the global operation, for example, by devising internal divisions of labour, by facilitating global learning, etc.

It appears that several of the investments ran into serious problems when attempting to integrate the Danish operations. Some subsidiaries experienced huge internal conflicts and others were divested. In the case of Four Soft, for instance, it almost led to a break-up of the company, and Reliance eventually gave up its R&D unit in Denmark. Also the strategic asset-seeking investments by Avesthagen ceased after an initial effort. Several explanations for these problems of integration can be offered. One is that these investments, as with all FDI, may run into difficulties, especially for acquisitions, which were common among the Asian investors. But there could also be explanations specifically related to the fact that these firms were from Asia. With high cultural distance, chances of clashes increase. Moreover, the firms, often being the vanguard of Asian investors, may have been inexperienced in operating subsidiaries in European countries, and lacked the organizational and managerial resources to integrate the subsidiaries.

10.5.7 Summary

So, are the Asian investments in Denmark conventional or latecomer types of investments? Essentially, we found evidence of both. On the one hand, we found that many of the Asian investors are investing in Denmark to upgrade global capabilities in higher-value-added activities related to sales, marketing, and R&D, as well as to consolidate and expand regional and global market positions in mainly business-to-business markets. Moreover, one of the hypotheses of conventional FDI literature is that Asian MNCs will seek market access in industries with mature technologies, where production is being phased out in Western countries owing to the huge production externalities and the growing cost-based competition from emerging markets. However, in our sample we see virtually no such examples. Indeed, the Chinese and especially Indian investors appear to be exploiting and developing advantages in frontier technologies both within services and manufacturing. For instance, several of the Indian investors are strong in knowledge-intensive industries such as renewables, pharmaceuticals, and IT, and appear to base their investment strategies on advanced technologies, high knowledge intensity, and on cutting-edge strategies and organizational modes. Likewise, Chinese investors such as BYD, with their investment in developing and testing battery-driven cars, are moving right to the technological frontier. The abilities of the Asian firms to combine high technology and know-how with a low-cost base cannot be underestimated.

In terms of entry modes, many of the investments were partial or full acquisitions. This could be in line with the latecomer theory as acquisitions are often instruments of accelerated internationalization. When the Asian investors maintained Danish ownership this appeared mainly to be aimed at aligning the interests of the previous Danish owner with that of the Asian firm. But where the investment was strategic asset-seeking in R&D, the Asian investors went for full control. We also identified many alternative entry modes such as representative offices and strategic alliances, suggesting, in accordance with the latecomer theory, that Asian investors are flexible and innovative in adopting entry patterns. Some of the market-seeking investors in Denmark did indeed adopt a staged entry, starting with small trade-supporting joint ventures, evolving into more ambitious operations. This was the case with the IT companies and Penta Shipping.

The Danish engagement has been far from positive for all Asian investors. Several investment projects never got off the ground, others were divested. Some of the surviving investments have performed badly, and it has proven very difficult for investors to capitalize on their investments and obtain global synergies. Thus, the linkage, leverage, and learning abilities seen as key characteristics of DCMNCs in latecomer theory find little support in our sample. So while the rapid acquisitions seemed to confirm the latecomer hypothesis, the failure to succeed appears to confirm hypotheses that we may see unsuccessful DCMNCs, owing to a volatile combination of weak organizational, managerial, and strategic capabilities and easy access to credit, predisposing problems in the operations phase.

10.6 Conclusions and implications

This chapter gave an overview of Chinese and Indian investments in Denmark and discussed whether these investments were expressions of something new or just conventional types of investments. To our knowledge, no similar analysis of Asian investments exists, and the study thus offers novel insights into Asian investments seen from the point of view of a small, open economy.

A lively debate continues within IB as to the nature of the growing Asian investments overseas. Some are arguing that these investments can be understood through the lens of conventional FDI theory, while others hold that they are expressions of a new type of investor arriving on the international business scene. Holding the patterns of Chinese and Indian FDI in Denmark up against the two theoretical positions, we find that the Asian investors are indeed unconventional in several respects. Rather than being staged market-seeking entries in mature industries, many of the investments are strategic asset-seeking in technological frontier industries, evidently aimed at augmenting capabilities upstream or downstream in the investing firms' value chain or improving the global strategic positioning of the investing firm. But it also appears that the strategic ambitions of the Chinese and Indian investors in many cases were shattered by problems of integrating and thus reaping the strategic rents of the investment. Moreover, many planned investments never materialized. This could support the hypothesis that the Asian investors lack the organizational and managerial capabilities to organize and integrate acquisitions. In other words, the Asian investors may have lacked the firm-specific advantages that could allow them to capitalize on their initial general advantages based on a low cost base and easy access to credit.

10.6.1 Implications

Where the welfare and policy implications of Danish investments in India and China have received much attention, very little has been said about Chinese and Indian investments in Denmark. Investments from China and India may currently be few and scattered, but they are almost certainly the vanguard of a much larger inflow of Asian investment in the future. As China and India move to the premier league of economies, it becomes increasingly important for a small, open economy like the Danish to secure investments from these countries. This is partly because Asian investments in Denmark are a prerequisite for accessing the low cost base of the Asian markets, in particular India's knowledge base and China's manufacturing base. But it is also because the Asian MNCs are becoming global leaders within their industries. Although their initial motive for investing in Denmark has been to access assets, in the longer run they may invest to further develop those assets, thus contributing to building Danish competitiveness. Companies like Four Soft and Suzlon are indicative of this possibility.

To attract investments from the Asian giants poses huge challenges for Danish FDI policy. For a small country like Denmark it is probably insufficient to rely on received advantages to attract Asian FDI. Denmark needs to differentiate itself among other large and small countries as it lacks the domestic market size to make it a natural investment target. In this situation, government promotion and facilitation of inward foreign direct investment becomes essential. In retrospect, it is clear that government action has been crucial to the first wave of Indian and Chinese investments, for example, tax policies, subsidies, infrastructure provision, support of higher education and research, and in general, the promotion of clusters. Thus, most of the Asian investors went for the Danish clusters in renewable energy, biotech, or shipping, which have been strongly advertised by Danish investment promotion authorities. However, the Asian investors were not just locating value-adding activity within these clusters: they were targeting R&D or the sales and marketing talent capabilities of these clusters. A possible policy implication could be that cluster development should focus not on general cluster development, but on building optimal conditions for the location of specific high-value-added functions within these clusters.

Notes

1. In particular, the Danish National Bank FDI database, a special run from FT FDI markets database, and Chinese and Indian Embassies' homepages.
2. For example, on Chinese investment in Italy (Pietrobelli, Rabellotti, and Sanfilippo, 2009), or Indian investments in Western countries in general (Anwar et al., n.d.; Pradhan, 2007).
3. Roughly equivalent to Dunning's (1988) ownership-specific and location-specific advantages in the OLI framework.
4. Sources: Four Soft's Annual Report 2008–9, information from Four Soft's homepage, www.four-soft.com, and interviews with management of Four Soft Nordic.
5. Sources: interviews with Penta Shipping Managing directors and Cosco Holdings Company, 2008 Report to the Hong Kong Stock Exchange.
6. A teus is the equivalent unit to the content of a 20-foot container, which amounts to 34 cubic meters.
7. Sources: Suzlon's Annual Report 2008–9, information from Suzlon's website, www.suzlon.com, and interview with Chief Executive Officer of Suzlon Wind Energy A/S and Suzlon Energy A/S.
8. Sources: interviews with management of Danish Investment Promotion Agencies, Invest in Denmark and Copenhagen Capacity; information from homepage of BYD, www.byd.com; conference paper by Hua Wang (2009), and World Bank (2009).
9. Sources: based on *BusinessWeek*, August 2009; *Fagligt Fællesforbund*, Juni 2004 (http://forsiden.3f.dk/article/20040624/LONARB/40624022); MidtJyllands Avis, 28.11.2009 (http://www.infomedia.dk/ms/GetArticleFull.aspx?outputFormat=Full&duid=e1c97255), ICIS Connect, June 2009 (http://www.icis.com/blogs/india-chemicals/2009/06/reliance-struggles-with-troubl.html).

References

Anderson, U., Johanson, J., and Vahlne, J-E. (1997), 'Organic Acquisitions in the Internationalization Process of the Business Firm', *Management International Review*, 37 (2), 67–84.

Anwar, A. I., Hasse, R., and Rabbi, F. (n.d.), 'Location Determinants of Indian Outward Foreign Direct Investment: How Multinationals Choose their Investments Destinations?', available at: http://www.google.dk/search?hl=da&source=hp&q=amar+anwar+hasse+location+determinants+indian+fdi&btnG=Google-s%C3%B8gning&meta=&aq=f&oq=.

Barney, J. (1991), 'Firm Resources and Sustained Competitive Advantage', *Journal of Management*, 17, 99–120.

Beausang, F. (2003), *Third World Multinationals: Engine of Competitiveness or New Form of Dependency?* Basingstoke: Palgrave Macmillan.

Buckley, P. (2009), 'The Impact of the Global Factory on Economic Development', *Journal of World Business*, 131–43.

Buckley, P., Wang, C., and Clegg, J. (2007), 'The Impact of Foreign Ownership, Local Ownership and Industry Characteristics on Spillover Benefits from Foreign Direct Investment in China', *International Business Review*, 16 (2), April, 142–58.

Danish National Bank Statistics Bank, http://nationalbanken.statistikbank.dk/statbank5a/default.asp?w=1280.

Danmarks Statistik (2009), *Udenlandske firmaer i Danmark,* Copenhagen, Danmarks Statistik.

Dunning, J. H. (1981), 'Explaining the International Direct Investment Position of Countries: Towards a Dynamic or Developmental Approach', *Weltwirtschaftliches Archiv,* 117 (1), 30–64.

Dunning, J. H. (1988), 'The Eclectic Paradigm of International Production: A Restatement and some Possible Extensions', *Journal of International Business Studies,* 19 (1), 1–31.

Dunning, J. H. and Narula, R. (1996), 'The Investment Development Path Revisited: Some Emerging Issues', in J. H. Dunning and R. Narula (eds), *Foreign Direct Investment and Governments: Catalysts for Economic Restructuring.* London: Routledge, 1–38.

Dunning, J. H. and Narula, R. (2004), 'Industrial Development, Globalization and Multinational Enterprises: New Realities for Developing Countries', in J. H. Dunning and R. Narula (eds), *Multinational and Industrial Competitiveness.* Cheltenham, UK: Edward Elgar, 38–77.

Dunning, J. H., Kim, C., and Park, D. (2008), *Old Wine in New Bottles: A Comparison of Emerging Market TNCs Today and Developed Country TNCs Thirty Years Ago,* SLPTMD Working Paper Series No. 11, Department of International Economics, University of Oxford.

Ernst, D. (2000), 'Inter-Organizational Knowledge Outsourcing: What Permits Small Taiwanese Firms to Compete in the Computer Industry?', *Asia Pacific Journal of Management,* 17 (2), 223–56.

Gereffi, G., Humphrey, J., Kalinsky, R., and Sturgeon, T. (2001). 'Introduction: Globalization, Value Chains, and Development', *IDS Bulletin,* 32 (3), 1–8.

Gerschenkron, A. (1962), *Economic Backwardness in Historical Perspective.* Cambridge, MA: Belknap Press.

Giddy, I. H. and Young, S. (1982), 'Conventional Theory and Unconventional Multinationals: Do New Forms of Multinational Enterprise Require New Theories?', in A. M. Rugman (ed.), *New Theories of the Multinational Enterprise.* London: Croom Helm, 55–78.

Grant, R., Almeida, P., and Song, J. (2000), 'Knowledge and the Multinational Enterprise', in C. Millar. et al. (eds), *International Business: Emerging Issues and Emerging Markets.* London: Macmillan.

Hay, F., Milelli, C., and Shi, Y. (2008), *Présence et Stratégies des firmes chinoises et indiennes en Europe: une perspective dynamique et comparative,* Direction Générale des Entreprises, Ministère de l'Economie, des Finances et de l'Emploi, Paris, mimeo.

Hobday, M. (1995), *Innovation in East Asia: The Challenge to Japan.* Aldershot, UK: Edward Elgar.

Hobday, M. (1997), 'Latecomer Catch-up Strategies in Electronics: Samsung of Korea and Taiwan', *Asia Pacific Business Review,* 4 (2–3), 48–83.

Jensen, P. Ø. (2009), 'Off-shoring of Advanced and High-Value Technical Services: Antecedents, Process Dynamics and Firm Level Impacts', PhD thesis, Copenhagen Business School, CBDS.

Johanson, J. and Vahlne, J. (1977), 'The Internationalization Process of the Firm – A Model of Knowledge Development and Increasing Foreign Market Commitments', *Journal of International Business Studies,* 8 (1), 23–32.

Khanna, T. and Palepu, K. G. (2000), 'Emerging Giants: Building World-class Companies in Emerging Markets', *Harvard Business Review*, 84, 60–9.

Kuada, J. (2004). 'Internationalization of Firms from Developing Countries: Towards an Integrated Conceptual Framework', paper presented to conference on 'Globalization, Internationalization of Companies and Cross Cultural Management', Ålborg, October.

Lall, S. (ed.) (1983), *The New Multinationals: The Spread of Third World Enterprises*. New York: John Wiley & Sons.

Lasserre, P. (2007), *Global Strategic Management*. New York: Palgrave Macmillan.

Lecraw, D. J. (1993), 'Outward Direct Investment by Indonesian Firms: Motivation and Effects', *Journal of International Business Studies*, 24 (3), 589–600.

Li, P. P. (2007), 'Toward an Integrated Theory of Multinational Evolution: The Evidence of Chinese Multinational Enterprises as Latecomers', *Journal of International Management*, 13, 296–318.

Mathews, J. (2006), 'Dragon Multinationals: New Players in 21st Century Globalization', *Asia Pacific Journal of Management*, 23, 5–27.

Meyer, K. (2002), *Entry Strategy Analysis: Towards an Eclectic Framework*, Copenhagen Business School, mimeo.

Narula, R. (2006), 'Globalization, New Technologies, New Zoologies, and the Purported Death of the Eclectic Paradigm', *Asia Pacific Journal of Management*, 23 (2), 143–51.

Oviatt, B. and McDougall. P. (1994), 'Toward a Theory of International New Ventures', *Journal of International Business Studies*, 25 (1), 45–64.

Pietrobelli, C., Rabellotti, R., and Sanfilippo, M. (2009), 'Chinese FDIs in Italy', paper presented to the 6th Asialics International Conference, June.

Pradhan, J. (2007), 'Growth of Indian Multinationals in the World Economy: Implications for Development', MPRA Paper No. 12360, MPRA Munich Personal RePEc Archive.

Ramamurti, R. (2008), 'What Have We Learned About Emerging-Market MNEs? Insights from a Multi-Country Research Project', Copenhagen Business School, Copenhagen, Denmark, October 9–10, 2–27

Ramamurti, R. (2009), 'FDI from Developing Countries', paper presented to the 3rd Vale Conference on Sustainable Investment, November.

Ramamurti, R. and Singh, J. (2008), 'Indian Multinationals: Generic Internationalization Strategies', in R. Ramamurti and J. Singh (eds), *Emerging Multinationals from Emerging Markets*. Cambridge: Cambridge University Press.

Rugman, A. and Li, J. (2007), 'Will China's Multinationals Succeed Globally or Regionally?' *European Management Journal*, 25 (5), October, 333–43.

Singh, L. and Jain, V. (2009), *Emerging Pattern of India's Outward Foreign Direct Investment Under the Influence of State Policy: A Macro View*. Patiala: Punjabi University for Development Studies.

Teece, D. (2000), 'Firm Capabilities, and Economic Development: Implications for NIEs', in *Technology, Learning and Innovation*, ed. L. Kim and R. R. Nelson. Cambridge, MA: Cambridge University Press, 105–28.

Tolentino, P. E. (2008), 'Explaining the Competitiveness of Multinational Companies from Developing Economies: A Critical Review of the Academic Literature', *International Journal of Technology and Globalization*, 4 (1), 23–38.

UNCTAD (2006), *World Investment Report: Developing Country FDI*. Geneva: United Nations.

UNCTAD (2009), *World Investment Report: The Role of FDI in Agriculture*. Geneva: United Nations.

UNCTAD (2010), *World Investment Report: FDI and Climate Change,* Geneva: United Nations.
Vernon, R. (1966), 'International Investment and International Trade in the Product Cycle', *Quarterly Journal of Economics*, 80 (2), 190–207.
Wang, H. (2009), 'Betting on Chinese Electronic Cars? Analyzing BYD's Innovation Capability', Paris, June.
Wells, L. T. (1983), *Third World Multinationals*. Cambridge, MA: MIT Press.
World Bank (2009), *2009 Benchmarking Study by World Bank of FDI Policies and Investment Promotion Agencies,* Washington, DC.

11

Chinese Outward Direct Investment in Europe and Belgium: Characteristics and Policy Issues

Filip De Beule, Daniel Van Den Bulcke,** and Haiyan Zhang****

11.1 Importance of Chinese outward foreign direct investment

The foreign ventures of Chinese enterprises such as Haier, Lenovo, CNOOC (China National Offshore Oil Corporation), and SAIC (Shanghai Automotive Industry Corporation) during the beginning of the twenty-first century drew so much media attention that even the general public has become aware of the expansion of multinational firms from emerging economies, especially from China. In Belgium more recently the significance of Chinese investors was underlined by the role played by the insurance firm Ping An as a minority shareholder in the saga about the nationalization and subsequent sale of the Fortis Bank to the French financial group BNP Paribas and the rejected bid by the Chinese auto producer Beijing Automotive Industry Corporation (BAIC) to take over General Motors' European Opel operations, including the plant in Antwerp, Belgium.

Yet, the importance of outward foreign direct investment (OFDI) on a global scale is still small, even though it is rising quite fast. According to OECD (2008), the flow of Chinese OFDI in 2006 reached US$ 17.6 billion, which was more than three times higher than in 2003 and more than seven times higher than the average flows during the 1990s. This amount represented 1.5 per cent of the worldwide OFDI flows in that year, which is almost double as high as China's share of global OFDI during 1982–9 and 1990–9, where it reached only 0.8 per cent during both periods. As a percentage of GDP, China's OFDI currently represents 0.7 per cent, compared to an average of 0.3 per cent during the 1980s and 1990s. This is far behind most of the developed countries. In 2007 China's outbound investment flow was comparable to small EU countries such as Austria and the Netherlands and 14 times smaller than US OFDI (Rosen and Hanemann, 2009).[1] In terms of stocks OFDI from China had accumulated US$ 118 billion in 2007 compared to US$ 75 billion in 2006, US$ 45 billion in 2004 and US$ 17.8 billion in 1995. As a percentage of global OFDI stocks China reached only 0.6 per cent, while it attained 2.9 per cent of the PRC's GDP.

The rise of the Chinese economy, on the one hand, and a number of highly publicized acquisitions of Western firms by Chinese multinational enterprises (CMNEs), on the other, alerted the investment promotion agencies (IPAs) from many countries to the potential of Chinese investment on their territories. An UNCTAD survey about the prospects (UNCTAD, 2005) for attracting investment from abroad surprisingly put China for the first time among the top five home countries worldwide behind the US, UK, and Germany for 2004–7, preceding Japan, which had previously been in fourth position. That especially the IPAs from developing countries had high hopes about Chinese OFDI is shown by the fact that they ranked China immediately behind the United States. Yet, while the positive expectations for OFDI from the US were quoted by more than half of the surveyed IPAs, for China it was less than one-fifth. However, responses in the *World Investment Prospects Survey 2009–2011* (UNCTAD, 2009b) brought China firmly in the lead with almost 60 per cent and ahead of the US (around 45 per cent), and the three other BRIC countries of India, Brazil, and Russia between one-third and one-fifth of the answers about the most favoured countries for FDI location.

There are some indications that Chinese outward investment might be underestimated. The investments, which are recorded by MOFCOM after having obtained authorization to venture abroad, most probably do not present a complete picture of Chinese outbound investments as they are unlikely to include all FDI from private sources. Also because the OFDI projects smaller than €280,000 only require approval from the local authorities many might escape the MOFCOM registration. Then, OFDI carried out by Chinese firms and subsidiaries from Hong Kong (or other host countries) will not be captured by MOFCOM's statistical system either. The consultant firm McKinsey (Hirt and Orr, 2006: 4) wrote: 'We estimate that actual outbound investment is two to three times higher than the official figures. China is therefore a material, if not yet massive, new force in the global market for business assets.' The OECD (2008) compared the figures about incoming FDI from China in its member countries with outgoing FDI as registered by China, and found that the stocks reported by MOFCOM are on average 40 per cent lower, with a few exceptions such as the US and Japan. The phenomenon of 'round-tripping' investment exaggerates both outward and inward FDI (Lunding, 2006) and distorts China's investment picture, even though the motivation for such FDI should disappear now that the corporate tax between domestic and foreign enterprises has been equalized. That the statistics about China's OFDI can also be confusing relates to the fact that China has been collecting these data according to the international standards only since 2003, when it started including reinvested earnings and intra-group loans. Also OFDI statistics about financial institutions were not available before 2006.

11.2 Characteristics of Chinese outbound FDI

Although some of these characteristics of China's OFDI will be developed in more detail below, it might be useful to draw attention to some of the main points at the beginning of this chapter.

China's economy started an outward internationalization process after the Chinese government initiated its open-door policy at the end of the 1970s (Cai, 1999). A first, mainly experimental stage up to the 1990s was characterized by strong supervision from the government. A second stage during the 1990s witnessed a large increase in the number of Chinese subsidiaries abroad, but with little strategic focus and with many of them reporting losses (Zhang and Van Den Bulcke, 1996; Cai, 1999; Quan, 2001). The third stage started with China's accession to the WTO, when a number of leading Chinese firms went international with a view to becoming global players in international markets (Child and Rodrigues, 2005). It seems that Chinese firms have come of age, and are demonstrating some spectacular improvements over previous stages.

First, in 2005 about one-fourth of Chinese OFDI, that is, US$ 3.2 billion, came from reinvested earnings by the subsidiaries. In a way this illustrates that Chinese affiliates performed relatively well and that they were confident to consider their operations abroad from a long-term perspective, rather than from an angle that concentrated on short-term profit-making.

Second, mergers and acquisitions (M&As) became a dominant entry form of Chinese firms to start operations abroad, although different waves have been distinguished (BCG, 2006a). In 2005, M&As represented half of China's OFDI in terms of value, as compared to only 18 per cent in 2003. Rosen and Hanemann (2009) state that around 60 to 70 per cent of total Chinese OFDI can be attributed to M&As. For instance, the proportion of takeovers in Germany by emerging economies went up from 5 per cent in 2005 to 12 per cent of total acquisitions in the country (Deloitte, 2007). Although this preference for M&As is one of the criticisms levelled at CMNEs, especially in the US, acquisitions are likely to remain their main entry mode (APFC, 2006; Globerman and Shapiro, 2009), even though, according to Luedi (2008), evidence suggests that the deals they concluded between 1995 and 2007 performed less favourably than those of the Western firms. However, according to the Boston Consulting Group (BCG, 2006a), a number of attenuating factors should be taken into account before drawing such a conclusion.

Third, according to MOFCOM's survey results, based on 6,426 Chinese overseas affiliates, Chinese investors clearly preferred wholly owned subsidiaries, branches, and representative offices. Only 4 per cent consisted of joint ventures with local partners. The APFC (2006) survey found that 90 per cent of China's OFDI projects were wholly owned or predominantly, that is, more than 50.1 per cent, owned by Chinese investors. Given that China for many years after the liberalization of inward FDI continued to insist that foreign companies – attracted by the potential size of the Chinese market or the advantageous cost conditions – should enter into joint ventures with local Chinese firms, this finding is somewhat surprising. Based on a survey of 138 Chinese outward investors, Cui and Jiang (2008) conclude that CMNEs are likely to choose a wholly owned subsidiary as a mode of entry if they enter a competition-intensive host country, seek complementary assets overseas, and pursue a global strategic motivation in FDI. Child and Rodrigues (2005) hypothesized that the apparent preference of CMNEs for acquisitions and organic growth rather than through joint ventures with non-Chinese MNEs suggests that they may prefer to retain their distinctive administrative heritage, which often consists of preferential links with government nstitutions.

Fourth, Europe represented only a small share of Chinese OFDI. In 2007 Chinese outbound direct investment to Europe was only US$ 4.5 billion in terms of stock and US$ 1.5 billion as a flow, which amounted to respectively 3.8 and 5.7 per cent of its total OFDI. For the EU the respective amounts and shares were US$ 2.9 and US$ 1 billion and 2.46 and 3.77 per cent. Yet, this surpassed North America for the first time, as it reached US$ 1.6 billion compared to US$ 1.3 billion.

Fifth, services became the most important sector of Chinese outward investment, as leasing and business services such as financial services took up one-fourth of total Chinese OFDI flows in 2006, followed by wholesale and retail activities (17 per cent) and transport and warehouse operations (10 per cent). Mining and petroleum represented nearly half of the OFDI flows, while only one-twentieth went into manufacturing activities. Also in 2003 mining and petroleum had accounted for almost half of OFDI, although manufacturing surpassed one-fifth in that particular year. Manufacturing accounted for one-tenth of China's OFDI in terms of stocks, compared with two-thirds for services, which consisted of 26 per cent of lease and business services, 17 per cent for wholesale and retail and 10 per cent for transport and storage. Mining reached nearly one-quarter of the total stock in 2006. The gradual switch to the tertiary sector by Chinese investors is expected to orient its investments more toward the OECD and EU countries (Rossi and Burghart, 2009; Rosen and Hanemann, 2009).

Sixth, the ownership structure of the Chinese multinational parent companies is changing – at least in terms of numbers – as a result of the expansion abroad of non-state-owned enterprises. During the first half of the 1990s state-owned enterprises (SOEs) dominated China's internationalization process (Zhang and Van Den Bulcke, 1996). The share of SOEs in the total number of CMNEs gradually declined, and dropped from 43 per cent in 2003 to 29 per cent in 2005. The private or non-state-owned enterprises are gradually becoming major players in China's outward FDI. Yet, in terms of value the SOEs still dominate outward investment. The share of OFDI stock held by SOEs under central government administration stood at around 84 per cent of the country's entire OFDI stock at the end of 2005 (OECD, 2008).

Seventh, especially since the end of the 1990s and even more so after it joined the World Trade Organization (WTO) in 2001, China has actively supported its investments abroad (Zhang, 2005; De Beule and Van Den Bulcke, 2010). Its 'go global' or 'go out' policy, which originally consisted mainly of an attempt to develop its one hundred largest SOEs into 'global players,' received an extra boost by the accumulation of massive foreign exchange reserves and the establishment of sovereign wealth funds (SWFs) (Cognato, 2008).

Eighth, over the years the media have devoted much attention to the failures of China's outward investment binge in terms of unsuccessful bids because of political or shareholder pressure—such as CNOOC with Unocal (2005) and Haier with Maytag in the US, Chinalco with Rio Tinto in Australia (2009), or disappointing results, for instance, by TCL with Thomson in France (2005), SAIC with Ssanyong Motor in South Korea (2009) and so on. Yet, according to the Boston Consulting Group, successes outnumber failures by about eight to one (*Financial Times*, 2009). Also, while the reasons of some of these so-called failures may be the result of outside factors such as political backlash and fear of China's dominance, others may relate to a lack of international experience of the Chinese managers or their underestimation of social and cultural aspects of the host countries, or simply their shortcomings in running an operation in a foreign country. In a number of cases the Chinese government even blocked the intended total or partial acquisition by a CMNE. Examples of such interventions are the Bank of China of the financial company de Rothschild (France in 2009), the China Development Bank of the Dresdner Bank (Germany in 2008), and by Tenzhong Heavy Industries of General Motors' production plant of the Hummer jeep (US in 2009).

Ninth, while the onslaught of the financial and economic crisis of 2008–9 caused a decline of inward and outward FDI in the developed countries with 29 per cent in 2008, the developing and the emerging economies only suffered a delayed decrease from the beginning of 2009 (UNCTAD, 2009a). In a way, Chinese OFDI ran in a countercyclical way, as it doubled in 2008 and continued to expand in 2009 (Davies, 2009). While the crisis certainly provided new investment opportunities to cash-rich investors, it also presented a challenge to Chinese firms that acquired ailing companies before the crisis struck (Nicolas, 2009).

Tenth, the majority of the Chinese outbound investments are based on market-seeking motives and also on strategic asset-seeking considerations, especially with respect to the developed countries. This is confirmed by practically all studies carried out about Chinese OFDI, that is, both by surveys based on questionnaires (for instance, APFC, 2005; IBM and Fudan University, 2006; Zhang, 2006) or econometric analyses (for instance, Buckley et al., 2007; Cheung and Qian, 2009). That resource-seeking OFDI is extremely important for China's future growth is shown by its important projects in the petroleum and mining sector directed to developing countries and resource-rich developed countries such as Australia and Canada.

11.3 Chinese OFDI in Europe from a global perspective

From the point of view of Europe as a host region of FDI at the end of 2003 the US was the largest investor by far (€772.67 billion) ahead of Japan (€72.96 billion), Singapore (€13.82 billion), and Hong Kong (€9.09 billion). Mainland China represented only one-hundredth (€0.75 billion) of the US investment in Europe. If one includes Mainland China, Hong Kong, and Taiwan into the so-called 'Greater China' the total amounted to €10.56 billion, however. And if one would also consider Singapore as a part of Greater China, as some authors tend to do, the amount would be twice as high with €24.38 billion. These figures show again that Europe does not figure very prominently as a destination for Chinese OFDI. The net overseas direct investment flows during 2004–7 mainly went to Asia and Latin America, albeit for different reasons. Yet, between 2004 and 2007 the amount of the OFDI flow quadrupled.

An analysis of net overseas direct investment flows from China illustrates the recent surge in Chinese outward direct investment (Figure 11.1). Most of the investment has gone to Hong Kong and some Latin American tax havens that typically serve as conduits to other countries or even back to China via the so-called 'round tripping.' Unlike most other countries, China's outbound investment does not go to developed economies, but rather to developing Asia, and even Africa. Clearly Europe does not rank all that high on China's 'most wanted' list. If one excludes these investment intermediaries, a more balanced distribution appears, however.

If Hong Kong and the Latin American tax havens such as the Virgin Islands, the Cayman Islands, and the Bahamas are excluded, Europe comes more into the picture as a host of Chinese investment abroad and reached levels that were more or less comparable to North America and Africa. These comparable lower levels for Europe, North America, and Africa are confirmed for the stocks of Chinese OFDI in 2007. Without Hong Kong and the Latin American tax havens, Europe and Africa in 2006 each hosted 17 per cent of Chinese OFDI compared to 14 per cent for North America. Latin America without the tax havens only represented 6 per cent compared to 7 per cent for Oceania. However, even without Hong Kong Asia attracted the largest share of Chinese OFDI and represented two-fifths (39 per cent) in the same year.

11.4 China's OFDI in Europe and the European Union

In 2004 about two-thirds (67 per cent) of the Chinese OFDI into Europe went to the European Union (EU), which consisted of 25 countries at that time. Russia hosted 16.54 per cent of Chinese European direct investment, followed

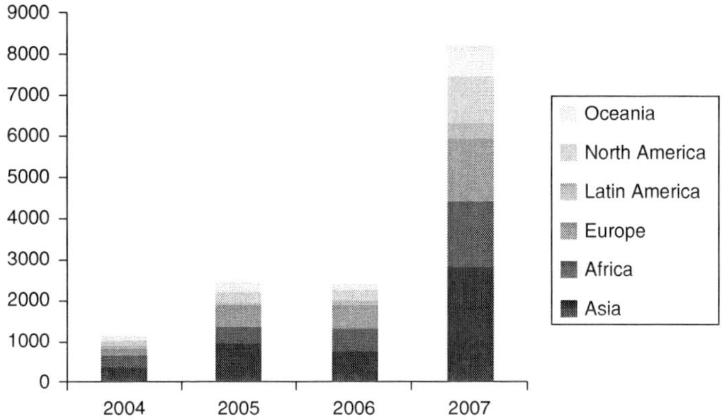

Figure 11.1 Geographical breakdown of outward Chinese foreign direct investment, excluding Hong Kong and Latin American tax havens (2004–7)
Source: National Bureau of Statistics of China, 2009.
Note: 2007 figures include financial ODI, but previous years do not.

by Romania (4.17 per cent), and Kazakhstan with 3.32 per cent of the Chinese OFDI stock of €746.66 that accumulated in Europe. In Poland a Chinese industrial park was set up in Koszalin (Godfrey, 2008). Germany, Spain, and the UK were the most favoured EU countries for CMNEs, and attracted respectively US$ 129, 128, and 108 million. Only US$ 1.64 million of this total amount found its way to Belgium. Germany has attracted many Chinese firms in the transportation and logistics sector as well as a high number of sales and distribution centres, of which many have clustered around the city of Hamburg. In the UK, London is the most favoured location for CMNEs, not only with sales offices but also with some R&D centres and regional headquarters, as well as banking and insurance activities and telecom activities. That the UK surpassed Germany, which was the leading receiver country during 2005 and 2006, as the preferred destination in the EU in 2007, is to some extent linked to the fact that financial ventures abroad have since then been included in China's OFDI statistics. Paris, the French capital, also counts Chinese representative and sales offices, while in the rest of the country there is also a certain Chinese presence in food, chemicals, and consumer electronics. In Denmark telecommunications and biotechnology are the preferred sectors, while in Spain petroleum and fishing dominate.

An analysis of the Chinese subsidiaries in Europe, based on the Amadeus database of European firms in Western and Eastern Europe, makes it possible to disentangle the geographical and sectoral breakdown of investment from Mainland China, Hong Kong, Taiwan, and Macao (Table 11.1).

Although Chinese multinationals have not targeted Europe as a primary destination for investment, some European countries have attracted relatively

Table 11.1 Number of 'Greater China's' foreign affiliates in Europe (2007)

Home country	**China**		**Taiwan**		**Macau**		**Hong Kong**	
Host country	N	%	N	%	N	%	N	%
Austria	10	0.2%	1	0.2%	0	0.0%	16	1.4%
Belgium	3	0.1%	0	0.0%	0	0.0%	0	0.0%
Denmark	6	0.1%	4	1.0%	0	0.0%	8	0.7%
France	28	0.6%	11	2.7%	2	33.3%	40	3.5%
Germany	947	20.0%	216	53.5%	0	0.0%	211	18.5%
Greece	1	0.0%	0	0.0%	0	0.0%	1	0.1%
Ireland	0	0.0%	1	0.2%	0	0.0%	4	0.4%
Italy	0	0.0%	0	0.0%	0	0.0%	0	0.0%
Luxembourg	0	0.0%	0	0.0%	0	0.0%	4	0.4%
Netherlands	68	1.4%	58	14.4%	0	0.0%	3	0.3%
Norway	1	0.0%	1	0.2%	0	0.0%	3	0.3%
Portugal	1	0.0%	0	0.0%	1	16.7%	2	0.2%
Spain	4	0.1%	3	0.7%	0	0.0%	30	2.6%
Sweden	0	0.0%	0	0.0%	0	0.0%	2	0.2%
Switzerland	1	0.0%	0	0.0%	0	0.0%	4	0.4%
United Kingdom	172	3.6%	76	18.8%	1	16.7%	794	69.5%
Total Western Europe	*1,242*	*26.3%*	*371*	*91.8%*	*4*	*66.7%*	*1,122*	*98.2%*
Bulgaria	117	2.5%	1	0.2%	0	0.0%	0	0.0%
Croatia	6	0.1%	0	0.0%	0	0.0%	0	0.0%
Czech Republic	1	0.0%	1	0.2%	0	0.0%	0	0.0%
Hungary	4	0.1%	0	0.0%	0	0.0%	0	0.0%

Latvia	0	0.0%	0	0.0%	0	0.0%	1	0.1%
Lithuania	0	0.0%	0	0.0%	0	0.0%	0	0.0%
Poland	10	0.2%	7	1.7%	0	0.0%	1	0.1%
Romania	2,342	49.6%	18	4.5%	1	16.7%	0	0.0%
Russia	1,003	21.2%	6	1.5%	1	16.7%	17	1.5%
Ukraine	0	0.0%	0	0.0%	0	0.0%	1	0.1%
Total Eastern Europe	*3.483*	*73.7%*	*33*	*8.2%*	*2*	*33.3%*	*20*	*1.8%*
Total Europe	**4,725**	**100%**	**404**	**100%**	**6**	**100%**	**1,142**	**100%**

Source: Authors' calculations based on Bureau van Dijk (2008).

many Chinese affiliates. Germany, for instance, has been the primary host country for Chinese affiliates in Western Europe for many years. Germany attracted close to a thousand Mainland Chinese subsidiaries, or three-quarters of all Mainland Chinese affiliates in Western Europe. The United Kingdom hosted 172 Chinese affiliates from the Mainland, or about 14 per cent. This share increases substantially to 38 per cent if all affiliates from Greater China (including Hong Kong, Taiwan, and Macao) are taken into account. The UK has especially attracted a lot of investment from Hong Kong, which is obviously due to its former colonial ties to the special administrative region of China. Germany is also strongly favoured by firms from Taiwan, with more than half of the Taiwanese establishments in Western Europe. According to this measure Germany is on the whole the most preferred country for investment in Western Europe, with about half of all Greater Chinese firms in the region, while the UK is a close second with nearly 40 per cent. The Netherlands have also attracted their fair share of Greater Chinese investment at almost 5 per cent. France has not nearly wooed as many CMNEs as its economic importance would suggest. Belgium has attracted very few Chinese firms and even lost some by relocation to other countries, like the Netherlands or Germany.

An analysis of the Greater Chinese affiliates in Europe in terms of sectors shows that CMNEs clearly prefer the service sector, and more in particular trading services (Figure 11.2). About 90 per cent of Greater Chinese subsidiaries are in services. This is true for firms from the Mainland, but also from Hong Kong and Taiwan. Taiwanese firms have made some investments in the manufacturing sector such as the production of radio, TV, and communication equipment, and the manufacture of office machinery and computers. The share of manufacturing firms by Taiwanese firms remains nonetheless at less than 6 per cent. Although Chinese firms have invested largely in the service sector, firms from Taiwan (12.2 per cent) and especially Hong Kong (24.1 per cent) have made these service investments in business activities, while firms from the Mainland have focused almost exclusively on the wholesale and retail trade, and hotels and restaurants. Much like their Japanese predecessors, China seems to focus mainly on exporting Chinese goods to Europe. Other service investments are made in support of these trading activities. More detailed data can be found in the Appendix.

11.5 Europe and future investments of Chinese MNEs

On the basis of the findings of a number of surveys it looks as though Europe does indeed not figure all that highly in future Chinese investments abroad either. The international consultant company Roland Berger (Von Keller and Zhou, 2005) investigated the future foreign investment prospects of the 50 largest CMNEs, and concluded that there was a steady interest in developed versus developing countries, as well as Asia and a continuing preference for North American over European markets among the developed regions. North

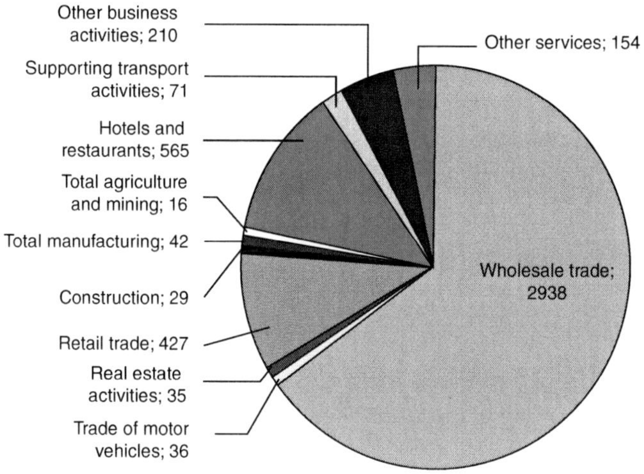

Figure 11.2 Number of Mainland China's subsidiaries in Europe, by industry (2007)
Source: Authors' calculations based on Bureau van Dijk, 2008.

America was labelled a 'priority target region' in the Berger study. Within Asia a diminishing orientation towards Hong Kong and Macau was identified. A comparison between the current geographical place of the top 50 Chinese MNEs with the so-called target place showed an intended expansion in South and North America, and the Commonwealth of Independent States (CIS), a stabilization in Southeast Asia and South Asia, and a decline in Oceania, Japan/Korea, and Western Europe (Von Keller and Zhou, 2005).

The CCPIT (2009) survey (with about 1,100 sampled firms) confirmed that over 60 per cent of the Chinese firms that have invested abroad, located in East Asia. The report states that 'Africa becomes a hotspot destination comparable with West Europe and North America by attracting 22 per cent of the Chinese enterprise' (CCPIT, 2009: 6). Twenty per cent of the surveyed enterprises opted for the US, and Hong Kong, which put these two economies in the leading positions in the ranking of the preferred economies for Chinese investors. Japan and Vietnam take third and fourth positions with respectively 10 and 9 per cent. Germany is placed fifth with 8 per cent, which puts it at the same level as Australia and precedes Singapore (6 per cent), Russia (5 per cent), and the UK and India (each with 4 per cent).

With regard to the future investment destinations the sampled companies in the CCPIT survey indicate that East Asia and Southeast Asia remain on top for Chinese outbound investment with about 60 per cent, compared to Western Europe and the US, each with 20 per cent, and Africa with 19 per cent. The Middle East, Eastern Europe, Latin America, and Oceania follow with respectively 16, 12, 7, and 5 per cent. When asked about the individual countries, it is somewhat surprising to find that Vietnam, with 28 per cent, precedes Hong Kong/Macao (21 per cent) and the US (20 per cent). Australia, Thailand, and Canada hover around 15 and 13 per cent of the expressed preferences, while Singapore and Germany are ranked eighth with 12 per cent. Again Germany is the only European country to be listed among the top ten potential destinations of Chinese investors.

To the question 'Which of the following countries/regions do you perceive will be the most likely destination for your company's overseas investment over the next 3–5 years' the APFC survey (2009) showed that only Germany was listed as a European destination among the nine most quoted countries/regions, on the one hand, for all sample companies and, on the other hand, for those that already had investments abroad. Hong Kong and Macao ranked first with respectively 16 and 21 per cent, followed by the USA (19 and 15 per cent), Vietnam (18 and 21 per cent), Thailand (14 and 12 per cent), Canada (14 and 10 per cent), and Singapore (14 and 9 per cent). For Germany the respective scores were 13 and 9 per cent. That the low interest in Europe is not the result of the protectionist measures of the European economies is shown by the ACPF survey (2009). According to this study Chinese investors perceive the openness of Europe toward Chinese FDI as positive and rank the UK, Germany, and France immediately behind the US, Canada, Australia, and Southeast Asia with a comparable score on a Likert scale from 1 to 5. These findings are confirmed in the CCPIT Survey (2009: 28) as the same countries are listed among the ten most open destinations for Chinese OFDI, again behind the US, Canada, and East Asia.

11.6 Belgium as a host country for Chinese outward direct investment

According to MOFCOM data, there were 13 Chinese subsidiaries in Belgium in 2004, with an approved amount of accumulated investment flows of US$ 9.49 million between 1979 and 2004. Only US$ 0.05 million of realized investment was registered in 2004 as compared to US$ 0.3 million in 2003, which amounted to only 0.07 per cent of the EU-15. The stock of Chinese realized OFDI in Belgium was estimated at US$ 1.64 million, representing only 0.33 per cent of the amount invested in the EU-15, which placed it in twentieth position in Europe and ninth in the EU-15. In 2004 only one new project was approved for investment in Belgium for US$ 70,000 as compared to five new initiatives in the Netherlands for a total investment of US$ 8.53 million.

The above figures (Figure 11.2) show that Belgium has not been very successful in convincing Chinese investors to locate on its territory. This conclusion is not only illustrated by the low level compared to other small, open economies such as Denmark, the Netherlands, and Sweden, but the low score is even much more striking when compared to its attractiveness for FDI in general. This is clearly shown if one relates both global and

Chinese inward FDI to the size of the population of a number of countries in 2004. Ireland (US$ 56,920), the Netherlands (US$ 26,370), and Belgium (US$ 24,900) occupy the leading positions for the amount of global FDI in their economies on the basis of per capita GDP. The same calculation on the basis of Chinese incoming FDI finds Denmark (US$ 12.45), Spain (US$ 3.01), the UK (US$ 1.82), and Germany (US$ 1.57) at the top of this ranking. As small nations with high levels of inward FDI Ireland, Belgium, and the Netherlands respectively only reach US$ 0.01, 0.16, and 0.55.

Given the limited presence of Chinese FDI in Belgium, it is somewhat surprising to find that during the 1990s there were some 30 Chinese firms in Belgium. Most of them were trading companies that were active in sectors such as chemicals, metals, and food. As early as 1978 there was a China–Europe Distribution Centre in Antwerp that had attracted about ten Chinese trading firms during the 1980s and 1990s. Yet most of those firms later on moved to Germany, especially Hamburg, and the Netherlands or closed down at the end of the 1990s. In 2005 only 12 Chinese firms were registered as members of the Association of Chinese Companies in Belgium. Most of them were quite small and counted few local managers or staff members. The Chinese companies tended to be concentrated in the major Belgian cities of Antwerp and Brussels.

In transportation and logistics COSCO, the major Chinese shipping company, has been present in Belgium since the 1980s, while China Shipping also moved to Belgium in 1999. Cosco owns 20 per cent of Antwerp Gateway, one of the largest container docks in the new 'Deurganckdok' in the port of Antwerp. The early (1986) entrant Sinobeltrans closed down in 2006. BBCA is a very diversified group that is active in logistics and distribution, while SPB assembles LCD-TVs for AMOI to avoid the EU common external tariffs, which is also the case for Hisense. Sales and marketing offices have been established by Hangzhou Westlake Automotive Spare Parts (HWL). The presence of Torin Jacks (hydraulic products) during 2003–6 was rather ephemeral. CNOOC Belgium bvba used the country as a platform to acquire 16.68 per cent of MEG, a Canadian company in oil sands. China National Blue Star (ChemChina) bought all the remaining shares controlled by CVC Capital Partners in Drakkar Holdings, the parent company of the French-based food company Adisseo.

11.7 Location factors for Chinese enterprises in Europe

In a survey by Bain & Co. (Reinert and Altrichter, 2005) the needs of Chinese investors in Germany were classified in three groups of location factors, namely support during establishment, support during the integration stage, and support of private activities. Based on a Likert scale from 1 to 5, requests for legal help and political support scored highest in the category of support during establishment and in the overall list of factors. With a score of 4.0, finding partners for the establishment and German-language courses for the category of support during the integration stage came *ex aequo* in second position. Third place was taken by a score of 3.9 for administrative support during the establishment stage and contact with neighbours for the integrative support stage. The scores in the category of support of private activities were generally lower and varied between 3.2 and 2.6 for the following aspects: Chinese food, established Chinese community, Chinese cultural organizations, Chinese schools, and Chinese clubs. A survey about Chinese firms in Hamburg (HWF, 2005) indicated that one-quarter of the surveyed companies mentioned the city's central location and the port facilities as determining factors, compared with 17 per cent each for the excellent infrastructure and the closeness of the market. Also 16 per cent appreciated the presence of the so-called Chinese network.

The survey of Liu and Tian (2007) about Chinese firms in the UK showed that of the 16 motives that were submitted to the Chinese firms 'access to EU markets' ranked highest with a score of 3.47 on a Likert 1–5 scale, followed by 'more expansion opportunities' (3.22) and, strangely enough, 'cultural and language proximity' (3.21). To seek and advance managerial skills and to seek local talent were fourth and fifth in this list of preferences, with respectively 3.06 and 2.76. In sixth position came lower political risk in the UK, while Chinese government support ranked seventh with 2.29. This result concurs with the more general finding that market expansion and growth are the dominating motives for Chinese OFDI, and specifies that the UK is regarded in China as a gateway to the European market and that even familiarity with the English language provides Great Britain with a location advantage.

According to Cross and Voss (2007), early (defined as before 2000) Chinese entrants in the UK were driven by international competitive pressures as the motive to develop new markets, while late (established after 2000) China entrants strove to access existing pools of knowledge to build or augment firm-specific advantages. This would mean that Chinese outbound investors are moving from a market-seeking strategy toward the European market to more strategic-asset seeking investments to obtain access to existing technology, patents, R&D, brands, and distribution channels. Cross and Voss (2007) distinguished between offensive market-seeking investment drivers for Chinese OFDI in the UK, defensive-driven strategies, and asset-seeking investment drivers. For both the early and late entrants 'the ease of exporting to the industrialized countries from the British market' scored highest on the 1–5 Likert scale.

The defensive driven investment strategies for both early and late entrants are judged as being similar by Cross and Voss (2007), and are mainly inspired by the desire to defend and further expand their close relationship with British customers. Other defensive motives, such as circumventing trade barriers set up by the EU, seemed to be more of an issue for the latecomers rather than for the early entrants. The responses of the asset-seeking drive pursued by Chinese companies in Britain illustrate the importance of the need to acquire new and advanced management skills and technologies to enhance their competitive position in the markets in which they operate. Cross and Voss (2007) express surprise at the finding that the surveyed Chinese companies were not interested in purchasing a British brand, and offer as an explanation that either the Chinese are sufficiently confident about their own brands or underestimate the importance of such brands. Another intriguing result of their study is that Chinese firms link their competitive advantages with their soft skills, for example, their business skills, which is rather doubtful, according to the authors. The extensive international corporate network and the strong support from the Chinese parent company offer a more convincing argument for explaining some of the ownership advantages of Chinese MNEs.

11.8 Location motives for foreign and Chinese firms in Belgium

The answers provided by American investors (Van Den Bulcke and Zhang, 2005) about the location factors in Belgium as compared to neighbouring countries measured by a Likert scale of 1–5 showed that the labour market and industrial relations scored best, followed by infrastructure and availability of sites, the quality of life, commuter, and transport facilities. Most negative items were the level of the personal taxation, corporate taxation, incentives, and regulation and business environment.

On behalf of the Belgian Federation of Belgian Industries (FEB-VBO) Zhang and Van Den Bulcke (2007) carried out a survey among the top managers of six Chinese companies established in Belgium. Although this number represented half of the members of the Association of Chinese Companies in Belgium the study relied mostly on interviews and was mainly qualitative. Additional insights were sought from meetings with Chinese journalists and diplomats with responsibilities in foreign trade and investment who were stationed in Brussels. According to the Chinese managers the availability of a multilingual workforce, measured with a 1–5 Likert scale, was the most important location factor for Belgium. With a score of 4 on the Likert scale six factors received the same evaluation, namely: equal treatment of all businesses, stability of business regulations, market liberalization of the utilities such as the postal service and energy, the availability of international railway connections, presence of international shipping links, and stability of the political environment. Immediately behind these latter factors were: quality of airport facilities, economic stability, central geographical location of the country, availability of skilled labour, and management and environmental regulations. Since this survey was carried out, Hainan Airlines has established a direct connection between the Belgian capital (Brussels National Airport) and China, although the number of daily flights had to be reduced after a few months.

The evaluation of the Chinese managers about the disadvantageous location factors of Belgium were very similar to the responses that were expressed by American managers in a much larger and representative sample of US firms in Belgium, which stressed the negative aspects of labour costs, complicated incentives, and level of taxation. Most negative from the Chinese perspective were gross employment costs and level of the employers' social security payments. Information on how to find out more about investment incentives and the administrative process about how to apply were considered to be wanting. The existing labour regulations were regarded as somewhat less negative than the costs, while corporate taxation as well as personal income taxation and employees' social security contributions were also evaluated as somewhat less negative.

11.9 European attitudes and policies with regard to China's OFDI

According to E. Chen, (1) it is necessary to distinguish between the attitudes of the government, the media, and public opinion with regard to Chinese OFDI. He stated that the attitude of the EU governments is rather moderately liberal, while the American federal government should be considered as conservative. The reactions of the media and the public in the EU towards Chinese OFDI is labelled as moderate during the 'honeymoon' period for newly established Chinese subsidiaries, but may occasionally become negative under the influence of the media. Chen also stressed that the attitude of the general public in the US is more controlled by the media and that it continually varies between negative and positive.

EU governments have generally been positive with regard to Chinese OFDI, and many have taken measures to increase the attractiveness of their countries for Chinese investors. The UK signed a China–UK Investment Partnership Agreement as early as 2001. This mainly acts as a forum to discuss and effectively deal with difficulties that might crop up in the investment process. It has been reported that the mayor of the city of London lobbied the China Investment Corporation, one of China's sovereign wealth funds, to set up a branch in London (*China Daily*, 2009). As a matter of fact the attitudes towards sovereign wealth funds in general and from China in particular have become much less negative since the economic crisis of 2008–9 (Fotak and Megginson, 2009).

Several EU countries (for example, Denmark, the Netherlands, Germany, and UK) have established Investment Promotion Agencies to target Chinese investors and have opened offices on the Mainland. Mahieu (2006) has noted that the French experience with Chinese investors was favourable enough to expand the office of 'invest in France' in China. Efforts have also been made to bridge the language gap by establishing websites in Chinese and the posting of documents in Mandarin. Early examples of such initiatives were in the

Netherlands (www.nfia-china.com) and Germany (www.invest-in-germany.de/cn/). In the Netherlands a Chinese business hotel was built near the city of Delft to lodge visiting Chinese businessmen and government officials in an environment that looks familiar and intends to lessen cultural differences. According to data published by the Netherlands Foreign Investment Agency (NFIA), China was the third most important foreign investor in terms of the number of projects for three years in a row (2006–8) behind the US and Korea. During this three-year period Chinese firms provided on average 10 per cent of the jobs in foreign-owned firms and ranked second, although far behind the US, both in 2007 and 2008 (NFIA, 2009).

Based on figures from the consulting and auditing firm Ernst & Young, GLAEconomics (2004) stated that firms from Greater China (including Singapore) created 46,300 jobs in Europe between 1997 and 2004, of which 20,500 (44 per cent) were in the UK and 1,000 in London. Yet, two-thirds of these jobs were generated by Taiwanese firms, even though they accounted for less than half (44 per cent) of the number of projects. Singapore carried out 13 per cent of the number of projects, but supplied only 3 per cent of the employment creation. The average employment per company was only 68 people for firms from the Mainland, compared to respectively 140 and 294 for companies from Hong Kong and Taiwan.

11.10 Evaluation of the Belgian investment climate for Chinese investors

At the time of the FEB-VBO study (Zhang and Van Den Bulcke, 2007) the Chinese managers, journalists, and officials who were interviewed were quite critical and thought that Belgium did not have much of a China policy. Their main objection was the complicated administrative and institutional system in Belgium. They claimed that Belgium lacked a unique 'image' or 'voice' abroad, especially from the Chinese perspective. Not only is Belgium less visible compared to larger European countries, its regional devolution into three regions, that is, Flanders, Brussels, and Wallonia, makes it difficult to develop a country identity. Moreover there is often competition rather than cooperation between these regions. The Chinese interviewees also regretted the absence of the national administration to represent Belgium in bilateral trade dialogue. They found it difficult for the Chinese central government and national trade organizations to develop active official channels with the regions in Belgium. While these remarks might be interpreted as though the Chinese wanted to change the constitutional reality of Belgium, it has to be admitted that a unique and strong image for the country will only be possible by respecting the division of power in the Belgian political structure.

The interviewed managers, journalists, and officials complained in particular about the relationship between China and Belgium, stating that there was no established contact point, such as an interactive China desk or department. According to these opinions, an expert support system or expert committee to facilitate coordination and decision-making about China should be established.[2] The interviewed Chinese regretted the absence of an effective framework at the federal level for trade promotion activities and thereby were ignorant of the reality of the Belgian political structure in which many domains, such as international trade, have been decentralized and have come under the authority of the regions. However, their complaints about the strict Belgian policy about obtaining a working permit and visa were even more severe.

The practical procedures to obtain a working permit and visa were considered as much too long and too complicated. While the so-called professional card is delivered by the Foreign Office of the federal government, the employment of foreign experts is controlled by the regional authorities. It was claimed that the request for an extension of the professional card was sometimes made dependent on the business performance of the company, thereby ignoring the fact that start-ups rarely have positive results at the beginning stages of their activities. Another handicap raised by the interviewees was that the procedures were long and not transparent. Business activities suffered from frequent interruptions because of repeated visa problems. If the visa and residential permit are not received on time or the renewal takes too long, it becomes difficult to travel abroad. This may result in the loss of business contacts and contracts during the waiting periods before the visa is finally delivered.[3]

It was suggested that the difficulties about extending and obtaining work permits and visas for Chinese managers might be responsible for the closure of Chinese firms or the decision to move to another European country. Examples of relocation of Chinese firms that were mentioned in the interviews were Beijing Drawn-work, Tianjin Distribution Centre, Henan Yueyang, and Shanghai Electricity.

A study carried out by Atos Consulting (2006) on behalf of the Ministry of Economics of the Netherlands has shown, however, that visa problems are not limited to Belgium. The Atos report compared the average number of days needed for visa requests at EU Schengen offices in four cities (Beijing, New Delhi, Moscow, and Riadh). Information was collected about the length of the visa procedure in those cities for six countries (the Netherlands, Denmark, Belgium, Italy, France, and Germany). The study confirmed that the visa procedure took longer in Belgium (and Denmark) as six days were needed, compared to four for Germany, three for the Netherlands and Italy, and only two for France. A surprising result from the comparison of the Belgian visa procedure between China–Beijing and India–New Delhi was that six days were needed in Beijing, while in New Delhi this could be handled in less than one day. An interesting finding is also that the size of the visa requests in Beijing for the earlier-mentioned Schengen countries was much higher for Germany and to a lesser extent also for France, than for Italy and especially the Netherlands and Belgium.

11.11 Promotion and marketing measures to attract Chinese enterprises to Belgium

Like most countries the federal government of Belgium as well as the regional governments and employers' associations regularly organize promotional visits and trade and investment missions to China. How effective such visits and missions are is difficult to find out as the opinions of the participants may be exaggerated, and signed 'declarations of intent' or 'memoranda of understanding' between enthusiastic future partners are not necessarily finalized.

Belgium was one of the first countries to conclude a bilateral agreement with China at the beginning of the 1980s. In 2005 a double taxation agreement between Hong Kong and Belgium was signed to facilitate the transfer of profits from the EU to China via Hong Kong. In the same year a collaboration agreement was concluded between the Belgian export and FDI investment insurance agency Ducroire-Delcredere and China's newly established Sinosure. Also in 2005 the China–Belgium Direct Equity Fund was launched to help small and medium-sized Belgian enterprises (SMEs) to get a foothold in China. The negotiations to make this into a two-way street by creating a 'mirror facility' to support Chinese firms with investment plans in Belgium have not yet resulted in a new agreement, however.

Apparently 2005 was a crucial year in which the Belgian authorities discovered the importance of Chinese OFDI. During that year the region of Flanders launched its China action plan, which consisted of the following items (Moerman, 2005):

- setting up a service centre in Flanders for Chinese companies as well as in China for Flemish firms;
- proactively approaching of Chinese companies, e.g., by setting up a website to provide information in Chinese to potential investors;
- cooperating in the life sciences, e.g., by establishing bio-incubators, clusters in the pharmaceutical and healthcare sector and in knowledge-based industries (such as IMEC and broadband technology);
- enhancing Flanders' position in logistics services (Flanders Institute for Logistics, Flanders Institute for Broadband Technology);
- stimulating mobility of researchers between Flanders and China.

On the basis of this plan, the Flemish regional government made the following four recommendations:

- promoting cultural exchanges (a Flanders House in China);
- developing a Chinese knowledge cluster by launching a virtual campus about Chinese culture, society, and language;
- establishing a Chinese school in Flanders;
- promoting Flanders as a destination for Chinese tourists.

11.12 Websites as leading sources of information about the business climate

A survey of American executives (Development Counselors International, 2008) about the sources of information on the business climate showed that online sources are becoming extremely important. With almost 30 per cent of the interviewed managers relying on online sources, this factor comes in fifth position in a list of 13 sources.[4]

When queried about the effectiveness of seven different market techniques for site selection in 2008, 55 per cent of the American managers rated internet/website at 4 and 5 on a five-point Likert scale, thereby registering the highest score and slightly ahead of planned visits to corporate executives and public relations/publicity, which took up second and third positions.[5]

There has been a marked evolution in the importance of different effective marketing techniques for site selection between 1996 and 2008, according to the ATOS survey. In 1996 the Internet/website was only chosen by 18 per cent of the American managers as an effective promotion tool. This doubled in 1999 to 37 per cent, stagnated to 34 per cent in 2002 and made another jump forward in 2002 to 53 per cent, which more or less equalled the level for 2008 of 56 per cent.[6]

11.13 Evaluation of Belgium's website for the promotion of Chinese OFDI

At the request of FEB-VBO and as a follow-up to a more general survey, Zhang and Van Den Bulcke (2007) evaluated the effectiveness of the Belgian websites that promoted foreign direct investment. The objectives of the study were:

- to benchmark the inward investment promotion websites of the Belgian federal government and the regional IPAs;
- to analyse the reliability and effectiveness of these websites for Chinese investors;
- to formulate suggestions for an effective web promotion strategy adapted to the needs of the Chinese investors.

The project was set up as some kind of 'laboratory test' and relied on ten Chinese students who obtained master's degrees at the University of Antwerp Management School (UAMS) as a proxy for potential Chinese investors.[7] During a three-hour computer session – carried out on 18 January 2007 – students were asked to use the Google and Baidu search engines to check if the Belgian inward investment promotion websites were accessible and to find out how relevant the information was for Chinese investors. The general idea was to check whether the Belgian IIP websites were successful in convincing Chinese firms to proceed further and consider Belgium as a favourable location when compared to the neighbouring countries.

Based on the checklist formulated by Loewendahl (2001) and the benchmark developed by MIGA (2006), the FEB-VBO study (Zhang and Van Den Bulcke, 2007) tested the Belgian inward investment promotion agencies on four key dimensions, namely information architecture, design, content, and promotional effectiveness, and worked out a combined score. Information architecture takes into account the speed of the connections, the time it takes to download documents, and the possibilities to carry out groupings according to key location factors. For the design the evaluation checked the extent to which the website was clear and had an easy layout. The relevance for the user as well as the availability of the necessary data were the elements on which the content was evaluated. The promotional effectiveness was evaluated by the extent that the needs of the investors were anticipated and by the availability of the information on the major search engines. The use of foreign language options—in this case Chinese—was also taken into account.

Belgium has two websites for investment promotion that were set up by the federal government, one by the Federal Public Service (FPS) Economy for SMEs, Self-Employed and Energy (FPS1) and the other jointly set up by FPS Economy, the FPS Finance and the FPS Chancellery of the Prime Minister (FPS2). The three regional IPAs with their own websites are Flanders Investment and Trade (FIT) for the Flemish region, Office for Foreign Investors (OFI) in Wallonia, and the Brussels Enterprise Agency (BEA) in the Brussels region. Given the institutional 'division of labour' the task of FSP1 and also FSP2 is to provide essential country information, while the regional IPAs should address the effective promotion of their region.[8]

As part of the laboratory test a separate search was conducted to compare the situation in Belgium with the promotional Internet efforts of the neighbouring countries. It was concluded that the Belgian websites from the point of view of the simulated Chinese investors were characterized by the following:

- lack of or incomplete information about the costs of amenities such as utilities, transportation, and real estate. This kind of information should be kept up to date and should also provide insights into recent economic developments relevant for foreign investors;
- unclear and incomplete information about the regulations of visa applications and other immigration matters;
- need for more information about technology transfer issues, product innovation systems, and intellectual property protection for investment in R&D activities;
- shortcomings in the provision of macro-economic data and market and sector information such as demographic data, identification of the major

players in the different industries, and availability of local suppliers. Links with professional and sectoral organizations might be most useful;
- danger of confusion and overlap between the two websites of the federal government;
- need for clear links between the websites of the federal government with those of the regions. Tailor-made information about the key location factors should be provided in which concerns of the potential investors should be anticipated;
- information should also be made available via downloadable documents and promotional brochures.

In the attempt to compare the location attractiveness of Belgium with neighbouring countries the laboratory test also asked participants to formulate their first three choices for the location of their virtual investments in the order of their preference. Eight out of ten listed Germany either as their first (4) or second (4) choice, compared to only four for the UK (2 + 2) and three for France (2 + 1). The Netherlands and Belgium were quoted each three times, with one for second and two for third choice for the Netherlands, and one for first and two for the third option for Belgium. This exercise confirms the high attractiveness of Germany, which was already referred to on the basis of investment data.

11.14 Policy implications and recommendations for European host countries

Investment promotion agencies from developed countries are still very much focused on direct investment flows from other developed countries as these take up most of global FDI. Yet, as OFDI from emerging economies such as China are making headway these IPAs are realizing the potential contribution from these firms to their economy as a source of diversification. The administrative aspects of immigration are non-priority issues for FDI from developed countries. European countries should be aware that the policy with respect to OFDI from emerging economies should be put in a larger framework and fully take into account immigration issues such as the procedures for obtaining visas and working permits for managers and experts from the emerging countries as this has often been an important roadblock. However, this should preferably be dealt with in a EU context.

European countries should consider renegotiating their bilateral investment treaties (BITs) with China and other emerging economies. Most of the BITs that were signed in the past consisted mainly of assurances that the activities of the MNEs from developed countries would receive guarantees about the repatriation of equity capital and profits to the country of origin if there would be a need to do so as well as the protection of their assets.

Agreements should become really bilateral and offer the same protection and guarantees to OFDI from emerging economies. The renegotiated German bilateral treaty with China could be seen as an example.

Now that emerging economies like China have come to a stage in which they actively promote OFDI through incentives and state support (De Beule and Van Den Bulcke, 2010) European governments and the EU Commission should make sure that Southern countries do not overextend their promotional efforts to encourage their companies to invest abroad. While the fear of the influence of the Chinese state should not be exaggerated, the policy measures could be more transparent. This should make it possible to avoid conflicts with China about the choice and aggressive support of their strategic companies, the generous extension of loans for investment abroad and the role of the sovereign wealth funds such as the China Investment Corporation. Therefore transparency should be insisted upon.

European IPAs should rely more actively on websites to provide information about investment locations in Europe to potential investors from Southern economies. Tailor-made websites in Chinese make a lot of sense as part of the promotion strategy of European countries. As Chinese private enterprises are more often engaging in activities abroad they should be considered as special targets for the European IPAs. Testimonials and case studies should also be included. The most important Chinese search engines for URL submission are Baidu, Sina, Sohu, Yahoo China, and Google China.

With regard to Belgium, the suggestions formulated in the studies commissioned by FEB-VBO resulted in some changes in the investment regime. The Belgian federal government announced that a special administrative procedure was to be set up for Chinese investors in order to facilitate their visa and work permit applications and to reduce the lead time necessary to obtain these essential documents for doing business in the country (BCECC, December 2006). A Chinese-language option was added to the website of the Flanders Investment and Trade agency (FIT), while a number of documents about Belgian investment regulations, location factors, and business opportunities were made available by FIT and the other regional investment promotion agencies. FEB-VBO held constructive discussions with Chinese diplomats and trade representatives in Brussels and the Belgian Embassy in Beijing to convince MOFCOM to include Belgium in the next edition of the official 'List of promoted countries and sectors for China's outward FDI'.

The positive attitude towards OFDI from emerging economies, especially China, is not generally shared. Okano-Heijmans and Van der Putten (2009) argue that to welcome investment from China should not mean that governments just sit back and enjoy the benefits, because on occasion they may run counter to the national interests of the host country. To check possible negative effects they propose to install a European case-by-case review system to improve the European bargaining power vis-à-vis China and to avoid the situation where countries are played off against each other. As an example they refer to the Committee on Foreign Investment in the US (CFIUS), which goes back to 1975 and was strengthened in 2007 by the Foreign Investment and National Security Act; it recently influenced a change in the Canadian investment regime (Bhattacharjee, 2009). Even though these authors admit that for the moment Chinese enterprises do not seek controlling interests in Europe and that the review system should not discriminate between non-EU investors on the basis of nationality, this suggestion is too much of a protectionist move to be acceptable as such. On the contrary, more attention should be devoted to the development of partnerships with Chinese investors to recapitalize and revitalize firms (BCG, 2006a, 2006b), for instance in the EU.

If certain sectors or companies are off limits for Chinese and other investors from emerging economies, this should clearly be indicated in advance (Brown, 2008: 13). Globerman and Shapiro (2009: 178) consider the main legislative instrument available to the US to be 'insufficiently precise and excessively vulnerable to abuse from domestic economic and political interest groups to serve the interests of the Americans.' On the other hand, it has to be admitted that 'Managing national security and national economic security in advanced economies requires better Chinese data on who is investing, where the investment is made, and who controls investment decisions' (Rosen and Hanemann, 2009: 14). The appeal for more transparency about Chinese OFDI had been made by several other analysts (Scissors, 2009). To hinder Chinese OFDI might go against the need to integrate the Chinese economy more fully within the global economy, although more statistical transparency should be expected. According to Rosen and Hanemann (2009: 2), 'China's OFDI data are out of line with international standards, and the value, destination, and sectoral mix of its OFDI are unclear.' To advise that China should concentrate on greenfield investments rather than acquisitions (particularly unsolicited bids and deals involving aggressive tactics) is not justified, however (Milhaupt, 2008), as is convincingly shown by Globerman and Shapiro (2009). China's global challengers, like those from other emerging economies such as India and Brazil, 'must accelerate their decisions about where they want to build defensible competitive positions and where they want to become leaders. Failure to make these hard choices may leave them in an unsustainable position—neither globally strong nor locally competitive' (BCG, 2009: 27). According to Rui and Yip (2008) and Peng (2009), one of the reasons for China's choice of M&As instead of greenfield ventures finds its origin in Chinese disappointment with the progress of accessing strategic assets through other modes of entry, such as international joint ventures.

Appendix

Table 11A.1 Number of 'Greater China's' foreign affiliates in Europe, by industry (2007)

Home country		China		Taiwan		Macau		Hong Kong	
Nace2	Description	N	%	N	%	N	%	N	%
	Agriculture and mining activities								
1	Agriculture, hunting and related service activities	11	0.2%	1	0.2%	0	0.0%	7	0.6%
2	Forestry, logging and related service activities	0	0.0%	0	0.0%	0	0.0%	3	0.3%
5	Fishing	0	0.0%	0	0.0%	0	0.0%	1	0.1%
11	Extraction of crude petroleum and natural gas	1	0.0%	0	0.0%	0	0.0%	3	0.3%
13	Mining of metal ores	1	0.0%	0	0.0%	0	0.0%	0	0.0%
14	Other mining and quarrying	3	0.1%	0	0.0%	0	0.0%	1	0.1%
	Total agriculture and mining	16	0.3%	1	0.2%	0	0.0%	15	1.3%
	Manufacturing								
15	Manufacture of food products and beverages	11	0.2%	1	0.2%	0	0.0%	3	0.3%
16	Manufacture of tobacco products	2	0.0%	0	0.0%		0.0%	0	0.0%
17	Manufacture of textiles	14	0.3%	1	0.2%	0	0.0%	2	0.2%
18	Manufacture of clothing	29	0.6%	1	0.2%	0	0.0%	6	0.5%
19	Manufacture of leather (products)	14	0.3%	0	0.0%	0	0.0%	2	0.2%
20	Manufacture of wood (products)	16	0.3%	1	0.2%	0	0.0%	0	0.0%
21	Manufacture of pulp and paper (products)	4	0.1%	0	0.0%	0	0.0%	0	0.0%
22	Publishing and printing	6	0.1%	0	0.0%	0	0.0%	7	0.6%
23	Manufacture of coke, petroleum products and nucle	1	0.0%	0	0.0%	0	0.0%	0	0.0%
24	Manufacture of chemical(s) (products)	15	0.3%	1	0.2%	0	0.0%	5	0.4%
25	Manufacture of rubber and plastic products	9	0.2%	5	1.2%	0	0.0%	6	0.5%
26	Manufacture of other non-metallic mineral product	7	0.1%	1	0.2%	0	0.0%	3	0.3%

(*continued*)

Table 11A.1 Continued

Home country		China		Taiwan		Macau		Hong Kong	
Nace2	Description	N	%	N	%	N	%	N	%
	Manufacturing								
27	Manufacture of basic metals	2	0.0%	0	0.0%	0	0.0%	1	0.1%
28	Manufacture of fabricated metal products	7	0.1%	0	0.0%	0	0.0%	5	0.4%
29	Manufacture of machinery and equipment	31	0.7%	5	1.2%	0	0.0%	6	0.5%
30	Manufacture of office machinery and computers	8	0.2%	8	1.9%	0	0.0%	0	0.0%
31	Manufacture of electrical machinery and apparatus	5	0.1%	4	0.9%	0	0.0%	10	0.9%
32	Manufacture of Radio, TV and communication equip	8	0.2%	13	3.0%	0	0.0%	8	0.7%
33	Manufacture of medical and optical instruments	5	0.1%	5	1.2%	0	0.0%	6	0.5%
34	Manufacture of motor vehicles	3	0.1%	1	0.2%	0	0.0%	1	0.1%
35	Manufacture of other transport equipment	4	0.1%	3	0.7%	0	0.0%	3	0.3%
36	Manufacture of furniture + manuf. N.e.c.	17	0.4%	2	0.5%	0	0.0%	12	1.0%
37	Recycling	5	0.1%	1	0.2%	0	0.0%	4	0.3%
	Total manufacturing	42	0.9%	25	5.9%	0	0.0%	34	3.0%
	Services and related activities								
40	Electricity, gas, steam and hot water supply	2	0.0%	0	0.0%	0	0.0%	0	0.0%
45	Construction	29	0.6%	2	0.5%	0	0.0%	9	0.8%
50	Trade of motor vehicles	36	0.8%	9	2.1%	0	0.0%	11	1.0%
51	Wholesale trade	2938	61.7%	204	47.8%	0	0.0%	383	33.3%
52	Retail trade	427	9.0%	29	6.8%	2	33.3%	50	4.3%
55	Hotels and restaurants	565	11.9%	3	0.7%	1	16.7%	25	2.2%
60	Land and pipeline transport	8	0.2%	0	0.0%	1	16.7%	5	0.4%
61	Water transport	8	0.2%	0	0.0%	0	0.0%	2	0.2%

62	Airtransport	2	0.0%	0	0.0%	0	0.0%	2	0.2%
63	Supporting transport activities	71	1.5%	7	1.6%	0	0.0%	39	3.4%
64	Post and telecommunications	10	0.2%	1	0.2%	0	0.0%	13	1.1%
65	Financial intermediation	13	0.3%	7	1.6%	0	0.0%	14	1.2%
67	Ancillary financial intermediation activities	9	0.2%	0	0.0%	0	16.7%	6	0.5%
70	Real estate activities	35	0.7%	2	0.5%	1	0.0%	55	4.8%
71	Renting of machinery and equipment	2	0.0%	1	0.2%	0	0.0%	2	0.2%
72	Computer and related activities	14	0.3%	19	4.4%	0	0.0%	42	3.6%
73	Research and development	11	0.2%	5	1.2%	0	0.0%	17	1.5%
74	Other business activities	210	4.4%	52	12.2%	0	0.0%	277	24.1%
75	Public administration and defense	5	0.1%	0	0.0%	0	16.7%	1	0.1%
80	Education	6	0.1%	0	0.0%	1	0.0%	1	0.1%
85	Health and social work	10	0.2%	1	0.2%	0	0.0%	3	0.3%
91	Activities of membership organizations	11	0.2%	1	0.2%	0	0.0%	0	0.0%
92	Recreational and cultural activities	17	0.4%	3	0.7%	0	0.0%	11	1.0%
93	Other service activities	25	0.5%	1	0.2%	0	0.0%	27	2.3%
95	Private households with employed persons	0	0.0%	0	0.0%	0	0.0%	2	0.2%
99	Extra-territorial organizations and bodies	1	0.0%	0	0.0%	0	0.0%	0	0.0%
	Total Services	4465	93.76%	347	81.26%	6	100.00%	997	86.62%
	Total	4762	100.0%	427	100.0%	6	100.0%	1151	100.0%

Source: Authors' calculations based on Bureau van Dijk, 2008.

Notes

1. Remarks made during a presentation during the 'Five Diamond Conference' organized by Columbia University, New York, April 2008.
2. A similar complaint has been formulated in the UK (Brown, 2009: 7–8).
3. According to the American Chamber of Commerce in China, the visa process for the USA is very 'lengthy, uncertain and personally humiliating.' Nearly half of the members declared that they lost significant sales opportunities due to visa problems for PRC visitors and that it drives away Chinese customers to rival companies in Europe and Japan (*China Daily*, ''Humiliating' US Visa Process Deters Chinese', May 17, 2006).
4. In the ATOS survey online information is preceded by: dialogue with industry peers (60 per cent), articles in newspapers and magazines (about 50 per cent), business travel (about 40 per cent), and meetings with economic development groups (somewhat less than 40 per cent). For Chinese managers the importance of the Internet is likely to be much higher, given their limitations in the use of some of the other information sources.
5. While planned visits to corporate executives during this period remained at the same level and public relations/publicity and the staging of special events went up, the losses occurred in advertising, direct mail, and telemarketing. Given that this question allowed for multiple answers, it can also be concluded that the Internet/website approach is still being combined with other marketing and promotion techniques for site selection.
6. While 'hosting special events' was ranked fourth, with more than 40 per cent, with a score of 4–5, direct mail, advertising, and telemarketing closed the ranks with approximately 18, 15, and 5 per cent respectively.
7. Although ideally the project should have allowed the researchers to use Chinese managers in China for this experiment, this was not feasible because of limited funding. More than half of these students had work experience in China of almost three years; some of them had management experience.
8. The participants in the 'laboratory test' spontaneously found 67 relevant terms, 38 of which were in Chinese and 27 in English. In total 385 keywords were created. They selected 132 websites/pages (hosted by 71 websites of which 37 were in Chinese and 34 in English) for providing the most useful information about their virtual investment plans. One-third of this information was found on the websites of government institutions, one-fifth by professional online information providers, and slightly less than one-fifth (18 per cent) could be accessed via IIP websites. Within this latter group 10 per cent was provided by the Belgian IIP websites FPS1 and FPS2, 6 per cent by Flanders Investment and Trade (FIT), 1.5 per cent by the Brussels Enterprise Agency (BEA) and less than 1 (0.8) per cent by the Office for Foreign Investors (OFI).

References

APFC (2005), *China Goes Global: A Survey of Chinese Companies Outward Direct Investments*, Asia Pacific Foundation of Canada and China Council for the Promotion of International Trade, September, Vancouver–Beijing.

APFC (2006), *China Goes Global II: Survey of China's Outward Direct Investment Intentions*, Asia Pacific Foundation of Canada and China Council for the Promotion of International Trade, December, Vancouver–Beijing.

APFC (2009), *China goes Global: 2009 Survey of Outward Direct Investment Intentions of Chinese Companies, Preliminary Results*, Asia Pacific Foundation of Canada and China Council for the Promotion of International Trade, Vancouver–Beijing.

Atos Consulting (2006), *Onderzoek naar de ervaren knelpunten rondom visumverlening*, Rapport Ministerie van Economische Zaken, The Hague, March.

BCECC (2006), *China is a Privileged Investor*, Belgian–Chinese Chamber of Commerce, Newsletter No. 6, December.

BCG (2006a), *China's Global Challengers: The Strategic Implications of Chinese Outbound M&As*, Boston Consulting Group, Report.

BCG (2006b), *The New Global Challengers: How 100 Top Companies from Rapidly Developing Economies are changing the World*, Boston Consulting Group, Report.

BCG (2009), *The 2009 BCG 100 New Global Challengers: How Companies from Rapidly Developing Economies are Contending for Global Leadership*, Boston Consulting Group, Report.

Bhattacharjee, S. (2009), *National Security with a Canadian Twist: The Investment Canada Act and the New National Security Test*, Columbia FDI Perspectives, No. 10, July.

Brown, K. (2008), *Chinese Overseas Direct Investment: What Kind of Opportunity?* Chatham House, London, January.

Brown, K. (2009), *The UK and China. Dealing with a New-Old Friend*, Chatham House, Asia Programme Briefing Note, London, June.

Buckley, P., Clegg, J., Cross, A., Liu, X., Voss, H., and Zheng, P. (2007), 'The Determinants of Chinese Outward Foreign Direct Investment', *Journal of International Business Studies*, 18, 499–518.

Bureau Van Dijk (2008), Amadeus Database, Brussels, www.bvdep.com.

Cai, K. (1999), 'Outward Foreign Direct Investment: A Novel Dimension of China's Integration into the Regional and Global Economy', *China Quarterly*, 160, 836–80.

CCPIT (2009), *Survey on Current Conditions of and Intention for Outbound Investment by Chinese Enterprises*, China Council for the Promotion of International Trade, Beijing.

Cheung, Y.-W. and Qian, X. W. (2009), *The Empirics of China's Outward Direct Investment*, Paper, February.

Child, J. and Rodrigues, S. (2005), 'The Internationalization of Chinese Enterprises: A Case for Theoretical Extension?' *Management and Organization Review*, 3, 381–410.

China Daily (2009), "City of London Woos China Investment Corporation", October 26.

Cognato, M. (2008), 'China Investment Corporation: Threat or Opportunity?', *NBR Analysis*, 19 (1), July, 9–36.

Cross, A. and Voss, H. (2007), 'Chinese Direct Investment in the United Kingdom: An Assessment of Motivations and Competitiveness', paper presented at international conference on Four Decades of International Business at Reading: Looking at the Future, University of Reading.

Cui, L. and Jiang, F. (2008), 'FDI Entry Mode Choice of Chinese Firms: A Strategic Behavior Perspective', *Journal of World Business*, 44, 4, 434–44.

Davies, K. (2009), *While Global FDI Fall, China's Outward FDI Doubles*, Columbia FDI Perspectives No. 5, May.

De Beule, F. and Van Den Bulcke, D. (2010), 'Changing Policy Regimes in Outward Foreign Direct Investment: From Control to Promotion', in K. Sauvant, W. Maschek, and G. MacAllister (eds), *Foreign Direct Investment from Emerging Markets: The Challenges Ahead*. New York: Palgrave Macmillan.

Deloitte (2007), *East Meets West. Inbound M&A Germany: Emerging Market Perspectives*, Berlin.

Development Counselors International (2008), *A View from Corporate America: Winning Strategies in Economic Development Marketing. A Continuing Survey of Corporate Executives with Site Selection Responsibilities*, July.

Financial Times (2009), 'China: Beijing's Bulls Expand at Home and Abroad', September 21.

Fotak, V. and Megginson, W. (2009), *Are SWFs Welcome Now?* Columbia FDI Perspectives, No. 9, July.

GLAEconomics (2004), *Enter the Dragon: An Analysis of Chinese FDI in London*, Greater London Authority, December.

Globerman, S. and Shapiro, D. (2009), 'Economic and Strategic Considerations Surrounding Chinese FDI in the United States', *Asia Pacific Journal of Management*, 26, 163–83.

Godfrey, M. (2008), 'Eastern Promise', *EuroBiz Magazine*, June.

Hirt, M. and Orr, G. (2006), 'Helping Chinese Companies Master Global M&As', *McKinsey Quarterly*, 4, 39–49.

HWF (2005), *Chinesische Firmen in Hamburg*, Hamburgische Gesellschaft für Wirtschaftsförderung.

IBM and Fudan University (2006), *Going Global: Prospects and Challenges for Chinese Companies on the World Stage.*

Liu, L. and Tian, Y. (2007), 'The Internationalization of Chinese Enterprises: The Analysis of the UK Case', paper presented at international conference Four Decades of International Business Research at Reading, University of Reading.

Loewendahl, H. (2001), 'A Framework for FDI Promotion', *Transnational Corporations*, 10 (1), 1–41.

Luedi, T. (2008), 'China's Track Record in M&As', *McKinsey Quarterly*, 3, 76–81.

Lunding, A, (2006), *Global Champions in Waiting: Perspectives on China's Overseas Direct Investment*, Deutsche Bank Research, Frankfurt.

Mahieu, E. (2006), *Investments from Large Developing Countries in France and Europe*, Invest in France, Paris.

MIGA (2006), *Providing Information to Investors, Investment Promoting Agency Performance Review*, Multilateral Investment and Guarantee Agency, World Bank Group, October.

Milhaupt, C. (2008), *Is the U.S. Ready for FDI from China? Lessons from Japan's Experience in the 1980s*, Deloitte–Vale Columbia Center, Investing in the United States, A Reference Series for Chinese Investors.

Moerman, F. (2005), *Flanders and China: An Excellent Future Together*, Flanders' China Strategy, Brussels.

National Bureau of Statistics of China (2009), *China Statistical Yearbook*, Beijing.

NFIA (2009), *Foreign Investors Still Favor the Netherlands*, Netherlands Foreign Investment Agency, The Hague, March.

Nicolas, F. (2009), *Chinese Direct Investment in Europe: Facts and Fallacies*, Chatham House Briefing Paper, London.

OECD (2008), *China 2008*, Investment Policy Review, Paris.

Okano-Heijmans, M. and Van der Putten, F.-P. (2009), 'Europe Needs to Sceen Chinese Investment', *Financial Times*, August 11.

Quan, Y. (2001), 'Access to the WTO and Internationalization Strategy of Chinese Companies', *Enterprise Studies*, 8, 12–24.

Reinert, U. and Altricher, S. (2006), *China Goes West: Eine Chance für die Deutsche Wirtschaft*, Bain & Co., Germany, Kompass.

Rosen, D. and Hanemann, T. (2009), *China's Changing Outbound Foreign Direct Investment Profile: Drivers and Policy Implications*, Peterson Institute for International Economics, Policy Brief, June.

Rossi, V. and Burghart, N. (2009), 'Chinese Investment in Europe: A Shift to Services', *China Business Review*, September–October, 26–8.

Rui, H. and Yip, G. (2008), 'Foreign Acquisitions by Chinese Firms: A Strategic Intent Perspective', *Journal of World Business*, 43, 213–26.

Scissors, D. (2009), *Chinese Foreign Investment: Insist on Transparency*, Backgrounder No. 2237, The Heritage Foundation, February.

UNCTAD (2005), *Emerging FDI from Developing Countries*, Trade and Development Board, Commission on Investment, Technology and Related Financial Flows, Note TD/B/COM.2.64, February.

UNCTAD (2009a), 'Transnational Corporations, Agricultural Production and Development', *World Development Report 2009*. New York/Geneva: United Nations.

UNCTAD (2009b), *World Investment Prospects Survey 2009–2011*. New York/Geneva: United Nations.

Van Den Bulcke, D. and Zhang, H. (2005), *Survey on US Direct Investment 2004–2005 and Business Confidence Survey: Doing Business in Belgium*, American Chamber of Commerce in Belgium, Brussels.

Von Keller, E. and Zhou, W. (2005), *From Middle Kingdom to Global Market: Expansion Strategies and Success Factors of China's Emerging Multinationals*, Roland Berger Strategy Consultants, Shanghai.

Zhang, H. and Van Den Bulcke, D. (1996) "International Management Strategies of Chinese Multinational Firms", in J. Child and Y. Liu (eds), *Management Issues for China in the 1990s: International Enterprises*. London: Routledge, 141–64.

Zhang, K. (2005), *Going Global: The Why, When and How of Chinese Companies' Outward Investment Intentions*, Canada in Asia, 5, Vancouver: Asia Pacific Foundation of Canada.

Zhang, H. and Van Den Bulcke, D. (2007), *Attracting Chinese Investors: An Assessment of the Belgian Inward Foreign Direct Investment Promotion Websites from an Investor Perspective*, Federation of Belgian Industries/University of Antwerp Management School.

12
The European Union, Southern Multinationals and the Question of the 'Strategic Industries'

Judith Clifton and Daniel Díaz-Fuentes

12.1 Introduction[1]

Much of the controversy around foreign direct investment (FDI) in European policy-making circles in the recent period has crystallized around the notion of incoming FDI (IFDI) as a potential threat to 'strategic industries'. Definitions of what constitutes a 'strategic industry' vary by country (Schulz, 2008) and even by government ministry, since those responsible for finance or competition will not necessarily share the same vision as those working in defence, employment, innovation, environment, transport or energy. In the recent period, debates and usage of 'strategic industry' to question and even block IFDI have come to the forefront in the European Union (EU). Probably the most controversial case of a Southern Multinational in the EU is Russia's state-owned Gazprom. Many policy-makers suspect that Gazprom has geopolitical, rather than commercial, interests in EU gas markets (Clifton, Díaz-Fuentes and Revuelta, 2010; Clifton and Díaz-Fuentes, 2010b). There have, however, been less high-profile instances where potential investors from the South have been unsuccessful in entering the EU, such as Mexican billionaire Carlos Slim's frustrated attempt to enter the Italian telecommunications market. Identifying and quantifying EU protectionism vis-à-vis Southern Multinationals in methodological terms is a challenge, however. Firstly, this is because details of why mergers & acquisitions (M&A) are blocked are usually quite opaque. Secondly, there is significant evidence of 'economic nationalism' as regards IFDI into certain 'strategic industries' from many countries, including other EU member states. Then Italian Prime Minister Romano Prodi spoke of an 'Italian solution' for Telecom Italia when foreign takeover by an American consortium was on the cards, while France's former Prime Minister Dominique de Villepin celebrated '*patriotisme économique*' (*Le Monde*, 2005) when faced with the prospect of the takeover of food company Danone by US multinational PepsiCo (Fuller, 2005). In Spain the 'Endesa saga' ended with the European Commission (EC) criticizing the government for avoiding a legitimate takeover by E.ON. So protectionism in the EU is not only applicable to IFDI from the emerging markets.

How, then, to evaluate recent EU policies affecting IFDI? This chapter analyses responses to IFDI from emerging markets in the 'strategic industries' from within the EU in a fast-changing environment. Diverse sectors are analysed though most attention is paid to two sectors that have been widely considered to be strategic by most countries around the world for several decades: energy and telecommunications. In order to understand the dynamics of the EU's international investment climate, particularly from the perspective of emerging markets, three main levels of analysis are required. First, the changing international context needs analysis, in particular the extent to which IFDI from emerging markets has challenged the status quo of the traditional investment climate, as well as the unfolding financial crisis and economic recession. Second, the European authorities, principally the EC, require analysis as the main institution responsible for forging the European Single Market and ensuring the 'four freedoms', meaning movement of goods, services, capital, and people. Third, individual member state behaviour needs examination, since it lies with national governments to establish FDI policy, and satisfy domestic political economy and welfare demands. This chapter is organized into four sections. In the second section, the EU IFDI regime for energy and telecommunications is set in international context. Thirdly, the evolution of recent European-level policy reform that directly or indirectly impinges on IFDI in these sectors is analysed, and the role of the Commission as 'neutralizer' of potential or real restrictive attitudes towards IFDI at the national level is considered. Conclusions follow in section four.

12.2 The changing EU FDI regime in international context

The EU boasts one of the world's most liberal FDI regimes (OECD, 2007). EU member states are hosts to multinationals in most sectors from virtually all corners of the globe, and many of the new FDI players from emerging markets opt for the EU as host. In the context of increased FDI flows from 2004, peaking at an historic US$ 1.8 billion in 2007, the EU – like most other countries – was rightly criticized for increasing the implementation of restrictive policies and practices with an aim to limit IFDI as and when governments thought barriers necessary or desirable (UNCTAD, 2008). The EU has also been criticized by various business executives from emerging markets for raising protectionist barriers to their firms, including Gazprom (Traynor, 2007) and Mittal (as chronicled by Bouquet and Ousey, 2008). The financial crisis and economic recession triggered by the collapse of the sub-prime market in the United States since 2007 changes the international context for FDI policy significantly. UNCTAD (2009) estimates that IFDI and cross-border mergers and acquisitions (M&A) to the EU would decline by around one-third in 2008: this represents the largest decline in any other part of the world. Similar or even larger declines are predicted for 2009. Governments in the EU are divided between requiring short-term capital investment to guarantee jobs and economic growth, and the need to satisfy medium to long-term political and economic concerns that fuelled the rise of FDI restrictions in the first place. These concerns could escalate if the temptation towards protectionism is not firmly resisted.

When comparing the openness of the EU IFDI regime at the international level using OECD (2007) methodology, the EU can be classified, on average, as being one of the most open regimes in the world, comparable to the US, and more open than Australia, Canada, Mexico, and New Zealand, as shown in Graph 12.1. Here, on a scale of 0 to 1, countries' openness to IFDI is shown, 0 meaning no legal restrictions and 1 meaning full restrictions. The EU is much more open than most emerging markets: of the BRIC countries, Brazil is the most open of the four, which helps to explain why OFDI from the EU is largely concentrated there. That said, openness is uneven, since there are important differences in the extent to which individual member states protect diverse sectors. Generally speaking, the EU's most open regimes are the UK, Ireland, Netherlands, Germany, Belgium, and Italy, while Norway, Finland, and Spain pose the greatest restrictions. As regards sectoral openness, EU countries tend to protect much more utilities and services than manufacturing (OECD, 2007: 140).

If much of the tension in the EU's IFDI regime is concerned with protecting 'strategic industries', it is interesting to see how that debate has evolved. Traditionally, concern focused on military-related sectors but, recently, increased attention is being placed on network industries (energy, communications, transportation, and water) and the financial and banking sectors. Though the EU is as open as the US in general, both its electricity and telecommunications sectors are more protected than their American counterparts. For the bulk of the twentieth century, these sectors, along with other network industries, were organized as state-owned monopolies, managed according to particular social welfare principles, and heavily unionized (Clifton, Comín and Díaz-Fuentes, 2008). Even at the beginning of the twenty-first century, they are still broadly perceived as being 'public services' and thought to require special regulation. Despite this, the telecommunication sector is much more open to IFDI than the electricity sector. Explanations can be found in geopolitics or political economy. Smaller EU countries located near to the Russian borders have established the greatest restrictions to IFDI in electricity. It seems that these countries are concerned about foreign takeovers of their energy sector, a concern exacerbated by their small size and their Russian neighbour (Klinova, 2007). France, however, also maintains above-average protection of its electricity sector. The most liberal electricity regimes are Belgium and Spain (which historically had regionally based companies, with limited competition, and significant private sector

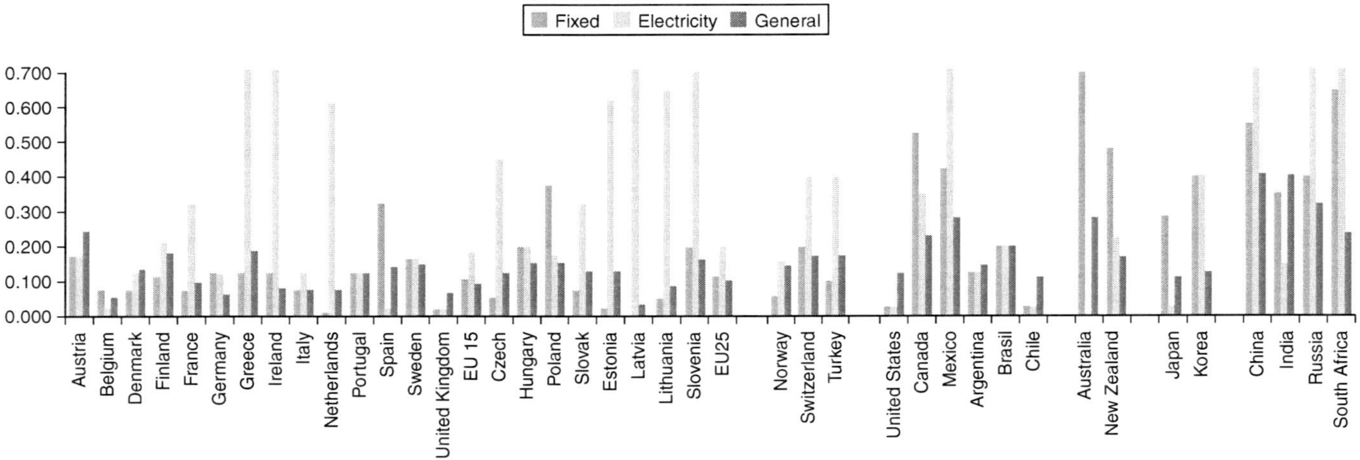

Graph 12.1 'Openness' to IFDI in general, fixed telephony and electricity
Source: Elaborated by the authors, based on OECD (2006), Golub (2003), and Koyama and Golub (2006).

involvement) and the UK (which implemented market-oriented reforms, including unbundling, in the 1980s). Somewhat paradoxically, these 'liberal' companies were taken over by other ex-incumbents (Electrabel by Suez-GDF, and Endesa by Enel and EDF). In the UK the main operators are E.On and RWE. In contrast, the telecommunication sector in the EU, which is often described as a 'strategic' sector in many countries, is on average as open to IFDI as any other industry sector in the EU.[2]

In terms of the direction of recent IFDI flows into EU member states, nearly 70 per cent were intra-EU flows, though in some countries, such as Austria, Belgium, Italy, Spain, Romania, Bulgaria, Poland, and the Czech Republic, this ratio was higher (Table 12.1). Albeit still marginal in terms of volume, IFDI from emerging markets has grown rapidly in recent years. The BRIC economies account for the larger part of these IFDI flows, some 1.4 per cent of total IFDI on average over the 2004–8 period (up from 0.7 per cent over 2004–6). Brazil and Russia account together for one per cent. Russian inflows have been mainly directed towards Germany, Austria, Bulgaria, and Spain, as well as towards other smaller countries such as Latvia, Estonia, and Cyprus (not included in the table). Meanwhile, Brazilian inflows have focused on Hungary,[3] Spain, the Netherlands, Portugal, Denmark, and Italy.

As regards the M&A track record, the EU regime is also relatively open when compared internationally. The entry of multinationals from emerging markets into both Northern and Southern markets has increasingly attracted the attention of scholars.[4] In recent years, dozens of 'Southern' Multinationals have entered the EU, including Tata, Mittal, Nanjing, Marcopolo, Cemex, Weg, Orascom, Lukoil, Gazprom, PEMEX, Hyundai, Sungwoo, Samsung, Sabó, Sonatrach, Grupo Bimbo, and Petrobras, to mention a few, sometimes taking over flagship European firms. Of course, a considerable number of the attempts by multinationals from emerging markets to enter the European energy and telecommunications infrastructure have failed, such as recent failures experienced by Russia's Gazprom and Mexico's Grupo Carso. However, just as emerging market multinationals have been frustrated, so have many multinationals based within the EU. To illustrate: Catalunya's Gas Natural and Germany's E.ON energy firms were frustrated in their attempts to take over Spanish Endesa; in 2006, Spanish Abertis was blocked when it tried to merge with Italian Autostrade, even though the Commission later ruled that Italy had violated EU law. While it is possible to catalogue a list of M&A failures and success stories, it is difficult to conclude whether the EU is becoming increasingly more protectionist in the light of the emerging Southern Multinationals or whether its increased protectionism is more general. One way to evaluate the EU's current climate for IFDI, especially from emerging markets, is to follow the way in which policy has evolved—which directly or indirectly affects the FDI regime of the EU and its member states. This is done in the next section.

Table 12.1 Inward foreign direct investment: total flows (million Euros) by main receptor country and percentage by zone and investing country, EU-27, 2004–2008

Inward Foreign Direct Investment; total flows (million euros) by main receptor country and percentage by zone and investing country; European Union (27 countries) 2004–2008

	Total IFDI (million EUR) 2004–2008	Percentage of total IFDI in the receptor country by investing country or group of countries								
		Intra-EU27	Extra-EU27	USA	BRIC	Brazil	Russia	India	China (excluding Hong Kong)	Hong Kong (SAR China)
European Union (27 countries)	2,356,976	70.9	29.1	12.7	1.4	0.56	0.44	0.15	0.11	0.16
United Kingdom	466,710	53.7	46.3	20.0	0.3			0.14		0.13
Luxembourg	447,448	55.7	44.3	9.0	–0.4	0.12	–1.18		0.47	0.25
France	352,469	76.6	23.4	13.8	0.7	0.07	0.12	0.02	0.09	0.41
Belgium	166,435	90.2	9.8	7.3	0.7			0.07	0.11	0.56
Netherlands	132,180	81.8	18.2	13.7	0.7	0.44	0.12		0.12	
Spain	128,501	87.8	12.2	7.0	1.7	0.77	0.81	0.03		0.04
Germany	124,400	78.7	21.3	1.5	3.3	0.06	2.60	0.08	0.42	0.10
Hungary	93,151	60.4	39.6	7.9	0.6	1.34	–1.07			0.35
Italy	85,818	92.4	7.6	2.7	1.0	0.39	0.19			0.36
Sweden	63,960	74.5	25.5	13.1	–0.3		–0.59		0.07	0.41
Poland	61,898	86.4	13.6	4.7	–0.8		–1.21	0.04	0.39	
Austria	46,546	92.7	7.3	1.8	2.2	0.28	1.18	0.15		0.60
Czech Republic	31,767	89.0	11.0	3.0	0.2			0.04	0.22	0.06
Romania	30,411	93.6	6.4	1.4	0.7		0.25	0.09	0.35	
Denmark	28,641	75.0	25.0	10.8	2.3	1.38	0.55	0.07	0.30	0.02
Bulgaria	24,577	84.2	15.8	2.6	2.9		2.82	0.02	0.02	0.03
Portugal	20,254	67.5	32.5	2.4	2.3	1.07	0.06	1.19		

Source: Elaborated by the authors based on Eurostat: Direct investment inward flows by main investing country, extracted on 24 August 2009 – last updated 15 June 2009, Hyperlink to the tables http://epp.eurostat.ec.europa.eu/tgm/table.do?tab=table&init=1&plugin=1&language=en&pcode=tec00049

12.3 EU and member state FDI policy: Recent developments

12.3.1 FDI governance and instruments in the EU

Because of its 'multilevel' governance structure, the EU offers an interesting arena for analysis of FDI policy. With different remits and objectives, policy developments in the Commission and at the national levels do not necessarily move in the same direction. The EU's liberal FDI regime both with regard to EU member states and third parties can be traced back to the Treaty of Rome (1957) where the 'four freedoms' were upheld: the free circulation of goods, services, people, and capital, as well as the right of establishment. However, the extent to which the four freedoms were implemented in the first decades of the EU was irregular and uneven. Though the main beneficiaries in these processes were the member states, increased liberalization at the international level occurred as a 'spillover effect': as non-member state capital entered the EU, it became increasingly difficult to discriminate against these capital flows. The Commission is legally responsible for overseeing member states' application of treaty law with regard to the free movement of capital.[5] The freedom of capital movement also applies to third countries, though Articles 57, 59, and 60 of the treaty allow for specific exceptions, sanctions, and safeguard measures. The Commission also establishes and supervises European law regarding cartels, antitrust, mergers, state aid, and takeovers. All of these rules must be implemented by the national government, and failure to do so can result in infringement cases taken against individual governments.[6] One of the aims of the Treaty of Lisbon is to increase the Commission's competence in investment policy, and this development is still ongoing.

In contrast, the FDI regime of each member state is decided at the national level and is usually implemented via bilateral agreements. It is the interaction of European and national layers of governance that causes friction. Generally speaking, the responsibilities of the Commission are economic and legalistic, while national governments are responsible for the political, economic, legalistic, *and* social dimensions of FDI, including national security and welfare. National governments have the final word in the defining which industries are 'strategic' for the nation, as well as the degree of protection these industries enjoy from IFDI. The Commission, on the other hand, has to ensure liberalized markets, unless this would threaten national security. In practice, this is a grey area in legal and political terms. Events, as usual, throw up new challenges. Most dramatically, the recent spate of terrorist attacks since September 11 targeted infrastructure (metros, trains, buses, planes) while mobile phones, postal services, and the Internet were used to orchestrate the attacks. This has led to renewed debate on how 'critical infrastructure' can be protected, including aspects about its ownership and regulation. For many Europeans, the cold month of January 2009 was accompanied by the threat or actual lack of gas due to the stand-off between

Russia and the Ukraine. Certainly, if there is a blackout, an energy or water failure, or paralysis in the urban transportation system, European citizens hold their national government accountable, regardless of who owns and runs the network (Clifton, Comín, and Díaz-Fuentes, 2007; Clifton and Díaz-Fuentes, 2010a). The same perception characterizes the current financial crisis: national governments are held accountable by their citizens. There is some evidence that this belief in national accountability is getting stronger: according to special Eurobarometer surveys regarding energy issues, in 2006, 57 per cent of Europeans stated that energy challenges should be managed at the local or national level, and not at the European level, up from 45 per cent in 2005 (EC, 2006). Unsurprisingly, this change was particularly strong in countries near the Russian border (Estonia, Latvia), near the Ukraine (Romania, Hungary), as well as smaller countries, such as Austria, Cyprus, Greece, and Ireland.

Another reason for the tensions between the Commission and member states is the need for the latter to attend to domestic political economy interests. A number of member states have opted to protect business in certain sectors using 'national champion' policies. In particular, former monopoly incumbents have enjoyed temporary 'respite' from the European liberalization directives by delaying opening up at home while aggressively pursuing expansion opportunities abroad. A case in point is Spanish Telefonica, which, while enjoying virtual monopoly privileges at home until 1998, expanded aggressively into the Latin American telecommunications markets, which were privatized from the early 1990s onward after the debt crisis in the region (Clifton, Díaz-Fuentes and Revuelta, 2010).

Particularly since the current financial crisis spread to most other areas of economic life, there have been many threats and declarations by governments and trade unions from various EU countries about the need to buy nationally produced goods. In the UK, strikes have taken place to protest about firms' hiring of non-British (Italian) workers. Protectionism, it would seem, could spiral out of control if left unchecked. At the same time, most of these threats have been countered by reminders as to the cause of the Great Depression and the futility of isolation. Political rhetoric and action are often contradictory, however.

The most common, formal instruments to restrict FDI are ownership restrictions, obligatory screening and approval procedures, and other formal restrictions, such as rules on the composition of the board, restrictions on the employment of foreign nationals, and so on. All of these instruments have been used by one EU member state or another in recent years. There are, of course, numerous other policies, which do not necessarily focus directly on IFDI, but work in other ways to restrict it. These mechanisms may be more subtle, such as the existence of complex regulatory frameworks or systems of corporate control. In addition, informal practices, such as the publicizing of opinions by policy-makers or members of the business community in order to steer an 'unfriendly' investment climate, are also likely to affect the climate for IFDI. An evaluation of the importance of these formal and informal instruments on FDI must be made carefully. Just as the WTO prefers 'transparent' tariffs to other forms of protectionism, since they are easier to quantify and therefore compare, formal instruments relating to FDI, such as laws, regulations, and screening mechanisms are easier to quantify than their informal counterparts. However, even though an analysis of formal FDI rules provides a useful – if impressionistic – picture of an economy's position vis-à-vis IFDI, of greater importance is the *use made* of the FDI framework. For instance, there have been some important cases of restricting FDI in EU member states using *existing* FDI regulations. To complicate matters more, it is not always straightforward to know the facts about why one deal is blocked and another accepted, and the real role of IFDI restrictions in that process. With these caveats in mind, this section analyses policy responses first by the member states themselves and then by the Commission. Two main areas are covered: the policy responses based on concerns about security, however defined, and EU member states' responses to the rise of sovereign wealth funds.

12.3.2 EU member states and IFDI policy

At the individual member state level, Germany has perhaps gone furthest in the introduction of new policies that restrict IFDI. In September 2008, the German cabinet approved a new bill that would allow prospective IFDI that involves 25 per cent or more of a company's stake by non-European firms to be screened for approval. According to German officials, one of the triggers for this reform was in 2003, when a US private equity investment firm acquired a German submarine manufacturer (Government Accountability Office, 2008: 61). Alarm was raised about the lack of legal clarity in the protection of German military and strategic interests and, the following year, section 7 of the German Foreign Trade and Payments Act was enacted, which established limits to the free movement of capital into Germany on the grounds of 'security'. IFDI would be subject to review if it involved acquisition of a domestic company producing or developing weapons or other military equipment. German Chancellor Angela Merkel claimed that Germany needed a 'light CFIUS' (Benoit, 2007) and, while the German government has downplayed the importance of this new bill, many local businesses have expressed their concern about the negative signals this may send to international markets. The stated concern behind this bill was the need to clarify German law in order to ensure 'strategic' industries were protected, and officials stress that Germany is only adapting its policy framework to the US or UK model. As shown in Table 12.1, Germany is more exposed relatively to Russian IFDI than most other EU member states, which could partly explain their concerns. In addition, as seen in Graph 12.1, Germany has been more 'open' to IFDI into the electricity and telecommunication sector than the EU member states' average. This confirms the interpretation that the new bill could be interpreted as a move away from relative openness towards the EU average, though it remains to be seen how the Commission will respond. This is already the second version of the bill, since the first version was rejected by the Commission (Walker, 2008).[7]

France has also attracted much attention for its recent IFDI reforms. In 2005, the French government compiled a list of 'strategic' and 'sensitive' industries in which foreign investors would be subject to government screening (UNCTAD, 2006; OECD, 2007).[8] The Decree (2005–1739) was criticized by the Commission, which stated that it did not respect the principle of 'proportionality", was unnecessarily unfavourable toward IFDI, included 'casinos' (which were already protected by another French law), and discriminated between EU and non-EU investors, since potential investors from non-EU countries would be required to provide more data to the review process board. In the face of criticism, the French government appealed to the principle of subsidiarity, and claimed that it had the ultimate duty to defend the 'national interest' as well as the legal responsibility to define what constitutes a 'strategic' industry. The Commission formally requested France to modify the decree in October 2006 and discussions were still ongoing throughout 2008. At the same time, concerns in French policy circles have grown about the security of their energy infrastructure and supply. Since winning the presidential elections in 2007, President Sarkozy has publicly declared his preference for an active industrial policy approach. In June 2007, inspired by developments in Germany, the French Parliament produced a report suggesting that the energy sector should be added to the list of protected industries. This debate has been 'uploaded' to the European level, as we shall see later in this section. Finally, with the onset of recession in 2008 and, in response to a concern that distressed assets in the EU could be bought up cheaply by foreigners, Sarkozy proposed the creation of a European Sovereign Wealth Fund in order to protect Europe's 'strategic' industries, though nothing has come out of this initiative so far. Appealing to populist sentiment, he was quoted as saying 'I don't want European citizens to wake up in several months' time and find that European companies belong to non-European capital, which bought at the share prices' lowest point' (Bennhold, 2008).

There are several other developments at the national level. Hungary has earned the disapproval of the Commission, which issued a formal letter of concern to its government about the new company law on FDI passed in 2007. The Commission perceives this law as incompatible with European law. While Hungarian authorities claim this law aims to secure the public supply of services such as energy and water, the Commission argues that it has two main and undesirable effects: firstly, the Hungarian government will have the right to place politicians on the boards of energy firms; and secondly, it will slow down and publicize potential M&A, which could eliminate the element of surprise, thus increase prices, and open up more opportunities to block operations (EC, 2007).[9] Hungary had also been asked by the Commission in 2006 to modify its privatization law, which, the Commission claimed, conferred golden shares to firms in sectors including the food industry, pharmaceuticals, financial services, telecommunications, energy, and defence.

The retention of 'golden shares' in privatized industries has been an area where the EU has been active vis-à-vis national governments. Infringement procedures have been initiated with regard to various countries and firms, and the Commission states that special rights are still being conferred on privileged investors, preventing capital from flowing freely. In January 2008, the Commission referred Portugal to the European Court of Justice over its alleged special rights in Portugal Telecom (EC, 2008a) and Energias de Portugal (EC, 2008b), while in July 2008, the European Court of Justice found the requirement that potential acquisitions of Spanish energy firms had to be approved by the Comisión Nacional de la Energía (National Energy Commission) to violate Community law (EC, 2008c).

Nation states' behaviour has thus been subject to review by the Commission in the areas in which it has competence. In general, the Commission functions as the 'liberalizing machine', correcting national economic policies if they violate the free movement of capital. Two important developments, however, have emerged at the supranational level that concern – directly or indirectly – IFDI flows: energy policy and responses to sovereign wealth funds.

European energy policy can be traced back to the Treaty of Rome (1957), particularly in regard to the European Coal and Steel Community Treaty and the Euratom Treaty on the civil use of nuclear energy. However, until the 1990s, little was done to forge an internal market in energy and other infrastructure, and providers were usually organized as national or local state-owned monopolies. From the late 1990s onward, market-oriented reforms began, particularly for telecommunications, electricity, and gas. Though belated, these reforms generated great expectations and, between 1993 and 2000, the worldwide 'race' for FDI was dominated by investment in telecommunications and energy utilities. Nearly two-thirds of world FDI during this period took place within the EU, and the utilities sectors were responsible for nearly three-quarters of privatization proceeds (Clifton, Comín, and Díaz-Fuentes, 2003). As world FDI flows dropped by around a half between 2000 and 2003, in the EU, delays dogged the implementation of European liberalization directives on electricity and gas, while the reforms already implemented did not always deliver what had been promised in terms of competition, price reductions, and market power. A second round of reforms was launched in 2003 (European Directives on Electricity, 2003/54/EC and Gas, 2003/55/EC) with the stated aims of providing more competition (highest priority), improving service quality and universal services, and ensuring the security of supply. Despite the rhetoric, the main focus of the Commission was economically driven: market competition was sought above all, at the expense of the other two objectives. One year later, the Commission found that 18 member states had not implemented the new directives adequately. In 2005, the Commission took Estonia, Greece, Ireland, Luxembourg, and Spain to court for failing to adapt national laws to the directives. The following year, the Commission took action against 17 countries for failing to implement legislation. After several years of attempted reform, the largest generator in the electricity market in EU member states often enjoys huge market shares. Thomas (2003) predicted that these liberalization reforms would lead to monopolistic competition between the 'seven brothers', though there were arguably only six or five by 2009. While some member states privatized and liberalized quite deeply (the UK and Spain), other member states were much more reluctant. Some electricity firms aggressively exploited opportunities opened up by liberalization programs abroad, while they enjoyed restricted or delayed liberalization at home. Smaller economies, particularly those located at the Russian borders, avoided M&A into their energy markets based on 'security' concerns (they had been highly dependent upon Russian gas since the Soviet era). Many governments and their firms were simply flouting the European legislation in terms of unbundling and liberalization. In 2006, a further directive (2005/89/EC) was passed concerning measures to safeguard the security of the electricity supply and infrastructure investment.

In 2007, the new energy policy was launched by the EU, which included issues beyond purely economically driven concerns, such as increased attention to the promotion of new or diverse energy sources, climate change, and the coordination of energy 'security of supply'. Security of supply is understood as an emphasis on diversity of energy types and sources, dialogue and agreements with trading partners, and preparation for an energy crisis (European Council, 2006). In the face of maverick firms and member states delaying or refusing to unbundle, the Commission has relaxed its policy stance somewhat, opting for 'competition for the market' rather than 'competition in the market.' Some European politicians claim that Russia's decision to cut off energy supplies to the Ukraine in 2006 triggered this shift in European energy policy. One development is that the Commission is seeking to impose a 'reciprocity' clause (sometimes called the 'Gazprom clause') so that companies buying EU energy transmission assets would have to abide by similar rules to those of the EU as regards liberal markets. A further clause stipulates that 'third-country individuals and countries cannot acquire control over a Community transmission system or transmission system operator unless this is permitted by an agreement between the EU and the third country'. The clause, once adopted as law, would remove national competence in the area and require that any bilateral energy agreements with third countries are dealt with exclusively at Community level. Current

Energy Commissioner Andris Piebalgs justified the reciprocity clause on the grounds that it would give third-country suppliers clear rules for investment in the European market (Euractiv, 2007; Wolf, 2007). Discussions are ongoing, and the Council adopted the development as part of the internal energy market package in February 2009.

The second area where significant developments have occurred is with regard to sovereign wealth funds. Already controversial before the current financial crisis and recession, the falling asset values in the EU have made this topic even more contentious. The main thrust of the development has been to work on guidelines for both the recipient country and the agent behind the fund in order to increase transparency and predictability of this kind of investment. Here, the ongoing work of the OECD (2009) has been helpful for EU policy-makers in drawing up key principles, and a common EU code was drafted at the end of 2008 (EC, 2008d).

Thus, the Commission has been active in reversing 'golden shares', rejecting or diluting national government's lists of 'strategic industries', and enforcing the free movement of capital both within the EU and with regard to third countries. Yet there remains a grey area between market liberalization on the one hand, and nationally defined 'security interests' on the other, into which the majority of disputes fall. Moreover, there are delays to the liberalization process of some industry sectors, such as energy, where for instance unbundling policies will not be easy to enforce.

12.4 Conclusions

The EU enjoys one of the most liberal FDI regimes in the world, and is increasingly a host for IFDI and multinationals based in emerging markets. At the same time, the EU is not immune to a generalized increase in concern about IFDI by governments around the world. Member states have, in recent years, introduced new measures that aim to restrict IFDI, particularly from third countries. Informal practices have also proved unfavourable to IFDI. The main reason provided by EU and national policy-makers to justify any increase in FDI restrictions revolve around questions of 'national security' and 'strategic industries'. Behind these concerns lies a diverse, contradictory set of interests, including bitter experiences with Europe's dependency on Russian gas, demands of incumbent business groups to protect national champions, economic nationalism sentiment and, perhaps most importantly, knee-jerk protectionist impulses based on fears about job losses and firm closure in the face of recession. The rise of Southern Multinationals is a newly emerging issue for EU leaders, and comes at an already 'difficult' time: the Single Market is mature though becoming blocked in 'complex' sectors. These internal tensions are only compounded and intensified as new global players from emerging markets strive to enter as recession sets in. Financial crisis and economic recession may make distressed EU assets attractive to international investors. From a purely economic point of view, this is to be welcomed, though when the other wider dimensions, such as national interests in the long term are considered, the picture is much less clear. The leading light in this period of relative darkness is the maturity of institutions repeatedly insisting on rational, thought-out collective action, an element missing in the 1930s.

Notes

1. We would like to thank Andrea Goldstein, Louis Brennan, and Karl Sauvant for their valuable comments on presentations of the preliminary versions of this chapter.
2. However, there are above-average levels of protectionism in Austria, Hungary, Poland, and Spain. In the case of Spain, the telecommunications sector was organized as a private monopoly, and its main players treated as 'national champions'.
3. This is largely via the investment of Sabó, a car component manufacturer that is a global supplier to Volkswagen. Sabó was founded by a Hungarian immigrant in the 1950s.
4. See, for instance, Lall, 1983; Amsden, 2001; International Finance Corporation, 2006; UNCTAD, 2006; Goldstein, 2007; Ramamurti and Singh, 2008; Sauvant, 2008; Aykut and Goldstein, 2008; Goldstein, 2008.
5. As a general rule, and according to the principles of subsidiarity and proportionality, policy should be, by default, conducted at the national level, with European-level policy only occurring when the EU enjoys legal competence to act, and where subsidiarity and proportionality are respected.
6. An ongoing list of infringement cases is available at: http://ec.europa.eu/internal_market/capital/analysis/index_en.htm.
7. Also in September 2008, the Commission made a final warning to the German government about the 'VW law', which was found in 2007 to violate the EU free flow of capital rules. This law prevents the car company from being taken over as the Lower Saxony state government owns 20 per cent of Volkswagen (Schäfer, 2008).
8. The decree protects: gambling and casinos, private security, R&D in substances of potential interest to terrorists, equipment designed to intercept communication, testing of information technology systems, products for information systems security, cryptology equipment, activities carried out by firms entrusted with defense secrets, research or production of arms or war materials, and activities carried out by firms for the design or supply of equipment for the Ministry of Defence.
9. Ongoing developments in the completion of the single market are available at: http://ec.europa.eu/internal_market/capital/analysis/index_en.htm.

References

Amsden, A. (2001), *The Rise of the Rest: Challenges to the West from Late-industrializing Economies*. Oxford: Oxford University Press.

Aykut, D. and Goldstein, A. (2008), 'Developing Country Multinationals: South–South Investment Comes of Age', in David O'Connor and Monica Kjollerstrom (eds), *Industrial Development for the C21st*. London: Zed Books.

Bennhold, K. (2008), 'Idea of Sovereign Wealth Funds Divides Europeans', *New York Times*, October 21.

Benoit, B. (2007), 'Germany Plans for Own CFIUS Deal Watchdog', *Financial Times*, September 27.

Bouquet, T. and Ousey, B. (2008), *Cold Steel: The Multi-billion Dollar Battle for a Global Industry*. London: Little Brown.

Clifton, J., and D. Díaz-Fuentes (2010a) "Evaluating EU policies on public services: A Citizens' Perspective" *Annals of Public and Cooperative Economics*, 81(2) pages 281–311.

Clifton, J. and Díaz-Fuentes, D. (2010b), 'Is the European Union Ready for FDI from Emerging Markets?' In K. Sauvant, W. Maschek and G. McAllister (eds), *Foreign Direct Investment from Emerging Markets: The Challenges Ahead*. London/New York: Palgrave Macmillan.

Clifton, J., Díaz-Fuentes, D., and Revuelta, J. (2010), The Political Economy of Telecoms and Electricity Internationalization in the Single Market', *Journal of European Public Policy*, 17 (7), 988–1006.

Clifton, J., Comín, F., and Díaz-Fuentes, D. (2003), *Privatization in the European Union*. Dordrecht: Kluwer.

Clifton, J., Comín, F., and Díaz-Fuentes, D. (eds) (2007), *Transforming Public Enterprise in Europe and the Americas: Networks, Integration and Transnationalisation*. Basingstoke: Palgrave Macmillan.

Clifton, J., Comín, F., and Díaz-Fuentes, D. (2008), 'The Rise of the New Public Service Transnationals', in H. Schroeter (ed.), *The European Enterprise: Historical Investigation in a Future Species*. Dordrecht: Springer.

EC (2006), *Special Eurobarometer: Energy Policy*, available at: http://ec.europa.eu/public_opinion/archives/ebs/ebs_258_en.pdf [accessed 10 November 2008].

EC (2007), *Free Movement of Capital: Commission Scrutinizes Amendments in Hungarian Company Law* [available at: http://europa.eu/rapid/pressReleasesAction.do?reference=IP/07/1681&format=HTML&aged=0&language=EN&guiLanguage=en].

EC (2008a), *Free Movement of Capital: Commission Refers Portugal to European Court of Justice over Special Rights Held by State in Portugal Telecom* [available at: http://europa.eu/rapid/pressReleasesAction.do?reference=IP/08/120&type=HTML&aged=0&language=EN&guiLanguage=en].

EC (2008b), *Free Movement of Capital: Commission Refers Portugal to European Court of Justice over Special Rights Held by State in EDP* [available at: http://europa.eu/rapid/pressReleasesAction.do?reference=IP/08/1357&format=HTML&aged=0&language=EN&guiLanguage=en].

EC (2008c), 'Commission v. Spain: Judgment of the Court of Justice in Case C-207/07' [available at: http://curia.europa.eu/en/actu/communiques/cp08/aff/cp080054en.pdf].

EC (2008d), *A Common European Approach to Sovereign Wealth Funds* [available at: eu.europa.eu/internal_market/finances/docs/sovereign_en.pdf].

European Council (2006), 'Presidency Conclusions', available at: http://ue.eu.int/ueDocs/cms_Data/docs/pressData/en/ec/89013.pdf [accessed 10 November 2008].

Euractiv (2007), '"Gazprom Clause" Issues Russia Ultimatum for Energy Co-operation', September 20, www.euractiv.com [31 accessed March 2008].

Fuller, T. (2005), 'French Fear Eye of "Ogre" is on Danone', *Financial Times*, July 21.

Goldstein, A. (2007), *Multinational Companies from Emerging Economies*. Basingstoke: Palgrave Macmillan.

Goldstein, A. (2008), 'Who's Afraid of the Emerging-market TNCs? Or: Are Developing Countries Missing Something in the Globalization Debate?' in K. Sauvant (ed.), *The Rise of Transnational Corporations from Emerging Markets*. Cheltenham, UK: Edward Elgar, 183–203.

Golub, S. (2003), *Measures of Restrictions on Inward Foreign Direct Investment for OECD Countries*, OECD Economic Studies No. 36. Paris: OECD.

Government Accountability Office (2008), *Foreign Investment: Law and Policies Regulating Foreign Investment in Ten Countries*. Washington: GAO, available at: http://www.gao.gov/new.items/d08320.pdf [accessed 10 November]

International Finance Corporation (2006), *Southern Multinationals: A Rising Force in the World Economy*, International Finance Corporation and Financial Times.

Klinova, M. (2007), 'Privatization and Transnationalisation of Russian Enterprises', in J. Clifton, F. Comín, and D. Díaz-Fuentes (eds), *Transforming Public Enterprise in Europe and the Americas: Networks, Integration and Transnationalisation*. Basingstoke: Palgrave Macmillan, 157–71.

Koyama, T. and Golub, S. (2006), *OECD's FDI Regulatory Restrictiveness Index: Revision and Extension to More Economies*, OECD Economics Department Working Papers No. 525. Paris: OECD.

Lall, S. (1983), *The Multinational Corporation*. London: Macmillan.

Le Monde (2005), *'Dominique de Villepin en appelle au patriotisme économique'*, July 29.

OECD (2006), *FDI Regulatory Restrictiveness Index*. Paris: OECD.

OECD (2007), *International Investment Perspectives 2007*. Paris: OECD.

OECD (2009), *Foreign Government-controlled Investors and Recipient Country Investment Policies: A Scoping Paper*. Paris: OECD.

Ramamurti, R. and Singh, J. (eds.) (2009) *Emerging Multinationals in Emerging Markets*, Cambridge University Press, New York.

Sauvant, K. (ed.) (2009), *The Rise of Transnational Corporations from Emerging Markets*. Cheltenham, UK: Edward Elgar.

Schäfer, D. (2008), 'Germany Handed Final Warning over VW Law', *Financial Times*, September 10.

Schulz, M. (2008), *A Return of Protectionism? Internal Deregulation and External Investment Restrictions in the EU*, Discussion Paper 08-04, Tokyo: Fujitsu Research Institute, Economic Research Center.

Thomas, S. (2003), 'The Seven Brothers', *Energy Policy*, 31 (5), 393–403.

Traynor, I. (2007), 'Gazprom Told to Slim to Compete in Europe', *Guardian*, September 20.

UNCTAD (2006), *World Investment Report 2006*. Geneva: United Nations.

UNCTAD (2008) *World Investment Report 2008*. Geneva, United Nations.

UNCTAD (2009) *World Investment Report 2009*. Geneva, United Nations.

Walker, M. (2008), 'Germany Tinkers with Foreign Takeovers Plan', *Wall Street Journal*, January 14.

Wolf, M. (2007), 'Why Plutocracy Endangers Emerging Markets', *Financial Times*, November 7.

13
The Emergence of SWFs and the European Perspective

Ruth Rios-Morales and Louis Brennan

13.1 Introduction

In the current highly volatile international financial system, sovereign wealth funds (SWFs) have emerged as significant global financial players. The emergence of these funds has drawn considerable attention from policy-makers, market players and scholars. There are two main reasons for this. First, SWF have been acknowledged to be the largest concentration of capital that the world has ever known. In 2008, SWFs exceeded the amount of US$ 5 trillion (UNCTAD, 2008). It is estimated that by 2015 they will reach the amount of US$ 12 trillion (Redicker and Crebo-Redicker, 2007). Secondly, the management of these funds has raised concern about the lack of transparency in the administration and investment strategies of these colossal funds. Strong sentiments of protectionism have been particularly expressed by some European countries. Much of these strong sentiments can be attributed to the unprecedented phenomenon that results from the accrual of large current accounts surpluses of some emerging and developing nations, who are keen to invest in the developed world. This remarkable shift of capital flows suggests the establishment of a new economic order. This chapter considers the emergence of SWFs as global financial players, the new regulations placed to lessen concerns around this phenomenon, the European approach towards SWFs and their impact on the global economy.

13.2 The emergence of SWFs as global financial players

While the establishment of SWFs is not a new phenomenon, the emergence of SWFs as global financial players is novel and their role is having a significant impact in the global economy. Despite the growing recognition of the role of these financial players, there is no consensus on the definition of sovereign wealth funds; however, the following definition incorporates some common features of SWFs:

> SWFs are defined as special purpose investment funds or arrangements, owned by the general government. Created by the general government for macroeconomic purposes, SWFs hold, manage, or administer assets to achieve financial objectives, and employ a set of investment strategies which include investing in foreign financial assets. The SWFs are commonly established out of balance of payments surpluses, official foreign currency operations, the proceeds of privatizations, fiscal surpluses, and/or receipts resulting from commodity exports.
>
> International Working Group of Sovereign Wealth Funds, 2008: 28

Although these government-owned investments, accumulated from various surpluses and receipts, have only been investing globally in recent years, SWFs have existed since as far back as the 1950s. The first SWF was created by the Kuwait government in 1953. The concept extended from the Middle East to Asia. In 1974, Singapore became the first Asian country to launch a SWF. At present, Singapore holds two of the largest SWFs: Singapore Investment Corporation and Temasek Holdings. Singapore holds the second largest SWF after Abu Dhabi (Table 13.1). In 1976, Abu Dhabi created its SWF, and it is the largest established SWF, holding assets to the amount of US$ 875 billion. Europe's largest SWF, the Norwegian Government Pension Fund, established in 1990, currently holds US$ 375 billion in assets. Only 17 out of the 70 SWFs held by 44 countries have been launched in recent years (UNCTAD, 2008). However, their rapid growth and proliferation have taken place since the early 1990s (IMF, 2007). In a large proportion (83 per cent), SWFs have their origins in emerging and developing economies (Rios-Morales and Brennan, 2009).

SWFs represent the outcome of the highly skewed imbalances between debtor nations and nations with surpluses. Although this is a widely debated issue, it is acknowledged that rising oil prices, financial globalization and rapid economic growth in some developing markets have resulted in the rapid accumulation of foreign assets (*The Economist*, 2008a). While SWFs have been largely associated with oil- and gas-producing countries, estimates suggest that 64 per cent of the total SWFs originate from oil and gas revenues; other countries such as China, Singapore and Australia, among others that have benefited from accumulated current accounts surpluses of non-commodity sources, account for the other 36 per cent. A large number of SWFs are based in the Middle East (46 per cent), while 35 per cent come from Asia, 13 per cent from Europe and 2 per cent from the Americas (SWF Institute, 2008).

SWFs are generally established to maintain the wealth of the nation and ensure that national resources and assets are being used to fulfil national

Table 13.1 The 20 largest sovereign wealth funds

Name of Funds	Year founded	Source	Billion US$
Abu Dhabi Investment Authority	1976	Oil	875
Singapore Investment Corporation	1981	Non-commodity	330
Norway Government Pension Fund-Global	1990	Oil	322
Saudi Arabia Various Funds	n/a	Oil	300
Kuwait Invetsment Authority	1953	Oil	250
China Investment Corporation	2007	Non-commodity	200
Hong Kong Monetary Authority Investment Portafolio	1998	Non-commodity	140
Stabilisation Fund of the Russian Federation	2003	Oil	127
China Investment Company	2003	Non-commodity	100
Singapore Temasek Holdings	1974	Non-commodity	108
Australia Government Future Fund	2004	Non-commodity	50
Libya Reserve Fund	n/a	Oil	50
Qatar Investment Authority	2000	Oil	40
US Alaska Permanent Fund	1976	Oil	40
Brunei Investment Agency	1983	Oil	35
Ireland National Pension Funds	2001	Non-commodity	29
Algeria Revenue Regulation Fund	n/a	Oil	43
South Korea Investment Corporation	2006	Non-commodity	20
Malaysia Khazanah Nasional	1993	Non-commodity	18
Kazakhstan National Oil Fund	2000	Oil, gas and metals	18

Source: Deutsche Bank Research, "Sovereign Wealth Funds, State Investment on the Rise", September, 2007.

financial objectives and plans (IWG, 2008). There are four main objectives usually considered by governments when establishing SWFs. Portman (2008) categorized these as follows:

(1) Macroeconomic stabilization – funds are utilized to balance fluctuating revenue flows and insulate fiscal policies of a country. SWFs can be used to build up reserves in times of growth and economic expansion. Then can be invested internationally to generate economic profits. In times of economic contraction, the investments can be withdrawn and scaled back in order to inject money back into the system.
(2) Future generations – funds aim to create a store of wealth for future generations by building portfolios to provide returns over a long period. This illustrates that SWFs also have the potential to act as a vehicle for spreading wealth over time.
(3) Domestic industries – funds are used to support the growth of local industry.
(4) Seeking higher returns – governments are trying to maximize returns rather than holding these funds in low-return and risk-free assets. For instance, the Norwegian SWF earns an average yield of 7 per cent (*The Economist*, 2008b). It can be noted that these main objectives of SWFs, are not mutually exclusive.

SWFs are vehicles of opportunity to generate a high return on a country's investments; an increasing number of countries that hold SWFs are making moves towards investment in the financial markets. Particularly at this time of high volatility in the global financial system dominated by risk aversion, liquidity pressures and asset write-downs, SWFs have emerged as significant financial players. A number of international investment banks have received financial resources from SWFs to alleviate their liquidity pressure brought by the 'credit crunch'. In Table 13.2 we observe that important sums of capital were invested during 2007 in international financial institutions. For instance, the Chinese Investment Corporation (CIC) invested US$ 3 billion, obtaining a 10 per cent stake in Blackstone, an American leading global financial institution. International banks such as Barclays, Citigroup and UBS among other financial institutions obtained important investments. During 2008, SWFs continued to invest in international banks, with Barclays and Credit Suisse obtaining capital from Qatar's investment authority (*The Economist*, 2008b). Given the sheer scale of investments made by SWFs, it is clear that they have an influential role in the global financial system.

13.3 The new SWF regulations: The Santiago Principles

The unprecedented emergence of SWFs as financial players has impelled a debate among policy-makers, market players and scholars regarding the

Table 13.2 Investment of sovereign wealth funds in 2007

Date of Investment	Investment of SWFs in Financial Institution	Amount (US$)
May 2, 2007	Dubai International Capital buys an undisclosed stake in British bank HSBC Holdings PLC.	n/a
May 20, 2007	China's state investment company buys 10 % stake in U.S. private equity firm Blackstone Group LP.	3 billion
July 13, 2007	Dubai International Capital purchases a 2.87 % stake in one of India's largest banks, ICICI Bank Ltd.	750 million
July 23, 2007	China Development Bank, a Chinese state agency agrees to buy 3.1% stake in British bank Barclays PLC	3 billion
	Temasek Holdings, a sovereign wealth fund in Singapore agrees to buy 1.77% stake in Barclays.	2 billion
Sept. 20, 2007	Abu Dhabi-based Mubadala Development Co. buys a 7.5% stake of the management operations of Carlyle Group	1.35 billion
Sept. 20, 2007	The Qatar Investment Authority acquires a 20% stake in the London Stock Exchange and nearly 10% of Nordic bourse operator OMX AB.	
Oct. 22, 2007	China's government-controlled Citic Securities Co. and U.S. Bear Stearns Cos. agree to invest $1 billion in each other for minority stakes that could be expanded. They will also operate a 5O-5O joint venture in Hong Kong to offer capital markets services across Asia.	1 billion
Oct. 29, 2007	Dubai International Capital, acquires 9.9% stake in Och-Ziff	1 million

Nov. 7, 2007	Central Huijin Investment Co. acquires 71% of China's joint-stock China Everbright Bank	2.7 billion
Nov. 26, 2007	Abu Dhabi Investment Authority acquires a 4.9% stake in Citigroup Inc.	7.5 billion
Dec. 10, 2007	Government of Singapore Investment Corp invest a 9% stake in UBS	9.75 billion
	Undisclosed strategic investor in the Middle East invest in UBS	1.77 billion
Dec. 19, 2007	China Investment Corporation's invested in Morgan Stanley	5 billion

Sources: Financial Times, Dealogic, Thomson Financial, AP Research.

potential risks and benefits that these funds can convey to the global economy (Johnson, 2007). While the significant role of SWFs has been widely acknowledged in the current highly volatile global financial system, the liveliest debate has tended to focus on concerns related to regulation of SWFs. The main concern has been the lack of transparency in the administration and investment strategies of these colossal funds. A number of authors have underlined the danger that SWFs may cause if they remain unregulated (Green and Torgerson, 2007; Truman, 2007a), suggesting that SWFs can act as vehicles of future global instability (Redicker and Crebo-Redicker, 2007). Other authors have emphasized the need to establish an international code of conduct in order to avoid protectionism that would be detrimental to the globalization process (Truman 2007a, 2007b). In contrast to the above perspective, other market players have underlined the variety of economic and financial benefits that SWFs present (Jen, 2007; Kern, 2007).

Beside market players and scholars, multinational organizations have also been involved in the above debate. Since 2007, the OECD has been working at the request of G7 finance ministers and other OECD members to develop guidance for recipient countries' policies towards investments from SWFs (Ervin, 2008). The European Commission has advocated tighter regulation on a number of occasions, in the form of a code of best practices, as being the best way to make SWFs transparent and thus dispel the mistrust felt by many towards them. The International Monetary Fund (IMF) had argued that SWFs can help to avoid extreme economic cycles, transfer surpluses of current accounts across generations and enhance revenues of investor nations (IMF, 2008). Nonetheless, this international institution has been prominent in raising the importance of establishing an international code of conduct (IMF, 2008). In April 2008, the IMF established the International Working Group on SWFs (IWG) at a meeting of 26 countries with SWFs in Washington, DC. The IWG's mandate was to identify a framework of generally accepted principles and practices that would reflect the appropriate governance, accountability and investment practices for all SWFs.

In October 2008 the International Working Group (IWG) of Sovereign Wealth Funds launched the Santiago Principles. There are 24 generally accepted principles and practices for SWFs that had been agreed by all 26 countries. In their furtherance, the IWG members either have implemented or intend to implement the following principles and practices, on a voluntary basis, *each of which is subject to* home country laws, regulations, requirements and obligations. The generally accepted principles and practices (GAPP) address three main areas of concern for SWFs: (1) the legal structure and relationship with the state, policy and investment objectives, and their degree of coordination with their home country's macroeconomic policies. (2) The institutional structure and governance mechanisms. (3) Recommendations in relation to investment and risk management frameworks (Emmerich, 2008).

The GAPP principles established by IWG (2008) follows.

- **GAPP 1. Principle:** The legal framework for the SWF should be sound and support its effective operation and the achievement of its stated objective(s).

  GAPP 1.1 Subprinciple The legal framework for the SWF should ensure the legal soundness of the SWF and its transactions.

  GAPP 1.2 Subprinciple The key features of the SWF's legal basis and structure, as well as the legal relationship between the SWF and the other state bodies, should be publicly disclosed.

- **GAPP 2. Principle:** The policy purpose of the SWF should be clearly defined and publicly disclosed.
- **GAPP 3. Principle:** Where the SWF's activities have significant direct domestic macroeconomic implications, those activities should be closely coordinated with the domestic fiscal and monetary authorities, so as to ensure consistency with the overall macroeconomic policies.
- **GAPP 4. Principle:** There should be clear and publicly disclosed policies, rules, procedures, or arrangements in relation to the SWF's general approach to funding, withdrawal, and spending operations.

  GAPP 4.1 Subprinciple The source of SWF funding should be publicly disclosed.

  GAPP 4.2 Subprinciple The general approach to withdrawals from the SWF and spending on behalf of the government should be publicly disclosed.

- **GAPP 5. Principle:** The relevant statistical data pertaining to the SWF should be reported on a timely basis to the owner, or as otherwise required, for inclusion where appropriate in macroeconomic data sets.
- **GAPP 6. Principle:** The governance framework for the SWF should be sound and establish a clear and effective division of roles and responsibilities in order to facilitate accountability and operational independence in the management of the SWF to pursue its objectives.
- **GAPP 7. Principle:** The owner should set the objectives of the SWF, appoint the members of its governing body(ies) in accordance with clearly defined procedures, and exercise oversight over the SWF's operations.
- **GAPP 8. Principle:** The governing body(ies) should act in the best interests of the SWF, and have a clear mandate and adequate authority and competency to carry out its functions.

- **GAPP 9. Principle:** The operational management of the SWF should implement the SWF's strategies in an independent manner and in accordance with clearly defined responsibilities.
- **GAPP 10. Principle:** The accountability framework for the SWF's operations should be clearly defined in the relevant legislation, charter, other constitutive documents, or management agreement.
- **GAPP 11. Principle:** An annual report and accompanying financial statements on the SWF's operations and performance should be prepared in a timely fashion and in accordance with recognized international or national accounting standards in a consistent manner.
- **GAPP 12. Principle:** The SWF's operations and financial statements should be audited annually in accordance with recognized international or national auditing standards in a consistent manner.
- **GAPP 13. Principle:** Professional and ethical standards should be clearly defined and made known to the members of the SWF's governing body(ies), management, and staff.
- **GAPP 14. Principle:** Dealing with third parties for the purpose of the SWF's operational management should be based on economic and financial grounds, and follow clear rules and procedures.
- **GAPP 15. Principle:** SWF operations and activities in host countries should be conducted in compliance with all applicable regulatory and disclosure requirements of the countries in which they operate.
- **GAPP 16. Principle:** The governance framework and objectives, as well as the manner in which the SWF's management is operationally independent from the owner, should be publicly disclosed.
- **GAPP 17. Principle:** Relevant financial information regarding the SWF should be publicly disclosed to demonstrate its economic and financial orientation, so as to contribute to stability in international financial markets and enhance trust in recipient countries.
- **GAPP 18. Principle:** The SWF's investment policy should be clear and consistent with its defined objectives, risk tolerance, and investment strategy, as set by the owner or the governing body(ies), and be based on sound portfolio management principles.

    GAPP 18.1 Subprinciple The investment policy should guide the SWF's financial risk exposures and the possible use of leverage.

    GAPP 18.2 Subprinciple The investment policy should address the extent to which internal and/or external investment managers are used, the range of their activities and authority, and the process by which they are selected and their performance monitored.

    GAPP 18.3 Subprinciple A description of the investment policy of the SWF should be publicly disclosed.

- **GAPP 19. Principle:** The SWF's investment decisions should aim to maximize risk-adjusted financial returns in a manner consistent with its investment policy, and based on economic and financial grounds.

  GAPP 19.1 Subprinciple If investment decisions are subject to other than economic and financial considerations, these should be clearly set out in the investment policy and be publicly disclosed.

  GAPP 19.2 Subprinciple The management of an SWF's assets should be consistent with what is generally accepted as sound asset management principles.

- **GAPP 20. Principle:** The SWF should not seek or take advantage of privileged information or inappropriate influence by the broader government in competing with private entities.
- **GAPP 21. Principle:** SWFs view shareholder ownership rights as a fundamental element of their equity investments' value. If an SWF chooses to exercise its ownership rights, it should do so in a manner that is consistent with its investment policy and protects the financial value of its investments. The SWF should publicly disclose its general approach to voting securities of listed entities, including the key factors guiding its exercise of ownership rights.
- **GAPP 22. Principle:** The SWF should have a framework that identifies, assesses, and manages the risks of its operations.

  GAPP 22.1 Subprinciple The risk management framework should include reliable information and timely reporting systems, which should enable the adequate monitoring and management of relevant risks within acceptable parameters and levels, control and incentive mechanisms, codes of conduct, business continuity planning, and an independent audit function.

  GAPP 22.2 Subprinciple The general approach to the SWF's risk management framework should be publicly disclosed.

- **GAPP 23. Principle:** The assets and investment performance (absolute and relative to benchmarks, if any) of the SWF should be measured and reported to the owner according to clearly defined principles or standards.
- **GAPP 24. Principle:** A process of regular review of the implementation of the GAPP should be engaged in by or on behalf of the SWF.

The aim of the Santiago Principles is to provide a clear understanding of the management of SWFs so that policy-makers and market players can welcome these funds and use them as tools of economic growth. FDI by SWFs can become the *avant-garde* of the global economy. It has been widely accepted that foreign direct investment is an important element of economic development in the new global economy (Blomstrom, 2001; Addison and Heshmati, 2003; World Bank, 2004; Lall, 2005). In the present global system, states are playing a central role in the determinants of international business activities (Dunning, 2006), and emerging and developing economies are becoming important investors increasing their role in the global economy.

13.4 Europe and sovereign wealth funds

In the debate around the potential risks and benefits of SWFs, the main concerns have been the lack of transparency in the administration and investment strategies of these colossal funds. While the launch of the Santiago Principles has in many ways appeased the concerns about the lack of transparency, Western countries have voiced strong apprehensions around the prospective investment strategies of SWFs. The argument is that SWFs could be used to seize control of strategic companies in sensitive sectors for their own political purposes (Siebert, 2007; Betts, 2008). Although the European Commission has highlighted the benefits of SWFs investment, France and Germany have expressed serious apprehension about the investment strategies of SWFs. Both countries have taken protectionist stances, with Germany planning to introduce legislation to block state-controlled investments along with pushing to enforce protectionist EU legislation. Angela Merkel's parliamentary leader, Volker Kauder, stated: 'This is about protecting important industrial sectors from the political influence of other states' (*Financial Times*, 2007a). The French president, Nicolas Sarkozy, speaking at the European Parliament, called for the creation of European SWF to buy stakes in companies with low share prices and protect them from non-European predators (Barber and Chaffin, 2008).

In light of the fact that some countries in Europe have welcomed investment from SWFs and other European countries have expressed serious concerns, the European Union at the beginning of 2008 published a report entitled *A Common European Approach to SWFs*, aiming to endorse a coherent approach towards SWFs by supporting increases in transparency, predictability and accountability (CEUC, 2008). The EU has been active in supporting the principles and practices of the GAPP. In October 2008, Joaquín Almunia, European Commissioner for Economic and Monetary Affairs, at the ministerial meeting of the International Working Group of Sovereign Wealth Funds, stated the following:

> The European Commission has pleaded from the very beginning for a cooperative and multilateral solution. In February 2008, the Commission

> issued a Communication on a common European approach to sovereign wealth funds. There we stated that: 'Europe must remain committed to its tradition of openness to capital investments, as they are a vital source of strength for the European economies in a globalised world.'
>
> (IWG, 2008)

The investment strategies of SWFs continue to be a serious concern in the Western world and in Europe, generating a protectionist reaction despite the fact that SWFs have been widely acknowledged as contributors to financial stability. Protectionism therefore is leading to economic inefficiencies, multilateral reduction of trade and an increased reliance on domestic firms (*The Economist*, 2008c). Worrying signals are emerging from European countries who are proposing the use of 'golden shares', which would allow governments to block takeovers of domestic companies without requiring a majority holding in those companies (Devlin and Brummit, 2007). Another protectionist technique being adopted by France is the establishment of its own SWF with the sole purpose of protecting domestic businesses. This is a marked departure from French free trade policy. The announcement was made on 20 November 2008 in light of Nicholas Sarkozy's expression of serious concern over SWF investment in the European economy (Caisse des Dépôts, 2008).

Protectionism is not the only issue of concern raised by the emergence of SWFs, but the 'new mercantilism', as some academics have labelled this phenomenon. New mercantilism refers to the most evolved form of state capitalism, since the public sector is gaining involvement in corporate activity (Gilson and Milhaupt, 2008). Through their cross-border investment activities, governments have begun accumulating various kinds of stakes in what were once purely private companies (*Financial Times*, 2007b). This means that as well as being able to plan the direction of the economy, the controlling government ensures that company-level behaviour results in country-level maximization of economic, social and political benefits. One of the ways this can be done is through the enforcement of corporate governance procedures in exchange for state investment (*The Economist*, 2008d). Therefore the widely promulgated notion that the public sector is not an efficient administrator of resources is being ignored by countries that hold, or are planning to establish, a SWF.

13.4.1 A European sovereign wealth fund

President Sarkozy's endorsement of the establishment of a European SWF is the result of the apprehension that these funds have created in the Western world. On 22 October 2008, while addressing business leaders in Annency, France, President Sarkozy stated: 'I will not be the French president who wakes up in six months' time to see that French industrial groups have passed into other hands' (*Financial Times*, 2008). There is some possibility that there will be the creation of a European SWF in the future. However, there are two main significant limitations that may impede the establishment of such a fund. First, the basis for the establishment of a SWF is absent in Europe. A SWF by definition is a government-owned investment, accumulated from surpluses of current accounts and reserves. In Europe there are only two countries that hold SWFs; Ireland and Norway, and the latter is not a member of the European Union. The Norwegian Government Pension Fund – Global was set up in 1990 and is the third largest SWF in the world, with assets in the range of US$ 322 billion. Ireland possesses its own SWF in the form of the National Pensions Reserve Fund (NPRF), established in 2001. Ireland has accumulated this fund through its large current account surpluses during the Celtic Tiger era. Nowadays, the common denominator among European countries is large current account deficits, which clearly hamper the sources for creation of a SWF. Secondly, the creation of a SWF from Sarkozy's viewpoint is to bail out European companies (Singh, 2008). As stated in section two of this chapter, governments keep in mind certain objectives when establishing SWFs. Bailing out national companies would then be a new SWF objective, which contradicts the original basis for the establishment of SWFs and implies a political motivation to their creation.

13.5 Implications of SWFs in the global economy

There has been a significant and rapid change to the landscape of the global economy since the emergence of SWFs as global investors. The emergence of SWFs has a major implication in terms of the shift in capital flows. The shift is not only that inward investment to the developed world has its origins in developing and emerging countries, but that investment is shifting from public sources to private companies. UNCTAD, in the *World Investment Report 2008*, indicated that over three-quarters of FDI from SWFs were invested in developed economies in 2007; that is, over US$50 billion has been allocated into Western banking institutions and investment firms (Cohen, 2008). By the same accounts, SWFs are providing more and more capital to private organizations around the globe. SWFs are typically acquiring around a 10 per cent stake in these companies – their investment portrays a shift from the public to the private sector. The shift of capital is contributing to the establishment of a new economic order, as stated in the introduction to this chapter.

Other implications of SWFs to the global economy can be framed as benefits and threats, opportunities and challenges. The most significant benefit of SWFs is that they are potentially significant sources of investment, providing much-needed liquidity into capital systems during the period of high volatility that the system has been undergoing. Protectionism, on the other hand, is the most significant threat to the global economy and can be detrimental to global economic growth. The Western world pioneered the concept of open borders, and now many economies look set to close them again in the face of the emergence of SWF investments. SWFs also present both opportunities and challenges for their home and host countries, as well as for the broader international financial community. Home economies can leverage their funds to generate returns, spread wealth over time, gain access to markets, pursue a political agenda, improve economic development and stabilize their economy. Host economies can benefit through enlarging the pool of global capital and acting as a long-term investor in domestic enterprises and government bonds. The international community faces the challenge of making sure that SWFs are not pursuing political, but rather financial objectives. The international financial community is fast approaching a watershed in its approach to SWFs, facing a choice of rejection or well-managed acceptance. This choice facing the international financial community will influence the global landscape for years to come.

13.6 Conclusions

There has been significant and rapid change to the landscape of the world economy over the past few years; SWFs are playing an important role in this rapid change. SWFs have gained importance predominantly through the need for liquidity in the financial system and the lack of investor confidence in the financial markets. This change continues to dominate the world's political and economic agenda. The growth and proliferation of SWFs in recent years has altered the traditional flow of capital in the global financial market. The change has been from the dominance of the developed countries to the surging importance of the emerging and developing countries. The change has also been predominantly from public capital to finance the private sector.

Despite the establishment of the GAPP principles, some policy-makers believe increased regulation is needed to administer these SWFs as they continue to grow and their investments become increasingly bigger and bolder. The debate among world leaders will continue, as one side is demanding transparency, the other insisting that regulation is not required. Careful regulation is the way to ensure that SWFs are not prevented from investing in Western economies. Similarly, the avoidance of barriers to the increased mobility of capital stemming from mutually beneficial SWF activity is the biggest concern of SWFs, who fear financial protectionism. Finally, European countries are fast approaching a watershed in their approach to SWFs. They face a choice of rejection or well-managed acceptance. The European approach will help to determine the global landscape for years to come.

References

Addison, T. and Heshmati, H. (2003), *The New Global Determinants of FDI Flows to Developing Countries,* United Nations University/WIDER, Discussion Paper No. 2003/45.

Barber, T. and Chaffin, J. (2008), 'Sarkozy Calls for European Wealth Funds', *Financial Times*, 21 October.

Betts, P. (2008), 'Sovereign Wealth Funds Hold Out for a Tough Bargain', *Financial Times*, 5 March.

Blomstrom, M. (2001), *The Economics of International Investment Incentives*, OECD Series, September.

Caisse des Dépôts (2008), *Creation of the Strategic Investment Fund*, 21 November.

Cohen, B. J. (2008), *Sovereign Wealth Funds and National Security: The Great Trade-off*, Department of Political Science, University of California, Santa Barbara, Working Papers, available at: http://www.polsci.ucsb.edu/faculty/cohen/working/pdfs/SWF_text.pdf [accessed: 14 January 2009].

Commission of the European Communities (CEUC) (2008), *A Common European Approach to SWFs*, Communication from the Commission to the European Parliament, the Council, the European and Social Committee and the Committee of the Regions, Brussels.

Devlin, W. and Brummit, B. (2007), *A Few Sovereigns More: The Rise of Sovereign Wealth Funds*, OECD Working Papers on Insurance and Private Pensions No. 14.

Dunning, J. (2006), 'Towards a New Paradigm of Development: Implications for the Determinants of International Business', *Transnational Corporations*, 15 (1), 173–228.

Emmerich, A. (2008) 'Sovereign Wealth Funds Adopt Voluntary Best Practices', *The Harvard Law School Forum on Corporate Governance and Financial Regulation*, available at: http://blogs.law.harvard.edu/corpgov/2008/11/01/sovereign-wealth-funds-adopt-voluntary-best-practices [accessed 8 January 2009].

Ervin, C. (2008), 'Sovereign Wealth Funds', *The OECD Observer*, 267, 21–2, May/June.

Financial Times (2007a), 'German Call to Curb Foreign Buyers', 13 July.

Financial Times (2007b), 'Funds that Shake Capitalist Logic', 29 July.

Financial Times (2008), 'Sarkozy's Fund of Bad Advice', 22 October.

Gilson, R. and Milhaupt, C. (2008), *Sovereign Wealth Funds and Corporate Governance: A Minimalist Response to the New Mercantilism*, Stanford Law and Economics Olin Working Paper No. 355 and Columbia Law and Economics Working Paper No. 328, February.

Green, R. and Torgerson, T. (2007), *Are High Foreign Exchange Reserves in Emerging Markets a Blessing or Burden?* Department of the Treasury, Office of International Affairs, Occasional Paper No. 6, March.

International Monetary Fund (IMF) (2007), *The Global Financial Stability Report: Financial Market Turbulence, Causes, Consequences and Policies*. Washington DC: IMF, October.

International Monetary Fund (IMF) (2008), *IMF Intensifies Work on Sovereign Wealth Funds*, 4 March, available at: http://www.imf.org/external/pubs/ft/survey/so/2008/POL03408A.htm [accessed 18 November 2008].

International Working Group of Sovereign Wealth Funds (IWG) (2008), *Sovereign Wealth Funds: Santiago Principles*, IWG.

Jen, S. (2007), 'Sovereign Wealth Funds: What They Are and What's Happening', *World Economics*, 8 (7), 1–7.

Johnson, S. (2007), 'The Rise of Sovereign Wealth Funds', *Finance and Development*, 44 (3), 56–7.

Kern, S. (2007), 'Sovereign Wealth Funds – State Investments on the Rise', *Deutsche Bank Research Current Issues*, 10 September.

Lall, S. (2005), 'Linking FDI and Technology Development for Capacity Building and Strategic Competitiveness', *Transnational Corporations*, vol. 11, 39–88.

Portman, C. (2008), 'The Economic Significance of Sovereign Wealth Funds', *Economic Outlook*, 32 (1), 24–33.

Redicker, D. and Crebo-Redicker, H. (2007), *Foreign Investment and Sovereign Wealth Funds*, Global Strategic Finance Initiative, New America Foundation, Working Paper No. 1, 25 September.

Rios-Morales, R. and Brennan, L. (2009), 'Sovereign Wealth Funds: The New Global Financial Player', *Centre Interdisciplinaire de Recherche sur le Commerce Exterieur et l'Economie, Les Cahiers de Recherche*, 12, 111–28.

Siebert, H. (2007), *Rules for Borders-Crossing Factor Movements*, The Kiel Institute for the World Economy, Working Paper No. 1381, October.

Singh, K. (2008), 'Protecting Europe's Wealth: Sovereign Wealth Funds and the Global Europe', *Global Research*, 27 October.

The Economist (2008a), 'Once Bitten, Twice Shy', 16 October.

The Economist (2008b), 'A Petro-Dollar Saved', 4 September.

The Economist (2008c), 'Beyond Doha', 9 October.

The Economist (2008d), 'The Rise of State Capitalism', 18 September.

Truman, E. (2007a), *Sovereign Wealth Funds: The Need for Greater Transparency and Accountability*, Peterson Institute for International Economics, Policy Brief No. PB07-06, August.

Truman, E. (2007b), 'The Management of China's International Reserves: China and a SWFs Scoreboard', paper prepared for Conference on China's Exchange Rate Policy, Peterson Institute for International Economics, October.

UNCTAD (2008), *World Investment Report 2008: Transnational Corporations and the Infrastructure Challenge*. New York/Geneva: United Nations, July.

World Bank (2004), *World Development Report 2005: A Better Investment Climate for Everyone*. Oxford: Oxford University Press.

Part V

Innovative Perspectives on Southern Multinationals

14

Exploring the Configuration of Emerging Country Multinationals – A Value Chain Perspective

J. S. Srai and D. E. Fleet

14.1 Introduction

This chapter explores the investment patterns of emerging country multinationals (EC-MNCs) to understand whether these differ from the traditional approaches used by firms from developed countries. Specifically we analysed investments in operations in production activities, but equally of interest were those investments that would constitute upstream (R&D, design, supply-side) or downstream investments (distribution/route to market, after-sales services). This 'value chain perspective' was of interest as it may provide particular insights into different internationalization patterns of EC-MNCs.

Before introducing our review of case data gathered from several studies on internationalization and mergers and acquisition (M&As), we consider at a more general level the globalization trends within production operations, patterns in foreign direct investment (FDI) from EC-MNCs, the role of M&As in their internationalization, and how a value chain operational perspective might provide insights to motives and investment patterns.

14.2 Globalization trends in production

The increasing globalization of goods and services, as signified by the growth in exports outstripping production and GDP growth (Figure 14.1), has resulted in dramatic changes in the patterns of supply and demand around the world.

As many authors have observed, the BRICs countries (Brazil, Russia, India and China) and other ECs are playing an increasingly important role in global production volumes, with new centres of production emerging that serve their fast-growing domestic markets, but also play a key role in international trade. FDI from ECs, often through international M&As, is a key mechanism for achieving international growth.

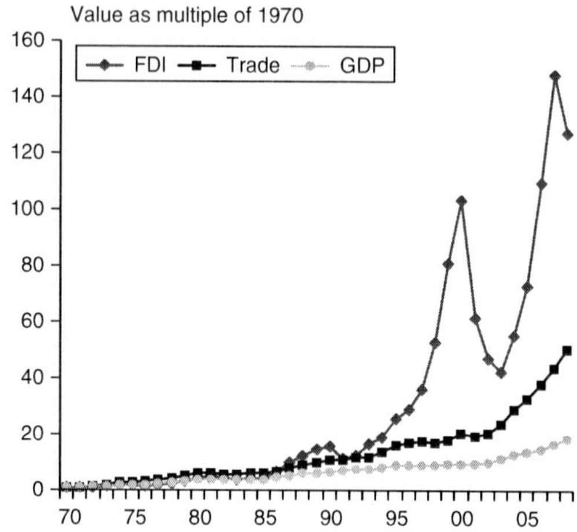

Figure 14.1 Growth in GDP, trade and FDI
Source: UNCTAD and IMF.

14.3 FDI trends from emerging countries

A key indicator of these changes in international trade is the amount of foreign direct investment (FDI), that is, the sums invested in one country from another. The statistics on FDI collated by the United Nations Conference on Trade and Development (UNCTAD) show that over the past four decades global FDI has generally increased much more rapidly than global GDP, but going through a number cycles of growth and decline. Most recently an apparently irresistible rise from the mid-1990s was reversed at the beginning of the new century, but growth picked up again from 2004, exceeding the earlier 2000 peak by 2006 and reaching a new record of US$ 20–21 trillion in 2007, only to fall back yet again as the global credit crisis started to bite in 2008 (Figure 14.1).

The growth in FDI reflects many influences, but a major factor is the requirement for firms to develop their competitive position in international markets – as supported by the observation that, over the past decade, mergers and acquisitions (M&As) have accounted for about 60 per cent of global FDI. A large part of this investment flows between developed countries as industries become more global, but the newly emerging economies are attracting increasing levels of FDI as companies in developed nations attempt to access their rapidly growing domestic markets and/or to take advantage of the low local cost of production. While the European Union, or EU, was the destination for about 38 per cent of global FDI over the years 2006–8 the BRICs countries (Brazil, Russia, India and China) received about 15 per cent – not so far behind the 16 per cent received by the United States.

A more recent, and less reported, trend has been the growth of FDI from the emerging economies themselves. Outward FDI from newly emerging countries was a minor contributor to the FDI peak in 2000, but it had climbed significantly by the time of the next peak in 2007. As an example of this growth, in 1996, before Hong Kong reverted to China, the combined outward FDI from the BRICs accounted for only 0.7 per cent of global FDI (compared to around 70 per cent for the countries currently in the EU), but this had risen to around 6 per cent over the years 2006–8 (and 9 per cent when Hong Kong is included), whereas FDI from the EU had fallen to just under 56 per cent of the global total. Another indication of the increasing FDI from these countries is that, while global FDI fell back by more than 13 per cent from 2007 to 2008, outward FDI from the BRICs increased by nearly a third. The fraction of the FDI from the BRICs in the form of M&A is around 40 per cent – that is, comparable to the fraction of EU FDI in the form of M&A. These figures have to be treated with some caution as, for example, practices such as 'round-tripping', the flow of capital from mainland China to Hong Kong and then back to the mainland to achieve financial benefits, may exaggerate trends a little, but there is no doubt that there is an increasing willingness and ability for companies in emerging countries to invest abroad.

The point at which the strong outward FDI growth started varies slightly from country to country. For Brazil, Russia and China, it seems to have been 2003–4, while for India growth was relatively modest from 2000, followed by strong acceleration in 2006. Recent studies by researchers at the Centre for International Manufacturing of Cambridge University's Institute for Manufacturing (IfM) suggest that while factors such as the inflow of FDI and recent national policy reforms have contributed to this growth in BRIC outward FDI, there were usually local companies ready to capitalize on these changes and emerge as multinationals to take on established companies from the West; we term these companies EC-MNCs (emerging country multinationals). There seemed to be striking similarities in the early growth of these EC-MNCs, which prepared then to compete with Western MNCs. Each was located in a large country with a huge domestic market in which local monopolies were often the case, or in which the companies were sheltered from intense international competition. As a result, they were able to gain scale and experience before facing the established international competition. Many of the companies we studied had engaged early in significant collaborations, which helped them develop their competencies. In some cases, this was with a Western joint venture partner hoping to penetrate their home markets, whereas in other cases the competence was developed as a contract manufacturer for an established company. The Chinese companies, in particular, that we studied seemed to have actively sought out manufacturing competencies to help them grow. Many of the Brazilian, Russian and capital-intensive Chinese companies started as state-owned enterprises;

the others were privately held companies of one form or another. In China, in the industrial regions of PRD and YRD, in relatively low capital-intensity manufacturing sectors, firms were privately owned having reached global scale within a relative short timeframe through contract manufacturing. Indian companies, on the other hand, were primarily family-owned with a dominant equity holder. As a result, all were free to take a longer-term view of strategy. Furthermore, in the Indian and Chinese cases, a key leader, often the founder, can be identified as the person behind the company's strategy and internationalization. Finally, most of these companies studied gained international experience well before the more recent outward FDI surge from their countries. Although no single pattern was observed to explain this early internationalization, their methods and motives appear to have been varied. Many of the companies made their early international investments in other developing markets, often with cultural or political links to the home economy, but those internationalizing to acquire raw materials had to invest where the resources were located!

During the last FDI peak in 2007 outward investment from the BRICs was approximately two per cent of GDP. This is still only approximately half the global average, and a third of the EU figure, but the percentage has been growing steadily, and with the growth of the GDP in these countries we can expect to see EC-MNCs becoming more active in international markets.

A key dimension to the outward FDI trends from ECs has been the relaxation of home country trade policies. In India for example, outward FDI was facilitated by the progressive relaxation of currency controls, which allowed Indian firms to acquire overseas firms with revenues substantially greater than their own. Similarly China's 'Going Global' policy of 2002 encouraged Chinese firms to invest overseas.

14.4 The role of M&A in internationalization

Although M&A plays a major role in the internationalization of companies, it is frequently reported that most M&A projects fail to meet their objectives (for example, Brewis, 2000; Habeck et al., 2000). The task of realizing operational synergies in M&As is complex and often not well managed (Srai et al., 2010), and is a key reason for such projects not meeting expectations.

One of the factors that have hindered an understanding of the problem of integration of manufacturing operations has been the lack of a common framework to describe the activities that occur during the M&A. The Operations Process Map for international M&As (see Figure 14.2; Srai et al., 2010) was developed to address this need. It can be used to identify the key operational activities that are required to support effective integration in international M&As in order to realize potential synergies between firm manufacturing and supply networks.

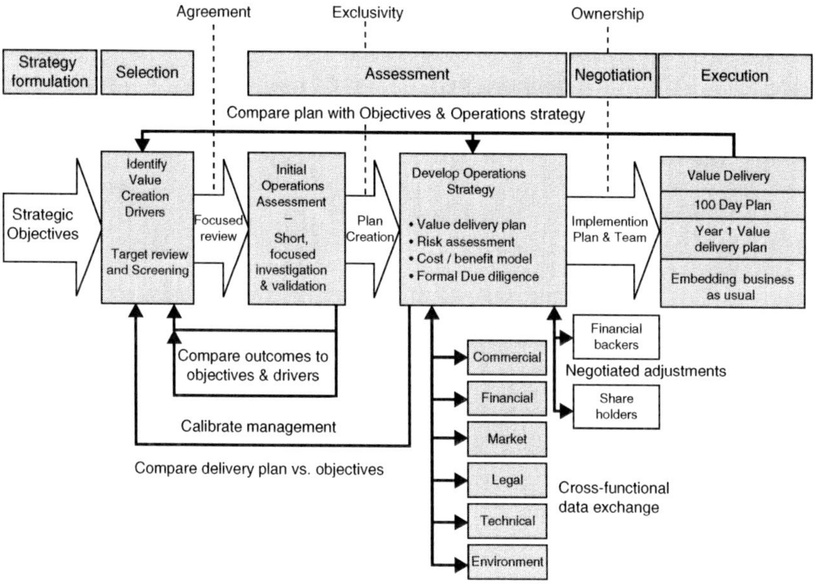

Figure 14.2 Understanding M&As – an operations perspective
Source: Srai et al. (2010).

Figure 14.2 shows three essential activities of M&A: *target selection* (identifying companies that could add value if acquired), *assessment* (confirming that the assumptions underpinning selection are correct), and *execution* (extracting the value in the deal, often by post-merger integration, PMI). Most M&As require PMI to release synergies and release the potential value in the deal (for example, Haspeslagh and Jemison, 1991). PMI is inevitably complex (Seaby, 1969; Shrivastava, 1986; Vester, 2002; Epstein, 2004), and the more complex this integration, the more likely there are to be problems. International M&A requires additional coordination across geographic areas, and the integration of operations is one of the most complex areas – for example, it has been argued that manufacturing integration takes longer than integration in other functions, owing to the number of people involved (Baden-Fuller and Boschetti, 1996), the difficulties in production system integration (Quah and Young, 2005), and the time-consuming nature of production facility change (Kitching, 1967). Hence international M&As that require operational integration are likely to be particularly risky.

Figure 14.3 shows the linkages between the key success factors (KSFs) reported in M&As, the operational activities required and their role in value creation (Srai et al., 2010). Srai et al. argue that the two principal routes to achieving operational synergies during *execution*, and hence unlocking value

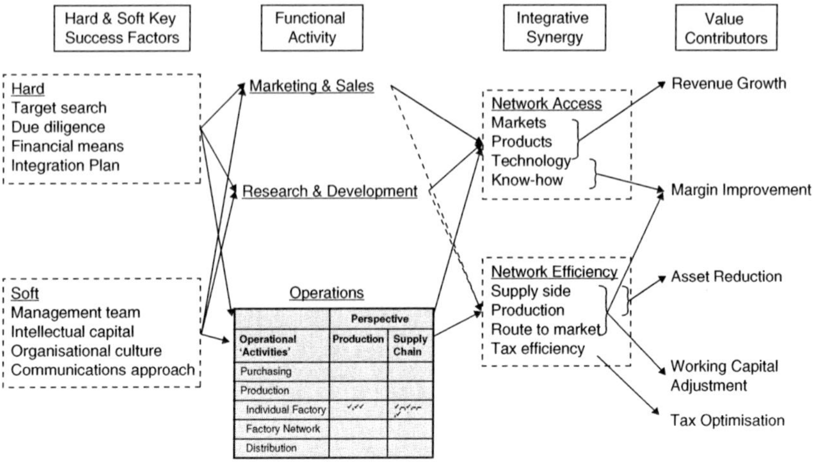

Figure 14.3 Drivers of M&A synergy
Source: Srai et al. (2010).

potential in M&As, are through enhanced *'network access'* (markets, products, technology, know-how) and *'network efficiency'* (optimizing manufacturing and supply chain resources), as shown in Figure 14.3. The dimensions supporting network efficiency in particular, representing central elements of the manufacturing value chain, are thus key aspects to observe in the internationalization behaviour of EC-MNCs.

14.5 The manufacturing value chain

A key aim of the present study was to understand whether EC-MNCs have different investment patterns in developed and emerging countries, and whether these investment patterns differ when compared with Western MNCs. Traditional analysis of manufacturing has focused on the production capabilities of the firm, typically the original equipment manufacturer (OEM). More recently, many studies have extended their analyses to the supply networks within which production sits – capturing the complex interrelationships, information and material flows between the various players in a product (product category) supply chain, both upstream suppliers and downstream distribution activities.

In this study, the value chain concept is used to ensure that a broader systems perspective is taken: one that incorporates R&D, operations and after-sales services into the analysis of investment strategies. While the value chain concept is not new, its use here, as an analysis framework to capture the alternative configurations EC-MNCs adopt during their investment and internationalization strategies, is novel with the aim of providing a new

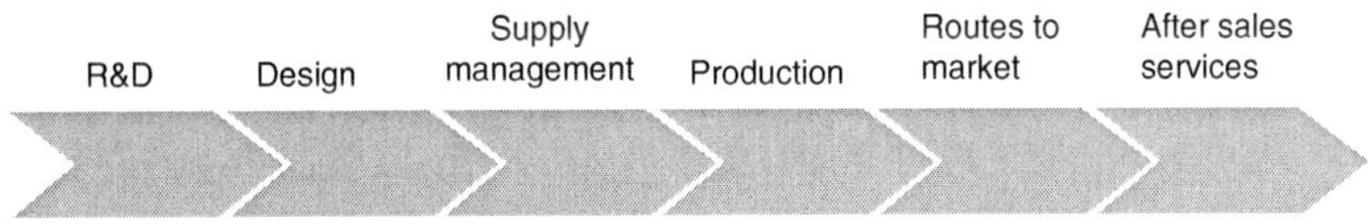

Figure 14.4 The manufacturing value chain

perspective on their motives and the challenges they potentially face in implementation.

The manufacturing value chain concept used in the case study analysis spans R&D and design, supply management, production, routes-to-market through to after-sales service, and is schematically presented in Figure 14.4.

The approach (as used in the IfM's input to the UK Government's Review of Science and Innovation Policy (Sainsbury Review, 2007); and studies on Chinese MNCs (Srai and Shi, 2008)) aims to identify the main drivers and trends at each stage of the value chain, the key linkages between stages and the importance or otherwise of their international location. This is particularly relevant for EC-MNCs whose manufacturing value chains are increasingly fragmented and globally distributed.

The operational dimensions considered in evaluating the configuration implications of the dispersion patterns of EC-MNCs were drawn from the literature on 'network configuration analysis'. Building on this value chain approach, various studies of international networks have focused in different stages of the value chain (Table 14.1).

The research considers how these network configuration dimensions of 'network structure', 'network dynamics', 'governance and coordination', 'support infrastructure' and 'product configuration' impact on MNC investment and internationalization strategies. In addition to the understanding of investments in international production networks, the approach enables upstream and downstream considerations to inform a more complete value chain assessment, against these key configuration dimensions, to identify investment patterns, and how they support internationalization strategies.

Reflecting on the cases used in this work, Table 14.2 summarizes the declared investment motives of developed and emerging country MNCs, captured against the various stages of the value chain.

14.6 Internationalization of EC-MNCs

While the popular image of overseas investment is of Western companies setting up greenfield operations in developing economies (developed to emerging, or D–E, investment) to develop sources of raw materials, for example,

Table 14.1 Configuration dimensions of international manufacturing operations

Configuration elements	**Engineering networks**	**Production networks**	**Supply networks**	**Service supply networks**
	(Zhang et al., 2007)	**(Shi and Gregory, 1998, Christodoulou et al., 2007)**	**(Srai and Gregory, 2008)**	**(Srai, 2010)**
Network structure	Geographic dispersion Resources and roles of engineering centres Rationale for network design	Plant role, characteristics Geographic dispersion Network evolution	Supply network tier structure and shape Geographical dispersion and supply network Mapping Integrating mechanisms	Multi-organizational network structure Service archetypes
Network dynamics	Operational processes supporting engineering information flows	Response mechanisms	Flow of materials and information between and within key unit operations Replenishment mode and supply–demand dynamics	Service supply contracting mode Through-life perspectives
Governance and coordination	Governance, including authority structure and co-ordination mechanisms	Horizontal and vertical coordination	Role of network leaders Inter-firm governance mechanisms	Service network governance modes
Support infrastructure	Support, including engineering tools and IT systems	–	–	Support systems
Network relationships		Intra-firm dynamic capability-building	Role of key network partners Inter-firm relationships	Partnering modes Firm and network value-sets
Product configuration		Product lifecycle and knowledge transfer	Product modularity Value density SKU portfolio/profile	Service offering Outcomes/effects

Table 14.2 Description of internationalization investment motives

MNCs invest to secure:					
D to D	To acquire advanced R&D/design capability	Only likely in resource-rich countries and for scarce resources	Only if transportation cost makes it cheaper to serve the market from this location	To acquire customers or developed routes to market	Generally to support sales of complex equipment
D to E	Cost advantages, understanding local requirements, politically important!	To secure sources of cheap or scarce materials	To access low-cost production (usually for proximate markets or to meet off-set obligations)	Not a major motive	To support sales of complex equipment
EC-MNCs invest to secure:					
E to E	Unlikely	To secure sources of cheap or scarce materials	To acquire production capacity close to target markets	Not a major motive	Unlikely
E to D	To acquire advanced R&D/design capability	Only likely in resource-rich countries and for scarce resources	To acquire production knowhow or reputation	To acquire customers or developed routes to market	Unlikely
	R&D/design	**Supply management**	**Production**	**Route to market**	**After-sales service**

Note: D = developed, E = emerging.

Unilever palm oil, or to tap emerging markets, for example, Unilever's investments in Nigeria in the 1920s, most investment by companies from developed economies is in other developed economies (D–D investment) and mergers and acquisitions (M&As) are now more a more common form of investment than greenfield investment (UNCTAD FDI statistics).

Given the recent growth in FDI from emerging economies it is interesting to examine the internationalization behaviour of EC-MNCs to see if it matches FDI behaviour by companies from developed economies. There are, of course, many well-known 'stages of growth' models (for example, growth v. internationalization) describing the way in which companies develop their international operations, but these were necessarily developed by observing the behaviour of companies from developed economies. As a first step to understanding whether these apply to internationalization by firms from emerging economies, we explore the investment behaviour across the manufacturing value chain (Table 14.2) for MNCs from both developed and emerging economies, and how these support the internationalization process.

The analysis presented in this chapter draws from case studies on internationalization strategies of MNCs (Sainsbury, 2007; Fleet and Shi, 2008), international M&A (Zhang, 2007) and particularly investments in BRICs economies (Srai and Shi, 2008). Whereas they represent a non-random set of cases drawn from separate studies of international manufacturing and supply networks, and international M&As, the investment patterns across the value chain captured within these case studies provide interesting insights. Table 14.3 summarizes the case study data we are drawing on and represents around a hundred individual international investments.

14.6.1 Internationalization by MNCs from developed economies

We first review briefly current internationalization trends by MNCs against which to compare the behaviour of EC-MNCs.

14.6.1.1 MNC internationalization in developed countries

Globalization can be seen as one of the primary drivers for MNCs investing in other developed economies (D–D internationalization). Whereas once it was necessary to have a leading market position in a country to be profitable, the erosion of tariffs and globalization of markets now requires a leading position regionally or even globally. Establishing such a position by organic growth is difficult and slow, particularly when confronted by incumbent firms in the contested markets. Hence M&As are now often the preferred route to achieve this aim. Examples include the repeated consolidations in the global pharmaceutical industry, reflected in the names of the surviving entities such as GSK, formed by the merger of SmithKline Beckman and the Beecham Group plc to form SmithKline Beecham plc, the merger of Glaxo and Wellcom to form Glaxo Wellcome, and finally the merger of Glaxo

Wellcome and SmithKline Beecham to form GlaxoSmithKline. One might term this behaviour 'horizontal internationalization' since the acquired companies focus on the same stages of the value chain as the acquirer.

Another behaviour we have observed might be termed 'vertical internationalization', in which companies are seeking to plug weaknesses in their global value chains. This might include the 'upstream internationalization' with the traditional aim of securing sources of raw materials, although companies can increasingly rely on reliable markets for this, or more commonly

Table 14.3 Case data used in the Analysis of Investment Patterns study data

Focal company	Home country	SBU/Business	Target location and number
Ranbaxy	India	Pharmaceuticals	USA/Europe Various (E–E)
Aditya Birla	India	Chemicals etc. Metals Textiles	Far East (E–E) Global/Aus Various (E–E) Canada
Haier	China	Refrigerators White goods Airconditioning	USA/Italy Various (E–E) USA
TCL	China	TVs	Various (E–E)
Wanxiang	China	Automotive components	USA
Petrobras	Brazil	Petrochemicals	Various (E–E, E–D)
Vale	Brazil	Mining	Various (E–D)
Norilsk Nickel	Russia	Mining + processing	USA/UK
Co#3	UK	Semiconductor equipment	USA
Co#4	Austria	Bricks	UK
Co#5	USA	Security seals	UK
Co#6	UK	Pumps	Italy
Co#9	UK	Power generation	Germany
Co#10	Italy	Household appliances	UK
Co#11	USA	Packaging products	UK
Unilever	UK/Neth	Foods Middle East subsidiary –FMCG FMCG	US/Global Middle East China
Midea	China	White goods	Africa
BAE Systems	UK	Aerospace	Australia
Johnson Electric	China	Electric motors	Europe
Airbus	France	Aerospace	China
Johnson Matthey	UK	Precious metals	Africa
Cussons	UK	FMCG	China

Note: D = developed, E = emerging.

the acquisition of R&D facilities to provide rapid access to new technology or a stream of new products – the UK semiconductor company's US acquisition (Table 14.3) is a good example. 'Downstream internationalization' might refer to acquiring outlets for product or routes to market (for example, the cases of the Austrian bricks company and the Italian household appliances company in Table 14.3) or establishing service operations to provide after-sales support for complex products (such as BAE Systems' acquisition of Tenix in Australia).

14.6.1.2 MNC internationalization in emerging countries

Looking first at 'horizontal internationalization', it seems the primary motivation for MNCs to invest in emerging economies is to reach new markets, hence it is not surprising that much of this activity has focused on the BRIC countries, for example, FMCG goods companies such as Unilever and Cussons establishing operations in China once that market was open to foreign investors. However, restrictions on foreign ownership or concerns about the risks in unfamiliar markets mean that joint ventures are often seen as the vehicle for entry in preference to M&As or greenfield investment. Companies investing in ECs often progress through a JV until sufficiently familiar with the market to establish a fully owned company, for example, Unilever re-established its operations in China via JVs but subsequently bought out the partners to establish a WFOE (wholly foreign owned enterprise). In certain industries manufacturing might be set up in an emerging economy as a condition of market access; the aerospace and automotive industries provide many examples where 'local content' requirements drive the investment decision.

Horizontal internationalization by relocating part of the existing value chain, typically manufacturing, to take advantage of low input cost factors, receives a lot of press, but is much less common than popularly supposed. Many companies who had this as one of their initial aims when entering China have found access to the local market to be far more important. While such 'off-shoring' may make sense when products have a high labour content, when transportation cost is low and when price competition is strong, the investment costs may be high and delivery times will increase. Nevertheless one sees examples of this 'near-shoring' strategy – particularly in Mexico for the US market and in Eastern Europe for the Western European Market. However, in other low-cost countries, many Western companies have outsourced all or part of their production operations to contract manufacturing service providers (CMSPs). These CMSPs may be local companies, but may also be international companies who take on the risk of manufacturing in emerging economies, often for firms who were traditionally the original equipment manufacturers (OEMs) in their home markets.

Within 'vertical internationalization' investments 'upstream' might be expected to secure sources of raw materials. This was once fairly common as Western companies invested in plantations, mines etc., but, as the economies of these countries have developed so that normal markets operate, this activity is less frequent than it once was. For instance, Unilever, which once had extensive plantations to secure its supply of palm oils, has progressively divested these assets and purchases oils on the open market. Unilever's divestment of its Malaysian Palm Oil operations is an example of this evolution. Nevertheless the petrochemical industry still has to follow this strategy.

A few MNCs have established their own research and design operations in emerging economies, especially India and China, but it is unclear whether this is driven by cost considerations, skills availability, identification with the potentially large local market or to comply with local political pressure. Some MNCs' local subsidiaries have evolved impressive research capabilities, which then require effective integration into the global network.

Outsourcing of development to emerging economies has been observed – particularly in the electronics industry, as many CMSPs have begun to offer design as well as production services (ODM). The close connection between manufacturing and design can makes this attractive to the brand owners, but there are obvious longer-term strategic issues to consider. CMSPs have themselves seen a conflict between CM growth and own brand development. Some have resorted to focusing on one or the other; others have separated out so that their roles are clear. Many remain trying to straddle both areas, posing a potential competitive threat to the OEMs they once served.

Downstream investments are not a major activity as MNCs can usually access sales and distribution channels and find customers fairly readily. We do see investment in service operations, however, when the MNCs are selling complex expensive equipment (for example, Airbus).

14.6.2 Internationalization by EC-MNCs

Clearly, not all EC-MNCs will exhibit exactly the same stages of growth, as their development will be influenced by the economic and political history of the home country, sector and product characteristics, and the market opportunities that have presented themselves. Nevertheless some common themes are emerging.

Most of the EC-MNCs we have studied were initially able to develop in market conditions that either encouraged local monopolies or sheltered them from intense competition from Western MNCs. Each was located in a large country with a huge domestic market. As a result, they were able to gain scale and experience before facing international competition.

Several of these companies engaged early in significant collaborations, which helped them develop their competencies. In some cases, this was with a Western joint venture partner hoping to penetrate their home market – for example, Ranbaxy (India) with Lapetit (Italy), Embraer (Brazil) with Piper Aircraft (USA), MTS (Russia) with T-Mobile (Germany), Birla (India) with

Kaiser Aluminium and Chemicals (USA), and TCL (China) with Thomson Electronics (France). In other cases, the competence was developed as a contract manufacturer for an established company – for example, Wanxiang (China) with Zeller (USA) and Haier (China) with Liebherr (Germany). The Chinese companies, in particular, seem to have actively sought out competencies to help them grow.

Industry structure clearly plays a role in investment strategy. As EC-MNCs have been recent additions to the industrial landscape, with manufacturing operations having reached global scale relatively quickly, many have invested in centralized production facilities in their home market, preferring to operate an export model manufacturing network. This supply from an EC-MNC base is more prevalent in very highly capital-intensive sectors (for example, TFTLCD screen manufacture) or where the combination of low factory labour costs and high product value-density combine to support an export-oriented supply model. These centralized manufacturing network models are supported by geographically concentrated closely coupled local suppliers; (within the same town/city) – often these are single-product category clusters operating in very close proximity to the production sites, providing rapid replenishment and risk-pooling advantages.

Ownership is also a key factor in investment behaviour. Most of the Brazilian, Russian and Chinese companies we studied started as state-owned enterprises (SOEs). The others were privately held companies of one form or another. The Indian companies were primarily family-owned with a dominant equity holder. As a result, all were free to take a longer-term view of strategy.

In the Indian and Chinese cases, a key leader, who was often but not necessarily the founder, can be identified as the person behind the company's strategy and internationalisation (for example, Aditya Birla at Birla, Parvinder Singh at Ranbaxy, Zhang Ruimin at Haier, Lu Guanqiu at Wanxiang and Dongsheng at TCL).

Family ties have been important factors in some cases. For example, in the early growth of what is now the Birla group the family linkages were more important than the business linkages between the various companies the family members controlled. Indeed, it is potentially misleading to talk of the growth of this company as if it had been a single entity. Beyond family, ethnicity has also been important in both Chinese and Indian companies, which have benefited from their diasporas. For example, Ranbaxy was able to bring back young Western-educated chemists and managers to build its capabilities in India, and Chinese companies have been assisted by Chinese nationals educated in the West and by Chinese contacts that could act as intermediaries in Western economies.

Most of these EC-MNCs studied gained international experience well before the recent upsurge in FDI from their countries. Often they were able to exploit their low-cost base advantage by attacking low-margin segments abroad – sometimes with branded products, but often as subcontractors for OEMs. The accumulation of funds from trade imbalances and inward investment has made it easier for these firms to use M&As as a means to pursue internationalisation objectives in recent years. Over the period 2004–6 more than half of the FDI from Brazil, India and China was in the form of M&As.

The next two sub-sections examine how investment patterns of EC-MNCs compare when investing in other emerging countries and when investment is in more economically developed nations.

14.6.2.1 EC-MNC internationalisation in emerging countries

Often EC-MNCs investing in emerging economies did so in countries with strong cultural or political links to the home economy (for example, Birla, Haier and TCL in Southeast Asia, Ranbaxy in sub-Saharan Africa and MTS in the former Commonwealth of Independent States).

As before, we can think of this in terms of horizontal and vertical internationalisation Many, but not all, of the EC-MNCs we studied began their internationalisation in other emerging countries – for example, the Birla group's early internationalisation was in textiles, where it expanded its operations to a number of Southeast Asian countries in the 1970s. Its chemicals group established operations there in the next decade, but this can be seen as diversification as well as horizontal internationalisation. Horizontal internationalisation appears to be the dominant form for EC-MNCs in emerging economies, particularly in industries where global-scale production is dispersed in nature; examples of horizontal internationalisation include Birla in Egypt and China; Ranbaxy in Eastern Europe, Africa, Southeast Asia and Brazil; Haier in Southeast Asia, Central Asia, the Middle East and Africa; and the expansion of MTS through the former CIS states. TCL's plant in Vietnam is another example, but those in Thailand, Mexico and Poland are better seen as former low-cost plants previously owned by its MNC partner, Thomson.

Examples of downstream vertical internationalisation to secure customers or routes to market in emerging economies were less evident, although Birla's establishment of fatty acid production in the Philippines as a way to add value and find an outlet for the product of its palm oil plantations might be classified as such. Other examples include Chinese firms in the white goods and electronic sectors, such as Midea, who have expanded into Africa, in downstream developments involving local distributors in the 'final assembly' of manufacturing kits (for example, fans) and in linking into extensive locally established distribution models that extend into the provision of after-sales service.

Upstream vertical internationalisation in emerging economies to secure raw materials was also observed, for example, Birla's establishment of a pulp plant in Laos and a sodium hydroxide plant in the Philippines to service its textile business; Petrobras's oil exploration activities, and the investment of Chinese companies in Africa, which accounted for a large part of China's US$ 5bn or so annual investment in Africa.

14.6.2.2 EC-MNC internationalisation in developed countries

Naturally the major attraction of developed countries is their rich markets, and most EC-MNCs will be primarily interested in horizontal internationalisation. Often they will want to exploit the advantage of their low cost base, and an export model will be attractive. However, the acquisition of local companies and their assets can help penetrate the target market, by providing a customer list and easing local concerns. Most of Ranbaxy's manufacturing acquisitions in the US and Ireland can be seen in this way, although in some cases they also provided product R&D expertise. Haier's acquisition of production facilities in Europe and North America is similar, although transportation costs dictate some local production. One of the most striking recent examples of horizontal internationalisation was the acquisition in 2006 of Inco (a Canadian mining company) by Brazil's Vale for US$ 17bn, which made it the second largest mining company in the world.

Many E–D investments represent 'entry' strategies with subsequent 'hollowing-out' of activities to the acquirer's home low-cost country (LCC), leaving only some final assembly in the country of the acquired company. The EC-MNC also thus acquires access to the markets, and sometimes the brands, of the acquired firm but is able to serve these from a lower cost base. This approach is exemplified in the acquisition strategies of Johnson Electric. Indeed, we have seen some firms KPIs include 'number of days to transfer component supply' to the LCC home base.

Vertical internationalisation aims to capture capabilities not present in the internationalizing organisation, and E–D activity provides many interesting examples. Many of these are downstream, which is not surprising as the aim is to penetrate the lucrative markets. Russia's Norilsk Nickel mining group acquired Norimet Ltd, a London-based metal trading company, to facilitate trading its output on the London Metal Exchange, and Stillwater Mining in the USA, which also had downstream production activities that provide a route to market for its metal. Wanxiang established itself as a contract manufacturer of automotive parts for Zeller, an auto parts supplier in the USA. Following a souring of the relationship, it started to export under its own name and eventually bought Zeller, hence acquiring its distribution channels. One of the most dramatic examples, however, is Birla whose aluminium and copper-producing company, Hindalco, purchased Novelis, a Canadian-based, global aluminium rolling and recycling company, for US$ 6.4bn.

Examples of upstream internationalisation for raw materials are also observed, but these tend to be restricted to former European colonies or dominions whose economies developed from exporting raw materials. For example, Birla has acquired mines in Australia and pulp mills in Canada, and recently China's Hanlong Mining has announced its intention to invest US$ 5bn in Australia over the next five years. However, the motivation here is the same as EC-MNC's in emerging economies or indeed MNCs, and does not illustrate differences in approach.

In the other area of upstream vertical internationalisation, the acquisition of R&D and design expertise, the behaviour is very different. This activity is hardly seen at all in emerging economies, but there are many examples in developed markets. Ranbaxy, initially a producer of 'me-too' generic products, purchased R&D operations in Ireland and the USA, and engaged in various collaborations to build its product expertise; this culminated in it acquiring its own patents and setting up major research facilities in India. Embraer was able to gain new technologies through its AMX military programme co-initiated by the Italian Air Force. The acquisition of MG Rover by SAIC was primarily to gain product and design knowledge.

14.6.3 Services

Although it has been discussed above it is interesting to compare approaches to investment in after-sales service operations. Here we see the differentiation between E–D and D–E, being largely shaped by industry norms. Whether this involves operations in developing or emerging markets, in many cases the need to provide effective after-sales service is required locally. In the example of aerospace, service operation investments are tightly controlled by OEMs, with near-identical support facilities whether they are in Europe or China. Airbus is a fine example where its facilities in China 'mirror' similar operations in its European hubs. In the case of electronics and white goods, local distributors and retailers, or specialist service providers are decoupled from OEMs and provide across-the-board service models that reflect market maturity and industry norms rather than models differentiated by the heritage of the OEM. Specialist service providers who operate within this last stage of the value chain will therefore reflect national approaches; a key exception is where closely coupled OEM–service provider arrangements provide an alternative business model offering distinct 'outcome'-centric product-service solutions. These are evident in both complex equipment service-provision (for example, UK defence 'availability' contracting for fighter aircraft and naval warships) as well as commodity white goods equipment supply-installation-servicing (for example, China). However, these service model arrangements differ from D–E markets driven by regulatory environments and the economic cost of servicing. In the case of complex equipment service provision, models involve either close-partnering with service providers or the eventual acquisition of the local provider (for example, the BAES acquisition of Tenix in Australia).

Table 14.4 summarizes the observations in our set of case studies to suggest the differences between the priorities of EC-MNCs in their first phase of internationalisation and the key behaviours of established MNCs.

Table 14.4 Internationalization behaviour across the value chain

MNC	D-D	+		++	++	(+) Complex equipment
	D-E		+	++		(+) Complex equipment
EC-MNC	E-E		+	+	+	
	E-D	++	(+) Only in specific countries	+	++	
		R&D, Design	Securing & Transporting Materials	Production / Core Company Operations	Securing Customers & Routes to Market	Service Provision
		Vertical Upstream		Horizontal	Vertical Downstream	

Table 14.5 Examples of internationalization behaviour

MNC	D-D	UK semi-conductors		USA Packaging USA security Seals	Austria Bricks, Italy HH appliances	BAES
	D-E		Petrochemicals Johnson Matthey	Unilever, Cussons		Airbus
EC-MNC	E-E		AB Textiles AB Chemicals	Ranbaxy, AB Textiles, Haier, MTS, TCL	AB metals & chemicals	
	E-D	Ranbaxy	**AB textiles and Metals**	Haier. Wanxing Johnson Electric	AB Metals, Norlisk Nickel, Ranbaxy, Vale	
		R&D, Design	Securing & Transporting Materials	Production / Core Company Operations	Securing Customers & Routes to Market	Service Provision
		Vertical Upstream		Horizontal		Vertical Downstream

Examining behaviours in different stages of the global value chain provides key insights to the differences observed.

Selected examples that provide some context to these generic findings are shown in Table 14.5.

14.7 Summary

This review has shown how EC-MNCs investment patterns differ from those of the traditional MNCs, and that their investments in emerging markets are largely supply-side *resource-* and demand-side *market-seeking*, and those in developed markets reflect objectives linked to *network access* (technology and markets). In contrast, traditional MNCs' international investments are driven by the need for *network efficiency* (particularly in the case of emerging markets) *and market access*-driven arrangements that integrate low-cost country (LCC) resources and emerging market potential.

From a research perspective, a value chain-based assessment of MNC investments, informed by operational models in M&A processes and network-configuration studies, provides insights not evident from the established FDI analytical approaches.

From an industrial context perspective, industry structure and dynamics, national regulatory differences and product characteristics remain key factors across the value chain, particularly in after-sales services, and significantly influence the investment options available to OEMs.

References

Baden-Fuller, C. and Boschetti, C. (1996), 'Creating Competitive Advantage through Mergers: The Lens of the Resource Based Theory', in H. Thomas and D. O'Neal (eds), *Strategic Integration*. Chichester, UK: John Wiley & Sons, 91–112.

Brewis, J. (2000), 'Most M&A Deals Fail to Add Value', *Corporate Finance*, 182, 8–9.

Christodoulou, P., Fleet, D. and Hanson, P. (2007), *Making the Right Things in the Right Places*. University of Cambridge IfM Publication.

Epstein, M. J. (2004), 'The Drivers of Success in Post-Merger Integration', *Organizational Dynamics*, 33 (2), 174–89.

Fleet, D. E. and Shi, Y. (2008), *Emerging Multinationals: Manufacturing in a Rapidly Changing Global Landscape*. CapGemini and IfM Publication.

Habeck, M. M., Kroger, F. and Tram, M. R. (2000), *After the Merger: Seven Strategies for Successful Post-merger Integration*. London: Financial Times/Prentice Hall.

Haspeslagh, P. C. and Jemison, D. B. (1991), *Managing Acquisitions: Creating Value through Corporate Renewal*. New York: The Free Press.

International Monetary Fund statistics: https://www.imf.org/external.

Kitching, J. (1967), 'Why Do Mergers Miscarry?' *Harvard Business Review*, 45, 84–107.

Quah, P. and Young, S. (2005), 'Post-acquisition Management: A Phases Approach for Cross-border M&As', *European Management Journal*, 23 (1), 65–75.

Sainsbury, D. J. (2007), *The Race to the Top: A Review of the UK Government's Science and Innovation Policies* (the Sainsbury Review), available at: www.rsc.org/ScienceAndTechnology/Parliament/sainsburyreview.asp, October.

Seaby, F. W. (1969), 'Control Postmerger Change', *Harvard Business Review*, 47 (5), 4–12, 154–5.
Shi, Y. and Gregory, M. J. (1998), 'International Manufacturing Networks – To Develop Global Competitive Capabilities', *Journal of Operations Management*, 16, 195–214.
Shrivastava, P. (1986), 'Postmerger Integration', *Journal of Business Strategy*, 7, 65–76.
Srai, J. S., Bertoncelj, A., Fleet, D. E. and Gregory, M. J. (2010), 'An Operations Process Framework for International M&A Value Creation', *European Journal of International Management*, 4 (1/2), 3–29
Srai, J. S. (2010), 'Supply Network Integration in Multi-organisational Network Systems', special issue of *International Journal of Manufacturing Research*, on Systems for Extended Enterprises (in press).
Srai, J. S. and Gregory, M. J. (2008), 'A Supply Network Configuration Perspective on International Supply Chain Development', *International Journal of Operations Management*, 5, 386–411, May.
Srai, J. S. and Shi, Y. J. (2008), *Understanding China's Manufacturing Value Chain*. University of Cambridge IfM Publication.
Srai, J. S., Bertoncelj, A., Fleet, D. E. and Gregory, M. J. (2010), 'An Operations Process Framework for International M&A Value Creation', *European Journal of International Management*, 4 (1/2), 3–29.
UNCTAD statistics: http://www.unctad.org/Templates/Page.asp?intItemID=1888&lang=1.
Vester, J. (2002), 'Lessons Learned about Integrating Acquisitions', *Research-Technology Management*, 33–41, May–June.
World Bank statistics: data.worldbank.org.
Zhang, R. (2007) 'Manufacturing Integration Processes in International Horizontal Mergers and Acquisitions', PhD thesis, University of Cambridge.
Zhang, Y., Shi, Y. and Gregory, M. J. (2007), 'Global Engineering Networks: The Integrating Framework and Key Patterns', *Proceedings of the Institution of Mechanical Engineers, Part B: Journal of Engineering Manufacture*, 221 (8), 1269–83.

15

Cadre-Capitalism Goes Global: Financial Market Reforms and the New Role for the People's Republic of China in World Markets

Jörn-Carsten Gottwald

15.1 Introduction

Chinese outward investment is making headlines: little-known Geely Automotive bids for Sweden's carmaker and European middle-class insignia Volvo (BBC, 2009), a completely unknown company from Sichuan for American icon Hummer (Stall, Terlap and King, 2009). State-owned energy companies invest in African oil, and the government of EU member state Greece turns to China to avoid bankruptcy (Reuters, 2010a). Three decades after the leadership of the People's Republic of China (PRC) initiated deep economic and social reforms, China joined other transition economies to emerge 'as significant outward investors' (UNCTAD, 2006: xxiii).

Inward foreign investment has played a crucial role for the policies of 'reform' and 'opening up' initiated under the leadership of Deng Xiaoping by the 3rd Plenum of the 11th Central Committee in December 1978. Turning Chinese enterprises from administrative units providing fundamental social and political duties to internationally competitive corporations proved one of the most difficult tasks in China's gradual transition towards its socialist market economy (Naughton, 2007: 298–304). In the 1990s, a new strategy called 'Go Global' was initially focused on overseas direct investment, international engineering and construction contracting, and labour services (Xiao Qinfu, 2004; Lou, 2009: 671–3). The aim set in 2002 was that ten to twenty state-owned enterprises would develop an international presence (Accenture, 2005). However, in addition to economic factors, the sensitivity of China turning from destination of FDI to source of FDI soon encountered political resistance. When China's oil company CNOOC bid for the US oil company Unocal (Lunding, 2006a: 1) the US government thwarted the deal. From a Western perspective, Chinese MNCs are too closely linked with the Chinese central leadership (Lunding, 2006b).

The strategy to 'Go Global' is a direct and logical consequence of the economic reforms initiated in the 1970s (Zheng, 2006), and it dovetails nicely with a major shift in international political economy: the rise of the so-called non-triad or Southern Multinational companies (UNCTAD, 2006; Goldstein, 2007) and their international expansion (Luo and Tung, 2007: 481–98). It complemented the Chinese attempts of 'bringing in' foreign investment by urging Chinese enterprises to 'go out' (Jiang Zemin, 2002). However, 'until recently the success of attracting inflows has overshadowed the outward investment strategy' (Cheung and Qian, 2009: 314) Based on the assumption of an intensifying globalization, 'the current financial crisis is presenting Chinese enterprises with a rare opportunity to go global' (*People's Daily Online*, 4 June 2009). Against the global trends, China's outward FDI continued to accelerate (Davies, 2009a). Chinese officials, however, stress the need to only provide 'market compatible' support for their own enterprises when venturing abroad (State Council, 2009). While total investment including portfolio investment in US treasury bonds reached nearly US$ 3,000 billion at the end of 2008, according to the State Administration for Foreign Exchange, SAFE (SAFE, 2009b), direct industrial investment is on course to meet the target of US$ 60 billion stated in the 11th Five-Year Plan (State Council, 2007).

Most studies on Chinese outward investment so far have been focused on resources, strategies (Morck, Yeung and Zhao, 2008) and the driving forces behind China's ODI (Lunding, 2006a, 2006b; Williamson and Ming Zeng, 2008). China's financial services sector, by contrast, only hit the spotlight when state-sponsored vehicles tried to acquire European or American enterprises (Heep, 2008b). While industrial companies act 'partly out of desperation' (Barboza, 2005), China's financial sector has been assigned a different role. The four big commercial banks have been carefully reformed and put into a new regulatory framework. Listing on international stock exchanges such as Hong Kong and New York, these banks are slowly raising their global profile through acquisitions while at the same time supporting Chinese industrial and service MNCs (PBC, 2009). At the same time, the Chinese government has encouraged its policy banks to increase their overseas activities. It created special investment vehicles, so-called sovereign wealth funds, to make better use of the huge foreign exchange reserves earned as part of the boom years since the 1990s. SAFE, the China Investment Corporation CIC, but also state-owned strategic bank such as China Development Bank have taken a far less cautious approach and have become the subject of heated debate. In the near future, China's financial services industry should find itself in a good position to use the power arising from its hybrid structure to accelerate its move abroad.

How did the PRC manage to turn around an ailing state-owned financial sector, forecast to break down in the early 2000s, into a vehicle for investments abroad? And what is the role for China's financial services industry in the 'Go Global' strategy now that the economic crisis has increased Chinese leverage and apprehensions in Europe and the US about a potential sell-out to Chinese enterprises? Looking at the way the Chinese leadership has reformed its major banks and stockmarkets, has set up its own sovereign wealth fund and has allowed SAFE to pursue targets abroad highlights the continuing and deepening involvement of the party–state leadership in China's socialist market economy. This again helps improve understanding of China's emerging capitalism and the role Chinese MNCs and government can play in the current renegotiation of the global economy.

15.2 The 'Go Global' strategy in the context of China's socialist market economy

Chinese observers and politicians stress the logical link between China's three decades of internal reforms and the decision to actively seek a prominent role for China's leading enterprises on global markets. While most governments around the world support their national champions, the links between the party–state and enterprises in China's socialist market economy are much tighter than in traditional liberal or coordinated market economies – and they are solidly institutionalized.

15.2.1 China's socialist market economy – adaptive cadre-capitalism

'The state has put into practice a socialist market economy' (Constitution of the PRC, 2004, 2008). The Chinese state is dominated by the CCP, the economic system is kept under the guidance of a Leninist party–state. While the use of the market as tool for the allocation of goods and services is respected, the issue of how far China's socialist market economy qualifies as a market economy is debatable. The EU flatly refuses to grant market economy status to this form of 'cadre capitalism' (Heilmann, 1996) on the grounds of China not fulfilling the relevant criteria (Remond, 2007). In international comparison, entrepreneurial freedom in China is average at best (World Bank, 2010).

China's reform policies have been described as the evolution of a Chinese capitalism (Breslin, 2004; McNally, 2006), the rise to power of a cadre-capitalism (Tsai 2005, 2007; Dickson, 2008) adapting to a changing international environment,[1] implementing Western techniques in the business of governing business (Pearson, 2005, 2007). China's socialist market economy exhibits an 'institutional amphibiousness' (Ding, 1994) of a market-oriented system based on strong involvement of a one-party state controlling the judiciary, the media and most of the large enterprises through partial ownership, selection of top management positions and privileged access to finance. While nobody would doubt the tremendous degree of change within the Chinese one-party state, progress towards a democratic multi-party system representing differing interests within the society, the implementation of a rule of law guaranteeing individual freedoms and private property rights even in confrontation with the CCP is still absent (Bergsten et al., 2007). Describing the changes taking place within the limits of the CCP-dominated and controlled Leviathan (Yang, 2005). The Communist Party of China has managed to preserve and even strengthen its grip on power by successfully co-opting new elites (Tsai, 2007;

Dickson, 2008). This includes the rebuilding of party committees in enterprises and social organizations (Shambaugh, 2008; Zheng, 2009: 6–15). The CCP provides access to entrepreneurial opportunities and economic rents. The party controls the elites in politics administration, law, major enterprises and leading societal organizations. While pursuing ambitious reforms of the legal system and proclaiming the objective of rule of law in China, there are only limited trends to bring the CCP under the control of the judiciary. Thus, the Chinese legal system rather aims at rule by law than rule of law (Clark, 2008).

15.2.2 Creating national champions through cadre-capitalism

According to international trade theory, enterprises develop their strategic size and experience in competitive domestic markets before venturing abroad. However, 'China's continental-sized economy is becoming extremely diverse' (Pearson, 2007: 719) and awaits a 'second economic transformation' (Meyer, 2007) to create national markets. In addition to limitations of size, China's piecemeal regulatory framework hampers the emergence of large enterprises. In fact, Chinese MNC took off before its domestic capitalism was well developed, suffering from 'highly imperfect markets for capital, resources, labour, property rights, and corporate control' (Williamson and Zeng, 2008: 83). As Huang Yasheng rightly points out, the most successful Chinese companies, such as Lenovo, are registered in Hong Kong and use the advantages the PRC offers to external investors even if the company's founders were scientists at China's prestigious Academy of Sciences (Huang Yasheng, 2008).

15.2.3 The Go Global strategy

Lacking the benefits of scale and experience derived from a large domestic market, China's enterprises move outwards either out of sheer despair, as an attempt to overcome domestic limitations – or following directions of the government. Discussing the 11th Five-Year Plan (2006–10),[2] the Chinese Ministry of Trade, in charge of the Go Global strategy, announced three new measures to improve the implementation of the strategy and to better promote Chinese enterprises: first, to speed up foreign direct investment and to penetrate deeper into global markets; second, to improve the innovative capacity of Chinese enterprises by pursuing various approaches to acquire leading technology and, finally, to expand cooperation into areas such as transport, telecommunications and engineering (Xinhua, 2006). Financial services were initially not considered to be a part of the strategy but were awarded an auxiliary role later on (sina. finance, 2009: 4). Only in 2009 did a special meeting of China's regulatory bodies for financial services declare that China's banks and investment companies had a significant role in the Go Global strategy (He Nanban, 2010).

These developments provide a fundamental shift in China's relations with the global economy: the state-sponsored coordination of enterprise reform dubbed by some observers 'China Inc.' (Fishman, 2005; Lanteigne,

2009) and the state-sponsored move abroad causing substantial distress in Western capitals and enterprise headquarters (Lohr, 2005; Heep, 2008b). The government's strategy to promote Chinese companies abroad and the companies' strategies are intrinsically linked (Chen Qingtai, 2005). The 'Go Global' strategy was officially announced in 2001 by then Vice-Premier Wu Bangguo at the China International Trade and Investment Fair in Xiamen (*People's Daily*, 12 September 2001). Following China's successful admission into the WTO, the PRC leadership sought to address the new opportunities provided under the global trade regime. The promotion of China's outward economic activities followed five objectives: a wider distribution of industries and regions; a better exploitation of overseas resources; development of overseas processing trade; preparing and supporting Chinese enterprises, particularly large enterprises, in their outward activities; and, finally, raising and diversifying the means of outward activities and promoting M&A activities of Chinese enterprises abroad (State Council, 2006). Most observers agreed that the new focus on outward activities was predominantly driven by China's need to secure resources (Davies, 2009b).

While Chinese authors stressed the importance of the strategy to further improve the market economic system and the competitiveness of Chinese enterprises (Chen Qingtai, 2005), some Western observers held a slightly different view: first, a high level of liquidity was triggering a need for more diversified and more profitable use of China's foreign exchange reserves; secondly, political motives such as buying US treasury bonds were an attempt to avoid public criticism of poor returns by investments in private companies and attempts by the Chinese government to buy goodwill of other governments in return for investments; and, finally, there were commercial reasons, including the acquisition of better management know-how and experience (Scissors, 2009). On many occasions, Chinese leaders have praised enterprises that excel in outward activities (State Council, 2009). The combination of state support and a coordinated strategy to help national champions to invest abroad has created 'hybrids with the flexibility and profit motive of a private enterprise, but which enjoy the support, albeit indirect, of one or more arms of the Chinese state' (Williamson and Zeng, 2008: 84). In 2005, a Chicago-based investment firm sold its stake in Chinese oil company CNOOC as it feared the latter might behave too much like a state company (Lohr, 2005).

In recent years, the 'Go Global' strategy has become part of a new drive to deal with an overall change in global trade and investment to create more sustainable patterns (*Caijing Online*, 3 July 2009a). High-tech enterprises, which were especially encouraged to invest abroad, should benefit from a closer co-operation of two rather odd partners, China's Central Bank and the Ministry of Technology, who announced better provision of finance for these activities (*Caijing Online*, 29 June 2009b).

15.3 Paving the way for the financial sector

In addition to promoting Chinese companies in resource exploitation and manufacturing, the Chinese government has increasingly pushed its main banks to internationalize and has set up special investment vehicles for outward portfolio investment. Drawing lessons from the Asian Financial Crisis in 1997/8, the Chinese leadership implemented three policies to make its ailing financial sector globally competitive: it changed the regulatory framework, emulating Western agencification; it beefed up the balance sheets of its main commercial banks through a series of direct transfers from the state coffers; and finally, it turned central administrative units into special vehicles for global portfolio investment.

15.3.1 Creating nominally independent regulatory agencies

Preparing the ground for global activities of China's financial industry has come a long way. Turning the state administration for financial resources into an open market for financial services is one of the most difficult tasks in the creation of China's 'socialist market economy'. Prior to the economic reforms of the 1980s, state-owned banks had administered the centrally planned allocation of capital to state-owned enterprises, which were foremost a social unit and less – if at all – as profit-oriented organizations for the provision of goods and services. Thus, the decision to open up the financial sector to external competition and to transform China's main banks had been delayed well into the 1990s (Schlichting, 2008).

Three major trends have appeared in the regulation of financial services on the national level over the last two decades: the administrative separation of the central bank from overall government; the introduction of independent bodies for the supervision of financial services in addition to the central bank; and in several countries the establishment of a single regulator for all financial services in banking, securities trading and insurance. All of these have had a significant impact on the degree and extension of self-regulation of the markets. In China, regulatory reforms since the 1990s have brought major changes: the complete overhaul of the central bank system, which freed regional branches from interference of provincial governments (Yang, 2006: 81–94; Naughton, 2007: 103), and then the introduction of China Securities Regulatory Commission (CSRC), China Banking Regulatory Commission (CBRC) and China Insurance Regulatory Commission (CIRC).

Between 1992 and 2003 the Chinese leadership set up three sectoral regulatory agencies for securities, banking and insurance. The CSRC, CBRC and CIRC are 'institutions directly under the State Council' (State Council, 2010) with ministerial status. While most agencies in OECD countries are under the supervision of a government department, usually finance, and the scrutiny of the parliament, in China it is the entire government. The People's Bank of China (PBC) provided substantial initial help to all the regulatory bodies, which draw heavily on the staff and resources of the PBC for their establishment. Thus, the role of the People's Bank of China (PBC) in developing and executing regulatory policies even in those areas where it has lost its official functions should not be underestimated. While formally following the international trend towards independent agencies, China's agencies are deeply embedded in the party–state through party control of leadership selection and staffing levels as well as subordination through party groups in the making of their policies. However, while the limits to their official independence have been pointed out in academic works (Heilmann, 2005a, 2005b; Pearson, 2005, 2007), it led to closer links with the global regulatory communities and changes in the content of regulation (Schlichting, 2008: 153–74).

15.3.2 Limited independence for the regulators and party–state embeddedness for the banks

All three regulatory bodies were set up with distinctive policy objectives that reached much further than the official market-creating and market-preserving principles that might have been copied and pasted from the standard recommendation of international watchdogs: in the case of the CSRC, it was the international promotion and domestic development of China's securities markets in order to raise new funds and spread the risks of China's highly indebted SOEs; for the CBRC, it was to speed up the process of cleaning the balance sheets of the main banks in order to allow for international listings of China's biggest banks. Conflicting policies were evident in the initial regulations regarding the listing of SOEs (Heilmann, 2002). Permission for listings was often based on the need to raise capital for debt- ridden companies and did not follow the market logic of allowing the most attractive enterprises to sell shares for future development. China's main growth engine over the last years, the private sector of the economy, has been largely excluded from IPOs and continues to face serious disadvantages in raising funds.

The highest authority for the supervision of financial services in China is technically the Chinese government, the State Council. All regulatory agencies and the People's Bank of China are either members of the State Council or organizations directly under the State Council. However, in the context of democratic centralism and the Leninist party–state, the power to define the direction and major contents of China's policies rests with the CCP. Thus, while the formal structure of financial services governance in the PRC leads to the state organs, crucial decisions concerning the scope, content, organization and staffing of the administration are decided by party organs, not by the state. The most important decisions to change China's economic governance were all taken within party organs such as the Central Finance Working Group or the Leading Finance and Economics Small Group. 'National Finance Work Conferences' that took place in 1997, 2002 and 2007 heralded fundamental policy decisions for financial markets

(Xinhua, 19 January 2007; PDO, 22 January 2007). 'Overall arrangements for financial work made by the Central Economic Work Conference' are duly discussed at follow-up meetings in the main bodies (PBC, 2010). Thus, while on paper the structure in China strongly resembles the organization of OECD economies in practice state organs play a much smaller role.[3]

In addition to the three regulatory agencies, the powerful National Development and Reform Commission, the State Asset Supervision and Administration Commission (SASAC), the Ministry of Finance, the People's Bank of China and the Central Huijin Asset Management Corporation are all involved in policy-making and policy implementation.

While competition and rivalry between regulatory organizations is also common within OECD countries, the high dynamics of institutional change and the opaqueness of the policy-making process in the PRC add to the turf wars between China's regulators. The PBC apparently succeeded in stretching its competencies into securities in 2005 (*FT*, 18 June 2005), the CSRC secured its say in bond markets 2007 (SCMP, 18 January 2007) but had to let SASAC in for the transfer of non-tradable shares to the National Social Security Fund (SCMP, 20 November 2006).

The ultimate battlefield for these turf wars lies behind the closed doors of the policy-making of China's communist party leadership. The leading personnel in all organizations and non-foreign enterprises in the area of financial services are part of the *nomenklatura*- and *bianzhi*-system (Brodsgaard, 2002, 2006; Brodsgaard and Zheng, 2006). 'Executives are rotated between institutions by government decree', as one observer described the human resources policies for China's top banks, regulators and ministries (*The Economist*, 4 February 2010). This provides the central leadership with a highly effective mechanism to keep a lid on the supposedly independent regulators, ministries, the central bank and courts. Re-establishing party committees and trade unions within Chinese and foreign financial service companies in China strengthens the capacity for party influence even if the exact working of these groups escapes generalizations: while some apparently exert real influence on the companies, others are described by their participants as predominantly groups for organizing social activities.[4]

The direct influence on banks became obvious when the Chinese leadership designed a 4 trillion RMB yuan macroeconomic stimulus package (c. US$ 400 billion). The banks immediately followed the central guidelines and provided roughly 110 per cent more credit in 2009 than the previous year – even against warnings of overheating and a potential rise in non-performing loans. Banks thus added another US$ 1.4 trillion of stimulus to the government package. In January 2010, when the Chinese leadership had achieved its objectives of keeping GDP growth above 8 per cent in 2009, the government ordered the banks to change their lending policies. And, contrary to several European countries, where governments found themselves hapless to cope with banks' restrictive lending policies even after massive state involvement, Chinese banks had to oblige no matter how sophisticated was their collaboration with central policy directives.[5] In January, banks in China ordered branches in various parts of the country to stop lending at all.[6] Raising the amount banks have to hold with the central bank and simply ordering bankers to stop lending illustrates perfectly the ambiguous nature of China's socialist market economy (Anderlini, Tucker and Hughes, 2010).

15.4 Going Global: China's Big Four, its development bank and other state vehicles

Deeply embedded in China's cadre-capitalism, China's commercial banks are consistently raising their international profile. Today, the Bank of China, China Construction Bank and China Bank of Commerce and Trade are listed in Hong Kong, New York and London. The Agricultural Bank of China is still awaiting its debut in Hong Kong and New York, while more banks are pushing towards the global scene. While the 'Big Four' have followed a rather low-profile approach, China's state-owned special investment vehicles have found themselves the object of intense public scrutiny at home and abroad.

15.5 China's commercial banks – The Big Four

The People's Republic of China has four banks owned by the central government: the Bank of China (BOC), the China Construction Bank (CCB), the Agricultural Bank of China (ABC) and the Industrial and Commercial Bank of China (ICBC). All banks suffered from heavy bad debts as a result of their close links with SOEs and underwent significant reforms. The central government used its foreign exchange holdings to set up special asset management companies to write the non-performing loans off the banks' books (Hansakul, 2004). The central government supervises bank lending closely and uses its influence to boost or stifle demand for credit (CDO, 22 February 2010). The boom in 2009 was partly triggered by the removal of strict lending limits. As Chinese banks earn less from fees than their international rivals, they rely much more on credit to create profits. The Chinese government, however, prefers credit quotas to changes in interest rates as a tool of their monetary policies. Thus, banks and the regulators find themselves regularly at odds about lending policies (MacMahon, 2010). Told to increase lending in 2008, Chinese banks lowered lending standards and faced the potential return of significant volumes of non-performing loans (Chan and Chu, 2009) as a result of being used as a transmission belt for government policies.

All banks are still controlled by the central government, but have diversified their ownership structure by opening up to foreign investors. The Bank of China is one of the oldest banks in China. It was founded in 1912 and was turned into a specialized state-owned bank in 1949. It became a state-owned commercial bank in 1994. In 2003, the Chinese government appointed BOC as a pilot bank for joint-stock reform. Today, its website states that it 'is one of China's four state-owned commercial banks. Its businesses cover commercial banking, investment banking and insurance. Members of the group include BOC Hong Kong, BOC International, BOCG Insurance and other financial institutions. Bank of China provides a comprehensive range of high-quality financial services to individual and corporate customers as well as financial institutions worldwide. In terms of tier one capital, it was ranked 18th among the world's top 1,000 banks by *The Banker* magazine in 2005' (BoC Investment Management, 2009). On 1 June 2006, during 'China's golden age for banking' (Briand, 2006), BOC raised US$ 9.7 billion through its IPO in Hong Kong. According to its website, BOC has over 600 operations worldwide (BOC, 2009). It held stakes in Morgan Stanley and Barclay's, which led to substantial write-offs in 2009, but continued to invest in European finance stocks such as French-based asset manager Rothschild (Luo J., 2009).

The Industrial and Commercial Bank of China started its overseas activities in 2006. A small acquisition in Indonesia was followed in 2007 by a US$ 590 million investment in Seng Heng Bank in Macau and a US$ 5.4 billion purchase of 20 per cent of South Africa's Standard Bank, 'the largest cross-border acquisition to date by a Chinese bank' (Rein, 2008; Anand, 2009). In 2009, it bid for stakes in the Canada-based East Asia Bank and finalized the takeover of 70 per cent of shares of the Bank of East Asia (Canada).

The Construction Bank of China has Bank of America (BoA) among its shareholders. Even during the onslaught of the financial crisis, BoA reduced its stake in 2009 but kept its involvement at a significant strategic level.[7]

The Agricultural Bank of China, the last of the Big Four to be restructured, was bailed out in 2008 by the government's Huijin Investment Corporation and the China Investment Corporation (CIC) who both took over 50 per cent of the stakes in preparation for a listing (Tschang, 2008). This bailout was part of the government's effort to boost demand in the countryside. The structure of having two vehicles of the central government own a rural development bank, which is marked for a listing in Hong Kong, again sheds some light on the firm grip of the party–state on formally profit-oriented companies in China's socialist market economy.

Even so called tier 2 banks, smaller and often regional banks, are raising their presence abroad: China Minsheng Bank, arguably the only private bank in China, offered US$ 205 million for a stake in San Francisco's UCBH Holdings in 2007, and Citic Securities invested nearly US$ 1 billion in Bear Sterns (Tschang, 2007). In these cases, the Fed had to sanction all investment beyond 5 per cent. From the Fed's view and particularly in the eyes of some American politicians, the objective of facilitating cross-border trade contrasts with the political issue of ceding influence on the US financial system to vehicles controlled by the Chinese party–state.

In addition to banks, China's insurance companies are following track – with mixed results so far. One of China's largest insurance companies, Ping An, faced massive public criticism after its 5 per cent stake in Belgian–Dutch insurer Fortis led to a write-off of US$ 2.3 billion in the third quarter of 2008 (Li Xiang, 2009). Similarly, China Development Bank lost around US$ 1.7 billion as a result of a 3.1 per cent stake in Barclay's, China Eastern Airlines lost more than US$ 900 million through wrong hedging of fuel costs and CITIC Pacific around US$ 2 billion in currency trading. In total, *China Daily* estimated the losses for Chinese companies 'overseas investments at US$ 30 billion, which led to diplomatic disputes between China and the US and China and Europe about the protection of Chinese investments (Xu Shenglan, 2008). Even the government had difficulties establishing the true extent of the exposure of Chinese companies abroad (Scissors, 2008).

Most of the banks have used Hong Kong as a testing ground and training facility to adapt to international practice before venturing out to Europe and the US. But even after going global, China's banks are still trapped in their dual function as profit-earning entities and transmission belts of government policy: 'addicted to loose credit' (MacMahon, 2010), their lending policies clearly follow government directives and rubbish all perceptions of them as independent private businesses. Informal telephone calls and non-disclosed changes in banking regulation make it difficult for outside investors to follow regulatory measures that 'bear little resemblance to how monetary policy typically is conducted in other economies' (MacMahon, 2010).

15.6 Direct government vehicles: China Investment Corporation and the State Administration for Foreign Exchange

China's main commercial banks are thus acting under guidance and control of the central party–state. But in addition to keeping the Big Four as important tools for macroeconomic policies, the Chinese leadership has explicit government-controlled vehicles for outward investments, the most important being the State Administration of Foreign Exchange (SAFE) and the China Investment Corporation (CIC).

In 2007, the Chinese government established the China Investment Corporation. Having amassed more than US$ 1,500 billion in foreign exchange by the end of 2006, rumours had been ripe about the leadership seeking better returns and more sophisticated venues to utilize this vast pool of resources. The management of these foreign reserves had been moved from the Central Bank to the State Administration for Foreign Exchange (SAFE). The investment strategy of SAFE, however, was restricted to relatively 'safe' instruments. Falling interest rates in the US reduced the attractiveness of buying high-interest US bonds and reselling them at lower rates to the domestic market (McGregor, 2008). Therefore, the leadership decided after careful consideration and after months of global speculation to follow the examples of Dubai, Norway and Singapore, and establish its own sovereign wealth fund.[8] Redirecting funds from the Central Bank via an exchange of reserves with the Ministry of Finance and merging the CIC with the Central Huijin Investment Company, the Chinese leadership transferred in the region of US$ 200 billion of funds to its latest investment tool. It is formally supervised by the Ministry of Finance and has two main objectives: to recapitalize leading domestic banks and to invest abroad. Addressing concerns about potential government influence on investment decisions, the Chinese leadership attempted to set up the CIC as close to the model of an independent profit-oriented entity as possible. However, the CIC found itself too often the subject of public debate in Europe and the US for alleged use of government money to buy into sensitive sectors of the host economy. But when early investments into US and European financial service institutions lost their value, the CIC found itself also at the heart of an angry debate inside China (Ma Wenluo, 2008; Gottwald, 2010).

In comparison with the CIC, SAFE has kept a lower public profile. Officially, its main task is the supervision of all foreign exchange markets in China. However, SAFE's managers are also responsible for, among other things, the 'management of foreign exchange reserves, gold reserves, and other foreign exchange assets of the state' and 'to take part in relevant international financial activities' (SAFE, 2009a). This brings it into conflict with the CIC. The official rationale for setting up the CIC was to diversify China's investments abroad and to make better use of its vast foreign exchange reserves. But SAFE, under the supervision of the Central Bank of China, secretly invested through its subsidiary in Hong Kong. Its stake in, for instance, BP was only admitted after serious pressure from Western and Chinese media. While most observers had expected CIC to take sole responsibility for these kinds of activities, apparently SAFE, backed by the People's Bank of China, emerged as a Chinese rival. In 2008, SAFE made international headlines when it bought Costa Rican government bonds at a highly subsidized rate under the condition the deal would not be made public – and within days of Costa Rica moving its diplomatic ties from Taiwan to the PRC (Anderlini, 2008). Then, Thomson Reuters published a list of SAFE's 45 investments in the UK totalling more than US$ 17 billion (Dow Jones, 2008). In Australia, SAFE holds investments in three of four of the country's largest banks.

Similarly, the National Social Security Fund (NSSF) and the China–Africa Development Fund (CAD) took a similar route. This underpins the growing sensitivity of outward investment by Chinese state-controlled vehicles as the interested public becomes highly critical of the poor performance of initial stakes in Blackstone, JP Morgan, Barclay's or Fortis who all have come under immense pressure during the global financial crisis. In February 2010, CIC disclosed holdings in US listed companies and funds of US$ 9.63 billion, with a focus on financial stocks and natural resources (Reuters, 2010b).

China's most important strategic policy bank, the China Development Bank, has gained a rather negative reputation in the European perception as a result of its 'record of creeping expansion, building strategic stakes in industries and countries around the world while remaining almost invisible' (Spencer, 2008). When the Chinese leadership discussed the reform of the financial sector in the run-up to and during the 17th National Congress of the Communist Party of China in 2007, Chen Yuan, the well-connected CEO of China Development Bank, attempted to use the occasion to push for a transformation of the CDB into an internationally active commercial bank. However, Chen Yuan's move initially made only limited progress apparently in face of resistance to the plans within the leadership. Rumours that he would take a non-executive director's seat at Barclay's in April 2008 raised concerns regarding the influence of a member of the State Council on one of the UK's most important financial institutions (*The Telegraph*, 20 August 2008). The officially announced transformation from policy-lender to commercial bank led to widespread rumours about CDB buying into existing commercial banks or seeking an investor itself (CDO, 20 March 2009). However, having received a banking licence for Hong Kong in June 2009 (CDO, 26 June 2009), the China Development Bank called for permission to upgrade its Hong Kong office into an overseas branch in July 2009 and to open up offices in Egypt and Moscow. This move into areas less affected by the global financial crisis was justified on the grounds of promoting China's Go Global strategy (Zhang and Zhang, 2009).

15.7 Conclusion: The role of the party–state in Chinese outwards investment

15.7.1 The central role of the party-state

China's socialist market economy exhibits an institutional ambiguity that makes it difficult for Western observers to come to terms with the type and character of Chinese enterprises entering the global market. Most of the resource-extracting companies are owned by the central government – and are yet more than just transmission belts for the government owing to bureaucratic policies (Liou, 2009). Chinese banks and investment companies have sought foreign investment without breaking out of the Leninist cadre control. Hence, they are even more difficult to assess. On the one hand, regulatory reforms, asset restructuring and listings in Hong Kong and New York have created globally competitive financial corporations. On the other hand, the regulatory structures are controlled by the one-party state, which resorts to formal and informal means considered alien to an ideal-type market economy in using the banks for implementation of national policies. In this regard, China's financial services sector highlights the uniqueness of its MNC in comparison to those in the US or Europe. While initial reactions to Chinese FDI have been mixed at best, the financial crisis had a profound impact. In the last few years, the governments of Pakistan, Argentina, Hong Kong, Belarus, Indonesia, Malaysia and South Korea have all turned to Beijing to receive support for their fledgling public finances (Von Hardenberg, 2010). What started out in the 1990s as an attempt to save China's weak banks and unprofitable SOE has become a major force in global politics and economics. Stepping up its profile in the new G20, the PRC will play its part in shaping the future rules of foreign investment, which, in turn, will strengthen the position of its MNC.

A by-product of the increased exposure of Chinese enterprises to the ups and downs of the global economy is growing public interest – in the West as well as in China. The nascent but at times vociferous public opinion in China predominantly expressed in blogs and online comments had already affected negotiations for admission into the WTO (Pearson, 1999). The Go Global strategy has thereby fed into a development in which the leadership is paying increased attention to public opinion, testing the ground by commissioned contributions to blogs and online comments and by using public opinion as a tool in international negotiations.[9] Public opinion has become a major factor in understanding China's foreign relations and foreign economic policies (Hao Yufan, 2007: 131–7). Chinese outward investment policy is thus directly linked into the political process in China. The role of the state continues to be central. In this regard, Chinese cadre-capitalism is well equipped to go global without losing its unique characteristics.

Notes

1. Although the underlying assumption of China in this way following a similar process of development to that in the UK, Prussia, the Netherlands or France in the nineteenth and early twentieth century is highly debatable for both empirical reasons (international context) as well as a normative one (the risk of entering a one-way street towards the evolution of a Western market economy).
2. According to the Chinese online source sina.com, the Go Global strategy had already been introduced during the 10th Five-Year Plan. See sina.finance (2009), *zouchuqu zhanlüe jiedu*, available at: http://finance.sina.com.cn/hy/20091123/13577002525.shtml [accessed 26 February 2010].
3. The role of the Chinese rubber-stamp parliament, the National People's Congress (NPC), while the ultimate organ for policy-making, according to the constitution of the PRC, has been very limited in practical terms. Nevertheless members of the NPC have occasionally influenced the evolution of the regulatory framework, most significantly when amending China's first securities law of 1998. Here, the NPC showed an astonishingly high degree of political autonomy within its institutional boundaries set by the CCP. See Heilmann (2005a, 2005b).
4. Interviews in Shanghai and Beijing in July 2009.
5. James Jubak eloquently describes the tradition of front-end loading credit in January to avoid stricter limits imposed by the government later in the year (Jubak, 2009).

6. In a similar case in 2008, banks in Shanghai received phone calls ordering them to stop all lending. Foreign banks asking for a written confirmation were left unanswered. Interviews with Shanghai bank officials, and 'China Tightens Reins on Loans', *The Wall Street Journal Asia*, 27 January 2010, available at: http://online.wsj.com/article/SB10001424052748703906204575026350912221106.html?mod=WSJ_hpp_sections_business [accessed 27 January 2010].
7. BoA held 16.6 per cent of CBC after completion of its sale in January 2009. See Tina Wang (2009), 'Western Partners Bail on Bank of China', *Forbes.com*, 14 January 2009, available at: http://www.forbes.com/2009/01/14/rbs-boc-china-markets-equity-cx_twdd_0114markets1.html [accessed 17 January 2009].
8. The Chinese leadership apparently commissioned a draft proposal from McKinsey. See Heep (2008a).
9. Wen Jiabao unofficially claimed to be left with no alternative but to defer the 11th China EU Summit due to take place in Lyons in December 2009, referring to public outrage at French President Sarkozy.

References

Accenture (2005), *China Spreads its Wings – Chinese Companies Go Global*, available at: http://www.accenture.com/NR/rdonlyres/6A4C9C07-8C84-4287-9417-203DF3E6A3D1/0/Chinaspreadsitswings.pdf [accessed 10 June 2009].

Anand, S. (2009), 'China's Largest Bank Expands in Canada', *BusinessWeek*, 6 June.

Anderlini, J. (2008), 'Beijing Uses Forex Reserves to Target Taiwan', *Financial Times Online*, 12 September 2008, available at: http://www.ft.com/cms/s/0/22fe798e-802c-11dd-99a9-000077b07658.html [accessed 24 September 2008].

Anderlini, J., Tucker, S. and Hughes, J. (2010), 'China Tells Banks to Halt Lending', *Financial Times Online*, 20 January 2010, available at: http://www.ft.com/cms/s/0/9d42f0f2-057e-11df-a85e-00144feabdc0.html [accessed 10 February 2010].

Barboza, D. (2005), 'China Seeks Known Brands to Go Global', *The New York Times Online*, 30 June 2005, available at: http://www.nytimes.com/2005/06/29/business/worldbusiness/29-ihtbrands.html [accessed 12 November 2009].

BBC News (2009), 'Ford Agrees Volvo Sale to Geely', 23 December 2009, available at: http://news.bbc.co.uk/2/hi/8428066.stm [accessed 27 December 2009].

Bergsten, F. C., Gill, B., Lardy, N. R. and Mitchell, D. J. (2007), *China, the Balance Sheet: What the World Needs to Know about the Emerging Superpower*. New York: Public Affairs.

BOC (Bank of China) (2009), *About Us*, available at: http://www.bankofchina.com/en/aboutboc/ab1/200810/t20081027_8295.html [accessed 30 June 2009].

BOC Investment Management (2009), *About Us*, available at: http://www.bociim.com/english.html [accessed 3 July 2009].

Breslin, S. (2004), *Capitalism with Chinese Characteristics: The Public, the Private and the International*, Warwick University Working Paper No. 104, June.

Briand, B. (2006), 'A Golden Age for China's Banking', *BusinessWeek*, 31 May 2006, available at: http://www.businessweek.com/globalbiz/content/may2006/gb20060531_906451.htm [accessed 10 January 2010].

Brodsgaard, K. E. (2002), 'Institutional Reform and the "Bianzhi" System', *China Quarterly*, 170, 361–86.

Brodsgaard, K. E. (2006), 'Bianzhi and Cadre Management in China', in Kjeld Erik Brodsgaard and Zheng Yongnian (eds), *The Chinese Communist Party in Reform*. London/New York: Routledge, 103–21.

Brodsgraad, K. E. and Zheng Yongnian (2006), 'Introduction: Whither the Chinese Communist Party?' in K. E. Brodsgaard and Zheng Yongnian (eds), *The Chinese Communist Party in Reform*. London/New York: Routledge, 1–14.

Caijing (2009a), 'Zhiku fenghui Zhou Xiaochuan fenxi quanqiiu jingji', *Caijing Online*, 3 July 2009, available at: http://www.caijing.com.cn/2009-07-03/110192749.html [accessed 3 July 2009].

Caijing (2009b), 'Zhonghang jiangyu kejibu zai liu lingyu hezuo', *Caijing Online*, 29 June 2009, available at: http://www.caijing.com.cn/2009-06-29/110190888.html [accessed 3 July 2009].

CDO (China Daily Online) (2009), 'CDB Has No Plan to Get Listed and Invite Strategic Investors', available at: http://www.chinadaily.com.cn/bizchina/2009npc/2009-03/09/content_7556575.htm [accessed 5 April 2009].

CDO (China Daily Online) (2009b), 'Hong Kong Grants Banking Licence to China Development Bank', available at: http://www.chinadaily.com.cn/bizchina/2009-06/26/content_8327303.htm [accessed 28 June 2009].

Chan, E. and Haibin Chu (2009), 'Analysing Bank Lending Data in China', *BIS Quarterly Review*, December, 20–1, available at: http://www.bis.org/publ/qtrpdf/r_qt0912x.htm [accessed 10 January 2010].

Chen Qingtai (2005), *'Shishi zouchuqu zhanlüede jige wenti'*, *Sina Finance News*, 8 May 2005, available at: http://finance.sina.com.cn/review/20050508/23061569479.shtml [accessed 1 June 2009].

Cheung, Yin-Wong and Xingwang Qian (2009), 'Empirics of China's Outward Direct Investment', *Pacific Economic Review*, 14 (3), 312–41.

Clark, D. C. (2008), 'China's Legal System: New Developments, New Challenges', *The China Quarterly, Special Issue*. London: Routledge.

Davies, K. (2009a), *While Global FDI Falls, China's Outward FDI Doubles*, Columbia FDI Perspectives No. 5, 26 May 2009, available at: www.vcc.columbia.edu/documents/DaviesPerspective-Final.pdf [accessed 10 June 2009].

Davies, K. (2009b), 'Outward Investment Rises as Countries Eye Many Benefits', *Shanghai Daily*, 8 June 2009, available at: http://www.shanghaidaily.com/sp/article/2009/200906/20090608/article_403369.htm [accessed 10 June 2009].

Dickson, B. J. (2008), *Wealth into Power: The Communist Party's Embrace of China's Private Sector*. Cambridge: Cambridge University Press.

Ding, X. L. (1994), 'Institutional Amphibiousness and the Transition from Communism: The Case of China', *British Journal of Political Science*, 24 (3), 293–303.

Dow Jones (2008), 'UPDATE: SAFE Steadily Building Stakes in UK – Thomson Reuters', *MarketWatch*, 12 September 2008, available at: http://www.marketwatch.com/news/story/-update-safe-steadily-building/story.aspx?guid=%7B1CC7BF6C-F4FA-4E1C-A16E-AC9AAAFEA328%7D [accessed 24 September 2008].

The Economist (2010), 'Red Mist: Who Matters in the World's Second Largest Financial System is Barely Understood', *The Economist*, 4 February.

Fishman, T. C. (2005), *China Inc: How the Rise of the Next Superpower Challenges America and the World*. New York: Scribner.

Goldstein, A. (2007), *Multinational Companies from Emerging Economies: Composition, Conceptualization and Direction in the Global Economy*. Basingstoke: Palgrave Macmillan.

Gottwald, J.-C. (2010), 'Europe and China: Convergence, Politicization and Assertiveness', *East Asia*, 27 (1), 79–97.

Hansakul, S. (2004), *China's Financial Sector: Institutional framework and main challenges*, DB Research, 9 January 2004, available at: http://www.dbresearch.com/PROD/DBR_INTERNET_EN-PROD/PROD0000000000072461.PDF.

Hao Yufan (2007), *Zhongguo waijiao juice. Kaifang yu duoyuanhua de shehui yinsu fenxi.* Beijing: Shehui kexue wenbu chubanshe, 131–7.

Hardenberg, C. von (2010), 'China wird zur neuen Weltbank', *Financial Times Deutschland*, 29 January 2010, available at: http://www.ftd.de/finanzen/maerkte/marktberichte/:geldgeber-china-wird-zur-neuen-weltbank/50066911.html [accessed 29 January 2010].

He Nanban (2010), *Zhongguo Renmin Yinhang, Zhongguo Yinjianhui, Zhongguo Zhengjianhui, Zhongguo Baojianhui chutai jinyibu zuohao jinrong fuwu zhich zhongdian tiaozheng zhenxing he yizhi bufen xingye channeg guo sheng de zhi*, available at: http://www.gzxz.gov.cn/Article/Print.asp?ArticleID=28688 [accessed 20 February 2010].

Heep, S. (2008a), *Chinas neuer Staatsfonds: Organisation, Finanzierung und Investitionsstrategie der China Investment Corporation (CIC)*, China Analysis 57, March 2008, available at: http://www.chinapolitik.de/studien/china_analysis/abstracts/no_57_kurz.pdf [accessed 10 November 2009].

Heep, S. (2008b), *Staatsfonds ante portas: Deutsche Reaktionen auf den wachsenden Einfluss staatlicher Investitionsgesellschaften*, China Analysis 65, November 2008, available at: http://www.chinapolitik.de/studien/china_analysis/no_65.pdf [accessed 10 November 2009].

Heilmann, S. (2002), *The Chinese Stock Market: Pitfalls of a Policy-Driven Market*, China Analysis No, 15, September 2002, available at: http://www.chinapolitik.de/studien/china_analysis/no_15.pdf [accessed 10 January 2010].

Heilmann, S. (2005a), 'Regulatory Innovation by Leninist Means: Communist Party Supervision in China's Financial Industry', *The China Quarterly*, 181, March, 1–21.

Heilmann, S. (2005b), 'Policy-making and Political Supervision in Shanghai's Financial Industry', *Journal of Contemporary China*, 14 (45), 643–68.

Huang Yasheng (2008), *Capitalism with Chinese Characteristics: Entrepreneurship and the State*. Cambridge: Cambridge University Press.

Jiang Zemin (2002), *Report to the 16th Party Congress*, available at: http://www.china.org.cn/english/features/49007.htm#9 [accessed 10 August 2009].

Jubak, J. (2009), 'The Tempest in the Teapot of China's Command Economy', *The Huffington Post*, 29 January 2010, available at: http://www.huffingtonpost.com/james-jubak/the-tempest-in-the-teapot_b_441921.html [accessed 29 January 2010].

Lanteigne, M. (2009), *Chinese Foreign Policy: An Introduction*. London/New York: Routledge.

Li Xiang (2009), 'Expensive Lessons for Overseas Investment', *China Daily Online*, available at: http://www.chinadaily.net/bizchina/2009-02/23/content_7501834.htm [accessed 20 June 2009].

Lohr, S. (2005), 'Who's Afraid of China Inc.?' *New York Times*, 24 July.

Liou Chih-shian (2009), 'Bureaucratic Politics and Overseas Investment by Chinese State-owned Oil Companies: Illusory Champions', *Asian Survey*, 49 (4), 670–90.

Lunding, A. (2006a), *Chinesische Firmen auf dem Vormarsch*, DB Research, China Spezial, Aktuelle Themen 364. Frankfurt/Main: DB Research.

Lunding, A. (2006b), *Global Champions in Waiting: Perspectives on Chinese Outward Investment*, DB Research, China Special, Current Issue, 4 August 2006. Frankfurt/Main: DB Research.

Luo J. (2009), 'Bank of China Said to Win Approval in Rothschild Deal', *Bloomberg.com*, 24 March 2009, available at: http://www.bloomberg.com/apps/news?pid=20601080&sid=aDKeDX9Caje4&refer=asia [accessed 10 May 2009].

Luo, Y. and Tung, R. L. (2007), 'International Expansion of Emerging Market Enterprises: A Springboard Perspective', *Journal of International Business Studies*, 38, 481–98.

Ma Wenluo (2008), 'China Overseas Investment Shifting to Real Assets', available at: http://www.chinastakes.com/2008/2/china-overseas-investments-shifting-to-real-assets.html [accessed 20 June 2009].

MacMahon, D. (2010), 'China Pushes to Wean Banks off Loans', *Wall Street Journal Asia*, 27 January 2010, available at: http://online.wsj.com/article/SB10001424052748703410004575028913349397820.html [accessed 10 February 2010].

McGregor, R. (2008), 'Beijing Starts to Pay for Forex Sanitization', *Financial Times Online*, 31 January 2008.

McNally, C. (2006), *Insinuations on China's Emergent Capitalism*, East–West Center Working Paper, Politics, Governance, and Security Series No. 15, February.

McNally, C. (2007), 'Reflections on Capitalism and China's Emergent Political Economy', in Christopher McNall (ed.), *China's Emergent Political Economy: Capitalism in the Dragon's Lair*. London/New York: Routledge, 17–35.

Meyer, M. (2007), 'China's Second Economic Transition: Building National Markets', *Management and Organization Review*, 4 (1), 3–15.

Morck, R., Yeung, B. and Zhao Minyuan (2008), 'Perspectives on China's Outward Foreign Investment', *Journal of International Business Studies*, 39, 337–50.

Naughton, B. (2007), *The Chinese Economy: Transitions and Growth*. Cambridge, MA/London: MIT Press.

PBC (People's Bank of China) (2009), *Zhongguo renmin yinhang yinjianhui zhengjianhui baojianhui guanyu jinyibu zuohao jinrong fuwu zhichi zhongdian chanye tiaozheng zhenxing he yizhi bufen xingyechan neng guocheng dezhidao yijian*, available at: http://www.pbc.gov.cn/detail_frame.asp?col=100&id=3463&keyword=&isFromDetail=1 [accessed 10 January 2010].

PBC (2010), *Implement the Arrangements of the Central Economic Work Conference and Promote Quality and Rapid Development of National Economy*, available at: www.pbc.gov.cn/english//detail.asp?col=6400&ID=1465 [accessed 9 March 2010].

PDO (*People's Daily Online*) (2001), 'China Launches Two Way Investment Strategy', 11 September 2001, available at: http://english.peopledaily.com.cn/english/200109/12/eng20010912_80006.html [accessed 9 June 2009].

PDO (*People's Daily Online*) (2009), 'Chinese Enterprises Should Better Prepare for Integration', 4 June 2009, available at: http://english.peopledaily.com.cn/90001/90778/90857/90861/6671939.html [accessed 10 June 2009].

Pearson, M. (1999), 'The Case of China's Accession to GATT/WTO', in David M. Lampton (ed.), *The Making of Chinese Foreign and Security Policy in the Era of Reform*, Stanford, CA: Stanford University Press, 337–70 [here 364–7].

Pearson, M. (2005), 'The Business of Governing Business in China: Institutions and Norms of the Emerging Regulatory State in China', *World Politics*, 57 (2), January, 296–325.

Pearson, M. (2007), 'Governing the Chinese Economy: Regulatory Reform in the Service of the State', *Public Administration Review*, July/August, 718–30.

Rein, S. (2008), 'Lessons for Chinese Companies as they Go Global', *Business Week*, 1 December 2008, available at: http://www.businessweek.com/globalbiz/content/dec2008/gb2008121_644935.htm?campaign_id=rss_as [accessed 2 January 2009].

Remond, M. (2007), 'The EU's Refusal to Grant China "Market Economy Status" (MES)', *Asia Europe Journal*, 345–56.

Reuters (2010a), 'Goldman Denies Made Greek Bank Sales Pitch to China', 27 January 2010, available at: http://www.reuters.com/article/idUSTRE60Q2RB20100127 [accessed 27 January 2010].

Reuters (2010b), 'UPDATE2: China's CIC Gives Breakdown of US Equity Stakes', available at: http://www.reuters.com/article/idUSTOE61802J20100209 [accessed 10 February 2010].

SAFE (2009a), 'Major Functions', available at: http://www.safe.gov.cn/model_safe_en/whjjs_en/whjjs_detail_en.jsp?id=1&ID=30202000000000000 [accessed 20 June 2009].

SAFE (2009b), 'The SAFE Releases China's International Investment Position for Year-end 2008', 2 June 2009, available at: http://www.safe.gov.cn/model_safe_en/news_en/new_detail_en.jsp?ID=30100000000000000,197&id=2 [accessed 1 July 2009].

Scissors, D. (2008), 'Chinese Investment (Mostly) Welcome', *The Heritage Foundation Web Memo*, 26 September 2008, available at: http://www.heritage.org/RESEARCH/ASIAANDTHEPACIFIC/wm2081.cfm#_ftn1 [accessed 1 July 2009].

Scissors, D. (2009), *Drowning in Cash: Chinese Foreign Investment – Who, Where, and Why*, available at: http://www.bfchina.de/index.php?option=com_content&task=view&id=209&Itemid=53&contentid=474 [acessed 30 June 2009].

Schlichting, S. (2008), *Internationalising China's Financial Markets*, Basingstoke: Palgrave Macmillan.

Shambaugh, David (2008), *China's Communist Party: Atrophy and Adaptation*. Berkeley, CA: University of California Press.

Sina.finance (2009), *zouchuqu zhanlüe jiedu*, available at: http://finance.sina.com.cn/hy/20091123/13577002525.shtml [accessed 26 February 2010].

Spencer, R. (2008), 'China Development Bank will Rival Big Names', *The Telegraph*, 1 April 2008, available at: http://www.telegraph.co.uk/finance/newsbysector/banksandfinance/2788573/China-Development-Bank-boss-Chen-Yuan-to-take-seat-at-Barclays.html.

Stall, J. D., Terlep, S. and King Jr, N. (2009), 'China Firm to buy Hummer', *The Wall Street Journal*, 4 June 2009, available at: http://online.wsj.com/article/SB124393928530076283.html [accessed 10 August 2009].

State Council (2006), 'Geng haode shishi 'zouchuqu' zhanlüe', available at: http://www.gov.cn/node_11140/2006-03/15/content_227686.htm [accessed 10 June 2009].

State Council (2007), 'Shangwu buzhang zhuli Chen Jian: Zhongguo qiye "Zouchuqu" xunzhao xin kongjian', available at: http://www.gov.cn/jrzg/2007-08/10/content_711929.htm [accessed 10 June 2009].

State Council (2009), 'Li Keming tiaoyan Guangdong zhongyang gongye youxian fuzeren gongsi Dongputao qiye', available at: http://www.gov.cn/gzdt/2009-04/08/content_1280373.htm [accessed 30 June 2009].

State Council (2010), *Institutions Directly under the State Council*, available at: http://english.gov.cn/2005-08/07/content_21039.htm [accessed 23 February 2010].

Tsai, K. S. (2005), 'Capitalists Without a Class: Political Diversity Among Private Entrepreneurs in China', *Comparative Political Studies*, 38 (9), November, 1130–58.

Tsai, K. S. (2007), *Capitalism Without Democracy: The Private Sector in Contemporary China*. Ithaca, NY: Cornell University Press.

Tschang Chi-Chu (2007), 'Chinese Banks Head for the US', *BusinessWeek*, 25 October 2007, available at: http://www.businessweek.com/globalbiz/content/oct2007/gb20071025_820673.htm [accessed 10 April 2009].

Tschang Chi-Chu (2008), 'Beijing Bank Bailout May Help Farmers', *BusinessWeek*, 22 October 2008, available at: http://www.businessweek.com/globalbiz/content/oct2008/gb20081022_730357.htm [accessed 10 April 2009].

UNCTAD (2006), *World Investment Report 2006: FDI from Developing and Transition Economies: Implications for Development*. New York/Geneva: United Nations.

Wang, T. (2009), 'Western Partners Bail on Bank of China', *Forbes.com*, 14 January 2009, available at: http://www.forbes.com/2009/01/14/rbs-boc-china-markets-equity-cx_twdd_0114markets1.html [accessed 17 January 2009].

Williamson, Peter J. and Ming Zeng (2008), 'The Global Impact of China's Emerging Multi-nationals', in C. A. McNally (ed.), *China's Emergent Political Economy: Capitalism in the Dragon's Lair*. London/New York: Routledge, 83–101.

World Bank (2010), 'China', in *Doing Business: Measuring Business Regulations*, available at: http://www.doingbusiness.org/exploreeconomies/?economyid=42 [accessed 10 February 2010].

Xiao Qinfu (ed.) (2004), *Zhongguo Zouchuqu Zhanlüe Yanjiu Baogao: Research Report on China's Go Global Strategy*. Beijing: Zhonggong Zhongyangdangxiao Chubanshe.

Xinhua She (New China News Agency) (2006), 'ShiYiWu' jiang caiqun sange jucuo tuidong qiye zouchuqu', 11 October 2006, available at: http://202.123.110.5/zxft/ft32/content_673359.htm [accessed 10 March 2009].

Xu Shenglan (2008), 'Ping An Seeks Govt Aid for Fortis Compensation', *China Daily Online*, available at: http://www.chinadaily.net/bizchina/2008-12/01/content_7257812.htm [accessed 7 June 2009].

Yang, D. L. (2005), *Remaking the Chinese Leviathan: Market Transition and the Politics of Governance in China*. Stanford, CA: Stanford University Press.

Zhang Yuzhe and Zhang Man (2009), *'Guokaihang haiwai buju Xianggang fenxing ba tou chou'*, *Caijing Online*, 26 June 2009, available at: http://www.caijing.com.cn/2009-06-26/110189721.html [accessed 28 June 2009].

Zheng Yongnian (2006), 'Zhongguo "zouchuqu" shoudao xifang zulan', *Huanqiu Shibao*, 26 June 2006, available at: http://news.xinhuanet.com/world/2006-06/24/content_4741860.htm [accessed 10 June 2009].

Zheng Yongnian (2009), *The Chinese Communist Party as Organisational Emperor: Culture, Reproduction and Transformation*. London/New York: Routledge.

Part VI
Implications for Theory and Theory Development

16

Internationalization Strategies of Firms from Emerging Economies: Is There a Strong Case for Theoretical Extension?

H. Emre Yildiz and Carl F. Fey

16.1 Introduction

Outward FDI flows from emerging economies have increased with an astonishing rate during the last several decades (Figure 16.1). While annual outward FDI flows originating from these economies were slightly less than US$ 12 billion in 1990, this figure increased by almost twenty-fold and reached US$ 253 billion in 2007 (UNCTAD, 2008). Concomitant with the mounting importance and prevalence of multinational firms from emerging economies, practitioners and academicians alike are becoming more interested than ever in understanding idiosyncratic strategies of these emerging multinationals (EMNEs). This interest reveals itself in special reports in practitioner outlets (for example, *The Economist*, 2008; BCG, 2009) along with focused issues in reputable academic journals such as the *Journal of International Business Studies* (Luo and Tung, 2007) and the *Journal of International Management* (Aulakh, 2007).

The common theme of the recent scholarly attention to EMNEs is that since these firms originate from home countries with distinct institutional, political, and economic contexts, they tend to adopt atypical internationalization patterns that cannot be explained by the received international business (IB) theories. Thus, extant research on EMNEs is geared towards deciphering their common features and international strategies that distinguish them from traditional models and frameworks of MNEs that are developed and rooted in the empirical setting of economically advanced regions across Triad (Guillen and Garcia-Canal, 2009). With this background, we aim to take a critical approach towards recent theorizing on multinational firms from developing economies. For that purpose, our primary aim is to decipher whether or not an EMNE is a *sui generis* form of entity such that new theories and frameworks are needed to understand its international strategies and growth patterns. In order to follow this line of enquiry, we will try to answer two interconnected questions: first, to what extent is the internationalization behaviour of EMNEs shaped by idiosyncrasies of their home country context compared to

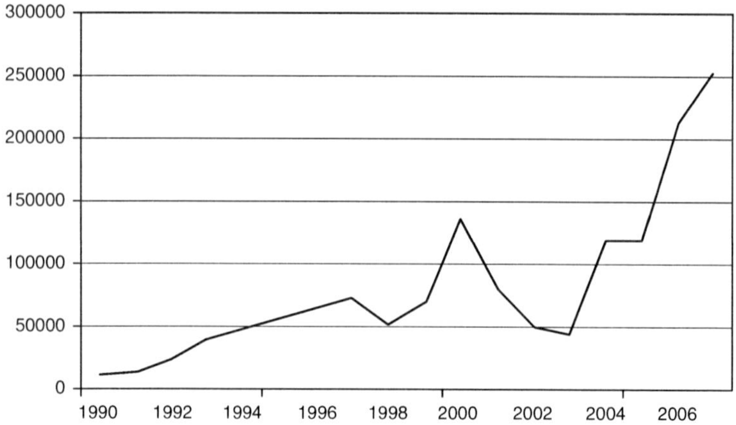

Figure 16.1 The increasing trend of outward FDI from emerging economies
Source: UNCTAD, 2008.

the effects of contingencies such as industry-level factors and characteristics of top-level managers? Second, beyond institutional and economic peculiarities of their country of origin, what are the reasons for EMNEs' deviation from the predictions of standard theories?

In this chapter, we initially suggest that delineating the external context (for example, institutional development and economic advancement of the home country) as the sole driver of EMNEs' unique internationalization behaviour is prone to the risk of jumping to quick generalizations. In other words, above and beyond country-level contingencies, other influences at the industry, firm, and/or individual level could be playing an equal, if not more important role in the international expansion patterns of EMNEs. Therefore, our contention is that multiple factors, over and above institutional and economic development, need to be considered while trying to understand internationalization strategies of EMNEs. In his enquiry into the necessity of developing new frameworks for understanding EMNEs' internationalization behaviour, Ramamurti (2009) touches on this point by emphasizing that a home country's level of development, which is the only operational difference between traditional FDI flows and outward FDI from emerging economies, may not be a strong enough contextual variable to render null and void the explanatory power of mainstream IB theories.

Related to our first premise, we further argue that there are two particular reasons alternative to country-of-origin effects for the espoused incoherence between received IB theories and the internationalization activities of EMNEs. First, in lieu of the *geographical shift* from developed countries to the developing countries, we claim that the *temporal shift* from past (viz. the period when the theory is developed) to present (viz. the period when the EMNE behaviour is observed) might be the underlying reason why standard IB theories are unable to explain the contemporary behaviour of MNEs, regardless of their country of origin (cf. Axinn and Matthyssens, 2001). It stands to reason that EMNEs and MNEs alike are *currently* adopting new kinds of internationalization strategies that are designed to deal with new issues and challenges that had been either absent or less widely used or relevant during times when traditional MNEs were originally developed. Second, based on the evidence that EMNEs operate on a much *smaller scale* than developed country MNEs (Deng, 2007), we will also try to make the case that some of the differences between EMNEs and MNEs are the reflections of size differences between two groups of firms rather than differences in home country environments.

We should be clear that there may be some unique aspects to EMNE's internationalization strategies, and we are strong proponents of the benefits of studying firms in diverse geographic contexts. Clearly, the extant literature is too developed country-based. Indeed, differentiating between EMNEs and MNEs from developed countries may be useful, but this differentiation seems unlikely to be the only explanation for why many EMNEs' behaviours differ from those predicted by classical internationalization theories. Our key point is that, by comparing firms from different points in time and of different sizes, many recent studies on EMNEs' internationalization have not clearly showed if the differences between MNEs from emerging economies and developed economies are really a result of this country-of-origin difference or other factors. We should also mention that in this chapter we limit our discussion to internationalization strategies. It may be that there are greater differences between EMNEs and MNEs from developed countries in other areas such as optimal management practices or advertising.

In the sections that follow, we will briefly review the theoretical foci and empirical findings of previous studies on the internationalization of EMNEs. Next, we will take on a critical approach towards earlier EMNE studies. Specifically, we will relate the discussion to the cases where industry- and firm-level effects prevail over country-level factors. Additionally, beyond country of origin, we will elaborate on possible reasons of incoherence between extant IB theories and EMNEs' strategies. Finally, we will enlist several theoretical and managerial implications of the ideas presented in previous sections.

16.2 Review of previous research on EMNEs

It is possible to divide the extant EMNE literature roughly into two subgroups. The first group from the late 1970s until mid-1980s had aimed at empirically understanding EMNEs' international expansion into other developing country markets. Major lines of enquiry in this earlier research were the unique characteristics of EMNEs (Lecraw, 1977), their motivations for international expansion (Wells, 1983), their pattern of international expansion (Chang and Grub, 1992), and the active role of governments in the internationalization process (Aggarwal and Agmon, 1990). On the theoretical front, this cohort of studies was not primarily directed towards new theory development. Instead, earlier works largely bordered on mainstream IB theories in order to explain international expansion strategies of firms from developing economies. For instance, based on the international product life cycle theory originally developed by Vernon (1966), Aggarwal and Ghauri (1991) emphasized that even if the market for a product becomes saturated in developed countries, it may be possible to introduce the very same product in other less developed country markets that are lagging behind technological innovations. As a result, this study argued that 'the process of FDI as undertaken by firms in the larger developed countries is likely to be repeated by firms from other small developed countries and eventually by firms from the [less developed countries]' (Aggarwal and Ghauri, 1991: 256). In a similar sense, by integrating product life cycle theory with the incremental model of international expansion (Johanson and Vahlne, 1977), Tolentino (1993) shows that outward FDI from developing countries evolve along sequential stages throughout which foreign investments move from physically close countries to distant ones in tandem with improvement in firms' innovative and managerial capabilities.

By and large, the first cohort of studies found that EMNEs indeed possess certain firm-specific advantages that can be appropriated in host countries with similar factor endowments, for example, factor costs, and comparable demand conditions and economic development levels. Furthermore, foreign operations of EMNEs are shown to be based on smaller scale, labour-intensive, and more flexible production technologies, which yielded these companies a competitive edge with respect to domestic firms and developed country MNEs operating in other developing economies (Lecraw, 1993). Thus, earlier theorizing and empirical evidence suggest that EMNEs are smaller and geographically distant replicas of conventional MNEs for both groups of firms seemed to follow comparable paths to multinationality based on similar sources of competitive advantage.

The second group of studies, which started to flourish by the early 2000s, is motivated by the need to explain recent investments of EMNEs in developed country markets. Perceiving the perplexing fact that EMNEs establish physical presence in economically advanced countries and globally competitive markets without necessarily possessing capabilities required to offer highly value-added products and services (Aulakh, 2007), this recently growing body of literature is geared towards developing more indigenous and genuine frameworks to understand the role of home country context on EMNEs' atypical internationalization behaviour (Mathews, 2006; Luo and Tung, 2007). To that end, one of the most commonly used theories in this stream of research is institutional theory,[1] which argues that organizations sharing the same environment usually choose similar strategies in order to achieve legitimacy and increase their likelihood of survival (DiMaggio and Powell, 1983). As a result of their deep embeddedness in institutional environments, organizations' practices and choices are often responses to and reflections of the rules and norms built within their immediate institutional contexts (Meyer and Rowan, 1977). From an institutional theory standpoint, then, the internationalization pattern of EMNEs is profoundly shaped by the institutional context of resource decisions at the firm and individual levels. In other words, even though the motivation and strategies to internationalize among EMNEs 'can be explained in terms of the same strategic factors that apply to western firms, namely the need to compete by exploiting or seeking assets, the decisions that they make about the pattern of internationalization will be informed by established mind-sets and existing practice, reinforced by institutional norms' (Child and Rodrigues, 2005: 405).

In a series of studies on Chinese EMNEs, Deng (2007, 2009) underscores the institutional environment as the main driving force behind asset-seeking outward FDI from China. More specifically, he reports that Chinese firms tend to make investment in other countries because of institutional pressures and cultural/cognitive influences emerging from the Chinese government's development plan by obtaining strategic assets so as to enhance the country's competitiveness in the global landscape. In addition to governmentally induced drives for global expansion, EMNEs also consider internationalization a way of escaping from institutional constraints of the home country. Weak law enforcement to protect intellectual property rights and difficulties in internal development of distinctive capabilities and technologies at the domestic scale create additional incentives for EMNEs either to conduct their R&D activities abroad or to acquire firms in a developed country that possess the desired assets. This point is also stressed in the springboard perspective developed by Luo and Tung (2007), in which the internationalization of EMNEs is portrayed as a springboard strategy to overcome latecomer disadvantages and competitive weaknesses by acquiring strategic resources that are not available at their home country environment because of institutional voids and underdeveloped markets.

Exploring regulatory transformations, liberalization measures and changes in the patent regulations that had been taking place in India during the 1995–2005 period, Chittoor et al. (2008) find that Indian pharmaceutical companies used internationalization as a means to develop and acquire new capabilities to respond better to the profound institutional changes in their home country environment. In their study of Mexican banking industry, Perez-Betres and Eden (2008) emphasize that sudden and profound regulatory punctuations taking place in emerging economies can create additional costs and risks for domestic firms. In order to cope with these types of changes in the institutional environment of the home country and to increase their likelihood of survival, firms from emerging economies are shown to expand into both developing and developed countries.

This strategy enables these firms to diversify business risks and to increase their abilities to respond to new realities of their home market institutions, and has proved useful to sense what the new trends are in different parts of the world, which may likely later be important also in home markets also. In-depth case studies of Thai business groups by Pananond (2007) also showed that the types of internationalization strategies employed by EMNEs are largely determined by home country institutional conditions. In particular, it is shown that Thai business groups rapidly internationalized across different sectors by relying on informal network ties whenever the home country institutional environment was characterized by weak intermediaries and substantial market imperfections. In the aftermath of the Asian financial crisis, however, the ongoing efforts to strengthen institutional intermediaries and mechanisms forced Thai EMNEs to rationalize their internationalization moves by focusing more on core industries and markets as well as formalizing their network relationships.

16.3 A critical assessment of the EMNE literature

16.3.1 Limits to the role of macro-level effects

As shown above, the technical difference between studying traditional MNEs and EMNEs is the economic and institutional characteristics of the home country context from which these two types of firms originate (Ramamurti, 2009). However, sampling firms from countries with per capita income below a certain threshold and/or with ongoing economic/political transformations, and presuming that these firms will have unique and unconventional patterns of international expansion on the basis of these sampling criteria deserve serious reconsideration. This type of research design would likely be built on over-aggregated models that would fail in explaining why firms from the same home country or industry (and with the same economic development levels, governmental policies, institutional transformations, etc.) tend to have heterogeneous internationalization experiences. Thus, as problematic as it is to lump all multinationals from different countries of origin together, we also argue that it is dubious to assume macroeconomic and institutional factors to be equally influential for all EMNEs operating within the same environment.

On a more general level, the present discussion can be related to the perennial debate on the role of structure v. agency, which is concerned with the extent to and ways which individual actors' capacity to make their own choices are determined and/or constrained by dominant norms and values residing in the institutional environment (Berger and Luckmann, 1966). In the strategic management literature, this debate sets up the theoretical foundations of two competing perspectives on firm-level behaviour, namely *external control* and *strategic choice* (Astley and Van de Ven, 1983). While proponents of external control envision characteristics of external environment (for example, resource availability, regulatory frameworks) as the main determinant of a firm's ultimate behaviour, advocates of strategic choice assign a more central role to the characteristics of firms (for example, age, size, experience) and executives (for example, educational background, personality, cognitive complexity etc.) who make choices and decisions to realize long-term goals and corporate objectives. Moving beyond the dualism of structure and agency, scholars have shown that elements of external control and strategic choice are interrelated and operative at the same time in firms' growth decisions in general (for example, Hitt and Tyler, 1991) and in EMNEs' internationalization behaviour in particular (for example, Rui and Yip, 2008).

Based on the aforementioned conjectures and findings, it is possible to observe firms having similar (different) responses to similar (different) environmental contingencies *as well as* similar (different) responses to different (similar) external factors (Figure 16.2). Each of the quadrants presented in Figure 16.2 represent a different phenomenon related to the internationalization strategies of EMNEs.

Contextuality refers to the cases when EMNEs originating from similar host country environments show similar internationalization patterns. For example, ZTE and Huawei of China, two upcoming EMNEs operating in global networking and the telecommunications industry, adopted very similar approaches to expanding their operations abroad. Both companies preferred to penetrate first into other emerging markets in order to avoid stiff competition while trying to reach critical economies of scale, which is crucial

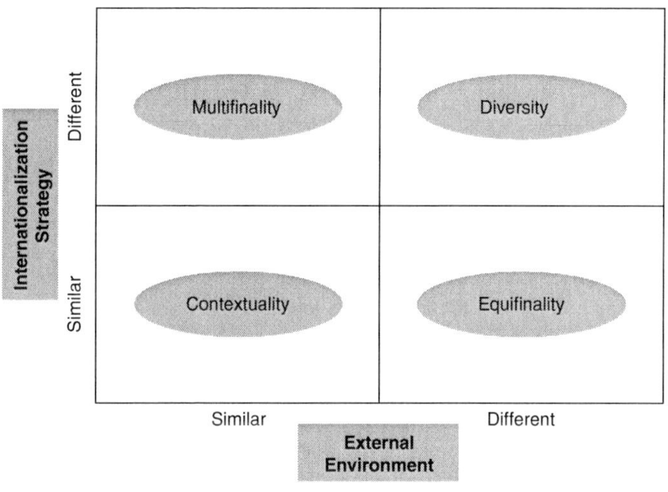

Figure 16.2 Distinct phenomena in the international expansion of EMNEs

for the success of their later entries into developed country markets where competition is mainly cost-based. To foster their innovation capabilities, ZTE and Huawei allocated a great proportion of their resources to internal R&D (c. 10 per cent of annual revenues), set up R&D subsidiaries in developed countries (for example, USA, Sweden) and formed strategic alliances and joint ventures with Western MNEs.

Diversity, where EMNEs from different environmental contexts implement different international strategies, is the exact mirror image of contextuality. As noted earlier, it is mistaken to assume all EMNEs fall into the same category for they are too diverse to lump together. One can easily realize this problem by noticing that, for instance, Indian pharmaceutical companies (for example, Dr Reddy's) had substantially different motivations for and trajectories of internationalization than those of Chinese energy giants (for example, CNOOC).

It is not moot to claim that firms from the same (different) external context would have convergent (divergent) internationalization patterns. However, contrary to the main premise of the institutional embeddedness perspective, we argue that it is possible to witness other cases where environmental differences can entail converging firm responses and vice versa. One such phenomenon is *equifinality*, in which EMNEs from different home country environments adopt similar internationalization behaviours. Such similarities, even in the presence of contextual differences, can be attributed to meso- and micro-level factors such as common industry structures and parallel mindsets and entrepreneurial orientations of key decision-makers (Hitt and Tyler, 1991). Arcelik of Turkey and Haier of China are two illustrative cases in point. Both of these white goods manufacturers decided to pursue an aggressive internationalization strategy by initially entering into developed country markets – UK in the case of Arcelik and US in Haier's case. They improved their innovation and marketing capabilities and gained strong footholds in these market niches by selling small refrigerators for dormitory and hotel rooms, a segment that was not very important to or profitable for established incumbents. However, once they had this base, they expanded their product range into other segments and expanded into other less competitive country markets. While both companies made substantial investments to increase the value of their own brands, they also bought several companies in other emerging economies (for example, Arcelik's acquisition of Arctic in Romania and Haier's acquisition of Anchor Electronics in India) in order to increase their production capacity and lower their manufacturing costs.

The last quadrant in Figure 16.2 is *multifinality*, which corresponds to the cases where EMNEs originating from similar environmental contexts adopt different internationalization strategies. Similar to equifinality, divergent international strategies within similar environmental contexts can be explained by differences in organizational cultures, corporate strategies, and executive decisions. Differences in the internationalization experiences of two Chinese consumer electronics manufacturers, TCL and Konka, are an exemplary case of multifinality. Based in Guangdong province of southern China, TCL had pursued a resolute entry strategy into global markets by making several acquisitions in Western Europe, namely Schneider of Germany in 2002 and Thomson and Alcatel of France in 2004. The primary motivation behind these acquisitions was to increase TCL's market share in the European market by obtaining premium brands, technical capabilities, and established distribution channels. The Chinese company Konka, on the other hand, internationalized its operations mainly by operating as an OEM partner for other MNEs. Konka opened up branch offices in several developed countries (for example, Canada, US, Germany) in order to respond better to customer requirements and follow trends, whereas all R&D was still undertaken internally in China. In order not to jeopardize its OEM business, Konka sold its own branded goods exclusively in the Chinese market, which comprise 30 per cent of its overall revenue.

16.3.2 Non-geographical sources of divergence

One of the ultimate issues motivating IB research explicitly focusing on international expansion of firms from emerging economies is the misfit between received theories of MNEs and peculiar internationalization behaviour of EMNEs. Based on this problem, scholars tend to stress the need for new theory development by epitomizing EMNEs as a different breed of firms with unusual internationalization strategies (Child and Rodrigues, 2005). For example, Mathews (2006) boldly claims that existing theories and frameworks of IB cannot explain the accelerated internationalization of firms from the periphery. In doing so, he points out that EMNEs' use internationalization not as a means to exploit their ownership advantages but as a way to access required resources by establishing linkages with source firms abroad, an explanation in stark contrast to some of the earlier theories and frameworks (Dunning, 1980; Caves, 1982). In the same way, in their recent work comparing EMNEs with the American model of the MNE, Guillen and Garcia-Canal (2009) note that the "new" multinationals internationalize faster by simultaneously penetrating into developed and developing economies and tend to use inorganic modes of entry (for example, alliances and acquisitions) to upgrade their competitive advantages.

Acknowledging their insightful analysis and parsimonious depiction of EMNEs, we agree with the above cited studies' claim that there are indeed new species of MNEs in the contemporary zoology of global economy. Correspondingly, internationalization behaviour of this new breed of MNEs displays an abnormal pattern vis-à-vis conventional theories and frameworks. However, contrary to these studies' identifying the *geographical shift* of economic activity from core to the periphery as the *raison d'être* of such abnormalities, we argue that incongruity between the theoretical predictions and empirical facts could be attributed to the *temporal gap* between the former's development and the latter's emergence. The implications of this temporality is nontrivial considering perpetual and profound changes that have been taking place in the global business environment during recent decades (for example, liberalization of economic policies, integration of financial markets, fast-paced technological changes and shortening product life cycles etc.). On the academic front, these changes reveal themselves in increasing evidence on the emergence of born-global firms (Oviatt and McDougall, 1994) and the use of international expansion as a way of sourcing technological capabilities (Song and Shin, 2008). In view of that, limits to the explanatory merits of incremental internationalization models (for example, Johanson and Vahlne, 1977) and theories of MNEs considering ownership advantages as the *sine qua non* of international expansion (for example, Hymer, 1976; Dunning, 1980) are not particularly germane to EMNEs but also to developed economy multinationals (for an elaborate discussion on this point, see Axinn and Matthyssens, 2001).

Over and above temporal changes in global business environment, mainstream IB theories inability to explain EMNEs' international expansion process can also be caused by the substantial scale differences between firms from emerging economies and developed country MNEs. Deng (2007) reports that the total assets, revenues and profits of the top 500 Chinese companies merely corresponds to 5.61 per cent, 7.3 per cent, and 5.22 per cent of those enlisted in Fortune's Global-500 list, respectively. Similarly, Ramamurti (2009) notes that only 49 EMNEs managed to hold a spot on Fortune's Global-500 list in 2007, even though it is likely to observe more EMNEs to replace incumbent global giants in the near future. These figures imply that there are still notable differences between traditional MNEs and EMNEs in terms of size and scale, which could have created divergent international expansion patterns in the first place. Endorsing this claim, one can easily note that distinguishing characteristics of EMNEs' strategies (for example, accelerated internationalization, resource constraints, importance of external links and networks etc.) are closely echoed in research on the internationalization of small and medium enterprises (cf. Jones, 1999). Granted that organizational size is a critical determinant of innovativeness (Damanpour, 1992), strategic flexibility (Penrose, 1959), and access to resources (Baum, Calabrese, and Silverman, 2000), we contend that using traditional models of MNEs to grasp international activities of EMNEs can create an apples-and-oranges problem.

16.4 Concluding remarks and implications for theory and practice

The core argument we tried to raise in this chapter is that EMNEs may not necessarily represent a new cohort of organizations having fundamentally different corporate objectives, adopting unique internationalization strategies and imposing unique competitive challenges compared with incumbent

MNEs. That said, our purpose is not to discourage recent academic interest in the rise of multinationals from emerging economies. Quite the contrary, we believe that studying EMNEs is a good opportunity to refine and overhaul extant IB theories and frameworks, most of which have been developed several decades ago.

In this vein, we suggest several avenues for further research on EMNEs. First, considering that emerging economies are typified by remarkable economic development and institutional transformations, it is likely that the composition of outward FDI from these economies will converge to the foreign investments undertaken by developed country MNEs. Indeed, the emergence and evolution of outward FDI from recently industrialized economies (for example, Japan, South Korea, Singapore) during the postwar era attests to this view. Therefore, it could be interesting to compare investment patterns of contemporary EMNEs with historical data on the international activities of firms that used to be classified as EMNEs. This type of research would be particularly useful in making projections about the future patterns of outward FDI from emerging economies as well as detecting prospective convergence in the international strategies of MNEs and EMNEs.

Currently there is insufficient systematic direct comparison of EMNEs and MNEs (see Petrou, 2007 as an exception). Extant studies on EMNEs usually collect data on firms from one or more emerging economies and contrast overall characteristics of their internationalization with findings of previous research on traditional MNEs. However, as we suggested earlier, the temporal gap between the two research streams and the scale gap between the two groups of organizations prevents direct and accurate comparisons. To better understand organizational and entrepreneurial similarities/differences between EMNEs and MNEs and to decipher how these are reflected in their internationalization strategies, future research can compare data from two groups of firms operating either within the same time period or on a similar scale, needless to say by controlling for other critical determinants of international expansion patterns (for example, industry structure, international experience).

In our critique of the over-aggregation problem in the extant EMNE literature, we briefly mentioned the perils of assuming that external environment would have a uniform effect on international activities of EMNEs. To overcome this problem, future research should be directed towards identifying the determinants of the extent to which of the EMNEs' internationalization strategies are the reflection of their home country context. To that end, it is possible to look at EMNEs' organizational (for example, ownership status, implementation of organizational practices used by developed country MNEs) and individual (for example, entrepreneurial characteristics of founder managers, personal network and social capital of key executives) characteristics, which can increase or decrease the degree to which institutional factors become influential in these firms' strategies. To single out effects of different factors operating at different levels of analysis (viz. country, firm, and individual), future studies can adopt multi-level research designs.

While the intended audience of this chapter is primarily other scholars interested in the rise of EMNEs, critical issues we emphasized in previous sections can help enlist a few managerial implications. First, it appears that there are commonalities among EMNEs originating from different emerging markets (for example, Haier and Arcelik) as well as differences among firms from the same country of origin (for example, TCL v. Konka). Consequently, it could be misleading for a developed country MNE to predict the behaviour of its competitors from emerging economies entirely based on their country of origin given that: (1) economic systems and institutional environments in emerging economies are evolving into those of developed countries, (2) the scale and size gap between EMNEs and MNEs are narrowing and (3) Western practices and managerial approaches are getting more acceptance across firms from emerging economies; this "new" group of competitors may not be so unprecedented and atypical vis-à-vis incumbent MNEs. Therefore, while it is important for developed country MNEs to prepare themselves for additional competition originating from the periphery, a more detailed analysis than simply considering if the MNE is from an emerging economy or transforming economy is likely to be necessary to understand likely internationalization strategies and gain competitive insights.

Note

1. It is important to note that institutional theory is not the only theoretical framework used to study EMNEs. Based on different theoretical perspectives, recent studies have also analyzed EMNEs' entry mode decision (for example, Filatotchev et al., 2007), location choices (for example, Makino, Lau, and Yeh, 2002), and paths to multinationality (for example, Cuervo-Cazurra, 2007), and have yielded results that are largely coherent with standard IB theories. This stands to reason that, when the effects of larger institutional context within which firms take their strategic decisions are controlled for, findings on the internationalization of EMNEs indeed fortify, rather than nullify, standard IB theories.

References

Aggarwal, R. and Agmon, T. (1990), 'The International Success of Developing Country Firms: Role of Government-Directed Comparative Advantage', *Management International Review*, 30 (2), 163–80.

Aggarwal, R. and Ghauri, P. N. (1991), 'The Evolution of Multinationals from a Small Economy: A Study of Swedish Firms in Asia', in P. J. Buckley and J. Clegg (eds), *Multinational Enterprises in Less Developed Countries*. London: Macmillan, 248–69.

Astley, W. G. and Van de Ven, A. H. (1983), 'Central Perspectives and Debates in Organizational Theory', *Administrative Science Quarterly*, 28, 245–73.

Aulakh, P. S. (2007), 'Emerging Multinationals from Developing Economies: Motivations, Paths and Performance', *Journal of International Management*, 13 (3), 235–40.

Axinn, C. N. and Matthyssens, P. (2001), 'Limits of Internationalization Theories in an Unlimited World', *International Marketing Review*, 19 (5), 436–49.

Baum, J. A. C., Calabrese, T., and Silverman, B. S. (2000), 'Don't Go It Alone: Alliance Network Composition and Startups' Performance in Canadian Biotechnology', *Strategic Management Journal*, 21, 267–94.

BCG (2009), *The 2008 BCG 1000 New Global Challengers: How Top Companies from Rapidly Developing Economies are Changing The World*, available at: http://www.bcg.com/publications/files/The_2009_BCG_100_New_Global_Challengers_Jan_2009.pdf [accessed 8 June, 2009).

Berger, P. and Luckmann, T. (1966), *The Social Construction of Reality: A Treatise in the Sociology of Knowledge*. Garden City, NY: Anchor Books.

Caves, R. E. (1982), *Multinational Enterprise and Economic Analysis*. Cambridge: Cambridge University Press.

Chang, T. and Grub, P. L. (1992), 'Competitive Strategies of Taiwanese PC Firms in their Internationalization Process', *Journal of Global Marketing*, 6 (3), 5–27.

Child, J. and Rodrigues, S. B. (2005), 'The Internationalization of Chinese Firms: A Case for Theoretical Extension?' *Management and Organization Review*, 1 (3), 381–410.

Chittoor, R., Ray, S., Aulakh, P. S., and Sarkar, M.B. (2008), 'Strategic Responses to Institutional Changes: "Indigenous Growth" Model of the Indian Pharmaceutical Industry', *Journal of International Management*, 14 (3), 252–69.

Cuervo-Cazurra, A. (2007), 'Sequence of Value-Added Activities in the Multinationalization of Developing Country Firms', *Journal of International Management*, 13 (3), 258–77.

Damanpour, F. (1992), 'Organizational Size and Innovation', *Organization Studies*, 13 (3), 375–402.

Deng, P. (2007), 'Investing for Strategic Resources and Its Rationale: The Case of Outward FDI from Chinese Companies', *Business Horizons*, 50, 71–81.

Deng, P. (2009), 'Why Do Chinese Firms Tend to Acquire Strategic Assets in International Expansion?' *Journal of World Business*, 44 (1), 74–84.

DiMaggio, P. and Powell, W. (1983), 'The Iron Cage Revisited: Institutional Isomorphism and Collective Rationality in Organizational Fields', *American Sociological Review*, 48, 147–60.

Dunning, J. H. (1980), 'Toward an Eclectic Theory of International Production: Some Empirical Tests', *Journal of International Business Studies*, 11, 9–31.

Filatotchev, I., Strange, R., Piesse, J., and Lien, Y. C. (2007), 'FDI by Firms from Newly Industrialized Economies in Emerging Markets: Corporate Governance, Entry Mode and Location', *Journal of International Business Studies*, 38, 556–72.

Guillen, M. F. and Garcia-Canal, E. (2009), 'The American Model of the Multinational Firm and the "New" Multinationals from Emerging Economies', *Academy of Management Perspectives*, 23 (2), 23–35.

Hitt, M. A. and Tyler, B. B. (1991), 'Strategic Decision Models: Integrating Different Perspectives', *Strategic Management Journal*, 12, 327–51.

Hymer, S. H. (1976), *The International Operations of National Firms: A Study of Foreign Direct Investment*. Cambridge, MA: MIT Press.

Johanson, J. and Vahlne, J. E. (1977), 'The Internationalization Process of the Firm: A Model of Knowledge Development and Increasing Foreign Market Commitments', *Journal of International Business Studies*, 8, 23–32.

Jones, M. V. (1999), 'The Internationalization of Small High-Technology Firms', *Journal of International Marketing*, 7 (4), 15–41.

Lecraw, D. J. (1977), 'Direct Investment by Firms from Less Developed Countries', *Oxford Economic Papers*, 29 (3), 442–57.
Lecraw, D. J. (1993), 'Outward Direct Investment by Indonesian Firms: Motivation and Effects', *Journal of International Business Studies*, 24 (3), 589–600.
Luo, Y. and Tung, R. L. (2007), 'International Expansion of Emerging Market Enterprises: A Springboard Perspective', *Journal of International Business Studies*, 38, 481–98.
Makino, S., Lau, C. M., and Yeh, R. S. (2002), 'Asset-Exploitation versus Asset-Seeking: Implications for Location Choice of Foreign Direct Investment from Newly Industrialized Economies', *Journal of International Business Studies*, 33 (3), 403–21.
Mathews, J. A. (2006), 'Dragon Multinationals: New Players in 21st Century Globalization', *Asia Pacific Journal of Management*, 23 (1), 5–27.
Meyer, J. W. and Rowan, B. (1977), 'Institutional Organizations: Formal Structure as Myth and Ceremony', *American Journal of Sociology*, 80, 340–63.
Oviatt, B. M. and McDougall, P. P. (1994), 'Toward a Theory of International New Ventures', *Journal of International Business Studies*, 25 (1), 45–64.
Pananond, P. (2007), 'The Changing Dynamics of Thai Multinationals after the Asian Economic Crisis', *Journal of international Management*, 13 (3), 356–75.
Penrose, E. (1959), *The Theory of the Growth of the Firm*. New York: Oxford University Press.
Perez-Betres, L. A. and Eden, L. (2008), 'Is There a Liability of Localness? How Emerging Market Firms Respond to Regulatory Punctuations', *Journal of International Management*, 14 (3), 232–51.
Petrou, A. (2007), 'Multinational Banks from Developing Versus Developed Countries: Competing in the Same Arena?' *Journal of International Management*, 13 (3), 376–97.
Ramamurti, R. (2009) 'Why Study Emerging-Market Multinationals?' In R. Ramamurti and J. V. Singh (eds), *Emerging Multinationals in Emerging Markets*, 3–22. Cambridge: Cambridge University Press.
Rui, H. and Yip, G. S. (2008), 'Foreign Acquisitions by Chinese Firms: A Strategic Intent Perspective', *Journal of World Business*, 43 (2), 213–26.
Song, J. and Shin, J. (2008), 'The Paradox of Technological Capabilities: A Study of Knowledge Sourcing from Host Countries of Overseas R&D Operations', *Journal of International Business Studies*, 39, 291–303.
The Economist (2008), 'The Challengers', January 10.
Tolentino, P. E. (1993), *Technological Innovation & Third World Multinationals*. London: Routledge.
UNCTAD (2008), *World Investment Report 2008: Transnational Corporations, and the Infrastructure Challenge*. New York/Geneva: United Nations.
Vernon, R. (1966), 'International Investment and International Trade in the Product Cycle', *Quarterly Journal of Economics*, 80, 190–207.
Wells Jr, L. T. (1983), *Third World Multinationals*. Cambridge, MA: MIT Press.

17

Indian Multinationals, Comparative Capitalism and Implications for Global and Host Country Economic Institutions

Andreas Nölke and Heather Taylor

17.1 Introduction: Who are the Indian multinationals, why are they important and why do we need an institutionalist perspective?

Although the current financial crisis is having rather harsh repercussions on Asian economies, most observers still expect the importance of Southern economies to rise significantly over coming decades (Figure 17.1). The role of Southern Multinationals will be crucial during this process.

For the purpose of this contribution, however, we will explicitly elaborate on Indian multinational companies because they have led the Southern multinationals pack in terms of brownfield investments, which will result in giving them complete control of the foreign target (Pradhan, 2007: 17–18). Between 1991 and 2001, when grouped together, 70 per cent of the total amount of outward foreign direct investment activities pursued around the globe by Indian MNCs can be classified as granting the Indian firm with a majority of 80 per cent ownership or more in the foreign target firm (Pradhan, 2007a: 13). Furthermore, Indian MNCs are unique because they have favoured acquiring triad companies (Figure 17.2), as opposed to pursuing brownfield investments in other non-triad markets as, for example, Chinese and Latin American firms have tended to prefer.

Finally, unlike other Southern Multinationals, which also are performing an outstanding number of takeovers, Indian MNCs have been primarily involved in the services sector and knowledge-intensive industries, thereby posing a potentially significant threat to the triad, given that these are areas in which most triad economies have dominated in the post-war period. In terms of the sector spread of Indian MNCs brownfields, the majority of acquisitions have been concentrated in the autos and autoparts, biotech/chemicals/pharmaceuticals, and IT & business services sectors (Taylor Nölke, 2010a) – each of these sectors has typically been dominated by triad-MNCs.

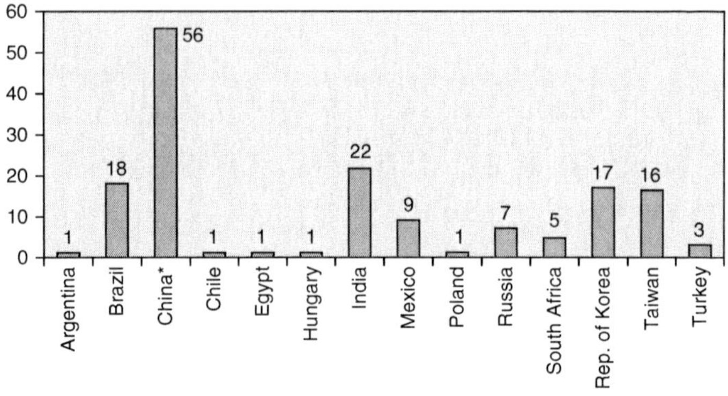

Figure 17.1 Non-triad multinational per non-triad nation
*China including Hong Kong.
Sources: Aguiar, Bhattacharya et al. (2006); Aguiar, Bhattacharya et al. (2007); UNCTAD (2005); Fortune (2007); Forbes (2007); *BusinessWeek* (2005).

As a result of these three tendencies, the surge of Indian MNCs may become a potentially conflict-ridden issue area within the triad over the years to come. This may pertain both to relationships between home and host economy, and to global economic regulation. The frenzied public debate surrounding the acquisition of Western firms by non-western firms is most often related to a fear that non-western firms will shutdown the newly acquired firms shortly after acquiring them. Indeed this fear is often related to the idea that once parent acquirer has obtained the resources of the target firm, the need for the target then becomes obsolete and will result in the parent firm shutting down the target. Significant tensions may arise associated with such a 'steal and thereafter shutdown' fear when related to the case of Indian firms acquiring western firms given that Indian MNCs have grown as global players in world markets based on low-cost advantages which are not suitable competitive advantages to compete on in Western markets.

Moreover, multinational companies are well known as key players in global economic regulation, on issues such as trade regulation, investment treaties, accounting standards or corporate social responsibility. Do Southern Multinationals play a similar role than triad MNCs? More importantly: do they share the preferences of triad MNCs? If not, we may envisage eminent conflicts in the years to come (Nölke and Taylor, 2010).

In order to understand potential tensions between the emerging Indian multinationals and their host economies, as well as with global economic regulations, we need an institutionalist approach. More particularly, we first need to understand the domestic institutional context that has allowed Indian MNCs to prosper. Moreover, institutions are core to both the home–host economy

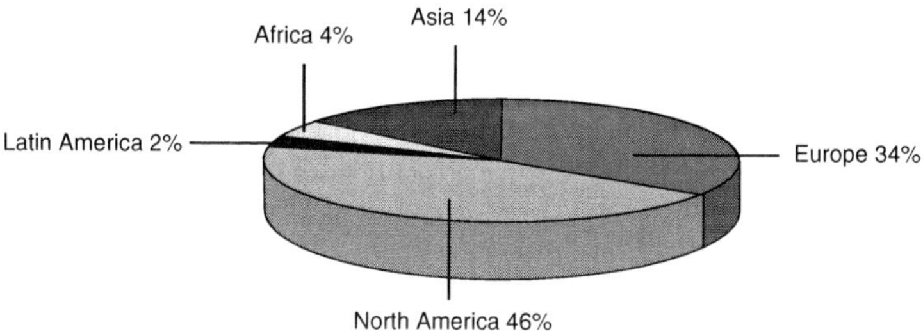

Figure 17.2 Global distribution of brownfield investments by Indian firms, 2000–7
Source: Pradhan (2007a).

confrontation, as well as to global regulation: the challenges that surface post-acquisition occur at both the firm and host country national institutional level. At the firm level, acquisitions can often act as shock to the path-pattern the target firm had previously been on and rapidly change the labour relations, corporate governance, corporate finance, etc. within the target firm. Whereas at the national level the impacts of a surge in Indian MNC acquisitions may not be as rapid, they may nevertheless have significant ripple effects on the overall stability of the national institutional compromises, that is, institutional equilibrium, fostering sector-specific industry growth within the host country. Given that the rise of Indian MNCs has been supported by certain domestic institutions, it is reasonable to expect that these companies will lean on these institutions when developing their preferences on global economic order. Conflicts might emerge if global economic regulation significantly differs from that in domestic Indian institutions.

Over recent years, a substantial literature on Indian multinationals and their success factors has emerged (for example, Bergman, 2006; Chadha, 2005; CRISIL, 2006; Das, 2007; Gupta, A. 2006; Kale, 2006; Kale, 2008; Khanna and Palepu, 2006; Kumar, 2007, 2008; Milelli, 2007; Mittal, 2006; Pradhan, 2007, 2007a, 2008, 2008a, 2008b; Sarathy, 2006; Wyatt, 2005). The main thrust of this literature, however, is on business strategies. Institutionalist theories, in contrast, do not play a major role. Analytical approaches derived from political science, however, are very rich on institutional categories. In particular the comparative capitalism (CC) perspective is useful in this respect, given its comprehensive analytical vocabulary on the different country-specific institutions that are supported by modern capitalism. In the following, we will apply the CC framework to Indian MNCs, in order to first understand their domestic background, and then study their conflict potential in host economies and in global economic regulation. Correspondingly, our claim is not to replace existing studies on Indian MNC business strategies, but rather to complement these studies with a more institutionalist approach.

The chapter will proceed in three steps. First, we need to understand the institutional framework that has assisted the recent rise of Indian multinationals. For this purpose we will use the comparative capitalism perspective as a heuristic framework that allows us to identify the most important institutional factors that have contributed to the rise of Indian multinationals. Second, we will address the contrast between home and host economy institutions by reflecting on the potential consequences of Indian MNC takeovers in Germany and the US, with a focus on industrial relations. Third, we will contrast the institutional environment of Indian MNCs with the current regulatory environment on a global scale, again in order to identify possible areas of conflict.

In all three cases, we are clearly unable to come up with systematic findings yet, given the early stage of studies on these issues. The focus rather is on the identification of a specific agenda for further empirical research, by formulating a number of hypotheses and elaborating on the research that needs to be carried out in order to test these considerations. While we can draw on some previous work on the institutional context of Indian multinationals (section 2), the most urgent case for empirical research is to be made for the issue of home–host interactions (section 3), particularly in a European context such as Germany; Indian multinationals are only beginning to set their sights on the issue of global economic regulation (section 4).

17.2 A comparative capitalism perspective on the rise of Indian multinationals

Western Europe, the US, and Japan have been the main focus of the 'comparative capitalism' research programme that has produced a large number of competing typologies (for example, Crouch and Streeck, 1997; Hollingsworth and Boyer, 1997; Whitley, 1999; Coates, 2000; Hall and Soskice, 2001; Amable, 2003; Schmidt, 2002, 2003; for a review, see Jackson and Deeg, 2006). The framework highlights the importance of five interdependent institutional spheres that are crucial for any understanding of contemporary economies: corporate governance, corporate finance, industrial relations, education and training systems and the transfer of innovations (Hall and Soskice, 2001a: 17–33, see also Jackson and Deeg, 2006, 11–20).

How can we make use of this framework to explain the drive of Indian multinationals toward acquisitions in the EU and the US? In order to address this question, we will highlight a number of institutional factors that have affected the Indian overseas investment drive (see Taylor and Nölke, 2010, 2010a for a more detailed account). However, we need to compensate for one major shortcoming of the VoC approach as developed by Hall and Soskice, that is, their neglect of the state as an agent of economic development. While this might already be questioned for advanced economies, it certainly would lead to a biased perspective on the development of economies such as the Indian.

Indian firms have typically risen as global players based on one or more of the following competitive advantages: low production costs, flexible production systems, strong engineering capacity, managerial expertise, a relatively lax regulatory environment, and ease of communication given strong English language capabilities. In terms of specialization in the Indian economy, we can infer that there is a focus on 'skill-intensive intermediate products and services' (Das, 2007: 140). These competitive advantages are supported by a system of corporate finance and corporate governance that is rather unlike the LME model, since most Indian MNCs are less dependent on (international) capital markets.

Regarding the Indian stock exchanges, while Indian exchanges may lay claim to having the largest amount of firms listed on their exchanges in the world (10,000), in fact the bulk of shares in the most significant markets are rarely actively traded as trading remains highly concentrated (Allen et al., 2006: 12–14). Furthermore, due to legal regulations listings on foreign exchanges such as NYSE, LSE, and Euronext are rare. As result, Indian firms have relied heavily on internally generated funds as well as informal loans (from family and friends) as a means to finance their outward investments.

Equally so, regarding corporate governance dispersed shareholders and the organized forces of global capital markets (mutual funds, pension funds, investment banks, hedge funds etc.) do not dominate Indian MNCs. Rather Indian MNCs are most often family-owned/kin-based or state-controlled. Indeed when looking at the firms that are listed on the Indian exchanges today, we find that in the majority of these firms the largest blocks of equity typically remain in the hands of the founding family or controlling shareholder (Allen et al., 2006: 21). Turning to the realm of industrial relations, organized labour tends to have a weak role in corporate decision-making and thus has in some case reinforced low levels of payment along with long working hours. Indeed a fairly flexible production system based on human capital has developed in accordance with a rather high degree of flexibility on the side of the workers. This last point does in fact complement the notion that the Indian economy has an overabundance of human capital even it cannot compete with the level of sector-specific skills in CMEs, nor with the level of the general skills education in LMEs.

The transfer of innovation throughout the economy is a crucial element enabling technological growth at the firm level for which institutional factors are important. The Indian government has played a crucial enabling role in this area by overtly choosing to specialize the economy in industries deemed of high priority. As a result, shortly after independence the government set up an institutional and regulatory environment that would foster growth in these industries. In doing so, barriers to entry were constructed in these sectors and regulations as to how large firms were allowed to become were set (Allen et al., 2006: 8).

Barriers were only lowered after the initial start-up phases of these industries at which point a new set of policies were created to encourage more domestic private firms to enter industries in order to make them more competitive. As these sectors became even more highly competitive post-1991, the pursuit of aggressive acquisition strategies abroad seemed like a natural transition strategy for Indian firms trying to survive in a new competitive landscape. The 'soft patent system to legalize reverse engineering' post-1970 (Goldstein, 2007: 95) should also be mentioned area as a key institutional mechanism which supported the possibility for technological upgrading of Indian firms early on. Nonetheless, with the entrenchment of a strict(er) IPR regime at the national level significantly altering the legislative scene for all industries, Indian firms can no longer rely on a lax IPR regime to support their product portfolio and technological growth. As such, many have increasingly utilized acquisitions in the triad as a means to improve their innovative capacity in the new regulatory environment (Goldstein, 2007: 63). As ODFI was also liberalized, Indian firms coped with fierce(r) domestic competition by setting their sights on markets, which would allow them to not only obtain comparatively easier profits, but also, more importantly, new skills, products, brands, knowledge, and technology (Ratnam, 1998; Pradhan, 2004, 2007a, 2007b, 2008b; CRISIL, 2006; Gupta, V. K. 2006; Narlikar, 2006; Pradhan and Alakshendra, 2006; Pradhan and Sahu, 2007; Das, 2007; Kale, 2008). Given that the government eased restrictions concerning what type of OFDI activities could be pursued and where they could be performed, a significant portion of firms set their sights on triad markets as those markets were the hubs of global innovation. However, the acquisition of companies of the triads can lead to serious strains within the host country environment, as discussed in the next section.

17.3 Indian multinationals and host economy labour institutions: a research agenda

The question whether multinational firms conform to host country practices, or rather import distinctive practices from their home country into their host country subsidiaries has attracted considerable attention over recent years (Hamill, 1984; Erramilli, 1996; Bae, Shyh-jer, and Lawlwe, 1998; Ferner and Quintanilla, 1998; Muller et al., 1998; Bruining and Boselie, 2005; Dobbin, 2005; Pulignano, 2006; Edwards, Colling, and Ferner, 2007. Among the most prominent approaches is new institutionalism, which seeks to highlight 'the relationship between the organization and its 'institutional environment', and the way in which this relationship shapes the organization's internal structures' (Ferner et al., 1998: 712). The relative degree of adaptation of the internal structure of the organization to the local environment is considered to represent local isomorphism (Powell and DiMaggio, 1991, 1991a). Isomorphic pulls are a result of the distinct variety of capitalism located within each country. However, given the distinct nature of each variety, firms are often tempted to import certain practices, especially with regard to human resource management and employment practices in their host country, rather than localize themselves. This is also based on the desire of the multinational to achieve consistency within the global organization as a whole. Since both tendencies collide, we might expect conflicts in the interaction between the MNC and the local institutional context.

Given the absence of empirical studies on acquisitions by Indian multinationals and their implications on the institutional context in host economies, a research project on these issues might depart from the assumption that these acquisitions lead to tensions with unions in the OECD area, given the very different institutional context in terms of industrial relations between India and triad countries. In particular we would assume that tensions might be caused between the need of Indian multinationals to preserve their low-cost production advantages and the rather elaborate (and expensive) industrial relations systems in most triad economies. Based on the comparative capitalism approach we may assume that the amount of these tensions heavily depends on the type of host country variety. Thus we study the impact of takeover operations by Indian multinationals on industrial relations within LMEs (the US) and CMEs (Germany). Below we sketch out this approach in some more detail.

In terms of specifics of the German labour market, roughly 27 per cent of the workforce is unionized. On top of this, employers' associations are considerably large and in addition play a key functional role in defining corporatist relations within Germany. Any firm with more than five employees (excluding apprentices and part-time workers) has the right to create a works council. The significance of the works council lies in its right to co-determination and ability to block decisions made by the firm, as result the right works council have in terms of being informed and being able to make recommendations to the firm on specific subject matters. The matters include among other things: work rules, working hours, holiday leave, fringe benefits, type of remuneration, as well as the use of devices to monitor and assess employees. Furthermore, a key aspect of co-determination is the call for employee representation on the board, thus giving employees a direct role in the internal governance of the firm. What is key to note here is that co-determination is legally enforced in Germany, whereas collective bargaining is not (Muller, 1998: 732).

Thus, firms have little room to change employee participation in the daily routines of the firm, while there is a considerably amount of room to maneuver in wage bargaining. As the example above has shown, domestic firms have made little use of this ability to maneuver; however, the choices made by foreign firms in Germany in this area may pose significant challenges to the continued existence and influence of collective bargaining. Finally, the labour market in Germany is quite inflexible, with stringent regulations on the ability of firms to hire and fire. Overall, the labour market tends to really on long-term labour contracts that protect workers from unexpected or unjustified layoffs. The long-term nature of employment in Germany also contributes to greater cooperative efforts between employees and employers, wherein both sides are encouraged to invest in employees obtaining company-specific skills (Hall and Soskice, 2001a). Furthermore, workers are also granted a minimum of 25 days of paid vacation in Germany (Ray and Schmitt, 2007: 12).

Overall, as a result of the strong institutional environment present in Germany, it can be inferred that there will be significant coercive pressures for firms to localize themselves when they enter the German market. If firms are unwilling to adapt to the German context, the probability of conflicts is high. The ability of firms to deviate in the German context can also be a strain on corporatist labour relations in Germany and may contribute to the erosion of the institutional complementarities within this system.

Labour relations in the US remain quite distinct when compared to their European counterparts mentioned above. Given the fluid nature of the labour market in the US, both domestic and foreign workers are not coerced in the same ways to conform to the strong institutional setting that is present in Germany, that is, they have considerable room to pursue various strategies without facing legal or institutional repercussions. The legal framework in the US does not stipulate the need for works councils. Furthermore, management is given unilateral decision capabilities, that is, they are not forced to answer to or cooperate with labour, which means that they have the ability to arbitrarily hire and, more importantly, fire. Unions are considerably weak in the US; however, they do have a stranglehold in a small minority of sectors.

Given the weak role of unions and the absence of employers' associations in the US, industry-wide collective bargaining does not take precedence, but rather plant-level and individual bargaining occur (Hall and Soskice, 2001b: 29–30). As a result the US relies, 'more heavily on macroeconomic policy and market competition to control wages and inflation' (Hall and Soskice, 2001b: 30). In terms of paid vacation, the US is the only OECD nation to have no statutory minimum, that is, there is no legal requirement to grant paid vacations. Furthermore, there is also no minimum amount of sick days granted, and the amount given remains extremely austere in each firm compared to policies followed in their European counterparts with regard to sick leave (Ray and Schmitt, 2007: 4). Since there is a relative lack of governance mechanisms regulating the labour market in the US, firms face few coercive pressures to localize.

To conclude, as a result of the strong institutional environment present in Germany, it can be inferred that there will be significant coercive pressures for firms to localize themselves when they enter the German market. We expect labour unions to be the primary pressure force intervening in the strategies firms are enabled to pursue. In contrast, Indian acquisitions in the US should work out more smoothly, given the far more conducive context in terms of industrial relations. In order to test our approach, we would need to systematically study the effects of acquisitions by Indian multinationals in Germany and the US. To do so, we would need to collect data on the kind of wage bargaining taking place in the three cases (India, Germany, and the US), the nature of the relations between employers and employees, and the role of the state in bringing these two actors around the table. We would need to collect data on bargaining rates and interview key persons with regard to level and kind of government involvement as well as the general character of industrial relations (cooperative or adversarial, differences between company, sector, and national level). Moreover, we would assemble information on fringe benefits given to labour, working rules and working conditions, type and length of contractual agreements between management and labour, employee turnover rates (in particular before, during, and after acquisitions), in addition to domestic labour market regulations. Finally, in-depth company studies would be necessary in order to find out whether the tensions mentioned above will indeed be caused by Indian acquisitions in Europe, most notably Germany.

17.4 Indian multinationals and the institutions of global (and European) economic governance: Future perspectives

What are the preferences of Indian multinationals with regard to transnational economic regulation? This question is of particular importance for the European Union. On the one side, the EU will face the preferences of Indian multinationals in global settings such as World Trade Organization (WTO) negotiation rounds. On the other hand, Indian multinationals may start lobbying in order to influence the regulations governing the Common Market, comparable to the approach taken by US multinationals within institutions such as AmCham.

As to the regulation of corporate finance, we may expect some tensions between global financial markets and Indian multinationals. Financial markets usually prefer company finance along the lines of LMEs, whereas Indian multinationals rather have highly concentrated ownership structures and therefore tend to neglect the protection of minority shareholders. The latter, however, is at the centre of many global regulatory institutions, be in the context of the OECD or the Financial Stability Board. Still, it may take some time for this conflict to be played out openly, since Indian multinationals may avoid it by either selectively, or not at all, implementing global standards, as indicated for the accounting standards developed by the EU-supported International Accounting Standards Board. The same assumption may be formulated for the case of corporate governance regulation. Again, Indian MNC preferences differ from the dominant LME model, and again this does not lead to open conflict (yet), but rather to highly uneven implementation of global standards.

In the field of industrial relations, we expect Indian multinationals usually to be unwilling to accept comprehensive global labour regulation by the International Labour Organization (ILO), because of the corresponding threat for the low (labour) cost strategy that has helped them to expand. Clearly evidencing the conflictive character of this issue is the opposing stance the Indian government has taken with regard to including a social clause within the free trade agreement it is currently negotiating with the EU. The main issue in the field of innovation transfer is intellectual property rights, another topic that has also been at the centre of controversy in negotiations on signing of the free trade agreement between India and the EU. Is there convergence on a common Indian position, or do we witness increasing divergence between preferences for a more liberal or a more strict IPR regime? And if so, how will this divergence be played out on the national and global levels respectively? In order to answer these questions, we need empirical research on the positions taken by different Indian companies and policy-makers, as well as on any articulation Indian companies have already undertaken in the fora of global and EU business regulation.

17.5 Conclusion

Our contribution has demonstrated how an institutionalist approach can add to the existing literature on Southern Multinationals in general and on Indian MNCs in particular. We identify this contribution in three main areas. First, an institutionalist approach can complement existing theories on the emergence and the business strategies of Indian MNCs. Second, an institutionalist account helps us to identify possible topics for tensions in the interaction between home and host economies. Third, an institutionalist account assists us in identifying future issues in global economic regulation, where the rise of Indian multinationals might lead to conflicts with existing rules.

Within the institutionalist camp, we have chosen a comparative capitalism approach as the heuristic framework for the development of our study. Based on this framework we have identified some typical institutional conditions that have supported the rise of Indian multinationals, including a limited reliance on global capital markets, a family-based system of corporate governance, a weakly enforced system of industrial relations regulation (in the services sectors), an education system that produces large numbers of graduate (but with uneven qualification), a not too strict system of competition policy, and – until recently – a rather lax IPR regime. Most prominently, however, we have highlighted the role of the Indian government as a far more important agent, as in most cases of Western capitalism.

Returning to the issue of the 'steal and thereafter shutdown fear', we may conclude that these fears might be partially valid in Germany, in contrast to the US. A growing number of acquisitions in Europe may thus lead to some tensions in EU–India relations. Moreover, not only at the firm level, acquisitions can often act as shock to the path-pattern the target firm had previously been on and rapidly change the labor relations, corporate governance, corporate finance, and innovation cooperation within the sector. Whereas at the national level the impacts of a surge in Indian MNC acquisitions may not be as rapid, they may nevertheless have significant ripple effects on the overall stability of the sector-level institutional compromises. Still, more country-specific empirical research, for example, on Indian acquisitions in Germany, is needed to come to conclusive findings.

In view of the early stage of research, it is also difficult to predict whether Indian MNCs will mobilize against the existing global economic order – while there are some tendencies for Indian MNCs to adapt to triad patterns, there are also some tendencies for different preferences. One obvious conclusion, however, can already be drawn: there is a much closer cooperation between Indian MNCs and their home governments, if compared with the relationships between triad MNCs and their home governments. Correspondingly, we generally expect less involvement of Southern Multinationals in transnational private self-regulation and transnational lobbying than we are used to in case of triad MNCs. Instead, North–South relations may become rather mercantilist and intergovernmental.

The main research interest of this contribution was to assess whether the rise of Indian multinationals would lead to tensions with the triad, in particular with EU member states. Based on our institutionalist approach, we come to nuanced hypotheses. While we have identified some specific issues for concern, both within the German host economy and on the level of global economic regulation, we do not expect a new North–South-conflict. Much more empirical research, however, is needed to test our findings in a more systematic way.

Bibliography

Aguiar, M., Bhattacharya, A. et al. (2006), *The New Global Challengers: How 100 Top Companies from Rapidly Developing Economies Are Changing the World*. Boston Consulting Group.

Aguiar, M., Bhattacharya, A. et al. (2008), *The 2008 BCG 100 New Global Challengers*. Boston Consulting Group.

Allen, F., Chakrabarti, R. S., De, S., Qian, J., and Qian, M. (2006), *Financing Firms in India*, European Finance Association, Zürich.

Amable, B. (2003), *The Diversity of Modern Capitalism*. Oxford: Oxford University Press.

Bae, J., Shyh-jer, C., and Lawlwe, J. J. (1998), 'Variations in Human Resources Management in Asian Countries: MNC Home-country and Host-country Effects', *International Journal of Human Resource Management*, 9 (4), 653–70.

Bergman, A. (2006), *FDI and Spillover Effects in the Indian Pharmaceutical Industry*, RIS Discussion Papers No. 113, New Delhi: Research and Information Systems for Developing Countries.

Bruining, H. and Boselie, P. (2005), 'The Impact of Business Ownership Change on Employee Relations: Buy-outs in the UK and the Netherlands', *International Journal of Human Resource Management*, 16 (3), 345–65.

BusinessWeek (2005), *The BusinessWeek Global 1200*. Accessed on April 1, 2007 <http://www.businessweek.com/pdfs/2005/0552_global.pdf>.

Chadha, A. (2005), *Trips and Patenting Activity: Evidence from the Indian Pharmaceutical Industry*, Departmental Working Papers WP0512, Singapore: Department of Economics, National University of Singapore.

Coates, D. (2000), *Models of Capitalism: Growth and Stagnation in the Modern Era*. Cambridge: Polity Press.

CRISIL (2006), 'Creating the Indian MNC', *CRISIL*, New Delhi: Center for Economic Research.

Crouch, C. and Streeck, W. (1997), 'Introduction', in C. Crouch and W. Streeck (eds), *Political Economy of Modern Capitalism: Mapping Convergence and Diversity*. London/Thousand Oaks, CA/New Delhi: Sage, 1–32.

Das, N. (2007), 'The Emergence of Indian Multinationals in the New Global Order', *International Journal of Indian Culture and Business Management*, 1 (1/2), 136–50.

Dobbin, F. (2005), 'Is Globalization Making Us All The Same?' *British Journal of Industrial Relations*, 43 (4), 569–76.

Dunning, J. H. (1995), 'Reappraising the Eclectic Paradigm in an Age of Alliance Capitalism', *Journal of International Business Studies*, 26 (3), 461–91.

Dunning, J. H. (1998), 'Location and the Multinational Enterprise: A Neglected Factor', *Journal of International Business Studies*, 29 (1), 45–66.

Edwards, T., Colling, T., and Ferner, A. (2007), 'Conceptual Approaches to the Transfer of Employment Practices in Multinational Companies: An Integrated Approach', *Human Resource Management Journal*, 17 (3), 201–17.

Erramilli, K. M. (1996), 'Nationality and Subsidiary Ownership Patterns in Multinational Corporations', *Journal of International Business Studies*, 27 (2), 225–48.

Ferner, A. and Quintanilla, J. (1998), 'Multinationals, National Business Systems and HRM: The Enduring Influence of National Identity or a Process of 'Anglo-Saxonization,' *International Journal of Human Resource Management*, 9 (4), 710–31.

Forbes (2007), 'The Global 2000', 1 April.

Fortune (2007) 'Global Fortune 500', available at: http://money.cnn.com/magazines/fortune/global500/2007/ [accessed 1 April 2007].

Goldstein, A. (2007), *Multinational Companies from Emerging Economies*. New York: Palgrave Macmillan.

Gupta, A. (2006), 'Emergence of Indian Multinationals', *Technology Exports*, 8, 1–12.

Gupta, V. K. (2006), 'Inventor Productivity in a Publicly Funded R&D Agency – the Case of CSIR in India', *World Patent Information* 26, 235–8.

Hall, P. A. and Soskice, D. (eds) (2001), *Varieties of Capitalism: The Institutional Foundations of Comparative Advantage*. Oxford: Oxford University Press.

Hall, P. A. and Soskice, D. (eds) (2001a), 'An Introduction to Varieties of Capitalism', in P. A. Hall and D. Soskice (eds), *Varieties of Capitalism: The Institutional Foundations of Comparative Advantage*. Oxford: Oxford University Press, 1–70.

Hamill, J. (1984), 'Labour Relations Decision Making within Multinational Corporations', *Industrial Relations Journal*, 15, 30–4.

Hollingsworth, J. R. and Boyer, R. (eds) (1997), *Contemporary Capitalism: The Embeddedness of Institutions*. New York: Cambridge University Press.

Jackson, G. and Deeg, R. (2006), *How Many Varieties of Capitalism? Comparing the Comparative Institutional Analyses of Capitalist Diversity*, MPIfG Discussion Paper 06/02, Cologne: Max Plank Institute for the Social Sciences.

Kale, P. (2006), 'Acquisitions in BRIC Economies: The Case of India', in S. Jain (ed.), *Emerging Economies and the Transformation of International Business*. Cheltenham, UK: Edward Elgar, 138–54.

Kale, D. (2008), *Internationalisation strategies of Indian pharmaceutical firms*. Paper presented at the Conference on Emerging Multinationals from Emerging and Developing Countries, October 9–10, 2008. Copenhagen: Copenhagen Business School.

Khanna, T. and Palepu, K. (2006), 'Emerging Giants: Building World Class Companies from Emerging Markets', *Harvard Business Review*, 84 (10), 60–9.

Kumar, N. (2007), 'Emerging TNCs: Trends, Patterns and Determinants of Outward FDI by Indian Enterprises', *Transnational Corporations*, 16 (1), 1–26.

Kumar, N. (2008), *Internationalization of Indian Enterprises: Patterns, Strategies, Ownership Advantages and Implications*. New Delhi: Research and Information System for Developing Countries.

Milelli, C (2007), *Outward Expansion by Indian Firms: The European Route*, Working Paper 2007-25, Paris: EconomiX.

Mittal, S. B. (2006), *India's New Entrepreneurial Classes: The High Growth Economy and Why it is Sustainable*, Occasional Paper No. 25, University of Pennsylvania: Center for the Advanced Study of India.

Muller, M. (1998), 'Human Resource and Industrial Relations Practices of UK and US Multinationals in Germany', *International Journal of Human Resource Management*, 9 (4), 732–49.

Narlikar, A. (2006), 'Peculiar Chauvinism or Strategic Calculation? Explaining the Negotiating Strategy of a Rising India', *International Affairs*, 82 (1), 59–76.

Nölke, A. and H. Taylor (2010), 'Non-Triad Multinationals and Global Governance. Still a North-South Conflict?', in M. Ougaard and A. Leander (eds), *Business and Global Governance*, London: Routledge, 156–178.

Pradhan, J. P. (2004), 'The Determinants of Outward Foreign Direct Investment: A Firm-Level Analysis of Indian Manufacturing', *Oxford Development Studies*, 23 (4), 619–39.

Pradhan, J. P. (2007), *Growth of Indian Multinationals in the World Economy: Implications for Development*, ISID Working Paper, 2007/04, New Delhi: Institute for Studies in Industrial Development.

Pradhan, J. P. (2007a), *Trends and Patterns of Overseas Acquisitions by Indian Multinationals*, ISID Working Paper, 2007/10, New Delhi: Institute for Studies in Industrial Development.

Pradhan, J. P. and Alakshendra, A. (2006), *Overseas Acquisitions versus Greenfield Foreign Investment: Which Internationalization Strategy is Better for Indian Pharmaceutical Enterprises?* Trivandrum: GLOBELICS.

Pradhan, J. P. (2008). 'Indian direct investment in developed region', Paper presented at Emerging Multinationals from Emerging and Developing Countries, October 9–10, 2008. Copenhagen: Copenhagen Business School.

Pradhan, J. P. (2008a), *'Indian direct investment in developing countries'* ISID Working Paper 2008/08. New Dehli: Institute for Studies in Industrial Development.

Pradhan, J. P. (2008b), *Indian Multinationals in the World Economy*. New Dehli: Bookwell.

Pradhan, J. P. and Sahu (2007), *Transnationalization of Indian Pharmaceutical SMEs*. New Delhi: Bookwell.

Powell, W. W. and P. DiMaggio (1991), 'Introduction', in W. W. Powell and P. DiMaggio (eds), *The New Institutionalism in Organizational Analysis*. Chicago: University of Chicago Press, 1–38.

Powell, W. W., and P. DiMaggio (1991a), 'The Iron Cage Revisited: Institutional Isomorphism and Collective Rationality', in W. W. Powell and P. DiMaggio (eds), *The New Institutionalism in Organizational Analysis*. Chicago: University of Chicago, 63–82.

Pulignano, V. (2006), 'The Diffusion of Employment Practices of US-based Multinationals in Europe: A Case Study Comparison of British- and Italian-based Subsidiaries', *British Journal of Industrial Relations*, 44 (3), 497–518.

Ratnam, C. S. V. (1998), 'Multinational Companies in India', *International Journal of Human Resource Management*, 9 (4), 567–89.

Ray, R. and Schmitt (2007), *'No-Vacation Nation'*, Washington: Center for Economic & Policy Research, Accessed July 22, 2010. http://www.cepr.net/documents/publications/NoVacationNation_asofSeptember07.pdf

Sarathy, R. (2006), 'Strategic Evolution and Partnering in the Indian Pharmaceutical Industry', in S. C. Jain (ed.), *Emerging Economies and the Transformation of International Business*. Cheltenham, UK: Edward Elgar, 229–49.

Schmidt, V. A. (2002), *The Futures of European Capitalism*. Oxford: Oxford University Press.

Schmidt, V. A. (2003), 'French Capitalism Transformed, Yet Still a Third Variety of Capitalism', *Economy and Society*, 32, 526–54.

Taylor, H. and A. Nölke (2010), 'Indian Multinationals and their Institutional Environment: A Varieties of Capitalism Perspective', in C. Esser and H. Egbert (eds), *Varieties of Capitalism: Dynamics, Economic Crisis, and New Players*. Saarbruecken: Lambert Academic Publishing, 41–54.

Taylor, H. and Nölke (2010a), 'Global Players from India: A Political Economy Perspective', in Karl P. Sauvant, W. Maschek and G. McAllister (eds), *Foreign Direct Investment from Emerging Markets: The Challenges Ahead*. New York: Palgrave Macmillian, 245–92.

UNCTAD (2005), *The Top 100 Non-Financial TNCS From Developing Countries Ranked by Foreign Assets*. New York/Geneva: United Nations.

UNCTAD (2006), *World Investment Report 2006: FDI from Developing and Transition Economies: Implications for Development*. New York/Geneva: United Nations.

Wells, L. T. (1981), 'Foreign Investors from the Third World', in K. Kumar and M. G. McLeod (eds), *Multinationals from Developing Countries*. Lexington, MA/Toronto: Lexington Books/D. C. Heath and Company, 23–36.

Wells, L. T. (1983), *Third World Multinationals: The Rise of Foreign Investment from Developing Countries*. Cambridge, MA/London: MIT Press.

Wells, L. T. (1986), 'New and Old Multinationals: Competitors or Partners', in K. M. Khan (ed.), *Multinationals of the South: New Actors in the International Economy*. London: Palgrave Macmillan.

Whitley, R. (1999), *Divergent Capitalisms: The Social Structuring and Change of Business Systems*. Oxford: Oxford University Press.

Wyatt, A. (2005), '(Re)imagining the Indian (Inter)national Economy', *New Political Economy*, 10 (2), 163–79.

18
The Impact of Financial Strategy on Internationalisation of EMNCs – a Neglected Factor?

Reinhard M. Meckl and Stephanie Graser

18.1 Emerging market multinationals in the financial crisis – point of departure

Emerging market multinational corporations (EMNCs) have made their way to the global business stage. They can increasingly be found in some of the most prestigious company rankings worldwide: for example, the Forbes Global 2000 list of 2009 includes 197 companies originating from BRIC countries (Forbes, 2009a), up from 79 in 2004 (Forbes, 2004). Some of these companies are even ranked among the Forbes Global High Performers (Forbes, 2009b). EMNCs have attracted considerable attention when announcing spectacular deals such as the acquisition of Jaguar and Land Rover by India's Tata Motors (ft.com, 2008), but not all of the headlines have been positive – for example, see Satyam – the 'Indian Enron' (*The Economist*, 2009a).

The financial crisis is and will continue to be a challenge for all companies – irrespective of size, industry or source country. This is shaking up the competitive landscape. Some companies will struggle, while others will survive and even prosper. For EMNCs, the financial crisis will be a tough test of the sustainability of their development, but it can also prove a unique window of opportunity (see, for example, *The Economist*, 2009b). As companies restructure and sell business units to raise funds, and in the face of relatively low stock prices, EMNCs looking for growth opportunities might find potential targets for both hostile and friendly takeovers readily available at low cost (KPMG, 2009). Financing could prove to be one of the key issues in this regard, as the availability of sufficient funds is a precondition to finance asset-seeking mergers & acquisitions (M&A) in industrialised countries. These are of particular interest for many EMNCs, in order to establish a leading position on global markets (Aykut and Goldstein, 2006: 24; Goldstein, 2007: 2).

EMNCs (see further Aykut and Goldstein, 2006; Goldstein 2007; Salehizadeh, 2007; Rugman, 2008; Sauvant, 2008; Ramamurti and Singh,

2009) are generally characterized as corporations from emerging (that is, transition and developing) countries (Aykut and Goldstein 2006: 7) such as China or Brazil. They are mostly smaller and less international than competitors from established markets, with a stronger regional focus. There is a link between the destination and the motives behind their investments: investments in other, often neighbouring developing countries tend to be led by asset-exploiting motivations, while investments into industrialized countries, which are of growing importance, are mostly asset-seeking-driven.

EMNCs are generally active in a broad range of sectors, but there are national biases in certain industries (for example, EMNCs from India in IT), and M&A deals also show temporary biases (for example, in metals and mining in 2006). Given their home country experience, EMNCs are strong at operating in a developing country environment, their production processes and products suiting developing country conditions and customer requirements. Although the ambition is there, in most cases they are not yet industry leaders in technology or branding. For example, there is no BRIC country company listed in the BusinessWeek & Interbrand 100 Best Global Brands list of 2008 (Interbrand Corporation, 2008). EMNCs have long benefited from a stable cash flow from home markets with strong growth. In some countries, like China and Russia, the role of government ownership or government influence plays an important part, whereas in other countries, private ownership, frequently by clans or families, or public listing are relevant characteristics.

The phenomenon of EMNCs progressively expanding their international activities and the unsolved question of the impact of financial strategy on internationalization has been the starting point for our research. For EMNCs, financial strategy may be the crucial deciding factor on their chances of establishing themselves in global markets as head-to-head competitors with established corporations from industrialized countries. As such, the question of whether and what influence financial strategy has on internationalization is highly relevant for EMNCs. This leads to the following research question: What role does financial strategy play in the internationalization of companies – and in particular in the case of EMNCs?

Financial strategy may merely play a passive role, characterized by 'finance essentially follows strategy'. In that case internationalization, for example through foreign direct investment (FDI), first paves the way for financial internationalization. On the other hand, the active role of financial strategy opens up new financing channels, for example a company listing on a foreign stock exchange to source new funds, enabling it to grow internationally. However, finance and internationalization can also factor independent of each other, with no significant relationship in terms of time (predecessor, successor) and content (where they are neither beneficial nor detrimental to the other).

Having identified this relationship we come closer to answering the question whether global financing as one form of global sourcing is the ultimate goal or whether it makes EMNCs more vulnerable to external shocks like a financial crisis. Presently, many EMNCs profit from their low involvement in international financial markets.

The following pages describe our research design for executing the project. The chapter is organized as follows: a literature review on finance and internationalization and the financial aspects of EMNCs, followed by an introduction of real and financial internationalization – two selected dimensions of internationalization. Furthermore, thoughts on possible relationships between these two dimensions are proposed in addition to some underlying assumptions on market imperfections and characteristics of EMNCs. Finally, we provide some details of the planned empirical research.

18.2 Literature review

18.2.1 Finance and internationalization

Little research has been done so far on the relationship between finance and internationalization (Agmon, 2006: 575). This is especially true at firm level, though more research can be found on the country level, for example, examining exchange rate effects on FDI flows. The lack of literature is rather surprising, given the important role that finance plays for the growth of a company and for internationalization as one method of corporate growth and expansion.

Most of the research on this topic within the field of international business has focused on the asset side of internationalization (Oxelheim et al. 2001: 382; Morgan, 2002: 275; Forssbaeck and Oxelheim, 2008a: 630), neglecting the liability side. Dunning (1993), for example, in his OLI paradigm, largely disregards financial factors. While his paradigm takes into account 'that the propensity of firms to own foreign income generating assets may be influenced by financial and/or exchange rate variables' (1993: 76), only few references are made to financial factors. Financial factors are included as an asset-type ownership advantage ('Oa', 1993: 150), and financial strength (1993: 77) is mainly linked to size of the company as well as to experience with and access to international financial markets (1993: 150, 162).

In the field of finance, the international dimension is far from neglected, but has a strong emphasis on valuation and risk management. Valuation includes, for example, how to value an FDI project, while risk management assesses issues such as how to manage exchange rate risks (Koller, Goedhart, and Wessels, 2005; Levi, 2005; Shapiro, 2006).

This gap in research has been explained with incongruent underlying assumptions: well-known theories of internationalization are based on the assumption of factor and goods market imperfections (see, for example, Dunning, 1993: 56, 76, 78), while central theories in finance are based 'on the two assumptions of complete and perfect [capital] markets' (Agmon, 2006: 576). But empirical research suggests that capital markets become more integrated and thus differ in their degree of segmentation (Stulz, 1999: 24), which has consequences for the market capitalisation and cost of capital of a company (Gozzi et al., 2008: 608, 630) and may therefore have implications for the relationship between finance and internationalization (Choi and Tsai, 2006: 20–1, 55; and see section '18.4 and 18.4.3).

There are a few exceptions to the disjointed view of finance and internationalization described above. According to Choi and Tsai (2006: 22), Aliber made the first attempt at trying to explain FDI through financial factors. He focused mainly on customs and currency (Aliber, 1970: 21). Morgan (2002) examines the effects of financial internationalization on MNCs from Germany, Japan, US and the UK, with particular reference to impacts on the corporate governance system.

Oxelheim and associated researchers (Oxelheim et al., 2001; Forssbaeck and Oxelheim, 2008a) have focused on finance-specific factors in terms of proactive financial strategies and the impact on FDI at firm level. They showed that finance-specific factors can indeed be an additional variable to the OLI paradigm in explaining FDI (Forssbaeck and Oxelheim, 2008b: 23, 26; 2008a: 631, 638, 640). This finding is based on the reasoning that a firm's cost of capital relative to those of competitors, as well as the availability of capital directly, impact on its relative likelihood to engage in FDI (Oxelheim et al., 2001; 382; Forssbaeck and Oxelheim 2008a: 631). Moreover, they argue that international financing is of particular importance for companies from developing countries (at least in terms of financial development), where the capital markets are segmented and less liquid than in industrialised countries (Oxelheim et al., 2001: 382; Randoy et al., 2001: 660; Forssbaeck and Oxelheim 2008b: 3, 16/17, 28; 2008a: 631). From their empirical research, it became clear that it is mainly equity-related factors that matter, for example, international cross-listing on a larger stock exchange (Forssbaeck and Oxelheim 2008b: 25; 2008a: 638).

Likewise, Choi and Tsai (2006) have shown that in addition to strategic factors, financial factors (especially internal financing und international diversification) also help in explaining FDI (2006: 21, 42, 51, 55).

On the contrary, Hassel et al. (Hassel et al., 2000a, 2000b, 2003) have found that internationalization in the real dimension and internationalization in the financial dimension are correlated at such a low level that they consider the distinction of these two different dimensions of internationalization valid (2000a: section 4.6; 2000b: 501, 517; 2003: 721). They label it the 'financial dimension', while choosing mainly equity-related parameters (ownership structure, foreign listing, accounting standard (2003: 714–15). Thus they have mainly shown the independency of the real dimension of internationalization and the equity-related dimension of internationalization. They themselves caution to what degree this finding (based on a sample of the 100 largest German companies in 1986 and 1996

(2000a: section 3; 2003: 712) is relevant to analysis on countries outside of continental Europe (2003: 718).

18.3 EMNCs and financial factors

Even less has been published on the financial aspects of EMNCs in specific detail. This is again surprising, as one would expect that multiple and diverse aspects of EMNCS have already been examined. After all, the phenomenon of EMNCs in itself is not new and there are a number of publications on the topic dating back to the 1970s and 1980s: see, for example, Heenan and Keegan (1979) and the pioneering research on 'Third World Multinationals' (TWMNEs) by Wells (1983), Lall (1983) or Lecraw (1977), to name just three.

Agmon and Lessard (1977) were among the early and few to discuss the impact of financial factors on the international expansion of developing country firms. At that early date, they already pointed out that 'financial factors are relevant to the multinational expansion of firms only if there are imperfections in financial markets' (1977: 197), which tends to be the case in developing countries. They argue that financial factors can, in such an environment, be constraints to international expansion (financing is limited to national sources) as well as motivation for international expansion: via FDI firms can get a foothold into a foreign market, which opens up access to financial sources in that country (1977: 211–14). Thus Agmon and Lessard concluded that financial factors, under the condition of imperfect capital markets, are indeed relevant to international expansion.

Salehizadeh (2007: 1155, 1157, 1159) found that most EMNCs are publicly listed (apart from Chinese companies, which are largely government-owned) and that many are even cross-listed on large international stock exchanges. According to Liuhto and Vahtra (2007), Russian companies have low standards of transparency and disclosure (2007: 125–6).

Goldstein (2007) includes a section on 'financial market issues' in his book on EMNCs. He mentions one particularity of EMNCs regarding financing, namely that several EMNCs have relatively easy access to cheap capital and/or subsidised loans, owing to their close relationship to their government (2007: 127). This would give them a comparative advantage in potential auction processes of M&A transactions. However Goldstein also questions whether national financing resources are sufficient to finance large international investments, or whether EMNCs will need to access international capital markets for financing (2007: 129), which affects the cost of capital (2007: 130).

Sauvant (2008: 9) does not see this bottleneck in finance for the international expansion of EMNCs, but it is not clear how he would assess the new setting of the capital markets during and after the world financial crisis of 2008–9.

As a conclusion of the analysis of relevant literature we find a need for research in the field of the relations of finance strategy and internationalization, especially regarding EMNCs.

18.4 Real and financial internationalization

18.4.1 Dimensions of internationalization

Before proceeding, the term 'internationalization' needs to be clarified and refined. In international business literature, 'internationalization' generally refers to the international expansion of a firm's business activities and/or assets, for example, engaging in international trade, making foreign direct investments, establishing alliances with companies from other countries. As financial sources can also be tapped in an international context, this definition of the term 'internationalization' is too ambiguous for the present purpose.

We will speak of *real internationalization* versus *financial internationalization* instead, in order to clearly distinguish between a firm's internationalization in the more traditional, real, dimension and a firm's internationalization in the new, financial, dimension. Thereby, 'traditional' and 'new' refer to the dimension's tradition of being subject to international business research (Hassel et al., 2000a: section 4). This distinction has previously been used by other researchers (including, for example, Hassel et al., 2003: 711 and Forssbaeck and Oxelheim 2008a: 630).

The forms and types of real internationalization are quite thoroughly described in the existing literature. Different modes of market entry, for example, export/import, cooperation, greenfield investment or M&A are a typical way of distinguishing strategies of real internationalization. This will serve as a guideline to specify the parameters for measuring the real internationalization of companies (export sales, foreign assets, etc.).

Regarding financial internationalization, Oxelheim has proposed 'alternative paths to internationalize the cost and availability of capital' (Stonehill and Dullum, 1998: 118; Randoy et al., 2001: 665). He suggests that a company with purely domestic financial market operations should move from issuing debt to listing and issuing equity on less liquid markets. With more experience and name recognition, they can proceed by listing and issuing equity on more prestigious foreign exchange markets (Stonehill and Dullum, 1998: 118–20; Randoy et al., 2001: 664–7; Eiteman et al., 2007: 411–13). Oxelheim's path model as well as his outline of proactive financial strategies (Oxelheim et al., 2001: 386–92) serve as guidelines to specify the parameters for measuring the financial internationalization of companies (for example, foreign ownership, cross-listing, foreign debt, cash flow and international accounting standards).

18.4.2 Positions on the relationship between real and financial internationalization

This research is aimed at understanding the relationship between real and financial internationalization of EMNCs at firm level. In order to do so, the spectrum of potential relationships as identified in the relevant literature, supplemented by the remaining theoretically possible relationships (to make the list completely exhaustive), needs to be worked out as a first step. The subsequent step is to look at which relationships can be empirically supported. The final point will be to discuss which relationships are preferable under which conditions.

A relationship between real and financial internationalization can exist in terms of time as well as in terms of content. In terms of time, one dimension of internationalization might systematically or accidentally precede the other, or they can happen in parallel. In terms of content, internationalization in the one or the other dimension might motivate, promote or hinder internationalization in the other dimension, or they can be without any impact on each other.

So there are three possible relationships:

1. Real internationalization precedes financial internationalization: This position says that real internationalization comes first. One argument often raised is that companies only or more easily have access to financial sources if they are already 'international' in real terms and have a foothold in the relevant country. This does, however, appear to be a rather outdated argument in times of proclaimed global capital flows. A slightly different, but nevertheless financial argument or motivation is that companies engage in real internationalization in order to diversify their cash flows by generating revenues in a country with different business cycles compared to their home country. This position is hardly ever explicitly verbalized, but often seems to be implicitly assumed.
2. Financial internationalization precedes/promotes real internationalization: This position is mainly proposed by Oxelheim and associated researchers, who have shown that an internationally oriented financial strategy is relevant for real internationalization (see section '18.2).
3. Real and financial internationalization are independent of each other: Hassel et al. came to the result (using an entirely German sample) that the correlation between financial and real internationalization is relatively low (see section 18.2).

18.4.3 Assumptions on capital markets and EMNCs

At this stage it appears that assumptions on capital markets and their fit with reality play a critical role in the reasoning: if a country's capital market is liquid and integrated, corporate financial internationalization should not make any difference in comparison to sourcing capital nationally. If these assumptions need to be relaxed – at least to some degree and/or for a certain time frame (Oxelheim 1998; Forssbaeck and Oxelheim 2008a: 631; 2008b: 2, 5, 6, 10), corporate financial internationalization might indeed make a difference and financial factors have additional explanatory power in explaining real internationalization (especially if it takes the form of M&As).

A second group of assumptions has to be made with regard to EMNCs. The question remains whether this group of corporations shows specific characteristics in comparison to conventional MNCs that might promote or disturb their standing on international capital markets. And indeed there seem to be some particularities: short track record but strong growth, weak corporate governance systems, strong government backing or government ownership (especially in the case of Chinese and Russian companies) and access to below-market cost financing options. As a consequence, we do see a specific position of EMNCs on international capital markets, which we use as an assumption for our further research.

18.5 Outline of planned research

Now that the hypotheses on the relationship between real and financial internationalization have been worked out as the first step of research, preparatory work for the empirical study needs to be done in the second step.

The measures of internationalization need to be defined in the two dimensions (real and financial internationalization). This means specifying the parameters for which data are to be collected, as well as deciding which parameter value is to be considered less international and which is to be considered more so. Ideally, this ranking is based on existing theory. If parameters of one dimension are at a certain stage to be aggregated, for example, to form an internationalization index, the respective weight of a parameter and/or the mathematical combination of parameters need to be chosen (for aggregating several parameters per real and per financial dimension, see Hassel et al., 2000a: section 4.6). Regarding the choice of parameters a multitude of suggestions are offered in the existing literature. Particularities of EMNCs are also to be considered. This will lead to two measurement constructs, which may be called real and financial EMNC internationalization indices.

A set of companies also needs to be chosen, based on criteria such as home country equity listing and/or ranking (different rankings from different sources using different criteria are available). Most likely, the companies as ranked by the Columbia Emerging Market Global Players Project (Columbia Program on International Investment, 2008) for Brazil, Russia, India and China (BRIC) will be selected for the sample. These country-wise rankings are considered particularly suitable as they list approximately the same number of companies per country, while ensuring a comparable ranking methodology (foreign assets). In order to avoid a bias towards capital-intensive industries owing to the primary criterion of foreign assets, the sample will be supplemented by companies that are large in terms of market capitalization (home country equity listing) as well as companies that are considered particularly interesting for reasons such as being included in the BCG Global Challengers List (Aguiar et al., 2007).

Once the preparatory work is done, data collection (from publicly available sources) can start, followed by statistical evaluation and discussion of the results.

The aim is not to develop a new theory of internationalization of EMNCs, but rather to take a first step in observing and understanding the interplay between real and financial internationalization, and their effects on EMNCs willing to expand their business abroad. Working from Buckley and Lessard's general thoughts on theory development in international business (2005: 597–8), this research intends to provide one more bridge between two main streams in current research (finance and internationalization theory). We believe this to be highly relevant, as EMNCs will prevail as an important factor in international markets.

Apart from being of academic interest, we are confident that the results will be of interest to both the management of EMNCs and their competitors in international markets. We hope to reveal an influencing factor, namely financial strategy, and its relevance for internationalization, with the possibility of deriving recommendations for managing this influencing factor or for estimating what the consequences for current market structures will be in, for example, the EU if EMNCs succeed in managing this factor well.

References

Agmon, T. (2006), 'Bringing Financial Economics into International Business Research – Taking Advantage of a Paradigm Change', guest editorial, *Journal of International Business Studies*, 37, 575–77.

Agmon, T. and Lessard, D. R. (1977), 'Financial Factors and the International Expansion of Small-country Firms', in T. Agmon and P. Charles (ed.), *Multinationals from Small Countries*. Kindleberger. Cambridge, MA/London: MIT Press, 197–219.

Aguiar, M. et al. (2007), *The 2008 BCG 100 New Global Challengers – How Top Companies from Rapidly Developing Economies Are Changing the World*. Boston Consulting Group, December.

Aliber, R. Z. (1970), 'A Theory of Direct Foreign Investment', in *The International Corporation*, ed. Charles P. Kindleberger. Cambridge, MA: MIT Press, 17–34.

Aykut, D. and Goldstein, A. (2006), *Developing Country Multinationals – South–South Investment Comes of Age*, Working Paper No. 257, OECD Development Centre, December.

Buckley, P. J. and Lessard, D. R. (2005), 'Regaining the Edge for International Business Research', *Journal of International Business Studies*, 36, 595–9.

Choi, J. J. C. and Tsai, E. C. (2006), 'Strategic and Financial Determinants of Foreign Direct Investments', *International Finance Review*, 7, 19–60.

Columbia Program on International Investment (2008), *Emerging Market Global Players Project*, available at: http://www.cpii.columbia.edu/projects/ [accessed 28 October 2008].

Dunning, J. H. (1993), *Multinational Enterprises and the Global Economy*. Wokingham, UK: Addison-Wesley Publishers.

Eiteman, D. K., Stonehill, A. I. and Moffett, M. H. (2007), *Multinational Business Finance*, 11th international edn. Boston, MA: Pearson/Addison-Wesley.

Forbes (2004), *The Global 2000 – Special Report*, available at: www.forbes.com, 2004 [accessed 13 July 2008].

Forbes (2009a), *The Global 2000 – Special Report*, available at: www.forbes.com, 8 April 2009 [accessed 5 May 2009].

Forbes (2009b), *The Global High Performers – Special Report*, available at: www.forbes.com, 8 April 2009 [accessed 5 May 2009].

Forssbaeck, J. and Oxelheim, L. (2008a), 'Finance-specific Factors as Drivers of Cross-border Investment – An Empirical Investigation', *International Business Review*, 17, 630–41.

Forssbaeck, J. and Oxelheim, L. (2008b), *Financial Determinants of Foreign Direct Investment*, IFN Working Paper No. 741, Research Institute of Industrial Economics, Stockholm, 19 March.

ft.com (2008), 'Jaguar Goes Tata', available at: www.ft.com, 27 March 2008 [accessed 11 May 2009].

Goldstein, A. E. (2007), *Multinational Companies from Emerging Economies – Composition, Conceptualization and Direction in the Global Economy*. Basingstoke: Palgrave Macmillan.

Gozzi, J. C., Levine, R. and Schmuckler, S. L. (2008), 'Internationalisation and the Evolution of Corporate Valuation', *Journal of Financial Economics*, 88, 607–32.

Hassel, A. et al. (2000a), *Dimensionen der Internationalisierung – Ergebnisse der Unternehmensdatenbank 'Internationalisierung der 100 größten Unternehmen in Deutschland'*, MPIfG Working Paper 00/1, Max-Planck-Institut für Gesellschaftsforschung, January.

Hassel, A. et al. (2000b), *'Zwei Dimensionen der Internationalisierung – eine empirische Analyse deutscher Großunternehmen', Kölner Zeitschrift für Soziologie und Sozialpsychologie*, 52 (3), 500–19.

Hassel, A. et al. (2003), 'Two Dimensions of the Internationalization of Firms', *Journal of Management Studies*, 40 (3), 705–23.

Heenan, D. A. and Keegan, W. J. (1979), 'The Rise of Third World Multinationals – Whether Viewed as a Threat or Opportunity, This Young Phenomenon is a Force to be Reckoned With', *Harvard Business Review*, 57 (1), 101–9.

Interbrand Corporation (2008), *Best Global Brands – 2008 Rankings*, available at: http://www.interbrand.com/best_global_brands.aspx, 2008 [accessed 15 October 2008].

Koller, T., Goedhart, M. and Wessels, D. (2005), *Valuation – Measuring and Managing the Value of Companies*, 4th edn, rev. and updated. Hoboken, NJ: Wiley.

KPMG (2009), *Emerging Markets Continue to Narrow the M&A Gap*, available at: http://www.kpmg.com/Global/IssuesAndInsights/ArticlesAndPublications/Pages/Emerging-markets-continue-to-narrow-the-MA-gap.aspx, 2 March 2009 [accessed 30 May 2009].

Lall, S. (1983), *The New Multinationals – The Spread of Third World Enterprises*. Chichester: John Wiley & Sons.

Lecraw, D. (1977), 'Direct Investment by Firms from Less Developed Countries', *Oxford Economic Papers*, 29 (3), 442–57.

Levi, M. D. (2005), *International Finance*, 4th edn. London: Routledge.

Liuhto, K. and Vahtra, P. (2007), 'Foreign Operations of Russia's Largest Industrial Corporations – Building a Typology', *Transnational Corporations*, 16 (1), 117–44.

Morgan, G. (2002), 'Multinationals, Corporate Governance and Financial Internationalisation', in *Management and Organization Paradoxes*, ed. Stewart R. Clegg. Amsterdam: John Benjamin, 275–93.

Oxelheim, L. (1998), 'From Market Segmentation to Market Integration', in L. Oxelheim (ed.), *Corporate Strategies to Internationalise the Cost of Capital*. Copenhagen: Copenhagen Business School Press, 23–33.

Oxelheim, L., Randoy, T. and Stonehill, A. (2001), 'On the Treatment of Finance-specific Factors within the OLI Paradigm', *International Business Review*, 10, 381–98.

Ramamurti, R. and Singh, J. V. (2009), *Emerging Multinationals in Emerging Markets*. Cambridge: Cambridge University Press.

Randoy, T., Oxelheim, L. and Stonehill, A. (2001), 'Corporate Financial Strategies for Global Competitiveness', *European Management Journal*, 19 (6), 659–69.

Rugman, A. (2008), 'How Global are TNCs from Emerging Markets?' in Karl P. Sauvant (ed.), *The Rise of Transnational Corporations from Emerging Markets*. Cheltenham, UK: Edward Elgar, 86–106.

Salehizadeh, M. (2007), 'Emerging Economies' Multinationals – Current Status and Future Prospects', *Third World Quarterly*, 28 (6), 1151–66.

Sauvant, K. P. (2008), *The Rise of Transnational Corporations from Emerging Markets – Threat or Opportunity*? Cheltenham, UK: Edward Elgar.

Shapiro, A. C. (2006), *Multinational Financial Management*, 8th edn. New York/Chichester: Wiley.

Stonehill, A. and Dullum, K. B. (1998), 'Corporate Strategies: A Conceptual Perspective', in L. Oxelheim (ed.), *Corporate Strategies to Internationalise the Cost of Capital*. Copenhagen: Copenhagen Business School Press, 117–32.

Stulz, R. M. (1999), 'Globalization, Corporate Finance, and the Cost of Capital', *Journal of Applied Corporate Finance*, 12 (3), 8–25.

The Economist (2009a), 'India's Enron', available at: www.economist.com, 8 January 2009 [accessed 11 May 2009].

The Economist (2009b), 'Not so Nano – The Financial Crisis May Have Strengthened the Hand of the Developing World's Emerging Giants', available at: www.economist.com, 26 March 2009 [accessed 11 May 2009].

Wells, L. T. J. (1983), *Third World Multinationals – The Rise of Foreign Investment from Developing Countries*. Cambridge, MA/London: MIT Press.

19

A Southern Multinational and an Emerging European State in an Entry Bargaining Process

Caner Bakir

19.1 Introduction

The relations between host state (HS) and multinational corporations (MNCs) have been subjected to extensive research in the International Business (IB) literature. Previous research on entry bargaining has focused on *the terms of the investment deal* (that is, outcome), which was regarded as the function of the relative bargaining strengths of HS and MNC. It has been noted that the MNC's actual entry conditions (or the bargaining context) are shaped by *economic* resources that are of interest to the other actor, the relative stakes that the two actors have in a given bargaining situation, and the similarity of interests between the two sides (Kobrin, 1987; Behrman and Grosse, 1990; Behrman and Grosse, 1992). This has been two-actor model of the MNC-centric view of entry bargaining (Vernon, 1971, 1977; Kobrin, 1987; Eden, Lenway and Schuler, 2005).

The primary concern of this study is neither MNCs' goals, resources, strategies, structures, and locational choices, nor an attempt to apply the existing bargaining models to understand HS–MNC relations. The theoretical motivation of this chapter is to provide a more complete account of entry bargaining process. Our findings lead to a conceptual model for taking account of how HS and MNC entry bargaining is a multi-level, and multi-actored *process*, and why *state capacity* in steering this dynamic bargaining process towards an agreement is fundamental. We argue that an investment agreement is more likely to be the outcome of the entry bargaining process when state capacity exists. Here state capacity refers to the ability of the state to formulate, pursue, and implement chosen objectives and goals towards the attainment of a vision despite resistance in the entry bargaining process. Our conceptual model is based on the state capacity, which is a function of informal, formal, and relational institutional foundations.

We benefit from the existing IB, comparative public policy, and governance literatures and from our in-depth analysis of an explanatory case. Specifically, we incorporate the state as a major political actor in the bargaining model.

The approach is novel in that it offers 'the state-led governance view of the entry bargaining process' by incorporating the concept of state capacity developed in political science literature into the bargaining process. In doing so, our model contributes to better understanding of the bargaining process between HS and MNC. It deals with bargaining among multiple actors, which takes place at local, regional, and national levels in the public policy process of emerging host countries. We view the entry bargaining as a process of governing or 'steering' by the state towards an investment agreement. Rather than treating the entry bargaining as a single event and focusing on an investment outcome only, we view it as a state-led governance process and recognize that the outcome has dual meaning of an investment and a non-investment decision. We show that a non-investment decision or the incompletion of an investment deal at the end of entry bargaining process is also an outcome that deserves explanation.

To this end, this chapter chooses the entry bargaining process that took place in 2006 when the world's 95th largest MNC, Hyundai Motors Corporation (HMC),[1] looked at the possibilities of setting up a US$ 1.5 billion car manufacturing plant in an emerging European country, Czech Republic, as an empirical setting to verify our model and propositions. Although there was a collaborative interaction at the national level between the Czech state and KIA Motors division of the HMC, the agreement was not signed owing to a conflict between the public actors and landowners over the sale of the land at Nošovice in 2004. A year later, in 2005, the entry bargaining process in the HMC investment witnessed a similar conflict stage. However, this time the conflict was resolved by the state and the outcome of the entry bargaining was an investment deal. This study is about explaining these two divergent bargaining outcomes.

Our study is novel in that our model looks at the entry bargaining processes between an emerging market multinational and the emerging European country through an interdisciplinary perspective. An analysis based on this entry bargaining case will also enable us to examine how emerging European states respond to policy challenges posed by inward FDI during the entry bargaining with Southern Multinationals.

Our resulting insights contribute to entry bargaining literature. Specifically, this chapter shows that the previous studies on entry bargaining have five major weaknesses. First, the bargaining model is outcome-oriented, ignoring the fact entry bargaining is a process that has mobilization, conflict, and resolution phases. Second, the perception of outcome is limited to a decision leading to an investment agreement between the HS and the MNC, ignoring the question of why some interactions among the key actors generate an investment agreement, while others do not. Third, the primary focus is on economic power potential of states and MNCs rather than political power where state has centralized legitimate authority and monopoly to regulate social relations territorially. Fourth, the HS is generally regarded as a static, monolithic, and secondary actor in the entry bargaining, ignoring the state's fundamental role in steering the bargaining process towards an investment deal. Finally, the entry bargaining is limited to bargaining between the two key actors (that is, HS and MNC) at national level, ignoring interactions among *various actors* such as supranational (for example European Union), international financial (for example, IMF) and various domestic (for example, civil society) organizations as well as individuals (for example, landowners) at *various levels*, such as systemic (that is, extraterritorial) and domestic (for example, national, regional, municipal, and local) levels.

An explanatory case study method is adopted in this study because 'how' and 'why' questions are posed; the researcher has no control over events; and the focus is a contemporary phenomenon in its real-life context (Yin, 1994). More specifically, we are dealing with how the entry bargaining process between the Czech state and the HMC took place and why the outcome was an investment deal in Czech Republic. The method of data collection was qualitative. Daily newspapers and weekly financial press published in the Czech Republic were widely used as media sources. Other textual sources included reports and press releases of the government and private agencies. The data are ordered chronologically and helped the formation of the theoretical framework.

The organization of this chapter is as follows. The next section presents the literature review and the adopted perspective. The results from the case study are analysed and the evidence that leads to propositions and a model is presented. The chapter concludes with an overview of the findings, the limitations of the study and suggestions for future research.

19.2 Literature review

This section has two parts. The first will introduce the main models on entry bargaining in the IB literature. These models are introduced in an order that reflects their historical development and relative influence. This will be followed by 'the state-led governance view of the entry bargaining process' that will guide the analysis of the case in the next section.

The traditional model of entry bargaining is widely known as the 'obsolescing bargain model' (OBM). This model reflects *conflictual* bargaining between developing country government and developed country multinational in natural resource industries in the 1960s and 1970s (Vernon, 1971, 1977; Moran, 1974, 1978; Bennett and Sharpe, 1979; Fagre and Wells, 1982; Jenkins, 1986; Kobrin, 1987; Brewer, 1992; Vachani, 1995; Mytelka, 2000). In this conflict model of firm/state interaction, the primary focus is on the HS's and MNC's *economic* sources of relative bargaining power as an ability or capacity *to* achieve their respective ends in the outcome, the investment deal (Vernon, 1971; Fagre and Wells, 1982; Kobrin, 1987). It is assumed that a MNC's bargaining power resources include ownership advantages such as capital and technology, while a HS's bargaining power resources include its location-specific advantages such as access to home market, natural resources, and cheap and skilled labour (Poynter, 1985; Boddewyn, 1988). This view focuses on the bargaining powers of the HS and the MNC: power of the MNC is highest at the time of entry but the balance of power shifts in favour of the state once initial investment is made. Sector-specific investments, as the argument goes, make the relatively immobile MNC vulnerable to opportunistic decisions of the HS, making the original bargain obsolete. The key vulnerabilities of MNCs include expropriations, adverse regulatory changes, renegotiation of contracts, and performance requirements imposed by the HS.[2]

However, with the advent of globalization and the adoption of neoliberal economic policies across market economies from the 1980s onward, there has been a gradual shift from conflictual to cooperative relations between HS and MNCs. Nation states increasingly compete with each other in order to attract inward FDI, which is seen as a significant means of achieving national economic growth and development objectives. As such, new models of HS and MNC emphasized cooperative relations among these key actors (Dunning, 1991; Stopford, 1994). It is noted that neither the states of host countries nor MNCs are able to achieve their ends by themselves. Collaborative interaction is required for the successful pursuit of their goals. Indeed, successful industrial and corporate strategy relies on collaborative interaction between governments and businesses (Lodge, 1990). As such, there is also a possibility for mutual gains among these actors: from the 1990s onward, interaction between HS and MNCs has changed from being 'predominantly adversarial and confrontational to being non-adversarial and cooperative' (Dunning, 1998: 280; Vernon, 1998).

The new political bargaining model (PBM) suggested a revitalization of the OBM by removing the twin emphases on 'entry' and 'obsolescing' (Eden, Lenway, and Schuler, 2005). Here, 'MNC–state relations are modelled as iterative political bargains between MNCs and governments over a wide variety of government policies at the industry level' (Eden, Lenway, and Schuler, 2005: 254). The PBM benefits from the liability of foreignness, transaction cost economics, and the resource-based views in the IB literature.

These entry bargaining views summarized above treat the host country as an actor and they focus primarily on the natural and human resources of the host country or nation. However, as Boddewyn and Brewer (1994: 125) noted, '[i]n reality, country borders contain various resources and institutions usually labelled as physical, economic, social, cultural and political. The first four characteristics coincide with the concept of nation, whereas the political one is associated with the existence of states. The theories commonly used to explain international business deal principally with the nation phenomenon...' The existing entry bargaining models focus on various physical and economic country resources rather than the state and its capacity to utilize these resources. There has been a failure to distinguish between country and state, as well as various types of state power, and thus a failure to appreciate the state's role in the entry bargaining process. It is widely assumed that cooperative/non-adversarial interaction between host government and MNC would eventually deliver an investment deal. These views omit the fact that the entry bargain is not limited to these key actors, and various dimensions of power exercised by the state should be taken into account. There is a need for a revision of the state and MNC-centric bargaining paradigm, because it fails to recognize the importance of other non-state actors. The dominant view has been increasingly become 'obsolete' due to the growing involvement of multiple actors such as supranational and international intergovernmental organizations, civil society organizations as well as individuals who may have veto power in the entry bargaining process. Indeed, in spite of such cooperative interaction between host governments and MNEs, the entry bargaining may be concluded with non-deal outcome due to antagonists who destabilize the bargaining process in the absence of state capacity to steer the process toward an investment outcome.

We aim to build a bridge between comparative public policy and IB fields by modifying the state capacity framework and adapting it to entry bargaining. Specifically, this study offers a state-led governance perspective (Pierre and Peters, 2000; Bell, 2003; Peters and Pierre, 2006) to the entry bargaining process. We follow a state-centric model of entry bargaining analysis because the state remains the key political actor in domestic political economy (Pierre and Peters, 2000). As Mann (2008: 355) notes, 'states provided power relations that were confined within a defined territory, which confined their subjects to that territory, and which derived from a central place. No other major form of power organization did this'.

The *State* is defined as a set of governing institutions that formulates and carries out a particular goal (Dunleavy and O'Leary, 1987). We focus on activities of government, public authorities, and bureaucratic agencies of the state aimed at steering entry bargaining processes. Following Peters and Pierre, *governance* is defined as 'a goal-directed', state-led steering activity, 'with the need to establish collective goals and develop the means of reaching those goals' (Peters and Pierre, 2006: 215). State-led governance perspective refers to state infrastructural power or political power, which is 'the capacity of the state to actually penetrate civil society and implement its actions across its territories' (Mann, 2008: 355; Katzenstein, 1985; Skocpol, 1985: 9; Atkinson and Coleman, 1989; Coleman, 1996; Weiss, 1998).

In comparative public policy literature, state capacity is conceptualized in terms of formal bureaucratic organizational foundations, which include autonomy (degree to which politicians and bureaucrats act autonomously from societal organizations) and concentration (degree to which ultimate decision-making power is concentrated in the hands of a relatively small number of officials). It is assumed that 'the more centralized, autonomous and elitist a state bureaucracy and its administrative core, the greater this [state] capacity' (Atkinson and Coleman, 1989: 52; Zysman, 1983: 300; Coleman, 1996). Accordingly, there are three major properties associated with formal state capacity: balance rather than conflict, concertation rather than competition, and concentration rather than fragmentation among *rowing* agencies, which are formally responsible for the day-to-day administration of particular sectoral policies in an economy. It is assumed that rowing agencies bring different perspectives and kinds of expertise to the policy process. The power of the state will be maximized when the institutional structure ensures that there is a *balance* between these various bureaucratic perspectives in the policy process. 'A balance permits formulation of policies that are more likely to address the competing objectives coming from financial services firms, their clients and the public interest' (Coleman, 1996: 74). When one agency clearly dominates the other, the state does not maximize its own political power potential and becomes more vulnerable to pressure from societal actors (see Coleman, 1996: 67). This balance should be achieved in an environment characterized by cooperation rather than bureaucratic competition. 'The positive coordination that comes from a concertation, problem-solving style helps create a synergy that optimizes overall policy performance' (Coleman, 1996: 74). The capacity of states to approach policymaking will be greater when there are smaller numbers of agencies that are responsible in policymaking. If the number of agencies involved in policymaking is small, it is more likely to pose fewer obstacles to coordination of bureaucratic perspectives and views. 'As the number of state actors participating in the policy process increases, the problems of coordination and consensus-building intensify' (Coleman, 1996: 67). As such, institutionalized mechanisms facilitating coordination and cooperation, and resolving conflict among public authorities are fundamental properties of the bureaucratic structure. In the absence of these properties, the state is too weak to provide strong leadership or direction for the FDI policies and in the entry bargaining process.

In addition to formal bureaucratic organization, Atkinson and Coleman emphasize knowledge and expertise of politicians and bureaucrats, bureaucratic and financial resources. They note that 'state strength is a function of bureaucratic centralization, the quality of bureaucratic elites, and the degree of control exercised by the State over financial resources' (1989: 54). Quality of bureaucratic elites include 'high-quality information, forums of active policy debate, and especially expert, dedicated, and experienced staff in key areas of policy formulation and implementation, [which] are also a vital component of state capacity' (Bell and Carr, 2003: 309). In a similar vein, the financial resources available for a state are vitally important for the realization of national interest. In the absence of such resources, a state's capability to pursue its objectives is constrained significantly.

19.3 State capacity framework in the entry bargaining process

We will benefit from these valuable insights on the state capacity framework summarized above. However, the major weakness of this framework is that it primarily focuses on formal institutional organization of the state, ignoring informal and relational institutional foundations. Thus, the current study views the state capacity in the entry bargaining process as a function of not only formal but also informal (that is, ideational) and relational (that is, ability to exercise various dimensions of power) institutional properties. We assume that the state capacity is a function of informal, formal, and relational institutional foundations (Figure 19.1). Specifically, the state's formulation of industrial strategy vision, the alignment of formal institutional structure with this informal structure, and its implementation through the exercise of political power is at the centre of the governance of the entry bargaining process. Accordingly, *state capacity* is defined as the ability of the state to formulate, pursue, and implement chosen objectives and goals toward the attainment of a vision despite resistance in the entry bargaining process. It plays a pivotal role in whether the entry bargaining will be concluded with an investment deal.

The informal aspect of the state capacity in the entry bargaining process includes state industry strategy vision, objectives, and goals toward inward FDI (for example, attracting productivity-enhancing inward FDI to achieve economic growth and higher levels of employment). Without having these

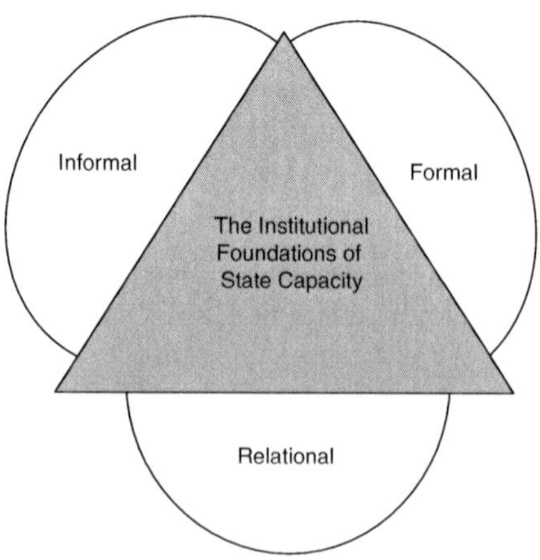

Figure 19.1 The institutional foundations of state capacity in the entry bargaining process

ideational properties a state cannot take a leadership role and develop the appropriate policy instruments to engage them. Such a vision plays a pivotal role in forming a consistency between objectives and goals as well as broader formal institutions. State industry strategy vision relates to ideas, which involve normative and cognitive parts. 'At cognitive level, ideas [like programs and paradigms] are descriptions and theoretical analyses that specify cause-and-effect relationships, whereas at the normative level ideas [like public sentiments and frames] consist of values, attitudes, and identities' (Campbell, 2004: 149). Ideas provide guidance for state actions. Inward FDI programs based on cognitive ideas have the notion that the investments of MNCs have beneficial effects on national economic growth and development, employment, technology transfer, managerial expertise, and capital provision. Thus HS increasingly adopt market-friendly policies towards MNCs in order to have these beneficial effects. Otherwise, domestic institutional environment not conducive to MNCs fail to attract FDI and struggle to have the beneficial effects as such. These programmatic ideas are legitimized publicly by states to facilitate their normative adoption by the public. In the present study, the informal institutional foundation concerns *industry strategy vision*, which is vitally important for the deliberate allocation of resources, as well as consistency and coherence of state objectives, goals, and policy instruments.

The formal institutional foundation involves a FDI policy regime including formal rules (for example, laws and regulations) that facilitate or constrain behaviour of actors, policy instruments, bureaucratic structure, and financial resources (see also Bell and Carr, 2003: 306–10). The FDI policy regime is related to the translation of the ideational properties of state capacity into actual policies. Formal rules relate to the legal framework, which includes relevant laws and regulations governing the inward FDI regime. Policy instruments include fiscal and financial incentives, public–private partnership, privatization, deregulation and so on. The legal framework and policy instruments are critical in facilitating coherence and consistency among vision, bureaucratic structure, and financial resources. Their utilization towards the realization of an industrial vision and goal is an important component of the state's capacity.

Inward FDI policy is directed by state bureaucratic agencies. Following the state capacity framework developed in comparative public policy literature, the bureaucratic organization, or the resources, expertise, and values of these agencies, and the interrelationships among them, play a crucial role in determining how policy is made and what form outputs take (Katzenstein, 1978; Zysman, 1983; Atkinson and Coleman, 1989; Coleman, 1996). Following Coleman (1996: 74), we specifically focus on the number of public sector actors involved in the entry bargaining process (the smaller the number of agencies involved, the greater the policy coordination and bureaucratic collaboration during the entry bargaining process), whether there is a balance among the perspectives of various public sector actors achieved through collaboration rather than competition (the higher the balance among the perspectives, it is more likely to address various policy challenges posed during the entry bargaining process), and whether this balance is achieved through collaboration rather than competition among the public sector agencies (the higher the collaboration, it is more likely to have bureaucratic synergy that optimizes overall policy performance). We assume that the HS with a smaller number of bureaucratic agencies sharing similar policy perspectives is more likely to steer an entry bargaining process towards an investment outcome.

Financial resources include a national budget surplus, resources from external budget support programs (for example, EU financial support), and the existence of an environment conducive to public–private partnerships, which are vitally important to a state's fiscal capability. Financial resources are needed in funding country-specific locational advantages such as transportation networks and the development of industrial and techno parks, which can also be tailored for specific inward FDI during entry bargaining. In a similar vein, they are also requisite for policy instruments such as job creation and training grants, and fiscal (for example, tax reduction) and financial (for example, subsidy) incentives, which may be used to forward an entry bargaining process towards an investment agreement. We assume that the HS with financial resources available to be utilized is more likely to steer entry bargaining toward an investment deal.

The relational foundation of state capacity involves how effectively a state is able to use various dimensions of power in the implementation of formal and informal foundations in the entry bargaining process. These three foundations are interrelated and an integral part of the state capacity. *Strong states* are able to realize their goals in the face of opposition from other actors, while *weak states* are not (see; Katzenstein, 1978; Skocpol, 1985; Atkinson and Coleman, 1989; Coleman, 1996). State strength here means the state's capacity to accomplish its objective(s), which may be in conflict with other actors whose interests are harmed by the state action. In this case, power relations involve resistance (Weber, 1978: 53). As Bacharach and Lawyer (1981: 200) note, 'power is not simply a part of bargaining, it is the essence of it'. The relational foundation of state capacity concerns the state's utilization of the three types of power to translate formal and informal foundations into policy outcomes. These are 'power to' accomplish your ends, 'power with' others to achieve your goal through collaboration, and 'power over' others by getting someone else to do what you want them to do despite resistance (for various types of power, see Lukes, 2005). We assume that these three dimensions of power constitute the relational bases of state capacity in various stages of the multi-actored entry bargaining process at national, regional, and local levels. Specifically, despite a collaborative interaction between states and MNCs, the conclusion of the final agreement may still be vulnerable to the resistance of antagonists who may destabilize the bargaining process, preventing the agreement. Accordingly, the state's exercise of power over 'destabilizers' to achieve the final agreement with the MNC becomes vital in the entry bargaining process. This power *over* is derivative of power *to* because it refers to a state's capacity to impose its will on antagonists (Lukes, 2005). In so doing, the state may demonstrate capacity to act despite resistance to the successful conclusion of investment agreement. In particular, the state's steering role is not only based on its legal and organizational capabilities to pursue its objective despite resistance, but also on coordination and fusion of public and private resources (see also Evans, 1997; Weiss, 2003). As such, how effectively a state is able to use various dimensions of power becomes a vital issue in state-led governance of the entry bargaining. We assume that the HS with relational power is more likely to resolve conflicts during the entry bargaining process toward an investment outcome.

Finally, the entry bargaining is not limited to interactions between states and firms. It takes place in the multi-actored and multi-level processes that move beyond the two-actor model. Apart from the state and the MNC various organizations (for example, interest organizations, civil society organizations, and international intergovernmental organizations) and individuals mobilize and demand government action to protect their own interests in the entry bargaining process. We define actors as individuals, and organizations that have political influence during the entry bargaining. These actors interact at local, regional, and national levels in the public policy process of host countries. We assume that these actors are guided by the maximization of their interests.

The next two sections present the case study. The analyses will focus on the question of whether the Czech state had the capacity to steer the process.

19.4 The Czech case

19.4.1 Informal institutional foundation

In regard to the informal properties of the state capacity, the Czech state had clear ideas about its inward FDI policy regime. The state adopted the Economic Growth Strategy Vision in 2005, which it defined as becoming a 'knowledge and technology centre of Europe with a growing standard of living and high employment rate' (Czech Government, 2005: 3). This vision provided an informal framework for the state objective and goal in industrial strategy, promoting the Czech state's collaborative interaction with the MNCs:

> The *objective* of the Economic Growth Strategy is to bring the Czech Republic as near as possible to the economic level of the developed EU member states while respecting the principles of sustainable development. Measured by GDP per capita, the country is capable of reaching the EU average level

> in 2013. To attain this *goal* the Czech Republic should use public-sector resources in support of goods and services with high value added, and make the business environment more attractive in order to induce efficient local companies to remain and new foreign ones to arrive.
>
> (Czech Government, 2005: 3, emphases added)

The major source of Czech economic growth is export-driven manufacturing production backed by inward FDI in the automotive sector (OECD, 2006: 16–17). According to CzechInvest, the government FDI promoting agency, between 1994 and June 30, 2005, automotive sector investments reached US$ 5.5 billion, with 148 firms, which constituted 42 per cent of total inward FDI and 29 per cent of total foreign-owned firms in the country (*Business News*, 27 September 2005).

The Czech state would progress towards meeting its vision, objective, and goal with the HMC investment. The HMC investment would be the largest foreign direct investment in the Czech Republic's history. With the addition of the HMC, the Czech Republic would become one of the EU's three largest car manufacturing countries, with an annual output of 1.1 million cars. Moreover, new suppliers would locate in the Czech Republic as a direct result of the HMC's investment in the country.[3] The Czech Industry and Trade Minister noted that the Hyundai factory in Nosovice would raise Czech GDP growth by about 1.1–1.2 percentage points in 2008 and by up to 1.5 percentage points in 2009, increase exports by US$ 2.5 billion and generate US$ 1.5 billion in the form of direct and indirect tax revenues to the budget (*CIA Daily News*, 31 March 2006).[4] For the national, regional, and municipal authorities, the HMC investment would help overcome economic stagnation in the Moravia–Silesia region. The settlement of the HMC was also expected to cut unemployment in the region, which at the end of August 2005 was the region's fifth highest at 14.5 per cent against the national average of 8.9 per cent, with 96,000 unemployed (*IntelliNews – Czech Republic*, 29 September 2005; *AWKnowledge – World Automotive Manufacturing*, 12 May 2006). The investment would cut the high unemployment rate by at least 2 per cent in the region and by 0.3 per cent in the country (*AWKnowledge – World Automotive Manufacturing*, 29 March 2006; *CTK – Business News*, 29 March 2006). The investment would create 3,000 direct and up to 20,000 indirect jobs in supply and service companies, according to CzechInvest estimates (*AfxAsia Newswire*, 27 March 2006). As such, the Czech state would progress toward increased GDP growth and higher levels of employment as envisaged in its informal institutional structure with the HMC investment.

In the words of the chairman of the HMC, 'Hyundai Motor, which has local production bases in most major regions in the world except Europe, has been mulling over the need of advancing into the European market' (*Financial Times*, 30 September 2005). There were three main reasons that made the Czech Republic 'an ideal candidate' for the location: the Czech

Republic's EU membership made the country an attractive gateway to the single EU market of 455 million consumers, its potential to grow as a financial hub for the East European market, and the HMC's need to have a plant in Europe that could serve as its global production network (see AfxAsia Newswire, 30 September 2005; *Yonhap News*, 30 September 2005). Indeed, following the collapse of the Berlin Wall in 1989, Central Europe has gradually emerged as a key driving force in the world's automotive sector. The Czech Republic, in particular, is now located in Europe's industrial backbone. The country is regarded as one of the best choices for investment in transport and logistics because of its perfect location in regard to EU markets, research and development (R&D), design, and production centres. The Czech Republic's geographical location bridging Western and Eastern Europe, the country's strong history in car manufacturing, as well as its long engineering tradition and skilled workforce served as local factors making it an attractive location. The manufacturing plant in the Czech Republic would be likely to provide Hyundai with 'the full range of local capabilities to serve the European market from design and engineering, to production, marketing, sales and after-service' (*Expansion Management*, 4 September 2007). Not surprisingly, there was a collaborative interaction between the Czech state and the HMC at the outset of the entry bargaining. The Czech state, guided by a national strategy growth vision, was well organized in its promotion of the country as a suitable investment location.

Proposition 1: *The greater the informal institutional foundations of the state, the greater the likelihood for a collaborative interaction with MNC.*

19.4.2 Formal institutional foundation

With regard to the formal FDI regime and policy instruments, the major strength of a state's FDI regime is its emphasis on public and private partnerships (that is, 'power with') in the productivity-enhancing infrastructure and human capital investments such as labour training and government provision and/or subsidization of infrastructure investment, including transportation and the preparation of industrial zones. For example, the Czech Prime Minister publicly promised 'all-out cooperation' by both the public and private sector to host the investment (see *AfxAsia Newswire*, 30 September 2005). Instead of a bidding war over largely ineffective corporate income tax cuts, the state focused on the improvement of local supplies of infrastructure and labour through direct public and private investment. The Czech FDI regime provided investors with several schemes including tax incentives, job creation and training grants, site support, and investment incentives in line with its strategic vision. Specifically, the Czech national investment scheme covered effective fiscal and financial incentives including corporate tax relief, and a tax holiday for ten years; job-creation grants of CZK 200 per employee in the region with the highest unemployment rate; training and retraining grants of 35 per cent of training costs in the regions where the unemployment rate is higher than the country's average; and a transfer of land acquired by the Czech state from private owners with infrastructure at a discount (*Intellinews*, 27 March 2006; *Czech Business Weekly*, 9 May 2006).[5] For example, the infrastructure in the North Moravia region was going to be improved through million-dollar public investments in the railroad transportation and the road network, including the extension of the road linking Nošovice with Zilina, where the HMC's subsidiary KIA Motors had a plant (*CIA Daily News*, 19 December 2005). Moreover, the government also injected public money into the preparation of the industrial zone. The Ministry of Labor and Social Affairs engaged in creating conditions to retrain several thousand workers that the HMC needed (*CIA News*, 10 October 2005).

In regard to bureaucratic organizational structure, there were several state elites and bureaucratic agencies involved in the bargaining process. The key public sector actors involved were the office of the Deputy Prime Minister of Economic Affairs, the Ministry of Industry and Trade, and CzechInvest operating at national level, as well as the governors of Moravskoslezsky and Zlinsky regions, and the mayor of Ostrava operating at regional and local levels (*CTK Business News*, 8 December 2005).

However, despite the high number of public actors involved in the bargaining process, the Czech state and its bureaucratic apparatus internalized a common vision. This served as an institutionalized mechanism facilitating coordination and cooperation among the public actors that helped in the formulation of a cohesive and integrated approach to the HMC bargaining process. The concerted *mobilization* of national, regional, and municipal authorities as well as CzechInvest toward attracting the HMC investment is highly illustrative. The Czech Deputy Prime Minister and the CEO of CzechInvest at the time visited South Korea at the end of August 2005 to promote potential sites and offered incentives to attract the HMC plant to the Czech Republic (*CIA News*, 6 September 2005). These public sector actors provided jointly shared policy responses to attract the HMC investment. For example, the regional and local authorities offered the HMC three attractive industrial zones while the Czech Government and CzechInvest focused on investment incentives to be offered in the initial mobilization stage of the entry bargaining. As such, the Czech Government, parliament, regional governments and municipalities, CzechInvest, and various ministries worked in concerted action toward the conclusion of the HMC deal.

A month later, the HMC senior executives met with public authorities including the Czech Prime Minister, and representatives of regional and municipal authorities and CzechInvest mobilized for initial negotiation talks (Czech Press Agency, 29 September 2005). Specifically, the then CEO of the HMC arrived in the country for the final site selection (*CTK – Business News*, 29 September 2005).[6] On 29 September 2005, the Hyundai CEO publicly expressed to the Czech Prime Minister the company's intentions to build the production plant. This was followed by the then HMC Vice President's announcement that the Ostrava district of Moravskoslelzsky region (hereafter North Moravia) was the HMC's preferred site for the possible investment (*Prague Post*, 20 October 2005). The HMC proposed a US$ 1.5 billion investment to create 3,000 new jobs in the region and 300,000 units per year from the Ostrava factory in the second half of 2008. This was followed by the visit of North Moravia regional governor and the Ostrava mayor to HMC headquarters in South Korea. When the Nošovice industrial park in Ostrava became the major contender for the investment, these public actors agreed to provide the land. Furthermore, in mid-November the Cabinet voted to add an additional CZK 1.5 billion to the CZK 3.25 billion in funds already earmarked to develop the Nošovice industrial park (*Prague Post*, 14 December 2005). As the Czech industry and trade minister noted, 'it was important to send a clear signal to Hyundai that the Czech Republic has invested in the locations suitable for Hyundai's investment' (*Prague Post*, 14 December 2005).

The significant role played by CzechInvest as a steering agency in this process deserves attention. This agency is regarded as being among the best investment promotion agencies in the world for its 'constructive and effective role' in FDI-related policies (UNCTAD, 2005: 212–13). CzechInvest has 'a well-defined mandate to provide policy advice on relevant issues' and 'the expertise and strong support to initiate and oversee the administration of a new incentive regime aimed at enhancing factor conditions underpinning R&D and innovation activities' (UNCTAD, 2005: 213). Moreover, it is 'well connected with key government ministries' (ibid.). It draws the attention of relevant government agencies to areas that are important for making the country more attractive for knowledge-intensive inward FDI.

In regard to financial resources, the Czech state benefited significantly from the country's EU membership.[7] Specifically, if inward FDI is in line with the competition rules and in conformity with the conditions for regional aid to large investment projects, the European Commission provides state support. North Moravia was covered by the Czech Government's and the EU's regional support programs with special incentives for investment and job creation (*AWKnowledge – Automotive Emerging Markets*, 19 May 2003). Thus, on 11 May 2007, the European Commission authorized an aid package of 111 million Euros (US$ 151 million) that the Czech Government planned to provide to the HMC for the setting up of the plant. The aid comprised a cash grant, transfer of land at a reduced price, and municipal aid (*Intellinews*, 14 May 2007). The HMC investment met EU competition rules because it would create 4,400 new jobs by 2011 in Nošovice. By 2007, the total regional aid that HMC received reached 194.49 million Euros for the investment cost of 1,148 billion (European Commission, 2007).

Proposition 2: *The greater the informal institutional foundations of the state, the greater the likelihood for formal institutional foundations facilitating collaborative interaction between HS and MNC.*

19.4.3 Relational foundation

The entry bargaining process was not limited to collaborative interactions among the Czech state and HMC at the national level. At the regional and municipal levels, the regional governor and mayor of the Ostrava region *mobilized* as supporters of the HMC investment to acquire the land, 30 hectares (74 acres) of which was owned by about 170 landowners, at the Nošovice industrial park. At the local level, the actors most threatened by the public authorities' attempts were some of the landowners and environmentalists. The key groups included local farmers mobilized via the Nošovice Agricultural Cooperative and environmentalists mobilized via their Dolni Lutyne Project. The farming cooperative growing cabbage aimed at protecting farming land, while environmentalists aimed at protecting a bird reserve on the site (*Prague Post*, 20 October 2005).

A *conflict stage* in the entry bargaining process, which took place over the sale of the land at Nošovice, erupted between the government, regional and local authorities on one side, and the farming cooperative and six landowners who had no interest in selling on other side (*Prague Post*, 20 October 2005; *New Europe*, 5 December 2005; *CTK Business News*, 16 December 2005). The regional and local authorities' land buyout initiative faced determined resistance from these opponents who had a strong potential to destabilize the entry bargaining process.[8]

A similar conflict had prevented the successful conclusion of the entry bargaining process with the investment of KIA Motors division of the HMC in 2004 (*Prague Post*, 20 October 2005). Although there was a collaborative interaction at the national level between the Czech state and KIA Motors, the agreement was not signed. This was due to a conflict between the public actors and landowners over the sale of the land at Nošovice. Specifically, the conflict took place at municipal, regional, and national levels and destabilized the entry bargaining process. At the municipal and regional levels, public authorities such as the governor and the mayor of the Ostrava region failed to persuade the landowners to sell their land. At the national level, the Czech Government's lack of legal resources justifying land expropriation led its failure to exercise *coercive power* over the landowners over the sale of the land to the local authorities for the KIA investment. This turned away the investment to neighbouring Slovakia where the HMC's first European manufacturing facility was established. The Czech Government failed to demonstrate the relational foundation of the state capacity as it could not exercise power over the landowners. Thus, in spite of collaborative interaction between the state and KIA, the entry bargaining process ended with a non-deal. This experience shows that the bargaining is a multi-actored/multi-level process that is vulnerable to the strong resistance of antagonists who destabilize the process.[9] Accordingly, despite collaborative interaction at the national level, bargaining that takes place at municipal and local levels may determine the direction of the entry bargain process. This arose through the veto powers of third parties such as landowners and/or municipal council members who may become part of the bargaining process.

A year later, in 2005, the entry bargaining process in the HMC investment witnessed a similar conflict stage. Although, by late November 2005, regional authorities had bought a majority of the land required, six landowners had not been persuaded to sell their plots in the industrial zone (*CTK – Business News*, 28 November 2005). The plots constituted 5 per cent of the targeted land for the HMC investment. In addition to local owners, in November 2005, civil society organizations such as Land for Life and the Environmental Legal Service were also mobilized against the HMC investment in the region, which was situated at the foothills of the Beskydy Mountains and near the Beskydy Nature Reserve (see *New Europe*, 5 December 2005). These civil society organizations sent an open letter to the HMC asking them not to build the plant in Nošovice (*Prague Post*, 15 December 2005). CzechInvest noted that the strong opposition groups might spoil the HMC investment and the construction of the automotive plant could be built in Poland instead (*Czech Republic Business Bulletin*, 30 November 2005; *AWKnowledge – World Automotive Manufacturing*, 14 December 2005).[10] However, it was the landowners rather than the civil society organizations that destabilized the progress of the entry bargaining process, which was otherwise moving towards a deal. The Czech Prime Minister confirmed the country's great national interest in the HMC's investment and expressed the government's willingness to help *resolve* the land buyout issue to the HMC Vice-President in a meeting held in Prague on December 7, 2005 (*CTK – Business News*, 8 December 2005). However, shortly after this meeting, on 11 December 2005, the regional authorities in North Moravia suspended the preparation of the industrial zone at Nošovice as they had failed to secure 100 per cent of the land needed (*CTK – Business News*, 12 December 2005). The Czech media reported that Hyundai could relocate its investment to Poland or Turkey if agreement could not be reached on the land issue (*AW Knowledge*, 14 December 2009).

As such, the state's willingness to carry out its will despite resistance becomes a significant component of state capacity in the governance of the entry bargaining towards the investment decision. Specifically, the conflict in the process can be *resolved* through the state's utilization of relational power. The Czech state considered the previous consequences of its failure to steer the entry bargaining. The KIA experience provided a significant feedback to the Czech state and contributed to its effective steering of the HMC entry bargaining. Thus not only persuasion at the regional and local level, but also inducement at the national level was used to exercise state power.[11] The state had given a strong signal to the HMC that it would acquire the land where there would be a conflict between landowners. Specifically, in August 2005, a new law on expropriation of land and buildings for reasons of public interest was approved by the legislative organ of the state, the lower house in first reading (*Czech Press Agency*, 30 September 2005). In October 2005, the Government introduced a bill that would force landowners to sell their property to the Government not only for major infrastructure projects but also for the development of industrial parks (*Prague Post*, 20 October 2005). The new expropriation bill as a policy instrument enhanced the state's relational foundation in the entry bargaining process. This move was guided by the state strategic vision. The Czech Prime Minister and the Industry and Trade Minister argued that the investment would bring new jobs and economic prosperity to the region, and that forced buyouts of land from private owners to build roads, motorways, railways and other projects were in 'the strategic public interest' (*CTK – Business News*, 30 September 2005). As such, landowners were required either to sell their Nošovice land to the government or face forced land expropriation as a legitimate action. In regard to the relational foundation of the state capacity, the Czech state exercised power over the landowners through the threat of land expropriation.

Proposition 3: *The greater the relational foundation of the state capacity, the less likely it is that antagonists will prevent an investment deal.*

19.4.4 Outcome: HMC investment decision

The Czech Prime Minister's subsequent threat of expropriation if the issue was not resolved by 22 December 2005 delivered the result: the regional authorities obtained the consent of owners for the sale of all necessary land (*CTK – Business News*, 16 December 2005). The Czech state steered the entry bargaining process via the utilization of the informal, formal, and relational institutional foundations of state capacity. On the one hand, 'power with' enabled the state to form a collaborative interaction with the HMC towards the investment deal, which was in line with the economic growth strategy vision. On the other hand, the Czech state exercised power over landowners (that is, destabilizers) by altering the incentive structure via the threat of forced land expropriation. As such, 'power over' and 'power to' enabled the state to pursue successful resolution of the conflict with the deal despite resistance. The Czech state had drawn lessons from the KIA experience for the HMC entry bargaining process.

On 27 March 2006, the parties signed a memorandum on the investment that included obligations of the parties (*CIA News*, 28 March 2006). A total financial and fiscal incentive offered by the Czech Government was US$ 280 million, which was 16.5 per cent of the total HMC investment of US$ 1.5 billion. Fiscal and financial incentives offered by the government included tax relief of US$ 59 million; US$ 9,000 subsidies for each new job (totalling

US$ 32 million for 3,500 employees);[12] a 45 per cent refund on job retraining costs (estimated at US$ 16 million); US$ 34 million discount on the land price; and a direct subsidy of US$ 109 million for the preparation of the industrial zone (*Czech Business Weekly*, 9 May 2006). The HMC proposed an investment of US$ 1.5 billion to create 3,000 new jobs in the region and 300,000 units per year from the Ostrava factory in the second half of 2008.

Proposition 4: *The greater the state capacity, the greater the likelihood for an investment outcome.*

19.5 Conclusion

This chapter has shown how state capacity can lead an entry bargaining process toward an investment outcome, by using a case study from an emerging European country. This analysis offers a state-led governance perspective, which suggested that effective state steering of various actors in a domestic policymaking process could deliver intended policy outcomes. Specifically, during the entry bargaining process various actors mobilize at national, regional, municipal, and local levels to pressure the HS to adopt a position that would accommodate their respective vested political, bureaucratic, and/or economic interests. As such, the bargaining outcome is influenced by the conflicting demands of allies and antagonists of the investment during the dynamic bargaining process.

Our findings show that the existence and effective utilization of the HS's informal, formal, and relational institutional foundations can be the key factor in the completion of this process with an investment deal. By bringing the state back into the entry bargaining process our study emphasizes state capacity or political power where the state has the centralized legitimate authority and monopoly to regulate social relations territorially. Thus, our contribution consists of a more complete specification of the entry bargaining process and the role of state steering therein. In this regard, there have been two main findings of this study. First, we show that entry bargaining is a multi-actored, multi-level process, which has mobilization, conflict, and resolution phases. Second, we emphasize the significance of state capacity, which has informal, formal, and relational foundations, to steer this entry bargaining process toward an investment deal.

The chapter points to the continued importance of political resources available to the state and state intervention despite the significance of economic resources and the advent of liberalization and globalization, which advocate a limited role for the state in markets. Our case study indicates that states should have ideational, legal, and organizational, as well as political power-based institutional foundations to deliver intended policy outcomes such as completion of an entry bargaining process with an investment deal. We have shown that entry bargaining is a multi-actored and multi-level governance process. An analysis based on the two-actor model of the MNC-centric view of entry bargaining focusing on the economic power resources of HS and MNC is perhaps less likely to help us in understanding why some interactions among the key actors generate an investment agreement, while others do not.

Our research findings draw on a single case study, so we need to be very cautious about making any generalizations at this point. Our study will hopefully stimulate more future research, which will take more case studies on how emerging European states respond to policy challenges posed by inward FDI during the entry bargaining with Southern Multinationals.

Notes

The authors would like to thank Nejat Capar for his valuable comments and encouragement.

1. Established in 1967, the HMC, which became the Hyundai KIA Automotive Group in 1998, is the biggest car manufacturer in South Korea, with more than 70 per cent of the domestic market and employing over 68,000 people worldwide, with a sales network extending to 193 countries. In 2001, the HMC's mission was to be one of the top five carmakers in the world by 2010. In terms of 2005 global sales ranking among automakers, the HMC ranked sixth with 3,715,095 cars (*Automotive News*, 5 June 2006).
2. Others, however, noted that the balance of bargaining power, especially in manufacturing, may shift toward the MNC rather than towards the HS. As Bennett and Sharpe (1979:87) argued, 'in a high-technology, consumer-goods manufacturing sector such as the automobile industry, the situation is often reversed.' Once car manufacturers have access to a market, they are integrated into the local economy and establish relationships within the host country, strengthening their bargaining power *vis-à-vis* the host government.
3. Indeed, several automotive supply companies arrived following the HMC investment decision. Examples include the Magneti-Marelli Company, which built an automotive lighting manufacturing plant worth 91.6 million Euros, creating 630 new jobs, and Sungwoo Hitech's new plant in Ostrava, which produces automobile body parts. This investment represents 87 million Euros with employment of 1,000.
4. However, the country's economy is regarded as the most concentrated among the EU-25 and heavily dependent on the automotive sector. Any decline in regional demand for cars would hit the Czech economy hard.
5. In principle, the total amount of the investment incentives must not exceed 50 per cent (with the exception of training and retraining) of the investment made into long-term tangible and intangible assets.
6. Although the Czech Republic was the HMC's main choice, HMC officials indicated that the Czech Republic, Poland, and Hungary had been short-listed for the investment.
7. At the supranational level, the EU also provides state aid in the form of investment incentives for FDI, which is compatible with the EU directives. The European Commission authorizes ad hoc aid packages to member countries under the EC Treaty state aid rules. The aid is evaluated by the EC and is calculated as a percentage of the total value of the actual investment. A new Act on Investment Incentives (Act No. 72/2000 Coll.) became effective on 1 May 2000. This act was discussed with the EC and follows European rules on state aid.

8. The land acquisition would secure the investment. In the words of Czech Prime Minister, 'If we secure the land in time, we have a big chance to receive the [Hyundai] investment' (*Prague Post*, 20 October 2005).
9. The destabilization effect of landowners and veto players operating at local and municipal levels is also seen in other jurisdictions. More recently, property developer Donald Trump's US$ 2 billion mega-development plan (1,400 acres) in a Scottish village failed in 2007 when a farmer refused to sell 23 acres of land and an Aberdeenshire Council committee blocked the plan (*Washington Post*, 7 December 2007).
10. Hyundai did not consider Slovakia, despite its KIA factory, due to serious problems it later faced, such as increased cost of building a factory and unresolved problems with landowners who eventually prevented construction of a new road leading to the plant (*Polish News Bulletin*, 13 September 2005; Slovak News Agency (SITA), 3 October 2005).
11. Persuasion refers to 'the act of convincing someone that something is in his or her interest. Inducement refers to the process of changing the incentive structure itself. Inducing someone to behave in a certain way entails changing the structure of rewards and penalties' (Caporaso and Levine, 1992: 161).
12. The parties agreed on the concrete number of new jobs (3,500) at the outset of negotiations.

References

AfxAsia Newswire, 30 September 2005.

AfxAsia Newswire, 27 March 2006.

Atkinson, M. M. and Coleman, W. D. (1989), *The State, Business and Industrial Change in Canada*. Toronto: University of Toronto Press.

Automotive News, 5 June 2006.

AWKnowledge – World Automatic Manufacturing, 19 May 2003.

AWKnowledge – World Automatic Manufacturing, 14 December 2005.

AWKnowledge – World Automatic Manufacturing, 29 March 2006.

AWKnowledge – World Automatic Manufacturing, 12 May 2006.

AWKnowledge – World Automatic Manufacturing, 14 December 2009.

Bacharach, S. B. and Lawyer, E. J. (1981), *Bargaining: Power, Tactics, and Outcomes*. San Francisco: Jossey-Bass.

Behrman, J. N. and Grosse, R. (1990), *International Business and Governments: Issues and Institutions*. Columbia, SC: University of South Carolina Press.

Behrman, J. N. and Grosse, R. (1992), 'Theory in International Business', *Transnational Corporations*, 1, 93–126.

Bell, S. (ed.) (2003), *Economic Governance and Institutional Dynamics*. Oxford: Oxford University Press.

Bell, S. and Carr, N. G. (2003), 'Governance Limits of the Australian State', in S. Bell (ed.), *Economic Governance and Institutional Dynamics*. Oxford: Oxford University Press, 304–20.

Bennett, D. C. and Sharpe, K. E. (1979), 'Agenda Setting and Bargaining Power: The Mexican State versus Transnational Automobile Corporations', *World Politics*, 32, 57–89.

Boddewyn, J. (1988), 'Political Aspects of MNE Theory', *Journal of International Business Studies*, 19, 341–63.

Boddewyn, J. and Brewer, T. (1994), 'International Business Political Behavior: New Theoretical Directions', *Academy of Management Review*, 19, 119–44.
Brewer, T. L. (1992), 'An Issue-Area Approach to the Analysis of MNC–Government Relations', *Journal of International Business Studies*, 23 (2), 295–309.
Business News, 27 September 2005.
Campbell, J. (2004), *Institutional Change and Globalization*. Princeton: Princeton University Press.
Caporaso, J. and Levine, D. (1992), *Theories of Political Economy*. Cambridge: Cambridge University Press.
CIA Daily News, 19 December 2005.
CIA Daily News, 31 March 2006.
CIA News, 6 September 2005.
CIA News, 10 October 2005.
CIA News, 28 March 2006.
Coleman, W. D. (1996), *Financial Services, Globalization and Domestic Policy Change*. New York: St Martin's Press.
CTK Business News, 29 September 2005.
CTK Business News, 30 September 2005.
CTK Business News, 28 November 2005.
CTK Business News, 8 December 2005.
CTK Business News, 12 December 2005.
CTK Business News, 16 December 2005.
CTK Business News, 29 March 2006.
Czech Business Weekly, 9 May 2006.
Czech Government (2005), *Economic Growth Strategy of the Czech Republic*, available at: http://www.hospodarskastrategie.org/.
Czech Press Agency, 29 September 2005.
Czech Press Agency, 30 September 2005.
Czech Republic Business Bulletin, 30 November 2005.
Dunleavy, P. and O'Leary, B. (1987), *Theories of State*. Basingstoke: Palgrave Macmillan.
Dunning, J. H. (1991), 'Governments and Multinational Enterprises: From Confrontation to Co-operation?' *Millennium – Journal of International Studies*, 20 (2), 225–44.
Dunning, J. H. (1998), 'An Overview of Relations with National Governments', *New Political Economy*, 3 (2), 280–4.
Eden, L. S., Lenway, S., and Schuler, D. (2005), 'From the Obsolescing to the Political Bargaining Model', in R. Grosse (ed.), *International Business and Government Relations in the 21st Century*. Cambridge: Cambridge University Press, 251–71.
European Commission (2007), *State Aid* (IP.07/659), May 11, 2007, available at: http://europa.eu/rapid/pressReleasesAction.do?reference=IP/07/659.
Evans, P. (1997), 'The Eclipse of the State? Reflections on Stateness in an Era of Globalization', *World Politics*, 50 (1), 62–87.
Expansion Management, 4 September 2007.
Fagre, N. and Wells, L. T. (1982), 'Bargaining Power of Multinationals and Host Governments', *Journal of International Business Studies*, Fall, 9–24.
Financial Times, 30 September 2005.
Intellinews, Czech Republic, 29 September 2005.
Intellinews, 27 March 2006.
Intellinews, 14 May 2007.

Jenkins, B. (1986), 'Re-examining the 'Obsolescing Bargain': A Study of Canada's National Energy Program', *International Organization*, 40, 139–65.
Katzenstein, P. J. (ed.) (1978), *Between Power and Plenty: Foreign Economic Policies of Advanced Industrial States*. Madison, WI: University of Wisconsin Press.
Katzenstein, P. (1985), *Small States in World Markets*. Ithaca, NY: Cornell University Press.
Kobrin, S. J. (1987), 'Testing the Bargaining Hypothesis in the Manufacturing Sector in Developing Countries', *International Organization*, 41 (4), 609–38.
Lodge, G. C. (1990), *Comparative Business–Government Relations*. New York: Prentice Hall.
Lukes, S. (2005), *Power: A Radical View*, 2nd edn. New York: Palgrave Macmillan.
Mann, M. (2008), 'Infrastructural Power Revisited', *Studies in Comparative International Development*, 43, 355–65.
Moran, T. (1974), *Multinational Corporations and the Politics of Dependence: Copper in Chile*. Princeton: Princeton University Press.
Moran, T. (1978), 'Multinational Corporations and Dependency', *International Organization*, 32 (1), 79–100.
Mytelka, L. (2000), 'We the People: The Transformation of State–TNC Relations at the Turn of the Millennium', *Journal of International Management*, 6 (4), 313–25.
New Europe, 5 December 2005.
OECD (2006), *Economic Surveys 2006: Czech Republic*. Paris: OECD.
Peters, G. and Pierre, J. (2006), 'Governance, Government and State', in C. Hay, M. Lister and D. Marsh (eds), *The State: Theories and Issues*. Basingstoke: Palgrave Macmillan.
Pierre, J. and Peters, G. B. (2000), *Governance, Politics and the State*. Basingstoke: Macmillan Press.
Polish News Bulletin, 13 September 2005.
Poynter, T. A. (1985), *Multinational Enterprises and Government Intervention*. New York: St Martin's Press.
Prague Post, 20 October 2005.
Prague Post, 14 December 2005.
Prague Post, 15 December 2005.
Skocpol, T. (1985), 'Bringing the State Back In: Strategies for Analysis in Current Research', in P. Evans, D. Rueschemeyer, and T. Skocpol (eds), *Bringing the State Back In*. New York: Cambridge University Press, 3–43.
Slovak News Agency (SITA), 3 October 2005.
Stopford, J. M. (1994), 'The Growing Interdependence between Transnational Corporations and Governments', *Transnational Corporations*, 3 (1), 53–76.
UNCTAD (2005), *United Nations World Investment Report 2005: Transnational Corporations and the Internationalization of R&D*. Geneva/New York: United Nations.
Vachani, S. (1995), 'Enhancing the Obsolescing Bargain Theory: A Longitudinal Study of Foreign Ownership of US and European Multinationals', *Journal of International Business Studies*, 26 (1), 159–80.
Vernon, R. (1971), *Sovereignty at Bay: The Multinational Spread of US Enterprises*. New York: Basic Books.
Vernon, R. (1977), *Storm over Multinationals: The Real Issues*. Cambridge, MA: Harvard University Press.
Vernon, R. (1998), *In the Hurricane's Eye: The Troubled Prospects of Multinational Enterprises*. Cambridge, MA: Harvard University Press.
Washington Post, 7 December 2007.

Weber, M. (1978), *Economy and Society: An Outline of Interpretative Sociology*, 2 vols, ed. Guenther Roth and Claus Wittich. Berkeley, CA: University of California Press.
Weiss, L. (1998), *The Myth of the Powerless State*. Ithaca, NY: Cornell University Press.
Weiss, L. (2003), *States in the Global Economy*. Cambridge: Cambridge University Press.
Yin, R. K. (1994), *Case Study Research: Design and Methods*, 2nd edn. London: Sage.
Yonhap News, 30 September 2005.
Zysman, J. (1983), *Governments, Markets, and Growth Financial Systems and the Politics of Industrial Change*. Ithaca, NY: Cornell University Press.

Part VII
Conclusion

20
Southern Multinationals and Their Impact on Europe: What Have We Learnt?

Louis Brennan

20.1 Introduction

The various contributors to this volume have sought to examine the emergence of Southern Multinationals and their impact on Europe. In this concluding chapter, the salient findings are summarised under a number of headings concerning the following issues:

- The extent of the phenomenon particularly as it relates to Europe;
- The drivers, motives and strategies of Southern Multinationals investing in Europe;
- Impact and policy considerations as they relate to Europe;
- Research implications.

20.2 The extent of the phenomenon particularly as it relates to Europe

In seeking to determine the impact that Southern MNEs have on Europe and to examine if (and how) this impact differs from traditional inward investors such as the USA and Japan, Buckley et al. show in Chapter 3 that such efforts are severely constrained by the lack of reliable and consistent data. The data deficit has also been alluded to by a number of other contributors (for example, Czakó in Chapter 6 and De Beule et al. in Chapter 11) to this volume.

Nonetheless, Buckley et al. show that the stock of FDI into the European Union by firms located in Southern countries has doubled over the period 2004 to 2008 while remaining small overall. Over the much longer time span of the past two decades, the proportion of global OFDI accounted for by the emerging world has recorded a similar increase. Mirza et al. in Chapter 2 contend that this trend is likely to continue given the relative strength of Southern Multinationals, their commitment to internationalization and the growing share of M&As deals accounted for by takeovers by such companies of developed world groups. While major firms have emerged in all sectors, the bulk of FDI from the emerging world has been in the tertiary sector. particularly business activities and finance. Mirza et al. also highlight that compared to their developed world counterparts, Southern Multinationals are more diversified, their international operations account for a smaller proportion of their overall assets, sales and employment and they have fewer foreign affiliates. Many of the largest Southern Multinationals are state-owned, and this is particularly so in the case of the primary sector.

This volume has considered the emergence of multinationals from a number of source countries. These include the Multilatinas – multinationals from Latin America – Chinese and Indian multinationals, Russian multinationals and those multinationals emerging from two of the former transition countries of Eastern Europe – Hungary and Slovenia.

In terms of Multilatinas and their venturing into Europe, their initial focus has been on countries with a lower cultural distance. Thus, Fleury et al. in Chapter 4 report that the countries of the Latin European cluster tend to be favoured by these firms in their first entry into Europe. Among the main Multilatinas, only about 20 per cent make their first internationalization step into Europe. However, a greater proportion of these firms that have proceeded beyond their first entry into other locations do so into Europe, with a greater proportion making these subsequent entries into the Anglo-Saxon European cluster. However, the presence of such firms in Europe and especially outside the Latin European cluster is small.

Wu has noted in Chapter 5 that despite the surge in OFDI from China in recent years, China's foreign direct investment into Europe has only accounted for about 2 per cent of China's total outward investment of China. Hay and Milelli report in Chapter 9 that the largest European economies such as the United Kingdom, Germany, France and, to a lesser extent Italy, have attracted about three-quarters of the total amount of Chinese and Indian investments since the 1990s. Torp et al. report in Chapter 10 that in the case of Chinese and Indian companies investing in Denmark, they represent only 0.5 per cent of total FDI stocks. By contrast, Mansilya-Kruz asserts in Chapter 7 that Europe's geographic and economic proximity helps to explain why Europe is by far the most important destination for Russian OFDI, which has surged over the past decade.

Czakó reports in Chapter 6 that OFDI from Hungary has increased dramatically from the mid-1990s and particularly over the past decade, albeit from a very low base. The major destinations are to other EU member countries, with other destinations based in non-EU-member neighbouring or close countries. The services sector dominated by financial services represents the largest share of Hungarian OFDI. Jaklič and Marjan consider in Chapter 8 that the emergence of Slovenian multinationals was spurred in large part by the loss of markets following the demise of the former Yugoslavia, with more than 70 per cent of their OFDI stocks located in the countries of the former Yugoslavia and the bulk of the remainder elsewhere in Europe. Following the crisis and the slowdown in Europe, Slovenian MNEs have started to extend their attention beyond Europe to encompass the fast-growing emerging economies of Brazil, China and India.

The emergence of sovereign wealth funds (SWFs) as global investors also represents a significant and rapid change to the landscape of the global economy. In Chapter 13, Rios-Morales and Brennan highlight that UNCTAD has reported that over three-quarters of FDI from SWFs were invested in developed economies in the year 2007. However, it can be noted that thus far the level of FDI engaged in by SWFs has been minor relative to overall global FDI.

Overall despite the data deficit, a picture emerges of an accelerating rate of investment into the countries of the EU by Southern Multinationals in recent years albeit from a very low base. However, while the bulk of investment by multinationals from Russia and the former transition countries of Eastern Europe has tended to be in Europe, thus far only a very small proportion of investments by multinationals from Brazil, China and India has been in Europe.

20.3 The drivers, motives and strategies of Southern Multinationals investing in Europe

In Chapter 2, Mirza et al. maintain that while there are similarities in the rationale for internationalization on the part of Southern Multinationals when compared to MNEs from developed counties, differences occur, however, when they invest in developed countries. In Chapter 3, Buckley et al. conclude that the impact of Southern investments on Europe will therefore differ significantly by MNE home country as well as by host economy. The value-chain perspective offered by Srai and Fleet reveals the differences between the investment strategies of Southern Multinationals and those of MNEs from the developed world. They show in Chapter 14 how Southern Multinationals' investments in emerging markets are largely supply-side resource-seeking and demand-side market-seeking, while their investments in the developed world tend to be motivated by network access in terms of technology and capabilities and markets. Traditional MNEs are motivated by network efficiency demands, especially in emerging markets, and by market access-driven arrangements that integrate low-cost country resources and emerging market potential. Nonetheless, they caution that industry structure and dynamics, national regulatory differences and product characteristics can also influence the choice of investment options.

The key drivers for Multilatinas are diverse, ranging from being part of global production network, resource-seeking, market-seeking and asset-seeking and operational support. Fleury et al. in Chapter 4 suggest a number of factors that serve to explain the small presence of the Multilatinas in Europe, including the institutional complexity of Europe and its cited reliance on social and environmental rules and norms to defend the region against foreign competitors as well as peculiarities of the consumer market and difficulties in accessing distribution channels. The lack of certain management competencies on the part of these firms also has a role.

In Chapter 5, Wu notes that while Chinese multinationals have many aspects in common with traditional MNEs generally, they also have their own special characteristics. These stem in part from the categories into which China's MNEs fall, viz. state-owned enterprises, private enterprise and foreign-invested enterprises, which are different from those of the developed world. While existing theories are useful in understanding the emergence of Chinese MNEs, Wu argues that there are some special considerations that need to be taken into account. These include institutional void, race to learn, vertical integration advantage and membership of a global supply network. While Chinese companies perform relatively well in locations that share a similar institutional environment to themselves, they perform less well in the developed world where the high cost and rigid labour market conditions militate against the success of these firms. This observation is consistent with the small proportion of Chinese investment into Europe. Chinese outward direct investment to Europe is motivated by technology-seeking and is concentrated in those sectors where the appropriated technologies are useful to China's next stage of domestic economic development. Ensuring the continued rapid economic growth of China remains the central motivator of outward investment by Chinese firms. Since the assets that Chinese companies acquire overseas or the facilities that they build in other countries must be complementary to the economic activities that those firms engage in and must facilitate the next stage of economic growth of China, outward foreign direct investment tends to be complementary in nature to the strengths of China's indigenous companies. This is in contrast to the theoretical model of a horizontal type of investment proposed by Hymer and the OLI paradigm explaining the existence of multinational enterprises.

Hay and Milelli suggest in Chapter 9 that market-seeking and asset-seeking are the predominant and oftentimes combined motives of Chinese and Indian firms investing in Europe. They note that while acquisitions are the main route to tap intangible assets, organic expansion is also used to set up development centres and design institutes within/or close to technological clusters in recipient countries.

Chinese and Indian firms investing in Denmark were found by Torp et al. in Chapter 10 to be motivated by market-seeking and strategic asset-seeking, with most of their investments in the form of acquisitions, either partial or complete. In the case of R&D-oriented investments, these tended to be strongly integrated in the Asian owners' global strategies, partly through full ownership control, partly through direct management oversight by the Asian owners, while integration of market-seeking investments tended initially not to happen.

Only in recent years has China extended its Go Global strategy to financial services. The Chinese government has increasingly pushed its main banks to internationalise and has set up special investment vehicles for outward portfolio investment. In advance of doing so it implemented a series of policies to restore the health of its financial sector and make it globally competitive, creating nominally independent regulatory agencies, cleaned up the balance sheets of its major commercial banks and turned central administrative units into special vehicles for global portfolio investment. However, Gottwald in Chapter 15 asserts that the regulators have limited independence and that the Chinese Communist Party retains the power to define the direction and major content of policies while it remains heavily embedded in the financial services companies themselves. While they remain deeply embedded in China's cadre-capitalism, China's commercial banks are increasingly raising their international profile, with three of the Big Four already listed overseas and the fourth due for imminent listing. Although some of the overseas equity investments in developed economies by China's financial sector have produced large losses, it still continues to expand into world markets.

Increased operational cash flows owing to high commodity prices and rapid domestic economic growth along with a change in public policy are cited by Mansilya-Kruz in Chapter 7 as having contributed to the surge in OFDI from Russia. Contrary to the general perception, only four out of the top 25 Russian non-financial multinationals are state-controlled firms. Much of Russian OFDI into Europe is motivated by combined market-seeking and strategic asset-seeking. This involves downstream integration with the appropriation of value-adding activities and increased market share, and has been largely associated with the oil and gas sector. The metal/mining sector has engaged in scale-seeking (efficiency) expansion with the appropriation of upstream activities For Russians firms mostly active in manufacturing, their strategic asset-seeking expansion into Europe has been described as product-line import. Similar to some Chinese acquisitions in Europe, this involves the purchase of a relatively smaller, but technically modern manufacturer in Europe and localizing the production of its products in Russia without necessarily terminating production in the acquired company locations.

While earlier studies on the motives for Hungarian OFDI cite resource-seeking, market-seeking and efficiency-seeking, Czakó in Chapter 6 notes that more recent findings suggest that market-seeking and strategic asset-seeking are dominant motives. Jaklič and Marjan report in Chapter 8 that Slovenian OFDI is dominated by a handful of large investors and that the manufacturing sector accounts for the greatest number of firms among the Top 25 non-financial services Slovenian MNEs. They note the trade and competitiveness benefits for these outward-investing firms. However, there remains the challenge for these firms of overcoming their management deficits in relation to operating internationally.

Overall it can be stated that market-seeking and asset-seeking are the dominant motives of Southern Multinationals investing in Europe. It has been suggested that there are differences in the rationale for internationalization on the part of Southern Multinationals when compared to traditional MNEs when they invest in developed countries. The insights obtained from adopting the value chain perspective on the investment strategies of Southern Multinationals and traditional MNEs also suggest differences between the two sets of MNEs. The case of Chinese MNEs and their investment strategy deserve special attention for a number of reasons. First, there is the primacy attached to the goal of facilitating China's next stage of domestic economic development in relation to Chinese OFDI. Second, there is the degree to which China's MNEs remain deeply embedded in China's cadre-capitalism. Third, there is a contrast between OFDI on the part of Chinese MNEs and some of the established theories.

20.4 Impact and policy considerations as they relate to Europe

Hay et al. in Chapter 9 note that in the case of Chinese and Indian companies investing in Europe they bring firm-specific advantages in terms of production process skills, increasingly combined with technological expertise and/or linkages with activities at home. They also benefit from proprietary assets, which can often arise in the case of Chinese firms from being state-owned while in the case of Indian firms they can arise from family ownership. However, Torp et al. argue that the lack of firm-specific advantages on the part of Southern Multinationals result in them being unable to capitalize on their low-cost base advantage and easy access to credit.

In considering the impact of Chinese and Indian firms on Europe Hay et al. consider that it is appropriate to do so in terns of FDI itself, bilateral trade, employment and qualifications, and on competition in product and service markets. Whether these impacts are complementary or competitive in nature depends on the individual country or region, sector and period of time.

There has been evidence of serious problems arising for acquiring Asian firms in Denmark in attempting to integrate their acquisitions. Torp et al. suggest in Chapter 10 that this may be due to the high cultural distance and inexperience in the operation of European subsidiaries, giving rise to a deficit in terms of appropriate organizational and managerial resources. Similarly, in the case of Russians manufacturing firms, Mansilya-Kruz in Chapter 7 notes that their strategic asset-seeking expansion has thus far had a low success rate, thus perhaps indicating that for distressed European manufacturers, Russian investment is not necessarily the panacea anticipated.

It is noteworthy that Torp et al. found that government policies have been crucial in attracting to Denmark the first wave of Indian and Chinese investments, for example, tax policies, subsidies, infrastructure provision, support of higher education and research, and in general the promotion of clusters. The investing firms targeted R&D or sales and marketing talent capabilities of related clusters. This suggests that creating optimal conditions for the location of specific high value-added functions within these clusters may be advantageous in the case of a small economy like Denmark in the attraction of investment from Southern Multinationals.

China has increasingly been viewed by investment promotion agencies as holding high prospects as a source of investment. As noted by De Beule et al. in Chapter 11, the gradual shift in the composition of China's outward investment to the tertiary sector is likely to orient its investments more towards the OECD and EU countries. Belgium has been less successful than some other open economies in the EU in attracting investment from China. De Beule et al. observe that labour costs, complicated incentives and the level of taxation were evaluated as negative factors from a location perspective on the part of Chinese managers in Belgium. Further, the challenges of dealing with the system of regional devolution in Belgium were highlighted, as well as what was experienced as strict policies on securing work permits and visas. Some European countries have established Investment Promotion Agencies to target Chinese investors, and have opened offices on the mainland and have also been proactive in attempting to overcome communication difficulties by establishing websites in Chinese and the posting of documents in Mandarin. However, an evaluation of Belgian federal and regional websites for investment promotion revealed significant shortcomings from the perspective of simulated Chinese investors.

Arising from the Belgium studies, some recommendations emerge for host countries in terms of increasing their visibility and attractiveness for investment by Southern Multinationals. The administrative aspects relating to the procedures for obtaining visas and work permits require scrutiny. Countries should reconsider renegotiating their investment treaties with home countries of Southern Multinationals so that they offer the same protection and guarantees to their investments as those afforded to developed countries' MNEs. Greater reliance should be placed on websites designed to provide useful information to potential investors to Europe. At the same time, given that attitudes to investments by Southern Multinationals are not always positive, greater transparency on the part of host countries of Southern Multinationals and their firms is required.

In considering the extent to which to which protectionism plays a role in Europe's response to the emergence of Southern Multinationals, Clifton and Díaz-Fuentes in Chapter 12 note that manifestations of protectionism are not confined to IFDI by Southern Multinationals. While the EU has one of the most open IFDI regimes in the world, that openness is uneven, as there are differences in the extent to which member states protect particular sectors. Thus, considering the 'strategic industries' of energy and telecommunications, the telecommunications sector is as open as any sector in the EU and much more open to IFDI than the electricity sector. While there have been incidences of Southern Multinationals failing in their efforts to enter Europe's energy and telecommunications sectors, there have also been examples of attempts by MNEs within the EU being thwarted in their takeover efforts in other European countries. Thus, according to Clifton and Díaz-Fuentes in Chapter 12, it is difficult to conclude whether the EU is becoming increasingly more protectionist in the light of the emerging Southern Multinationals or whether its increased protectionism is more general. Among the instances of a move away from openness has been the introduction by Germany of a new bill that would allow prospective IFDI that involves 25 per cent or more of a company's stake by non-European firms to be screened for approval. In 2005, the French government compiled a list of 'strategic' and 'sensitive' industries in which foreign investors would be subject to government screening. While the EU Commission has been active in enforcing the free movement of capital both within the EU and with regard to third countries, it is noteworthy that it has more recently diluted its focus on competition in the energy market to encompass considerations around security and diversity of supply.

While Southern Multinationals offer Europe a new source of investment, their emergence raises new challenges for the Europe in maintaining its openness to IFDI.

Although the European Commission has highlighted the benefits of sovereign wealth fund (SWF) investment, France and Germany have expressed serious apprehension about the investment strategies of SWFs. Both countries have expressed protectionist stances, while more recently the French President argued for the creation of a European Sovereign Wealth Fund in order to protect Europe's 'strategic' industries, and prevent their acquisition by non-European companies. The European Commission has advocated on a number of occasions tighter regulation, in the form of a code of best practices, making SWFs transparent and thus dispelling the mistrust felt by many towards them. While some countries in Europe have expressed serious concerns in relation to SWFs, other countries have welcomed their investments. The EU Commission has attempted to develop a common European approach to SWFs by supporting increases in transparency, predictability and accountability on the part of SWFs. In a similar vein, the EU has been actively supportive of the Santiago Principles that were produced in 2008 to reflect appropriate governance, accountability and investment practices for SWFs. In addition to representing inward investment to the developed world from developing and emerging economies, SWFs also represent investment from the public to the private sector.

From the perspective of established MNEs, the peril of embracing a generic one-size-fits-all approach to Southern Multinationals based on their country of origin is emphasised by Yildiz and Fey in Chapter 16. They argue that a more detailed analysis is likely to be necessary to understand their likely internationalization strategies and to gain competitive insights.

As Southern Multinationals grow and expand, Nölke and Taylor suggest in Chapter 17 that they are likely to articulate their preferences on matters relating to global economic governance, including economic and trade regulation, investment treaties, accounting standards and corporate social responsibility, and will increasingly influence the nature of global economic governance.

The emergence of Southern Multinationals has implications in terms of policy development for policy-makers in host governments and in international organizations. In considering the increasing competition between established MNEs and Southern Multinationals Mirza et al. argue that there is a need for policies at national and international level that maximise the benefits and simultaneously reduce the costs of such competition.

20.5 Research implications

Buckley et al. consider that the motivation pattern for Southern investment into the European Union call for further in-depth, firm-level analyses. In highlighting differences between the affiliates of Southern Multinationals in turnover per enterprise and per employee across European countries, and making comparisons with developed countries' firms, they again argue for in-depth, firm-level attention as this can reveal insights on the competitiveness of Southern Multinationals and hence their impact on Europe. Fleury et al. propose that research is also needed to ascertain the relative importance of the factors that have limited investment into Europe by Southern Multinationals.

Chinese and Indian investments in Denmark were found by Torp et al. to be both of a conventional nature and of the latecomer type. While the variety of entry modes employed give credence to the latecomer theory that these Southern Multinationals are flexible and innovative in adopting entry modes, little support emerges for the linkage, leverage and learning abilities of these firms. Wu argues that the nature of Chinese firms' outward foreign direct investment contrasts with the theoretical model of the horizontal type of investment proposed by Hymer and the OLI paradigm in explaining the existence of multinational enterprises.

Consideration of the internationalization strategies of Southern Multinationals and their relationship to those of traditional MNEs should extend beyond home country factors to encompass in addition industry, firm, individual and temporal considerations. Yildiz and Fey make the point in Chapter 16 that by comparing firms from different points in time and of different sizes, many recent studies on EMNEs' internationalization have not clearly showed if the differences between MNEs from emerging economies and developed economies are really a result of country of origin difference or other factors. They illustrate with examples the limits to the role of macro-level effects in the internationalization strategies of Southern Multinationals and point to non-geographic sources of divergence from conventional theories. Multi-level research is needed to establish the role of different factors.

Using the case of India, Nölke and Taylor argue in Chapter 17 that an institutionalist approach is needed to understand potential tensions between Southern Multinationals and their host economies as well as with global economic regulations. They suggest that such an approach would also complement existing studies on the business strategies of Southern Multinationals. To understand the institutional framework that has contributed to the emergence of Southern Multinationals, they embrace the comparative capitalism perspective as a heuristic framework that enables the identification of the most important institutional factors. However, in adopting the varieties of capital approach within that perspective, they acknowledge the need to compensate for the neglect of the state as an agent of economic development within that approach.

The role that financial strategy plays in the internationalization of MNEs and of Southern Multinationals in particular has received relatively little attention. Meckl and Graser highlight in Chapter 18 the need for research at the firm level into the relationship between finance strategy and internationalization, especially regarding Southern Multinationals. A distinction can be drawn between real internationalization and financial internationalization. The authors hypothesize that financial strategy may play either a passive or an active role in the internationalization of these multinationals, or financial and internationalization strategies may operate independently of one another in terms of time and content. Their proposed research is not aimed at developing a new theory of internationalization for Southern Multinationals but to develop an understanding of the relationship between real and financial internationalization and its effect on these multinationals. In so doing, the research can provide a bridge between two main fields of current research, internationalisation theory and finance.

Entry bargaining between host governments and MNEs may yield a non-deal outcome owing to antagonists who destabilize the bargaining process in the absence of state capacity to steer the process towards an investment outcome. Bakir in Chapter 19 modifies the state capacity framework developed in the comparative public policy literature and adapts it to the governance of the entry bargaining process using the case of a Southern Multinational and an emerging European state. Thus he has provided a bridge between the comparative public policy and international business fields. His work demonstrates the significance of state capacity in steering the entry bargaining process towards an investment deal. This approach offers useful insights for European states as many increasingly seek to secure investments from Southern Multinationals.

Overall in terms of research implications, a number of considerations emerge:

- There is a data deficit in terms of the emergence of Southern Multinationals and their impact that needs to be addressed.
- The completeness of existing theories in explaining the emergence of Southern Multinationals requires further exploration.
- Since consideration of the internationalization strategies of Southern Multinationals and their relationship to those of traditional MNEs should extend beyond home country factors to encompass in addition industry, firm, individual and temporal considerations, multi-level research is required.
- In depth firm-level analyses are required to elaborate and clarify the motivation pattern of investment by Southern Multinationals into Europe, their competitiveness and their impact.
- Research is needed to determine the relative importance of factors that limit investment by Southern Multinationals in Europe.
- Research on the emergence of Southern Multinationals that bridges different fields of enquiry offers the prospect of greatly improved insights and understanding.

Index